Gowaart Van Den Bossche

Literary Spectacles of Sultanship

Islam – Thought, Culture, and Society

Volume 10

Gowaart Van Den Bossche

Literary Spectacles of Sultanship

Historiography, the Chancery, and Social Practice in Late Medieval Egypt

DE GRUYTER

Winner of the 2020 BRAIS – De Gruyter Prize in the Study of Islam and the Muslim World

BRAIS
British Association for Islamic Studies

ISBN 978-3-11-221390-2
e-ISBN (PDF) 978-3-11-075302-8
e-ISBN (EPUB) 978-3-11-075313-4
ISSN 2628-4286

Library of Congress Control Number: 2023938293

Bibliographic information published by the Deutsche Nationalbibliothek
The Deutsche Nationalbibliothek lists this publication in the Deutsche Nationalbibliografie; detailed bibliographic data are available on the internet at http://dnb.dnb.de.

This volume is text- and page-identical with the hardback published in 2023.
Typesetting: Integra Software Services Pvt. Ltd.
Printing and binding: CPI books GmbH, Leck

www.degruyter.com

Acknowledgements

This book is a substantially revised version of a dissertation researched and written between 2014 and 2018 at Ghent University. In those four years and in the following four years of on and off working on revisions I have been lucky to receive assistance and advice from several people. The initial project was supervised by Jo Van Steenbergen. His critical readings and thoughtful comments on early and late drafts of the dissertation profoundly shaped the form of the dissertation and thus the core of what is found in the present book. He also provided helpful comments on the final draft of this book. I am grateful for his guidance over several years now. During the dissertation years Kristof D'hulster served as something of an unofficial co-supervisor due to his proximity at the neighbouring office desk. I have benefited from his willingness to try to answer many random questions as they came up during my research. I also greatly benefited from his critical reading of my translations from the Arabic in the first full draft of this book. Additionally, I am grateful to Konrad Hirschler and Frédéric Bauden for providing many key insights as committee members of the dissertation and in conversations in the following years. Maaike van Berkel and Wim Verbaal also sat on the committee and helped me think through some arguments that have influenced the current form of the book.

From 2019 until early 2022 I worked as a postdoctoral fellow at the ERC-funded KITAB project at the Aga Khan University Institute for the Study of Muslim Civilisations in London (European Union's horizon 2020 research and innovation programme grant agreement no. 772989). I am grateful to the project's PI Sarah Bowen Savant for providing insightful feedback on this book project in its dissertation form and for allowing me to use part of my time to work on the book. The KITAB project provided a stimulating environment where I could broaden my research interests significantly. This has helped me bring better into focus what was unique about the historical moment studied in this book and where it was connected to earlier and later developments.

Over the years I have benefited from companionship of several colleagues and peers, many of whom have also provided helpful feedback on presentations at conferences and on draft papers and chapters circulated at seminars. At Ghent University this includes Stijn Van Nieuwenhuyse Fien De Block, Maya Termonia, Mohamed Maslouh, Kenneth Goudie, Zacharie Mochtari de Pierrepont, Tarek Sabraa, Rihab Ben Othmen, Daniel Mahoney, and Mustafa Banister. To Mustafa I owe special gratitude for his proofreading of the final draft of the present book. In London I initially worked closely with Maroussia Bednarkiewicz, who read through the dissertation in 2019 and provided many helpful comments and suggestions. I additionally thank Claire Savina, Mathew Barber, Aslisho Qurboniev, Peter Verkinderen, and Lorenz Nigst for helping me think through issues voiced during various team meetings

https://doi.org/10.1515/9783110753028-202

or collegial chats. Outside of my direct colleagues I am grateful to Boriz Liebrenz, Matthew L. Keegan and Alasdair Roberts for providing advice on specific issues or sharing material with me. Most such individual contributions are noted in the footnotes throughout this book.

The present publication project is results from my dissertation winning the BRAIS-De Gruyter dissertation prize in 2020. I remain grateful to the organisation for honouring my dissertation with this prize, and for providing me with the jury feedback which was useful for the revision process. The team at De Gruyter—Torsten Wollina, Katrin Mittmann, and Sophie Wagenhofer—was supportive and flexible from the start: I am grateful to them for allowing me to take the needed time and for their feedback. The two anonymous peer reviewers they enlisted also provided me with many helpful suggestions and insights.

Writing books is a lonely endeavour but they are not written in an academic vacuum. For regularly pulling me out of the vacuum I want to thank my parents, siblings, friends, and fellow musicians. I thank especially my dearest Zoé for her support throughout the period I spent working on this book. I dedicate this book to the memory of my friend Sarah, who shared my love for Arabic but did not live to see the publication of this love letter to that language.

Contents

Acknowledgements —— V

Note on transliteration and abbreviations —— XI

Introduction —— 1

I Beyond legitimacy —— **7**
II Literary spectacles of sultanship —— **11**
III The historical background —— **16**
IV Outline of the book —— **22**

Chapter 1
The *sīra* corpus: Authors and texts —— 25

1.1 Muḥyī al-Dīn b. ʿAbd al-Ẓāhir —— **26**
1.1.1 The *sīra* of Baybars —— **30**
1.1.2 *Tashrīf al-Ayyām* —— **33**
1.1.3 *al-Alṭāf al-Khafiyya* —— **35**
1.2 Shāfiʿ b. ʿAlī —— **36**
1.2.1 *al-Faḍl al-Maʾthūr* —— **39**
1.2.2 *Ḥusn al-Manāqib* —— **40**
1.2.3 The *sīra* of al-Nāṣir Muḥammad —— **42**
1.3 Other family members —— **43**
1.4 Conclusion —— **45**

Chapter 2
The discourse of *Sīra*: Historiography, memory, and performance —— 46

2.1 Historiography: Literarisierung, narrative, meaning —— **48**
2.2 Defining *sīra* —— **51**
2.3 The arguments for *sīra*: Titles and introductions —— **57**
2.3.1 Ibn ʿAbd al-Ẓāhir's sīra of Baybars —— **59**
2.3.2 *al-Faḍl al-Maʾthūr* —— **64**
2.3.3 *Ḥusn al-Manāqib* —— **69**
2.4 Conclusion —— **74**

Chapter 3
***Sīra* as an act of narrative construction —— 76**

3.1 Ibn ʿAbd al-Ẓāhir's *sīra* of Baybars —— **78**
3.2 *Ḥusn al-Manāqib* —— **86**
3.3 *al-Faḍl al-Maʾthūr* —— **88**

3.4 *Tashrīf al-Ayyām* — **95**
3.5 *al-Alṭāf al-Khafiyya* — **98**
3.6 *Sīrat al-Malik al-Naṣīr* — **100**
3.7 Conclusion — **106**

Chapter 4
***Sīra* as chancery practice: Composition and compilation — 107**
4.1 Chancery — **110**
4.2 Career paths and patronage — **117**
4.3 *Sīra* as expression of *inshāʾ* identity — **124**
4.4 Compiling documents — **129**
4.4.1 The diplomatic correspondence between Aḥmad Tegüder and Qalāwūn — **131**
4.4.2 Documents before history: the re-use of letters as historical narrative — **140**
4.5 Conclusion — **143**

Chapter 5
***Sīra* as literary communication — 145**
5.1 The literary field — **147**
5.2 *Sīra* in the literary field — **154**
5.2.1 Poetry — **154**
5.2.2 Prose: *muʿāraḍa* — **164**
5.3 Conclusion — **169**

Chapter 6
Sīra as courtly phenomenon — 170
6.1 Defining court: terms, spaces, practices — **174**
6.2 Performing court: Ritual, ceremony, and the courtly habitus — **179**
6.3 Court and literary culture — **183**
6.4 Court and *sīra* — **188**
6.5 Conclusion — **199**

Chapter 7
Final conclusions — 200

Note on transliteration and abbreviations

I have followed the IJMES transliteration system for Arabic. I have not rendered the assimilation of sun-letters and I have only marked the case endings where I felt it was useful to do so. Words for which a commonly used English rendering exists—such as sultan and vizier—as well as names of localities such as Cairo and Damascus have not been transliterated.

In the body text and notes I have used the following abbreviations:

- BnF: Bibliothèque nationale de France
- BSOAS: *Bulletin of the School of Oriental and African Studies, University of London*
- EI2: *Encyclopaedia of Islam, Second Edition*, eds. P. Bearman, Th. Bianquis, C.E. Bosworth, E. van Donzel, W.P. Heinrichs (Leiden: Brill, 1960–2005), in https://referenceworks.brillonline.com/browse/encyclopaedia-of-islam-2
- EI3: *Encyclopaedia of Islam, THREE*, eds. Kate Fleet, Gudrun Krämer, Denis Matringe, John Nawas, Everett Rowson (Leiden: Brill, 2007–present), in https://referenceworks.brillonline.com/browse/encyclopaedia-of-islam-3
- Eir: *Encyclopœdia Iranica*, online edition (New York, 1996–present), in https://www.iranicaonline.org/
- IJMES: *International Journal for Middle East Studies*
- JAL: *Journal of Arabic Literature*
- JAOS: *Journal of the American Oriental Society*
- MSR: *Mamluk Studies Review*
- ZDMG: *Zeitschrift der Deutschen Morgenländischen Gesellschaft*

https://doi.org/10.1515/9783110753028-204

Note on transliteration and abbreviations

Introduction

قالَ لي من رأى صباح مشيبي عن شمال من لِمَّتي ويمين
أيُّ شيء هذا؟ فقلت مجيباً لَيلُ شكٍّ محاهُ صُبحُ يقين

The one who observed my old age dawning
all across my hair locks asked me:
"What is this?" So I said in response:
"A night of doubt, effaced by a dawn of certainty."[1]

On the 17th of Shaʿbān of the year 730 AH / 5th of June 1330 CE an old man died in Cairo. Two years before his death he was visited by the biographer Khalīl b. Aybak al-Ṣafadī (d. 764/1363). The pair engaged in a poetical exchange about the time-worn topic of old age—despite al-Ṣafadī being only 32 lunar years old at that point—to which the old man contributed the above quoted epigram. As a result of this meeting, al-Ṣafadī also received an *ijāza* (a permission to transmit information on the authority of a specific person) containing several more of his poems as well as a list of 25 books the man had written throughout his long life. He also collected books: al-Ṣafadī relates on the authority of a mutually acquainted bookseller that the deceased left behind 18 book cases (*khazāʾin*) filled with "literary gems" (*nafāʾis adabiyya*).[2] Yet al-Ṣafadī also tells us that the old man had been blinded by an arrow

1 Al-Ṣafadī reproduces these lines in a biographical notice he reproduced in at least four different works: *Aʿyān al-Aṣr wa-Aʿwān al-Naṣr,* 6 vols., eds. Abū Zayd e.a. (Beirut-Damascus: Dār al-Fikr al-Muʿāṣir & Dār al-Fikr, 1998), 2:505; al-Ṣafadī, *Alḥān al-Sawājiʿ Bayna al-Bādī wa-l-Murājiʿ,* 2 vols., ed. Ibrāhīm Ṣāliḥ (Damascus: Dār al-Bashāʾir, 2004), 1:356; al-Ṣafadī, *al-Wāfī biʾl-Wafāyāt,* 25 vols., ed. Hellmut Ritter e.a. (Wiesbaden: Franz Steiner, 1982), 16:47; al-Ṣafadī, *Nakt al-Himyān fī Nukat al-ʿUmyān,* ed. Aḥmad Zakī Bak (Cairo: al-Maṭbaʿah al-Jamālīyah, 1911), 165. This biographical notice was copied by Ibn Ḥajar al-ʿAsqalānī, *al-Durar al-Kāmina fī Aʿyān al-Miʾa al-Thāmina,* 5 vols., ed. Muḥammad Sayyid Jād al-Ḥaqq (Cairo: Dār al-Kutub al-Ḥadītha, 1966), 2:282, and Ibn Taghrī-Birdī, *al-Manhal al-Ṣāfī waʾl-Mustawfā baʿda al-Wāfī,* 13 vols., ed. Muḥammad Muḥammad Amīn (Cairo: Dār al-Kutub waʾl-Wathāʾiq, 1990), 6:198. The poem is also recorded in the independent biography given by Ibn Ḥabīb, *Tadkhirat al-Nabīh fī Ayyām al-Manṣūr wa-Bānīh,* 2 vols., ed. Muḥammad Muḥammad Amīn (Cairo: al-Hayʾa l-Miṣriyya l-ʿāmma li-l-kitāb, 1976–86), vol. 2:209. The word I have translated as "old age" (*mashīb*) means more literally "grey hairs" and is thus intimately related to the hair lock of the second hemistich of the first *bayt,* where an association is made between hair locks and fortune. The word *mashīb* also appears in al-Ṣafadī's own poem which triggered this response. For an alternative translation of the poem, compare: Livnat Holtzman, "The Dhimmi's Question on Predetermination and the Ulama's Six Responses: The Dynamics of Composing Polemical Didactic Poems in Mamluk Cairo and Damascus," *MSR* 16 (2012), 35.

2 Ibn Taghrī-Birdī adds "and others" (wa-ghayruhā), *Manhal,* 6:198. For an idea of what may have been meant by "literary gems," compare the books owned and/or consulted by al-Ṣafadī himself as studied by Élise Franssen, "al-Ṣafadī: the Scholar as a Reader" in *Authors as Readers in the Mamlūk*

https://doi.org/10.1515/9783110753028-001

during the Battle of Homs against the Mongols in the year 680/1281, when he was only 29 years old.[3] Apparently, this blindness did not impede his appetite for books: al-Ṣafadī next recounts how the blind man was able to identify each book in detail when handed the manuscript. He could even recall the time he bought the book and the exact amount he paid for it. His wife, whose name has not been transmitted, is said to have known the value of each of these books as well and was able to secure a pension of sorts by selling them off one by one before leaving Cairo seven years after her husband's death.

The protagonist of this anecdote is Nāṣir al-Dīn Shāfiʿ b. ʿAlī b. ʿAbbās b. Ismāʿīl b. ʿAsākir al-Kinānī al-ʿAsqalānī al-Miṣrī,[4] commonly known as Shāfiʿ b. ʿAlī. The bookish focus of the anecdote is not coincidental: Shāfiʿ spent a significant part of his life as a scribe (*kātib*, pl. *kuttāb*) in the elite composition bureau (*dīwān al-inshāʾ*) of the chancery of the late medieval sultanate of Cairo.[5] His career and that of his peers—including his visitor al-Ṣafadī—revolved around their command of the written word and thorough knowledge of the tenets of Arabic literary expression. Shāfiʿ and other scribes never missed an opportunity to display their literary prowess, both in rhyming cadenced prose (*sajʿ*) which they employed especially in

Period and Beyond, ed. Élise Franssen (Venice: Edizione Ca'foscari, 2022), 83–152. One of the works from Shāfiʿ's personal library was recently identified by Muḥammad ʿAlī Abū Ḥamza on Twitter (https://twitter.com/Alsonamyhart). This copy of al-Bandanījī's (d. 284/897) *Kitāb al-Tafqīh fī al-Lugha*, first produced in 591/1195, bears the note *li-Shāfiʿ b. ʿAlī ʿafā Allāh ʿanhu* ("belonging to Shāfiʿ b. ʿAlī , may God forgive him) on its title page. Istanbul Süleymaniye Kütüphanesi MS Aya Sofya 4670, 1a.

3 Al-Nuwayrī describes the event of his becoming blind in more vivid detail: "He was hit by a Mongol arrow in his head, and then that which blinded him poured forth from his brain to his eyes." *Nihāyat al-Arab fī Funūn al-Adab*, 33 vols. ed. Ibrāhīm Shams al-Dīn (Beirut: Dār al-kutub al-ʿilmiyya, 2004), 33:239. The most extensive treatment of this event can be found in a *tarjama* by al-Jazarī, which includes a first-person account of the event attributed to the blind man himself *Ḥawādith al-Zamān fī Anbāʾihi wa-Wafayāt al-Akābir wa-l-Aʿyān min Abnāʾihi*, 2 vols., ed. ʿUmar Tadmurī (Ṣaydā/Beirut: al-Maktaba al-ʿAṣriyya, s.d.), 2:428–429. See chapter one, section 1.2. for a translation of this account.

4 Al-Ṣafadī writes these *nisbas* as "al-ʿAsqalānī, then [*thumma*] al-Miṣrī," which could mean that he moved from ʿAsqalān to Egypt at some point, but more likely refers to his paternal family's ancestral ties to that city.

5 This study follows a recent research trend to avoid designating this sultanate or the period of its rule by the anachronistic misnomer "Mamluk." For the rationale behind doing so, see below in this introduction ("The historical background"). An in-depth discussion of the issue may be found in Jo Van Steenbergen, "Revisiting the Mamluk Empire: Political Action, Relationships of Power, Entangled Networks, and the Sultanate of Cairo in Late Medieval Syro-Egypt," in *The Mamluk Sultanate from the Perspective of Regional and World History: Economic, Social and Cultural Development in an Era of Increasing International Interaction and Competition*, eds. Reuven Amitai and Stephan Conermann (Bonn: V&R unipress/Bonn University Press, 2019), 75–106.

epistolary writings, and poetry, which they also wrote a good deal of as in-house panegyrists and as a more general literary pursuit. These men of the pen harnessed the various media of courtly and state communication as elite forms of literary performance, both within and without chancery contexts. This is very much the case for Shāfiʿ: although al-Ṣafadī and all his other biographers imply that his official career in the chancery ended after he was blinded, in his own works Shāfiʿ would have his readers believe that he continued to work as a prominent scribe for several decades—his last known claim to having composed an official document is dated to 708/1309, nearly thirty years after the event that blinded him.[6]

The works in which Shāfiʿ informs his readers about his scribal activities are predominantly biographies (*sīra*, pl. *siyar*) he composed of sultans whom he either served directly or with whom he lived contemporaneously. Three of these survive whole or in part. They respectively depict the reigns of sultans al-Ẓāhir Baybars (r. 658–676/1260–1277), al-Manṣūr Qalāwūn (r. 678–689/1279–1290), and the latter's son and second successor al-Nāṣir Muḥammad (r. 693–694/1293–1294, 698–708/1299–1309, 709–741/1309–1341). These three biographies were written in direct conversation with the foundational biographies of sultans written by Shāfiʿ's maternal uncle Muḥyī al-Dīn ʿAbd Allāh b. Rashīd al-Dīn b. ʿAbd al-Ẓāhir (d. 692/1293), generally known as Ibn ʿAbd al-Ẓāhir.[7] He was the leading chancery official under Baybars and remained in service in the higher echelons of the chancery until his death. His first and most widely circulated biography also deals with the sultanate of Baybars. A second and third biography deal with the reigns of Qalāwūn and his son al-Ashraf Khalīl (r. 689–693/1290–1293).[8] It is this corpus of six *sīra*s which will form the core focus of this book. These writings are generally considered some of the most authoritative sources for the political history of late 7th/13th century Egypt and Syria. The corpus covers about half a century of history, though unevenly: while the entire reign of Baybars is covered, as is most of Qalāwūn's, for both al-Ashraf Khalīl and al-Nāṣir Muḥammad the corpus is fragmentary.

---

6 Al-Nuwayrī mentions that Shāfiʿ "was forced [to resign] following the Battle of Homs." (*qad uḍirra ʿaqīb waqʿat Ḥimṣ*) *Nihāya*, 33:239. Paulina Lewicka, one of two scholars who edited Shāfiʿ's *sīra* of Qalāwūn, *al-Faḍl al-Maʾthūr*, consulted an ophthalmologist on this regard and was informed that complete loss of sight while preserving all other brain functions would have been impossible. She thinks it is more likely that he was blinded in one eye and later gradually lost his entire sight. Lewicka, *Šāfiʿ Ibn ʿAlī's Biography of the Mamluk Sultan Qalāwūn* (Warsaw: Dialog, 2000), 91.

7 In the following pages, I will use the name Ibn ʿAbd al-Ẓāhir only to refer to Muḥyī al-Dīn b. ʿAbd al-Ẓāhir. When referring to his father, son, and grandson (all of whom also had this family name) I will use fuller versions of their names to distinguish them from each other.

8 Shāfiʿ claims to have written a *sīra* devoted to al-Ashraf Khalīl as well, but no manuscript of such a text has been identified so far. Al-Ṣafadī, *Aʿyān*, 2:502.

The close familial and professional links between these authors make this into an exceptionally close-knit corpus. Although only their biographies of Baybars are directly related—Shāfiʿ's *sīra* of Baybars is explicitly presented as an abridgement (*mukhtaṣar*) of his uncle's earlier *sīra*—their other texts also adhere to a consistent conceptualisation of *sīra*. Even though the regnal biography was a well-established genre in Arabic historiographical writing by the 7th/13th century, I argue that these two authors' take on the genre constituted a unique iteration of a longer tradition. They built on the work of predecessors, especially the biographies devoted to Ṣalāḥ al-Dīn (r. 532–589/1174–1193) by his officials Bahāʾ al-Dīn b. Shaddād (d. 632/1234) and ʿImād al-Dīn al-Iṣfahānī (d. 597/1201) about a century earlier, but they went further than them in using the basic framework of accounts about one sultan's life and times as a central node in the preservation of historical memory.[9] For Ibn ʿAbd al-Ẓāhir and Shāfiʿ b. ʿAlī, memorialising the reign of a particular sultan also presented the occasion to memorialise the particular form of his *dawla*, the household formation of the state around the power networks of the sultan, in which the authors were important participants as prominent chancery officials. Memorialising a sultan's state also presented the opportunity to memorialise their own contribution to that state. It is notable in that sense that they applied the *sīra* format not just to a single paradigmatic sultan but to every major sultan they served. In most cases they also appear to have written large parts of their texts while the sultan was alive and not as retrospective memoirs. This indicates that the valence of *sīra* and the impulse to compose such a text was somewhat different in the late 7th/13th century than it had been for Ṣalāḥ al-Dīn's biographers, both of whom wrote their texts retrospectively and only devoted biographies to a single sultan. For these earlier authors, writing biography was a way to safeguard the memory of a sultan whose reign they saw as ideal, especially in the face of changing conditions of rule by his successors.

9 Bahāʾ al-Dīn b. Shaddād and ʿImād al-Dīn al-Iṣfahānī respectively devoted one and two historiographical works to (parts of) the life of Ṣalāḥ al-Dīn, none of which was explicitly titled *sīra*, although manuscripts of these texts did later circulate with such designations. The only text of these three written at least in part contemporaneously to Ṣalāḥ al-Dīn's reign is al-Iṣfahānī's *al-Fatḥ al-Qussī fī al-Fatḥ al-Qudsī*, allegedly composed to celebrate the conquest of Jerusalem initially, but in its present state going up to the death of Ṣalāḥ al-Dīn (no manuscript attestation exists of the alleged earlier version of the text). Neither author composed such works for Ṣalāḥ al-Dīn's successors. On this corpus, see among others P.M. Holt, "Saladin and His Admirers: A Biographical Reassessment," *BSOAS* 46:2 (1983), 235–239; Anne-Marie Eddé, *Saladin*, transl. Jane Marie Todd (Cambridge, MA: The Belknap Press of Harvard University Press, 2011), 4–6; Gowaart Van Den Bossche, "Narrative Construction, Ideal Rule, and Emotional Discourse in the Biographies of Ṣalāḥ al-Dīn and Louis IX by Bahāʾ al-Dīn b. Shaddād and Jean Sire de Joinville," *al-Masaq* 30, no. 2 (2018), 133–147.

That there was a boom of biographical writing in late 7th/13th century Cairo is confirmed by the existence of at least two other biographies of Baybars written by prominent cultural agents of the period. One was composed by the Syrian historian ʿIzz al-Dīn b. al-Shaddād (d. 684/1285). It is still extant in part and will feature regularly throughout this book.[10] Of a second biography supposedly written by the well-known jurist and prosopographer Ibn Khallikān (d. 681/1282) we only know that Ibn Khallikān compared Baybars to Genghis Khān in it.[11] This distinctive production of biographical writing did not continue into the early 8th/14th century, when several historians instead composed large scale works with a wider chronological focus: on the one hand voluminous universal histories, and on the other hand more regionally focussed chronicles with a strong presence of obituaries.[12] I posit that this 8th/14th century development amounts to a shift of dominant historiographical paradigm and that the 7th/13th century form of *sīra* itself also constituted such a temporarily dominant paradigm. Studying such a corpus is thus not only relevant to understand the modalities of history writing in a particular time and place, but also to gain insights into why such shifts occur and how historians' agency interacted with historically contingent events.

In this book I closely read the six texts in the *sīra* corpus alongside other available material written by their authors. I consider how their extant corpora straddle the domains of history, state communication and literary performance. In studying

---

10 ʿIzz al-Dīn b. Shaddād, *Taʾrīkh al-Malik al-Ẓāhir*, ed. Aḥmad Ḥuṭayṭ (Wiesbaden: Franz Steiner, 1983). The single known manuscript (Edirne Selimiye MS 2306) contains only the second of two original volumes. Additionally, several quotations from the first volume survive in the work of later historians. For a discussion of the text's contents, see: Yoel Koch, "ʿIzz al-Dīn ibn Shaddād and his Biography of Baybars," *Annali: Istituto Universitario Orientale, Sezione Slava* 43, no. 2 (1983), 249–287.

11 Reportedly, Ibn Khallikān was almost made vizier after he had the biography shown to Baybars, but this was prevented by the machinations of Ibn Ḥinnā, who served as Baybars' vizier at the time. Ibn Shākir al-Kutubī, *Fawāt al-wafāyāt*, 5 vols., ed. Iḥsān ʿAbbās (Beirut: Dār Ṣādir, 1973), 1:112. The information is paraphrased by Mathieu Eychenne, *Liens personnels, clientélisme et réseaux de pouvoir dans le sultanat mamelouk (milieu XIIIe-fin XIVe siècle)* (Beirut-Damascus: Presses de l'Ifpo, 2013), chapter four. I am grateful to Mustafa Banister for drawing my attention to this information.

12 These two groups have been distinguished as Egyptian and Syrian schools of historiography respectively. The idea originates with Donald P. Little, *An Introduction to Mamluk Historiography: An Analysis of Arabic Annalistic and Biographical Sources for the Reign of Al-Malik An-Nāṣir Muḥammad Ibn Qalā'ūn* (Wiesbaden: Franz Steiner Verlag, 1970), 98. See also Li Guo, "Mamluk Historiographic Studies: The state of the Art" *MSR* 1 (1997), 31–32; and a recent re-evaluation in: Jo Van Steenbergen "Introduction – History Writing, *Adab*, and Intertextuality in Late Medieval Egypt and Syria: Old and New Readings" in *New Readings in Arabic Historiography from Late Medieval Egypt and Syria: Proceedings of the Themed Day of the Fifth Conference of the School of Mamluk Studies*, eds. J. Van Steenbergen & M. Termonia (Leiden: Brill, 2021), 6–7.

these books as deliberately conceived wholes, I react against decontextualised readings of Islamic historiography. Instead of cherry-picking anecdotes from the rich historical and other assorted materials they include, I look at the textual fabric in which information was embedded. While such an approach is admittedly not viable for expansive, diachronically inclined research projects, I argue that a return to the sources as complete textual constructions is imperative if we want to develop more nuanced interpretations of the material contained in them. For similar reasons I directly involve the manuscripts through which these texts have come down to us in our discussions. As Ali Karjoo-Ravary recently noted with reference to a late 8th/14th century Persian text from Anatolia that is akin in spirit to the *sīra* corpus: "books in the premodern Islamicate context were produced with the complete appearance of the book in mind."[13] While many good text editions contain a discussion of the manuscripts on which they are based, these are usually informed by a historical critical mentality of establishing the relation of a certain manuscript to a holograph manuscript, or amount to little more than discussion of its completeness. Questions of materiality are usually only treated marginally, and paratextual details are often not discussed at all. Considering that most of our texts are only known in single manuscripts and that many of them are likely holographs it is straightforward and hence vital to study their materiality, for example for the ways in which they use layout to communicate meaning. These manuscripts offer important clues as to how authors wished their audience to understand their contents, and as a result they must be considered alongside their textual contents.

Through the holistic analysis of texts, this book aims to understand how two authors from similar backgrounds but diverging professional trajectories developed a coherent interpretation of a particular historiographical genre in the socio-political contexts of late 7th/13th and early 8th/14th century Egypt and Syria. I argue that these two authors endeavoured to construct literary edifices that constituted significant symbolic capital by which they negotiated their own position at court and their relationship to their peers. In doing so I argue against a common interpretation of these sources as essentially serving a legitimising end. This interpretation has fundamentally guided how these texts have been read as historical sources. The panegyric inclinations of the *sīra*s are thought to distort a balanced rendering of the past and necessitate a critical reading to disentangle the facts from

13 Ali Karjoo-Ravary, "Adorning the King of Islam: Weaving and Unraveling History in Astarabadi's *Feasting and Fighting*," *MAVCOR Journal* 6, no. 2 (2022). For a similar assessment on pre-modern books in general, compare Roger Chartier's statement that "the historically and socially distinctive significations of a text [. . .] are inseparable from the material conditions and physical forms that make the text available to readers." *Forms and Meanings: Texts, Performances, and Audiences from Codex to Computer* (Philadelphia: University of Pennsylvania Press, 1995), 22.

the fanciful, so to speak. As will become clear, I propose to largely abandon such a reading and focus instead on the authorial motives that governed choices of what to include in a *sīra*, how to make narrative sense of the recent past, and how to frame diplomatic and poetic material within a *sīra* context.

In the following section I discuss the issue of legitimacy in more detail. This is followed by a section where I present my alternative interpretation of the *sīra* corpus as "literary spectacle." Then follows an overview of the historical background constituting the context in which the *sīra*s were written as well as a critical discussion of some of the secondary literature on state formation insofar as it is relevant to understand the social position of our authors and the importance of their literary acts. The introduction is then concluded by a brief outline of the chapters of this book.

I Beyond legitimacy

Most of the texts in the *sīra* corpus are well known in the field because the authors were eyewitnesses of the genesis and early decades of the Cairo Sultanate, a period for which otherwise relatively few contemporary sources survive compared to an abundance of 8th/14th and 9th/15th century historiographical texts. Scholars have noted that many of these later texts rely substantially on some texts from the *sīra* corpus for their accounts of the reigns of the early sultans.[14] Despite this privileged position as direct sources for the period, scholars have routinely posited that because of their authors' close ties to the courts of former-slave-soldiers-turned-sultans, these texts' main interest lies in how they give expression to sultanic legitimisation strategies, instigated by the sultans themselves and executed by an able but servile scribe. They posit that such legitimisation was necessary because of the sultans' lack of noble lineage, their outsider status as ethnic Turks, and the fact that many of them came to power through usurpations, sometimes involving the assassination of their predecessor. The issue of legitimacy was applied to the *sīra* corpus first by P.M. Holt who wrote several articles dealing with parts of the *sīra* corpus. His basic assumption was that historiographical narratives were needed to legitimise the reigns of sultans Baybars and Qalāwūn, both of whom came to power through complex, sometimes violent machinations among the elites from which they emerged as strong leaders. Holt argued that the *sīra*s written by Ibn ʿAbd al-Ẓāhir and Shāfiʿ b. ʿAlī formulated

14 Ulrich Haarmann, *Quellenstudien zur frühen Mamlukenzeit* (Freiburg: Robischon, 1969), 97; P.M. Holt, "Three Biographies of al-Ẓāhir Baybars," in *Medieval Historical Writing in the Christian and Islamic Worlds*, ed. David O. Morgan (London: School of Oriental and African Studies, 1982), 19–29.

a propagandistic image of the ideal sultan and twisted historical facts to fit heroic narratives of rulership and to erase memories of usurpation. These narratives were not set in stone but were dependent on the time in which they were written—hence why Shāfiʿ b. ʿAlī's abridgement of his uncle's *sīra* of Baybars could diverge in important respects from the work it abridged—but the core issue remained to legitimise either the sultan to whom the biography was dedicated or a later sultan whose reign followed directly or indirectly on the reign depicted in the *sīra*.[15]

Holt's ideas have been widely received. Chase F. Robinson for example invoked the legitimisation thesis in his textbook *Islamic Historiography*. Robinson's discussion of later iterations of the ideal type historiographical form of "biography"—as distinct from "chronography" and "prosopography"—is even based in large part on Holt's work.[16] More recently, scholars have moved away from the problematic dichotomy of historical facts distorted by legitimising discourse and focussed instead on the legitimisation strategies themselves so as to interpret the modalities of ideological communication and the propagandistic use of historical memory. This is often done by combining readings of material in the *sīras* with other historical texts, diplomatic documents, and epigraphy.[17] One of the most extensive such

15 Holt's most comprehensive argumentation on the corpus can be found in: "The Sultan as Ideal Ruler: Ayyubid and Mamluk Prototypes," in *Süleyman the Magnificent and His Age: The Ottoman Empire in the Early Modern World*, eds. Metin Kunt & Christine Woodhead (New York: Longman, 1995), 122–137. He formulated the basic argument already much earlier in two articles focused on select texts: "The Virtuous Ruler in Thirteenth-Century Mamluk Royal Biographies," *Nottingham Medieval Studies* 24 (1980), 27–35; and "Three Biographies." Variations on the themes of this articles can furthermore be found in the following specific studies on Shāfiʿ b. ʿAlī's writings: "Some Observations on Shāfiʿ b. ʿAlī's Biography of Baybars," *Journal of Semitic Studies* 29 (1984), 123–130; "A Chancery Clerk in Medieval Egypt," *The English Historical Review* 101/400 (1986), 671–679; and "The Presentation of Qalāwūn by Shāfiʿ b. ʿAlī" in *Essays in Honor of Bernard Lewis: The Islamic World. From Classical to Modern Times*, eds. C.E. Bosworth, C. Issawi, R. Savory, & A.L. Udovitch (eds.) (Princeton: The Darwin Press, 1989), 141–50. The biographies are also used in his monograph *Early Mamluk Diplomacy (1260–1290): Treaties of Baybars and Qalāwūn with Christian Rulers* (Leiden: Brill, 1995), where he translated treaties and other assorted excerpts found in the texts of Ibn ʿAbd al-Ẓāhir and Shāfiʿ b. ʿAlī.

16 Chase F. Robinson, *Islamic Historiography* (Cambridge: Cambridge University Press, 2003), 121, 166.

17 See, among others, several of the articles compiled in: Denise Aigle, *The Mongol Empire between Myth and Reality: Studies in Anthropological History* (Leiden: Brill, 2015). See also: Anne-Marie Eddé, "Baybars et son double: De l'ambiguïté du souverain ideal," in *Le Bilad Al-Šam face aux mondes extérieurs: La perception de l'autre et la représentation du souverain*, ed. Denise Aigle (Damascus/Beirut: Presses de L'Ifpo, 2012), 73–86; Amina A. Elbendary, "The Sultan, the Tyrant, and the Hero: Changing Medieval Perceptions of al-Zāhir Baybars." *MSR* 5 (2001), 141–157; Remke Kruk, "History and Apocalypse: Ibn Al-Nafīs' Justification of Mamluk Rule." *Der Islam* 72, no. 2 (1995), 324–337; Tahar Mansouri, "Le portrait du sultan al-Manṣūr Qalāwūn d'après *al-Faḍl al-ma'ṯūr min sīrat al-Malik al-Manṣūr* de Šāfiʿ b. ʿAlī." in *Le Bilad Al-Šam*, 87–97; Anne Troadec, "Les

evaluations is Anne Broadbridge's study of legitimacy in the interactions between the Mongol Ilkhanate and the Cairo Sultanate as a battlefield of ideology, in which she focussed especially on diplomatic relations. She defines "Mamluk ideology" as directly linked to the question of legitimacy:

> [Mamluk ideology] hinged consistently and exclusively on antiquated Islamic concepts and on a vision of the Mamluk sultan as a martial Guardian of Islam and Islamic society. The Mamluk sultans used this outdated model because they suffered from two serious, linked problems: the institution of slavery and a lack of lineage. The Mamluk slave institution meant that the Mamluks were singularly ill-suited to justify themselves as ruler.[18]

The *sīras* take up a position of primary importance as sources articulating this project of Islamic legitimisation because they contain so much information about and specimens of diplomatic exchange with the Mongols. One such case of diplomatic exchange during the reign of Qalāwūn has been much discussed in scholarship and will form the focus of a case study in chapter four of this book (section 4.4.1.), where I will show how these accounts and documents need to be understood within their textual embedding.

The focus on the discourse of legitimacy has certainly brought many relevant insights to the study of late medieval political culture and textual production, but it has also created an interpretative monoculture. In this view *sīra* functions as panegyric and essentially comes into existence in a top-down process in which the scribes who wrote these texts are relatively constrained in what they can write by state-sanctioned legitimising propaganda.[19] This kind of interpretation stands in contrast to in-depth studies of literary dynamics in earlier periods which have interpreted panegyrics as multi-dimensional negotiations of authority between patron, panegyrist and the wider courtly habitus in which they participated.[20] Where the idea of legitimisation posits a unidirectional act of communication—an author

Mamelouks dans l'espace syrien: stratégies de domination et résistances (658/1260–741/1341)" (Unpublished PhD thesis, Ecole Pratique des hautes-études, 2014).

18 Anne F. Broadbridge, *Kingship and Ideology in the Islamic and Mongol Worlds* (Cambridge: Cambridge University Press, 2007), 12. See also her article "Mamluk Legitimacy and the Mongols: The Reigns of Baybars and Qalāwūn," *MSR* 4 (2000), 91–118.

19 For an important criticism of the idea of propaganda as a framework to understand literary expression in the Ayyubid period, see Matthew L. Keegan, "Rethinking Poetry as (Anti-Crusader) Propaganda: Licentiousness and Cross-Confessional Patronage in the *Ḫarīdat al-qaṣr*," *Intellectual History of the Islamicate World* (2022 forthcoming). I am grateful to Matthew for sharing a pre-print of this article with me. See also Keegan, "*Adab* without the Crusades: The Inebriated Solidarity of a Young Officer's Hunting Epistle," *Al-ʿUṣūr al-Wusṭā* 28 (2020), 272–296.

20 Beatrice Gruendler, *Medieval Arabic Praise Poetry: Ibn Al-Rumi and the Patron's Redemption* (Abingdon: Routledge, 2003); Margaret Larkin, *al-Mutanabbi: Voice of the Abbasid Poetic Ideal* (London: OneWorld, 2008).

expressing a sultan's legitimacy as an act of service to that sultan—these modern evaluations of panegyric instead see legitimisation as but one layer of a complex communicative act. Expressions of legitimacy share the stage with the panegyrist's display of literary dexterity and the concomitant performance of his social pre-eminence. While evaluations of this kind have been voiced for literary texts in the courtly orbit in late medieval Egypt and Syria, the interpretation remains marginal in historiography.[21]

The present study proposes to focus squarely on the contents of the *sīras* as they are presented to the reader. I read these texts along the grain and consider the late $7^{\text{th}}/13^{\text{th}}$ century iteration of the genre of *sīra* on its own terms.[22] I take seriously the presentation of history these texts offer and disregard questions of whether the facts presented in them are historically ascertainable and what legitimising concern these narratives may have served. My primary concern will be with how the historical presentation functions as a self-contained discourse on power, with special attention to the relationship of power to the written word. I argue that Ibn ʿAbd al-Ẓāhir and Shāfiʿ b. ʿAlī were not in the first place concerned with formulating arguments in favour of a given sultan's legitimacy. Rather, their primary concern was to appropriately render a sultan's legacy into literary form to ensure the preservation of its memory through the ages. Following Paul Ricoeur, I investigate how they reconfigured their experience of time through the interpretative and narrative act of writing history.[23] Legitimacy plays a role in these narrative configurations, especially in the presentation of how sultans came to power, but reading these texts as only speaking to issues of legitimacy leads to a distorted understanding of their objectives.

I suggest that authors reimagined *sīra* as a textual genre sitting at the heart of chancery practices because it presented a particularly fitting textual form to compile chancery documents relevant to a sultan's reign. In many cases these documents were composed by the authors themselves. The high-blown format of panegyric history also provided them with the opportunity to make extensive use of registers employed within the chancery when composing their historical accounts and allowed ample space for literary digression. These texts as such contain a strong

---

21 For a pioneering study of this ilk on a short historical work with strong literary inclinations, see Jo Van Steenbergen, "Qalāwūnid Discourse, Elite Communication and the Mamluk Cultural Matrix: Interpreting a 14th-Century Panegyric," *JAL* 43 (2012), 6.

22 I am grateful to Konrad Hirschler for suggesting the notion of reading texts "along the grain."

23 See especially this programmatic statement in Paul Ricoeur's *Temps et récit 1: L'intrigue et le récit historique* (Paris: Editions du Seuil, 1983), 10: "[L'intrigue d'un récit] <<prend ensemble>> et intègre dans une histoire entière et complète les événements multiples et dispersés et ainsi schématise la signification intelligible qui s'attache au récit pris comme un tout."

layer of literary performance, which I argue, should be understood within the framework of the relationship of patronage. Following Pierre Bourdieu, I argue that we should closely investigate the writing of regnal biography and the cultural capital deriving from it as one of several possible ways to negotiate a social position in the late medieval literary field of the Cairo sultanate.[24]

II Literary spectacles of sultanship

With Paul Ricoeur and Pierre Bourdieu serving as theoretical benchmarks informing my interpretation, I conceptualise the outcome of the process of narrative reconfiguration of time in the *sīra* corpus as "spectacle." I extrapolate this idea from Ibn ʿAbd al-Ẓāhir's metaphorical definition of *sīra* as "a mirror in which the spectator (*nāẓir*) may see the power of the first kings."[25] This programmatic designation partakes of a common idea of history as a mirror (*mirʾāh*), popularised not long before Ibn ʿAbd al-Ẓāhir's time by Sibṭ b. al-Jawzī (d. 654/1256) who entitled his universal chronicle *Mirʾāt al-zamān fī tawārīkh al-aʿyān* ("The Mirror of Time: Historical Accounts of the Notables"). This title and Ibn ʿAbd al-Ẓāhir's metaphor participate in a discourse of history being a domain of "likeness," not in the sense of *mimesis*, but in the sense that it presents the past in such a way that the reader may evaluate events of the past and reflect on similarities across history and the present.[26] There is a strong continuity here with advice literature, which frequently made use of historical exempla to make certain points about the ideal (or, conversely, undesirable) comportment of rulers.[27] The nature of ideal rule is central to the presentation of history in the *sīras* of Ibn ʿAbd al-Ẓāhir and Shāfiʿ. For them this was a genre testifying of a particular regnal form of historical memory—history encapsulated and given meaning within the framework of one sultan's life and reign—in which the spectator could understand the meaning and importance of a sultan's state. The benefit of *sīra* was that the reader could ponder the meaning of history in one cohesive whole instead of embedded in a larger discourse of annalistic historiography

---

24 While broadly inspired by his work, I have made most direct use of Pierre Bourdieu's article "Le champ littéraire," *Actes de la recherche en sciences sociales* 89 (1991), 3–46.

25 *Rawḍ*, 45. See chapter two (section 2.3.1.) for a more thorough discussion of this phrase in its context.

26 Note that similar ideas about mirrors were very much present in Latin Europe, especially in the idea of "mirrors for princes" which inculcated ideas of proper comportment to rulers. See, among others, Sabine Melchoir-Bonnet, *Histoire du miroir* (Paris: Editions imago, 1994), chapters 5 and 6.

27 Louise Marlow, "Advice Literature," *EI3*. On the intersection of advice literature and historiography in the format of the regnal biography, see Van Den Bossche, "Narrative Construction."

covering longer periods. Rather than the great "mirror of time" posited by Sibṭ b. al-Jawzī, theirs were as it were pocket mirrors, offering a smaller but also more detailed reflection of the recent past. The unusual English plural "spectacles" which I have used in the title of this book and its possible misreading as referring to glasses is in that sense not even unwelcome: the discourse of *sīra* may also be understood as offering the reader a way of seeing the past, as if they were offered a set of spectacles by which they might see more clearly the importance of a certain event of history and the author's literary reimagining of it.

In addition to Ibn ʿAbd al-Ẓāhir's underlining of the role of the "spectator," my reading of *sīra* as spectacle has been inspired by Kristie Fleckenstein's analysis of norms of social comportment in late medieval Europe as "decorous spectacle." She argues that these norms came into existence through a nexus of the increasing material presence of mirrors in the wealthy circles of high and late medieval Europe, ethical discourses in "mirrors for princes," and forms of elaborate textual discourse in letter writing (the *ars dictaminis*). Proper comportment became increasingly codified and associated with conceptions of resemblance, imitation, and self-assessment. She argues that this was reflected especially in rhetorical norms, which became increasingly stringent.[28] This theorisation of rhetoric as socially codified linguistic interaction typified by spectacle appears to me as useful in reading *sīra* literature even if the details for late medieval Egypt and Syria are different—for one, the material presence of mirrors has not been studied as extensively as far as I am aware. It draws attention to the "spectacular" fashion in which both our authors wrote their texts and their reliance on clichés that may appear as tiresome to a modern reader but which were appreciated by many contemporary readers as continuous engagement with and valorisation of the literary tradition.[29] The linguistic and compositional command displayed in these texts was meant to awe the audience and to integrate author, patron and the memory of the sultan—insofar as he was not himself the patron—into a multi-levelled performance of cultural pre-eminence: writing a text was a marker of considerable cultural capital, but so was the patron's understanding of its rhetorical and intertextual depths.

The spectacular is also relevant to the ways in which pre-modern Arabic literary criticism conceptualised the effects of literary language. As Lara Harb has shown, the central principle in criticism concerned the evocation of "an experience of wonder" through poets' creative usage of the Arabic language's rich treasure house of polysemic

---

28 Kristie S. Fleckenstein, "Decorous Spectacle: Mirrors, Manners, and Ars Dictaminis in Late Medieval Civic Engagement," *Rhetoric Review* 28, no. 2 (2009), 111–127.

29 On the concern of "originality" and the use of "clichés," see the insightful comments by Adam Talib in *How Do You Say Epigram in Arabic? Literary History at the Limits of Comparison* (Leiden: Brill, 2018), 76–77.

words and expressions.[30] While such evaluations were almost exclusively concerned with the workings of the literary experience in individual lines or even half-lines of poetry, it is possible to scale that idea up to the level of a single text and even to the level of a single author's output if seen as an accumulation of wondrous expressions. There is some precedent in this in the theory of *naẓm*, the "binding whole" of a text. Usually the term *naẓm* is applied to the textual category of poetry and to specific poems, but there is an interesting case in the present corpus where Shāfiʿ b. ʿAlī employs the verbal form *naẓama* to denote his uncle's composition of his *sīra* of Baybars.[31] Its original lexical meaning of "organisation" and "arranging" is doubtlessly important to this, as it accommodates both the meticulous arrangement of lexemes into the stringent order of metered poetry and the more flexible organisation of words in prose.

The stress on evoking wonder also brings into focus an important layer of the communicative directionality of these texts, already hinted at in my criticism of the idea of legitimisation. As outlined above, I interpret spectacle as denoting the involvement of writer and audience in the space of a text, but this audience is in fact largely implicit. Earlier scholars have routinely interpreted the audience of the *sīras* to have been the sultans and their entourages, and possibly a vaguely defined broader audience to whom legitimising propaganda should be addressed. I problematise this supposition in the final chapter of this book based on the material transmission of the *sīras*, most of which survive in holograph manuscript copies, but only one of which explicitly mentions a patron—most certainly not a sultan and likely a chancery agent. Given this conspicuous absence of directly identifiable patrons and the texts' rhetorical strategies I posit that the primary audience of these texts was relatively limited and primarily consisted of the authors' peers. More than the sultan, leading chancery officials and the powerful agents involved in overseeing the *dīwān al-inshāʾ*—especially the viziers and *dawādārs*—surface as the most likely audience towards whom many of these texts performed their literary pre-eminence. Given that the chancery functioned as the most stable professional prospect for those with literary ambition at the time, it became a major avenue for the performance of literary spectacle.[32]

30 Lara Harb, *Arabic Poetics: Aesthetic Experience in Classical Arabic Literature* (Cambridge: Cambridge University Press, 2021), 4 and passim.

31 Shāfiʿ b. ʿAlī, *Ḥusn al-Manāqib al-Sirriyya al-Muntazaʿa min al-Sīra al-Ẓāhiriyya*, ed. ʿAbd al-ʿAzīz al-Khuwayṭir (Riyadh 1989, second edition), 56. For a theorisation of *naẓm* as the "binding whole" of a text, see Rebecca Gould, "Inimitability versus Translatability," *The Translator* 19, no. 1 (2013), 81–104.

32 Consider for example the attention given to the chancery in Thomas Bauer's biographical sketch of arguably the most important 8th/14th century poet: "Ibn Nubātah al-Miṣrī (686–768/1287–1366): Life and Works Part I: The Life of Ibn Nubātah," *MSR* 12, no. 1 (2008), 9. See also the repeated invocation of the chancery as a central state and literary institution in Muhsin al-Musawi, *The Medieval Islamic Republic of Letters: Arabic Knowledge Construction* (Notre Dame, IN: University of Notre Dame Press, 2015), 117–118 and passim.

This last point brings us to another widely held supposition in the field, namely that literary culture in late medieval Egypt and Syria increasingly developed outside of the court which had dominated literary production in preceding periods. Literature now became communicative in socially horizontal directions, with poems and works being offered to peers instead of to persons in positions of authority, thus forming new kinds of patronage that were less directly built around hierarchical social relationships.[33] This line of interpretation has been useful to understand the changing dynamics of literary culture in the so-called post-classical period,[34] but as some scholars have recently highlighted, it runs the risk of obscuring the continued importance of the court as a significant locus of cultural production and performance which interacted in manifold ways with the wider literary field.[35] The corpus studied in this book lies neatly at the intersection of the courtly and literary fields: the authors were active in the prestigious composition bureau and directly served the sultan and other persons of high authority, but they also exchanged significant amounts of poetry and prose with their peers independently of their chancery roles. The *sīras* initially give the impression of being entirely courtly phenomena, but when read closely it emerges that they engaged in many ways with the broader literary field.

My methodology in re-interpreting legitimacy and literary culture in the space of the *sīra* corpus is broadly inspired by New Historicist readings of the contexts in which authors wrote and by Clifford Geertz's "thick description" method to reconstruct the cultural frameworks informing acts of cultural expression.[36] That is, I

---

33 Thomas Bauer, "Mamluk Literature as a Means of Communication," in *Ubi sumus? Quo vademus? Mamluk Studies – State of the Art*, ed. S. Conermann (Bonn: V&R unipress/Bonn University Press, 2013), 23–56.

34 In that sense the interpretation was pioneered by James T. Monroe & Mark F. Pettigrew who argued that a less court-focused literary field allowed new "popular" genres to develop. They specifically highlight the *zajal* and the *maqāma* in the 4th/10th century—respectively in Andalusia and Iraq—and the shadow play in 7th/13th century Egypt. "The Decline of Courtly Patronage and the Appearance of New Genres in Arabic Literature," *JAL* 34 (2003), 138–177.

35 Two important recent books have discussed this issue at some length for the early 10th/16th century: Kristof D'hulster, *Browsing the Sultan's Bookshelves: Towards a Reconstruction of the Library of the Mamluk Sultan Qāniṣawh al-Ghawrī (r. 906–922/1501–1516)* (Bonn: V&R unipress/Bonn University Press, 2021); Christian Mauder, *In the Sultan's Salon: Learning, Religion, and Rulership at the Mamluk Court of Qāniṣawh Al-Ghawrī (r. 1501–1516)* (Leiden: Brill, 2021). See also Syrinx Von hees, "Ein Lobgedicht auf den obersten Staatssekretär zum Anlass eines 'House-sitting': Überschneidungen von Herrschaftshof und Bildungsbürgertum und ihre Reflexian bei an-Nawāǧī" in *The Racecourse of Literature: An-Nawāǧī and His Contemporaries*, eds. Alev Masarwa & Hakan Özkan (Baden-Baden: Ergon Verlag, 2020), 213–262; Matthew Keegan "Review of Adam Talib, *How do you Say Epigram in Arabic?*," *Middle Eastern Literatures* 21, nos. 2–3 (2018), 251–252.

36 H. Aram Veeser (ed.). *The New Historicism* (London: Routledge, 1989); Clifford Geertz, "Thick Description," in *The Interpretation of Cultures* (New York: Basic Books, 1973). For a similar approach

endeavour to understand cultural, political, and other references within the cultural framework available to the authors who wrote these texts. In this book I do so by first forming a broad understanding of the presentation of *sīra* and the grand narrative constructions operating across these texts in chapters two and three, and then specifically zooming in on how the different fields—chancery, literary field, court—influenced the form and contents of the *sīra*s in chapters four to six (a more detailed breakdown of the chapters of this book is given at the end of this introduction).

To be able to make this interpretation a broad understanding of the broader political history of the period is necessary. In the next section I present an overview of the period's political history aligned with my reading of the issue of legitimacy and with discussions of state formation, as these have contributed to my understanding of where our authors fit within the structures of the state and its political history. As a visual summary, see also Figure 1, which provides a timeline

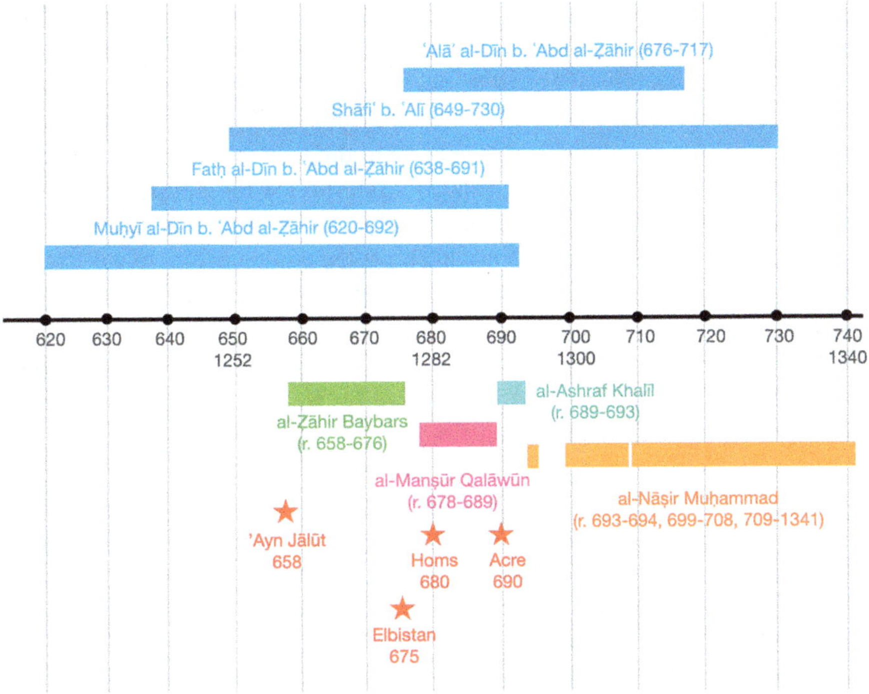

Figure 1: Timeline of author's lifetimes, sultanic reigns and major military engagements of the 7th/13th and early 8th/14th centuries.

---

to the study of political theory, but explicitly aligned with the Cambridge school of conceptual history, see Mohamad El-Merheb, *Political Thought in the Mamluk Period: The Unnecessary Caliphate* (Edinburgh: Edinburgh University Press, 2022), 32–34.

with the reigns of the most important sultans—that is, those to whom biographies were devoted—overlaid with the lifetimes of our authors and their direct family members. The most important military endeavours are also highlighted as these will be referred to regularly throughout the book.

III The historical background

The establishment of the Cairo Sultanate is conventionally situated in 648/1250, when the last Ayyubid sultan of Egypt al-Muʿaẓẓam Tūrān Shāh (r. 647–648/1249–1250) was assassinated by his military commanders (*amīr*, pl. *umarāʾ*, commonly rendered as amir in English) during the drawn-out military confrontation with Louis IX's invading forces in Egypt. These amirs, the majority of whom were freed military slaves, then delegated authority to one of their own. They would continue to do so until 923/1517, when the Ottomans executed the last sultan of Egypt. These rulers had started their careers as *mamlūk*s in the retinue of either the sultan—the Arabic term *mamlūk*, pl. *mamālīk* means "owned" and was commonly used to refer to slaves, especially in military contexts—or one of his high-ranking amirs. They were then manumitted and could rise in the military hierarchy to become amirs themselves. Scholars have routinely interpreted the mid-7th/13th century takeover of rule by these amirs from Ayyubid family members as a coup and have made much of the supposed establishment of a unique form of government dominated by the institution of military slavery, despite these events not being altogether unique in Islamic history. They have also designated the sultanate as the "Mamluk sultanate," even if early authors such as those studied in this book did not refer to the sultans whom they served as "Mamluk," let alone as part of a Mamluk regime.[37]

The polity's designation as "Mamluk" has received criticism in recent years and some researchers have stopped using the term altogether because of its unhelpful associations. While a field of "Mamluk studies" is well established at the point of writing and my choice to forego using this designation at times results in an awkward discrepancy between the body text and critical apparatus of this book, the choice has significant bearing on the core issue of legitimacy and its relationship to historiography. Because of the slavery and usurpatory background of the two earliest sultans to whom *sīra*s were devoted—Baybars and Qalāwūn—it has

37 See for an overview: Koby Yosef, "Dawlat al-Atrāk or Dawlat al-Mamālīk? Ethnic Origin or Slave Origin as the Defining Characteristic of the Ruling Elite in the Mamluk Sultanate," *Jerusalem Studies in Arabic and Islam* 39 (2012), 387–411. And a critical discussion: Van Steenbergen, "Revisiting the Mamluk Empire."

been commonly argued that these sultans were in dire need of legitimisation: their non-Arab and non-Islamic heritage was considered to create problems of legitimacy that needed to be whitewashed. Even for later sultans who were born as free Muslims, their genealogy going back to former slaves is considered to have been problematic. The fact that these two later rulers were members of a veritable dynasty established by al-Manṣūr Qalāwūn—itself following a short-lived Baybarsid dynasty—and that throughout the ensuing centuries dynastic reflexes repeatedly came into the political picture already highlights the problem with overly relying on a designation of the sultanate as "Mamluk," even if it cannot be denied that former *mamlūk*s at nearly all times dominated the most powerful factions in government. This has been especially problematic for the "Mamlukisation" of political theory and literary expression, that is, for its application of a "Mamluk" lens to all phenomena of the period, even if contemporary observers in fact made little of the slave background of their rulers.[38]

This is not to say that the political transformations of the mid-7th/13th century were not significant, but that they are too often seen as a strict political watershed. If anything, the *sīra*s which discuss the transition from Ayyubid to "Mamluk" rule paint a picture of continuity and especially of recovery once Baybars took the throne. The standard narrative of the Mamluk genesis explains how the Ayyubid ruler al-Ṣāliḥ Ayyūb (r. 637–647/1240–1249) had greatly increased the numbers of his personal *mamlūks* to strengthen his personal grip on power. These *mamlūks* then became so powerful that they almost inevitably usurped power. They did indeed do so when they assassinated al-Ṣāliḥ Ayyūb's son and successor Tūrān Shāh in 648/1250. Almost immediately after arriving in Egypt Tūrān Shāh had alienated his father's amirs by appointing his own amirs to positions of power—an action that repeatedly lead to conflicts between young rulers and established factions.[39] He is also often presented as indulging in frivolous activities in times of military distress.[40] After the crusader force was defeated and Louis IX captured, a number

---

38 "Mamlukisation" is a neologism coined by Jo Van Steenbergen to designate how in the later period of the sultanate an idea of an essential "Mamluk" identity of the sultanate became prevalent, which was then projected onto the earlier period, despite these early rulers in fact appearing much more in line with Ayyubid principles of rule. Because of the prevalence of 9th/15th century "Mamlukised" sources in studies of the field, the idea of a distinctly Mamluk sultanate has had wide currency. This is not to imply that slavery was not a widespread phenomenon in late medieval Syro-Egypt. However, reducing political practice in the period to factional rivalry between erstwhile military slaves significantly misrepresents the complexity of what is evident from the sources.

39 Angus Stewart, "Between Baybars and Qalāwūn: Under-age Rulers and Succession in the Early Mamlūk Sultanate," *Al-Masaq: Journal of the Medieval Mediterranean*, 19, no. 1 (2007), 47–54.

40 This run of events is a topos of medieval Arabic historiography. Similar stories are told about al-Saʿīd Baraka Qān and al-Ashraf Khalīl (see below). It has been argued that the depiction of Tūrān

of Ṣāliḥī amirs, among them Baybars and the leader of al-Ṣāliḥ's elite Baḥriyya regiment, Fāris al-Dīn Aqtāy, eventually conspired to kill Tūrān Shāh. After this regicide, power briefly passed to al-Ṣāliḥ's wife Shajar al-Durr and then to one of al-Ṣāliḥ's own amirs, who took up the regnal title al-Muʿizz Aybak (r. 648–655/1250–1257). Ayyubid rulers in Syria refused to recognise either sultan however, even though Aybak quickly installed the figurehead Ayyubid child sultan al-Ashraf Mūsā whom he claimed to serve as guardian. This and his marrying Shajar al-Durr are conventionally understood as measures to establish his reign as continuous with that of al-Ṣāliḥ Ayyūb.

In the sources these events are usually not painted as a usurpation but as a reaction against Tūrān Shāh's unacceptable innovations in the political system at the expense of al-Ṣāliḥ's elites. While scholars have situated the establishment of a fully "Mamluk" system of rule only during al-Ẓāhir Baybars's long reign, the sources rather depict his taking of power after a chaotic decade as a restoration of the paradigmatic political practice of al-Ṣāliḥ Ayyūb. The intervening decade was not so much problematic because of political innovation or because the rulers were illegitimate, but rather because they were incompetent and personally unsuitable. This was not because of their slave background but because of avarice, military undecidedness, and general weakness of character.

In 651/1254 al-Muʿizz Aybak had the leading amir Fāris al-Dīn Aqṭāy killed, as he had grown out to be a major challenge to Aybak's position of power. Afterwards Aybak took over direct rule of the sultanate. Fearing for their own lives, Baybars and many other Ṣāliḥī amirs fled towards Syria, where they sought refuge with various Ayyubid princes, especially the sultan of Damascus and Aleppo, al-Nāṣir Yūsuf (r. 634–658/1236–1260). Shāfiʿ b. ʿAlī would later denote this flight as a *hijra*,[41] using the same term as that designating the Prophet Muḥammad's flight from Mecca to Yathrib/Medina. As the event that marks the start of the Islamic calendar, its symbolic value should not be underestimated, and Shāfiʿ's equation thus stresses the prime historical importance of this later *hijra*.[42] As we shall see, Ibn

Shāh in some of the period's historiography is characterised by a high level of dramatisation, similar to how historical characters are fictionalised in later popular epics. Thomas Herzog, "Romans populaires arabes: de l'historiographie au roman, du roman à l'historiographie," in *Écrire l'histoire de son temps (Europe et monde arabe)*, ed. Richard Jacquemond (Paris: L'harmattan, 2005), 101.

41 Shāfiʿ b. ʿAlī, *al-Faḍl al-Ma'thūr min Sīrat al-Sulṭān al-Malik al-Manṣūr*, ed. ʿUmar Tadmurī (Ṣaydā/Beirut: al-Maktaba al-Aṣriyya, 1998), 61, 114.

42 Such a comparison was not unprecedented. ʿImad al-Dīn al-Iṣfahānī named the conquest of Jerusalem by Ṣalāh al-Dīn in 1187 a "second *hijra*" which he took as point of departure for his historical work on the last years of that sultan's life. Al-Iṣfahānī, *al-Fatḥ al-Qussī fī al-fatḥ al-Qudsī*, ed. Carlo de Landberg (Leiden: Brill, 1888), 6.

ʿAbd al-Ẓāhir similarly conceptualised this event as historically crucial, giving the events of this period a central position in the narrative arc of his *sīra* of Baybars.

When Mongol forces lead by Hülegü (r. 654–663/1256–1265) continued westward after their conquest of Baghdād and the killing of the Abbasid caliph resident there in 656/1258, Baybars decided to join with the Egyptians to confront the Mongols who had gone on to pillage Syria. The Egyptians were by now lead by sultan al-Muẓaffar Quṭuz, who had prevailed in Egyptian power struggles after Aybak's demise. After conquering Damascus Hülegü returned eastwards to attend to the succession of the Mongol Great Khan and left behind a smaller force lead by the amir Kitbughā to deal with the Egyptian forces. This Mongol army and the Egyptian army clashed on the 25th of Ramaḍān 658/3rd of September 1260 at ʿAyn Jālūt in the Galilee, where the Egyptian army somewhat unexpectedly won the battle. This defeat and the Mongol rout that followed it would eventually result in the relative stabilisation of the border with the Mongol Ilkhanate east of the Euphrates. Perhaps even more important than this victory, which is often lauded as the first Muslim victory against the Mongols who were hitherto considered invincible, was what happened on the victorious army's return journey. A conspiracy of several amirs, according to some sources lead by Baybars, killed Quṭuz and power subsequently passed to Baybars who took the regnal title al-Malik al-Ẓāhir.[43]

Baybars' seventeen-year reign is conventionally seen as a period in which the groundwork for the "Mamluk" sultanate's enduring political system was laid.[44] He was the first long-reigning sultan since al-Ṣāliḥ Ayyūb and was gradually able to bring both Egypt and most of the Syrian lands under his direct control. Baybars is also credited with initiating two important institutions that would define politics for the following centuries: the reinstatement of the Abbasid caliphate in Cairo shortly after his accession to the sultanate and the installation of four chief *qāḍīs* for each of the four law schools (*madhhab*, pl. *madhāhib*) in 663/1265.[45] His persona would continue to loom large in later periods: al-Ẓāhir Barqūq (r. 784–801/1382–1399, with

43 These events were a core concern of P.M. Holt's works on the *sīra* corpus. See, among others, "The Sultan as Ideal Ruler", 134–135; "Shafi ibn Ali's Biography", 126.

44 William W. Clifford, *State Formation and the Structure of Politics in Mamluk Syro-Egypt, 648–741 A.H./1250–1340 C.E.*, ed. Stephan Conermann (Bonn: V&R unipress/Bonn University Press, 2013), 18.

45 Both innovations have been much debated. For the former, see the most recent discussion in: Mustafa Banister, *The Abbasid Caliphate of Cairo: Out of the Shadows* (Edinburgh: Edinburgh University Press, 2021). For the latter, see an overview of the debate in: Yossef Rapoport, "Legal Diversity in the Age of *Taqlīd*: The Four Chief *Qāḍīs* Under the Mamluks," *Islamic Law and Society*, 10, no. 2 (2003), 210–213.

a brief intermission) would for example employ Baybars' image in his "restoration" project after putting an end to the Qalāwūnid dynasty in the late 8th/14th century,[46] and in Ottoman times a popular epic, the *Sīrat Baybars*, would grow to enormous popularity. In modern history he was even appropriated as a national hero of Kazakhstan and a Syrian soap opera called *al-Ẓāhir Baybars* was devoted to his life and reign. Much of that image derives from his achievements in conquering several of the remaining Latin Crusader outposts on the Syrian littoral, most prominently Antioch and Caesarea, and successfully fighting off another Mongol invasion at the battle of Elbistan/Abulustayn (675/1277) in Anatolian Seljuq territory. This latter battle was the culmination of years of tense relations between local Anatolian elites, the Egyptian sultanate, and the Ilkhanid Mongol state. Shortly after his return to Damascus from that battle, he died and was buried in the mausoleum he had erected in Damascus.

Despite Baybars' preparations for a smooth succession by making his son al-Saʿīd Baraka Qān[47] co-sultan and marrying him to the daughter of one of his most prominent amirs, Baraka's reign did not last long. Similar to Tūrān Shāh before him, Baraka tried to strengthen his power base by dismissing amirs from Ṣāliḥī and Ẓāhirī backgrounds to appoint his own amirs to positions of authority, and in the process alienated these still powerful earlier elites. Our sources tell us that Qalāwūn al-Alfī, who had in the latter years of Baybars' sultanate grown much in prominence in his retinue, emerged as de facto leader of these disgruntled amirs. The situation eventually came to a head and after mediations Baraka abdicated and retired to Karak. He was replaced by his infant brother al-ʿĀdil Sulāmīsh, who reigned for only one month, after which Qalāwūn deposed Sulāmīsh and ascended the throne himself.

Qalāwūn's reign was in many ways a continuation of Baybars': he actively propounded his image of a warrior sultan by defeating a new Mongol invasion at the Battle of Homs in 680/1281 and conquering a handful of further fortresses and settlements held by the Franks, most prominently the fortress of Marqab and the city of Tripoli. Qalāwūn's grip on power was not unchallenged however, and he had to spend the early years of his reign dealing with, among other setbacks, a defection of one of the most powerful amirs in the sultanate, Shams al-Dīn Sunqur al-Ashqar,

46 Clément Onimus, *Les maîtres du jeu: Pouvoir et violence politique à l'aube du sultanat mamlouk circassien (784–815/1382–1412)* (Paris: Editions de la Sorbonne, 2019), chapter three: "Légitimation et restauration de la dignité sultanienne," section "La restauration de l'autorité de Baybars."

47 I follow Hans-Ulrich Kühn in transcribing his name like this instead of the commonly used Bereke Khān. Kühn, *Sultan Baibars und seine Söhne: Frühmamkūkische Herrschaftssicherung in ayyūbidischer Tradition* (Bonn: V&R Unipress/Bonn University Press, 2019), 120–122.

who proclaimed himself sultan in Damascus.[48] Much of his reign had to deal with restoring order in Syria. Aside from his martial undertakings, Qalāwūn's reign is also important for the foundation of one of the largest endowed institutions of Cairo up to that point: the Manṣūriyya complex, which included a hospital (*bīmaristān*), a *madrasa*, and a mausoleum (*qubba*). It was situated in Cairo's symbolic and ceremonial thorough-fare *Bayn al-Qaṣrayn* ("Between the two palaces"), partly occupying the space that had heretofore been occupied by the Fatimid palaces the area is named after.

Qalāwūn had prepared to be succeeded by his son al-Ṣāliḥ ʿAlī, but the latter's premature death in 687/1288 obliged the sultan to reluctantly name his other adult son al-Ashraf Khalīl as successor. During the preparations for the conquest of Acre, the last remaining major Latin settlement, Qalāwūn died unexpectedly. The conquest was completed by Khalīl in 690/1291 who thus started off his reign with a major victory that was widely praised in correspondence and poetry. The rest of his short reign was however mired in struggles akin to those of al-Saʿīd Baraka before him: in trying to replace the earlier balance of power he promoted amirs of his own choice but this resulted in clashes with the powerful factions who had dominated politics before his ascension. Al-Ashraf Khalīl was murdered by a group of amirs on a hunting trip. These amirs then put his underage brother Muḥammad on the throne with the regnal title al-Malik al-Nāṣir.

Neither al-Ashraf Khalīl's murder, nor al-Nāṣir Muḥammad's first reign are recorded in any of the surviving parts of the *sīra* corpus, which is most detailed for the reigns of Baybars and Qalāwūn and peters out for the following years due to incomplete manuscript survival. It suffices to note here that al-Nāṣir Muḥammad's initial reign was quickly cut short when he was deposed and succeeded by al-ʿĀdil Kitbughā, and then al-Manṣūr Lājīn, both powerful amirs from Qalāwūn's Manṣūriyya regiment.[49] When the latter was murdered, the new strong men among the amirs reinstated al-Nāṣir Muḥammad in 698/1299. He would now reign for a longer period but remained dominated by the two amirs Baybars al-Jāshnikīr and Sayf al-Dīn Sallār. Only a few months after being reinstated he had to lead an army to confront a new Mongol invasion. The Syro-Egyptian forces were humiliatingly

48 Linda Northrup has called this an "attempt to restore Syria to its status as an autonomous province in the Ayyubid tradition." Northrup, *From Slave to Sultan: The Career of al-Manṣūr Qalāwūn and the Consolidation of Mamluk Rule in Egypt and Syria (678–679 A.H./1279–1290 A.D.)* (Stuttgart: Franz Steiner, 1998), 178.

49 On this regiment, see Amir Mazor, *The Rise and Fall of a Muslim Regiment: The Manṣūriyya in the First Mamluk Sultanate, 678/1279–741/1341* (Bonn: V&R Unipress/Bonn University Press, 2015), especially chapter two: "The Manṣūriyya from Qalāwūn's death to the third reign of al-Nāṣir Muḥammad ibn Qalāwūn (689/1290–709/1310)."

defeated at Wādī al-Khaznadār (699/1299), but this did not lead to a full-scale occupation of Syria by the Mongols. In 702/1303, the Mongols returned but were halted at the Battle of Shaqḥab (also known as the Battle of Marj al-Saffar/Suffar). The surviving part of Shāfiʿ b. ʿAlī's *sīra* of al-Nāṣir Muḥammad starts shortly after this battle took place. However, the most developed bit of the text deals with al-Nāṣir Muḥammad's defection to Karak, his resignation of the sultanate, and the ascension of Baybars al-Jāshnikīr as sultan with the regnal title al-Muẓaffar. He reigned for a mere nine months, after which al-Nāṣir Muḥammad finally returned to Cairo for his third and longest reign, which would last until his death in 741/1341. The manuscript of Shāfiʿ's *sīra* does not take us far beyond this third ascension, however, as it is cut off in the year 710/1310 and we do not know at which point he concluded the text. We do know from several other contemporary and later sources that al-Nāṣir Muḥammad would during this third reign become arguably the most powerful ruler of the sultanate, establishing his absolute authority through ruthless purging and reorganisation of the sultanate's elites. A final peace was settled with the Mongols in 722/1323.[50]

In the following chapters, more details will be given about specific historical events as they are reflected in the *sīras* and other sources. In the remaining space of this introduction, I provide brief summaries of the six chapters of this book.

IV Outline of the book

In the first chapter of the book, I provide brief biographies of the two main agents to whom this book is devoted, as well as brief discussions of the six *sīra* texts they wrote, especially the manuscripts in which they are attested and the editions that have been published of them. These are meant as reference descriptions and the information given here will be built on throughout the rest of the book to provide much fuller reconstructions of the authors' lives and descriptions of the textual contents. Chapter three especially will provide more details on the contents of the works, while biographical information related to the authors' chancery careers will be discussed in chapter four.

---

50 The wide-ranging implications of this third reign have been discussed in: Amalia Levanoni, A *Turning Point in Mamluk History: The Third Reign of al-Nāṣir Muḥammad Ibn Qalāwūn (1310–1341)* (Leiden: Brill, 1995). See also Willem Flinterman & Jo Van Steenbergen, "Al-Nasir Muhammad and the Formation of the Qalawunid State," in *Pearls on a String: Art in the Age of Great Islamic Empires*, ed. Amy Landau (Baltimore/Seattle: The Walters Art Museum/University of Washington Press, 2015), 87–113.

In the second chapter I endeavour to write a conceptual history of *sīra* as it appears in the works of our authors. After a brief overview of the term throughout Islamicate history, I then look in detail at the rhetoric of the introductions preserved for three of the *sīra* texts. I also evaluate the horizons of expectation implied by four securely preserved book titles from the corpus. A common conception of *sīra* emerges from these three texts, revolving essentially around the interplay of memorialisation of a sultan's *dawla* and of the scribe's personal contribution to that *dawla*. The role of the scribe as participants makes them into the ideal candidates to undertake the project of historiographic memorialisation.

In chapter three I investigate how our authors translated the ideas put forward in their introductions and in the titles of their texts into narrative constructions of the past. For this, I read each text from a macro perspective and discuss the narrative constructions operating across single texts, insofar as possible given the fragmentary survival of some texts in the corpus. While I discuss each *sīra* individually, I also highlight narrative choices found across multiple texts from the corpus and the ways in which later texts built on the example of earlier ones. One of the major themes to emerge from this general overview is the centrality of the chancery to the presentation of history. More than a panegyric of a given sultan's heroism, these narratives sing the praises of a sultan's *dawla*, and especially its textual management, that is, the role of the chancery in that *dawla*.

Chapters four to six zoom in more specifically on the contexts that informed the textual forms and the material included in the texts and serves as a broader study of how particular contexts provided the terms in which these authors could write about the past. I start with the chancery in chapter four. This chapter starts with a critical re-evaluation of the chancery as an institution. A careful reading of how our authors talk about the chancery provides us with a much more fluid organisational pattern and more complex perspective than that typically presented by scholars who have based themselves on normative literature dating to later periods. Instead, the workings of the household formation of the state are here also reflected in the importance of personal relationships between scribes and between sultans and scribes. I then evaluate compiled chancery material in the texts, on the one hand documents that are quoted literally and on the other hand documents that were heavily reworked before being included. I specifically highlight the importance of evaluating how such materials are embedded and the performative implications of this material within the textual framework of *sīra*.

Chapter five is devoted to the literary field. I evaluate the use of linguistic registers within the texts and the usages of compiled material that is not directly related to the chancery. I specifically consider the position of poetry and of the literary practice of *muʿāraḍa*. For the former, I highlight how especially Ibn ʿAbd al-Ẓāhir made creative use of the citation of poetry to link himself to great poets of the past.

This reconfigures the common scholarly interpretation of the *sīra* texts representing sultans' actions re-enactment of heroic feats of celebrated rulers of the past to also include the agency of scribe writing those narratives of re-enactment. The practice of *muʿāraḍa*, found in the *sīra* corpus in the form of the inclusion of multiple different documents or literary texts pertaining to the same historical moment, also highlights scribal agency.

Finally, in chapter six I zoom in on the court, which has traditionally been foregrounded as the central locus for the production and performance of *sīra* materials. This chapter does not challenge the court's centrality but aims to provide a better understanding of how the court sits in relation to the chancery and the literary field, as well as in broader processes of state formation. I engage with recent conceptualisation of the court and provide some remarks based on the 7th/13th century sources. I consider how our authors wrote about the court and from there revert to the issue of legitimacy and the audience of these texts. These audiences have traditionally been assumed to be courtly, but a close reading of the material survival of the corpus highlights that this supposition might have to be revisited.

Chapter 1
The *sīra* corpus: Authors and texts

أيا ناصر الدين انتصر لي فطالما ظفرتُ بنصرٍ منك بالجاه والمال
وكن شافعًا فالله سمّاك شافعًا وطابقتَ أسماءً بأحسن أفعال
وقدرك لم نجهله عند محمد لأن ابن عباس من الصَحب والآل

Oh Nāṣir al-Dīn, come to my help, for how often
have I been successful through your spiritual and material aid!
Be a mediator, for God has named you accordingly
and you have made names correlate with the best actions
We are not ignorant of your standing with Muḥammad
because Ibn ʿAbbās is both a companion and a family member[51]

These lines were written by the poet Sirāj al-Dīn al-Warrāq (d. 695/1296), one of the literary heavyweights of late $7^{th}/13^{th}$ century Cairo.[52] They were addressed to Shāfiʿ b. ʿAlī and were meant to urge Shāfiʿ to intercede with his cousin Fatḥ al-Dīn Muḥammad b. ʿAbd al-Ẓāhir (d. 691/1292) in favour of al-Warrāq. To attract his dedicatee's goodwill, al-Warrāq sets up a rather elaborate interpretation of different parts of Shāfiʿ's name: in the first two lines he reads the first word of his *laqab* Nāṣir al-Dīn ("the helper of religion") as well as his given name Shāfiʿ ("mediator") literally,[53] and in the third line he reads his patronymic through early Islamic references. He reads the given name of Shāfiʿ's cousin, Muḥammad, as a direct reference to the Prophet, and the patronymic of his father, Ibn ʿAbbās,[54] as a reference to the companion of the Prophet of the same name (d. 68/687), who was indeed both a family member and a companion of the Prophet. The poem is a nice specimen of literary communication between literary scholars of the period (on which, see chapter five below), but it is also telling for how contemporaries perceived the

---

51 Al-Ṣafadī, *Wāfī*, 16:84–85; al-Ṣafadī, *Aʿyān*, 2:510. In *Aʿyān* (same page) al-Ṣafadī additionally quotes a second poem sent by Sirāj al-Dīn al-Warrāq to Shāfiʿ.
52 Like most literary figures of the period, he remains severely understudied. Thomas Bauer notes that Sirāj al-Dīn al-Warrāq's hunting epistle established the format followed by most later examples of the genre from $7^{th}/13^{th}$ and $8^{th}/14^{th}$ Syro-Egypt. Bauer, "The Dawādār's Hunting Party: A Mamluk *Muzdawija Ṭardiyya*, probably by Shihāb al-Dīn ibn Faḍl Allāh," in *O Ye Gentlemen: Arabic Studies on Science and Literary Culture in Honour of Remke Kruk*, eds. A. Vrolijk & J.P. Hogendijk (Leiden: Brill, 2007), 303.
53 I have rendered this by the phrase "named you accordingly" in the first hemistisch of the second line. In fact, al-Warrāq is punning on Shāfiʿ's name here, using it the first time as "mediator" and the second time as a given name.
54 That is, Shāfiʿ's father was ʿAlī and his father in turn was ʿAbbās. Ibn ʿAbbās would thus be the patronymic of ʿAlī.

https://doi.org/10.1515/9783110753028-002

family relation between the two authors who wrote the corpus of *sīra*s studied in this book and its professional implications.

It is part of the contention of this book that the close family relation of our two authors resulted in them establishing a conception of *sīra* that is coherent across the six such works they composed. The present chapter will provide more information about the authors and those individual works, the manuscripts in which they are attested, and the editions that have been published of these texts. I will also provide details in footnotes on the digital versions I created of these texts which have been integrated into the OpenITI corpus, a large and diverse corpus of digital Islamicate texts which can be used for multiple computational operations. I rely on these digital texts for text reuse results as well as some textual statistics in the following chapters.[55] I have grouped the works per author prefaced by brief biographical sketches for both Ibn ʿAbd al-Ẓāhir and Shāfiʿ b. ʿAlī. For most books the descriptions will be brief and more specific information will be given in subsequent chapters, especially chapter three, but for the first text a more thorough discussion is in order because of textual issues.

While I will only discuss the two authors who will be the focus of this book at some length here, it bears repeating that they were part of a family dynasty of scribes, occasionally referred to as the Banū ʿAbd al-Ẓāhir.[56] In Figure 2 I have visualised their familial relations. This visualisation includes a few other family members who are named only in passing and about whom little more is known. Ibn ʿAbd al-Ẓāhir's son Fatḥ al-Dīn and grandson ʿAlāʾ al-Dīn b. ʿAbd al-Ẓāhir are discussed in a third section of this chapter.

1.1 Muḥyī al-Dīn b. ʿAbd al-Ẓāhir

Muḥyī al-Dīn Abū al-Faḍl ʿAbdallāh b. Rashīd al-Dīn b. ʿAbd al-Ẓāhir b. Nashwān b. ʿAbd al-Ẓāhir b. Najda al-Saʿdī al-Rūḥī al-Judhāmī was born on the 9th of Muḥarram 620 / 12th of February 1223 and died on the 3rd of Rajab 692 / 9th of June 1293.[57] His

55 For a detailed overview of the OpenITI corpus and its management see the documentation at http://kitab-project.org/docs/openITI On the software passim and the methods of text reuse, see http://kitab-project.org/methods/text-reuse

56 In his famous chancery manual *Ṣubḥ al-Aʿshā fī Ṣināʿat al-Inshāʾ* (Dawn for the Blind: On the Art of *Inshāʾ*), al-Qalqashandī uses this designation and notes that family members rose to prominent positions in the chancery during the reigns of Baybars and Qalāwūn. *Ṣubḥ al-Aʿshā fī Ṣināʿat al-Inshāʾ*, 14 vols., no editor (Cairo: Maṭbaʿat Dār al-kutub, 1922), 14:70. Compare a brief discussion of other such families in Thomas Bauer, "Ibn Nubātah al-Miṣrī (686–768/1287–1366): Life and Works. Part I: The Life of Ibn Nubātah," *MSR* 12, no. 1 (2008), 10.

57 Information compiled from various incomplete dates given by: al-Ṣafadī, *Wāfī*, 17:257–290, at 258; al-Jazarī, *Ḥawādith*, 1:175; Ibn al-Ṣuqāʿī, *Tālī kitāb wafāyāt al-aʿyān*, ed. Jacqueline Sublet

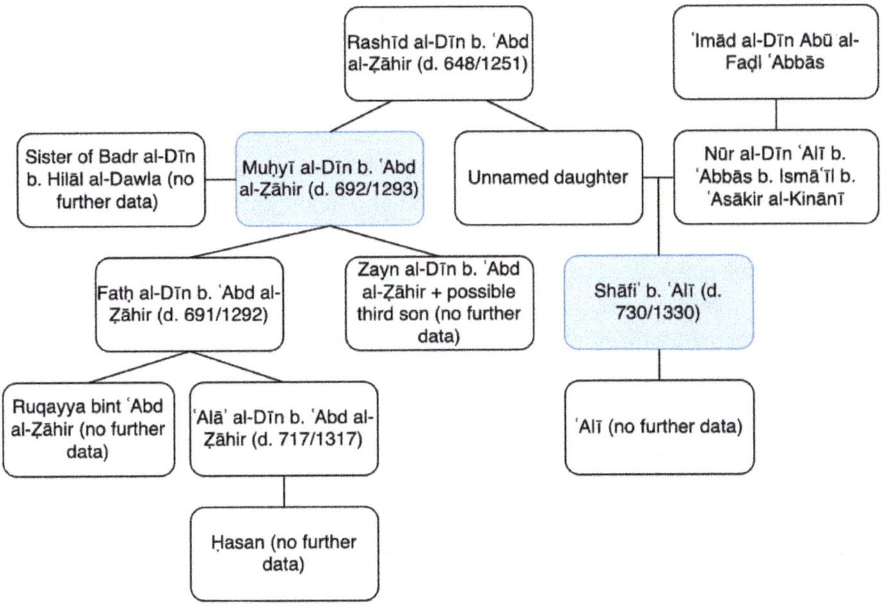

Figure 2: Family tree of the Banū ʿAbd al-Ẓāhir.

father Rashīd al-Dīn b. ʿAbd al-Ẓāhir (d. 649/1251) was famed as the most important Qurʾān reciter of his time in Cairo but he does not appear to have had any links to the chancery.[58] We do not know how Ibn ʿAbd al-Ẓāhir gained his position in the chancery. In the early 640s/1240s, we have attestation of him writing official letters for an Ayyubid ruler (see 4.2. below for a more thorough discussion). By the time al-Ẓāhir Baybars took over the reins in Egypt, he was already a prominent member of the chancery there and subsequently rose to become *ṣāḥib dīwān al-inshāʾ*,

(Damascus: Presses de l'IFPO, 1973), 118–121; Ibn Taghrī-Birdī, *Manhal*, 7:98–99; al-Maqrīzī, *al-Muqaffā l-Kabīr*, 8 vols., ed. Muḥammad al-Yaʿlāwī (Beirut: Dār al-gharb al-islāmī, 1991), 4:580. Modern biographies of the author have been compiled by Frédéric Bauden, "Ibn ʿAbd al-Ẓāhir," *EI3*; Gowaart Van Den Bossche, "Muḥyī al-Dīn b. ʿAbd al-Ẓāhir," in *Arabic Textual Sources for the Crusades*, ed. Alex Mallett (Leiden: Brill, forthcoming); Ḥusayn ʿĀṣī, *Muḥyī al-Dīn b. ʿAbd al-Ẓāhir, Aṣruhu wa-Turāthuhu al-Taʾrīkhī* (Beirut: Dār al-kutub al-ʿilmiyya, 1413/1993); Eliyahu Ashtor (published under surname Strauß), "Muḥyī'ddîn b. ʿAbdaẓẓâhir," *Wiener Zeitschrift für die Kunde des Morgenlandes* 45 (1938), 191–202; Paul Casanova, "L'historien Ibn ʿAbd aḍh-Ḍhâhir," in *Mémoires publiés par les members de la Mission Archéologique française au Caire, vol. 6*, ed. M. Urbain Bouriant (Paris: Ernest Leroux, 1893), 493–505.

58 One of the earliest biographies of him is given in Aḥmad b. Muḥammad al-Ḥusaynī (d. 695/1295), *Ṣilat al-Takmila li-Wafayāt al-Naqala*, 2 vols., ed. Bashshār ʿAwād Maʿrūf (Dār al-gharb al-islāmī, 2007), 1:240.

leader of the composition bureau. We know that he continued writing in the chancery during the reigns of Qalāwūn and al-Ashraf Khalīl, but he seems to have relinquished his leading position as *ṣāḥib* for what may have amounted to an honorary position, possibly due to faltering eyesight.[59] His son Fatḥ al-Dīn b. ʿAbd al-Ẓāhir took over the leading role in the chancery under Qalāwūn and gained especially in prominence under his successor al-Ashraf Khalīl. In any case, several official documents were still drawn up by Ibn ʿAbd al-Ẓāhir during these later reigns. He would continue to be considered one of the leading literary figures of his time by several of his contemporaries and throughout the next centuries.[60]

The primary memory of Ibn ʿAbd al-Ẓāhir in these later texts is as a gifted poet and prose stylist. This contrasts with the fact that today he is mostly known as a historian. It is notable in that sense that the text of his of which most manuscripts have come down to us is a *dīwān* of his poetry, although its compilation and transmission history remains unclear.[61] That is not to say that his historical writing was ignored by his contemporaries: in fact, his *sīra* of Baybars was regularly cited by later historians. Additionally, his work on the topography of Cairo, *al-Rawḍa*

59 This claim of faltering eyesight is made by Shāfiʿ b. ʿAlī, who claims that he used to read out letters for his uncle in the final years of the reign of Baybars when there was little light at dawn (*saḥaran*). He mentions this specifically in the context of al-Saʿīd Baraka's marriage to Qalāwūn's daughter in 674/1276. On this occasion, however, the reading of Ibn ʿAbd al-Ẓāhir's letter took place during full day light, so Shāfiʿ's help was not needed. Shāfiʿ b. ʿAlī, *Ḥusn*, 326.

60 The renowned 8th/15th century prose stylist Ibn Ḥijja al-Ḥamawī (d. 838/1434) for example at one point evaluates a rhetorical flourish of the equally renowned litterateur Ṣafī al-Dīn al-Ḥillī (d. 749/1349) by comparing it negatively to the greatness of Ibn ʿAbd al-Ẓāhir's prose ("*ayna huwa min ʿuluww maqām al-qāḍī Muḥyī al-Dīn b. ʿAbd al-Ẓāhir!*"). Ibn Ḥijja al-Ḥamawī, *Khizānat al-Adab wa-Ghāyat al-Arab*, ed. ʿIṣām Shuʿaytū (Beirut: Dār Maktabat al-Hilāl, 2004), 40. By the 12th/18th century, the Ottoman literary scholar and statesman ʿIṣām al-Dīn al-ʿUmarī (d. 1193/1779) cited four poems by Ibn ʿAbd al-Ẓāhir in his biographical dictionary of littérateurs, *al-Rawḍ al-Naḍir fī Tarjama Udabāʾ al-ʿAṣr*, ed. Salīm al-Nuʿaymī, 3 vols. (Baghdad: al-Majmaʿ al-ʿilmī al-ʿIrāqī, 1975), 1:69, 1:154–155, 1:458, 2:237–241.

61 Three manuscripts are known. The only dated copy is Dār al-Kutub wa'l-Wathāʾiq MS Shiʿr Taymūr 101, dated to 12 Shaʿbān 1298/10 July 1881. This manuscript was likely copied from al-Azhar MS Adab 657 (general number 7244) which is missing an unknown number of folios at the end but which ends on the same poem as the Dār al-Kutub MS. Finally, Leiden MS Or. 2688 appears to be organised differently than the Egyptian manuscripts. The final two folios contain extracts from letters written by Ibn ʿAbd al-Ẓāhir, written in a different hand than the poetry. This last manuscript is described as "recent" by Jan-Just Witkam, *Inventory of the Oriental Manuscripts of the Library of the University of Leiden, volume 3: Manuscripts Or. 2001 – Or. 3000, registered in Leiden University Library in the Period between 1871 and 1883* (Leiden: Ter Lugt Press, 2008), 184. Tarek Sabraa is of the opinion that it was compiled by a student of Ibn ʿAbd al-Ẓāhir. Personal communication. The text has been published with an accompanying study: Ibn ʿAbd al-Ẓāhir, *Dīwān: Dirāsa wa-taḥqīq*, ed. Gharīb Muḥammad ʿAlī Aḥmad (Cairo: Maṭbaʿat Dār al-Bayān, 1990).

al-Bahiyya al-Zāhira fī Khiṭaṭ al-Muʿizziyya al-Qāhira, was also cited in later topographical works by al-Qalqashandī and al-Maqrīzī. Only a fragment of the original work has been identified in manuscript form.[62] Another text that is extant is *al-Darr al-Naẓīm min Tarassul ʿAbd al-Raḥīm* ("The Well-Organised Achievement: from ʿAbd al-Raḥīm's Letters"), which contains Ibn ʿAbd al-Ẓāhir's selection of letters written by al-Qāḍī al-Fāḍil.[63] Finally, a manuscript containing a diverse selection of official and literary correspondence between Ibn ʿAbd al-Ẓāhir and some of his peers has been preserved in the National Library of Bulgaria in Sofia. It was identified as such in an Arabic catalogue of its holdings compiled by Yūsuf ʿIzz al-Dīn but remained otherwise unknown to scholars.[64] As I only discovered the existence of this text when I had already submitted the first draft of this book, I have only been able to add a few references to it in this book.

Several texts were at one point or another attributed to Ibn ʿAbd al-Ẓāhir but are not know to have survived. Al-Qalqashandī and al-Maqrīzī cite a text on the pigeon post called *Tamāʾim al-Ḥamāʾim* ("On Carrier Pigeons") but its attribution to Ibn ʿAbd al-Ẓāhir has been challenged by Eliyahu Ashtor.[65] Two different biographical dictionaries of poets or anthologies are attributed to him as well: one is referred to as *Shuʿarāʾ al-Maʾiyya al-Sābiʿa* ("Poets of the seventh century") by al-Ṣafadī as one of the sources he used to construct his own massive biographical dictionary *al-Wāfī biʾl-Wafāyāt*.[66] A similar work is cited as *al-Nujūm al-Durriyya fī al-Shuʿarāʾ al-Miṣriyya* ("The Glittering Stars: the Egyptian Poets") by al-Maqrīzī.[67] Finally, independent copies of a particularly eloquent *risāla* (epistle) of his survive, but all of these appear to be relatively recent reproductions of the text as it is included in al-Ṣafadī's literary commentary *Tamām al-Mutūn fī Sharḥ Risālat Ibn Zaydūn* ("The Complete Texts in Explanation of the Epistle of Ibn Zaydūn").[68] A work named

62 This fragment survives in a single codicological unit (British Library Or. 13317 folios 142–180). The edition of the text was reconstructed on the basis of that fragment expanded with quotations from the text by these later authors. Ibn ʿAbd al-Ẓāhir, *al-Rawḍa al-Bahiyya al-Zāhira fī Khiṭaṭ al-Muʿizziyya al-Qāhira*, ed. Ayman Fuʾād Sayyid (Cairo: al-Dār al-ʿArabiyya liʾl-Kutub, 1996).

63 *Al-Darr al-Naẓīm min Tarassul ʿAbd al-Raḥīm*, ed. Aḥmad Aḥmad Badawī (Cairo: Maktaba Nahḍat Miṣr, 1959).

64 Sofia, St. Cyril and Methodius National Library, MS Or. 2026. Yūsuf ʿIzz al-Dīn, *Makhṭūṭāt ʿArabiyya fī Maktabat Ṣūfiyā al-Waṭaniyya al-Bulghāriyya (Kīril wa-Mītūdī)* Baghdad: al-Majmaʿ al-ʿilmī al-ʿIrāqī, 1968), 115.

65 E. Strauß (Ashtor), 'Muḥyî'ddîn b. ʿAbdaẓẓâhir', 202.

66 al-Ṣafadī, *Wāfī*, 1:61.

67 al-Maqrīzī, *Muqaffā*, 5:359 and 6:266. The two extracts cited concern the poets Ibn Zayn al-Kātib (d. 621/1224) and Fakhr al-Dīn b. al-Jinān al-Shāṭibī (d. 653/1254), so it is possible that this text and the one cited by al-Ṣafadī are the same.

68 See the introduction to chapter five of this book for references and a translation of its opening lines.

Taḥarrī al-Ṣawāb fī Tahdhīb al-Kitāb ("The Proper Inquiry: on the Refinement of the Book") is listed with its opening words by the Ottoman bibliographer Ḥajjī Khalīfa who notes that it dealt with "instruction in the principles of calligraphy" (*qawāʿid al-khaṭṭ taʿlīman*).[69] A similar text is referred to by as *Faltat al-Yarāʿa wa-Laftat al-Barāʿa* ("The Slip of the Pen and the Turnabout of Excellence") by al-Ṣafadī: he cites an epigram by our author from it about a pen box. This poem is also found on a physically preserved pen box produced in the year 704/1304 or 1305 and currently preserved in the Louvre Museum (no. OA 7531).[70] The appearance of these poems on such luxury objects highlights the cultural impact made by members of the Banū ʿAbd al-Ẓāhir as poets.

1.1.1 The *sīra* of Baybars

The first text of Ibn ʿAbd al-Ẓāhir that was published in a modern edition was his *sīra* of Baybars. This text exists in two manuscripts, both of which are lacking folios at the start and at the end. As a result, no colophon nor title page has been preserved for either manuscript, but both are pre-modern copies. Their layout also suggests that both were produced before the Ottoman period. The text's first edition by Syedah Fatima Sadequi *Baybars I of Egypt* was based exclusively on the British Library manuscript Or. Add 23331, of which it also provides a translation.[71] This

69 Ḥajjī Khalīfa, *Kashf al-Ẓunūn ʿan Asāmī l-Kutub waʾl-Funūn,* 2 vols. ed. Mehmed Şerafeddin Yaltkaya (Beirut: Dār Iḥyāʾ al-Turāth al-ʿArabī, n.d.), 1:59.

70 Frédéric Bauden, "'The Calligrapher Is an Ape!' Arabic Epigrams on Pen Boxes (Sixth/Twelfth-Ninth/Fifteenth Centuries" in *Inscriptions from the Islamic World,* ed. Bernard O'Kane, Andrew Peacock, and Mark Muehlheusler (Edinburgh: Edinburgh University Press, forthcoming), 489–491 (translation and discussion of the poem), 519–521 (description of pen box, including photographic reproduction). I am grateful to Frédéric Bauden for sharing a pre-print of this chapter with me. The article contains several more examples of poems attested on 22 such pen boxes. One of the other such poems, attested on two pen boxes (including the same one from the Louvre), was written by Ibn ʿAbd al-Ẓāhir's son Fatḥ al-Dīn and we are told by al-Ṣafadī that Fatḥ al-Dīn had it engraved on a pen box to be gifted to his father. In another recent article, Doris Behrens-Abouseif writes about the same pen box held by the Louvre and suggests that this may be the very pen box produced for Ibn ʿAbd al-Ẓāhir by his son, but that its dating was altered by a later owner. She also extensively discusses the pen box's visual programme with several reproductions. Behrens-Abouseif, "A Mamluk Pen Box Connected to the *Thousand and One Nights* and the Historian Ibn ʿAbd al-Ẓāhir," *Muqarnas* 39 (2022), 23–36.

71 Syedah Fatima Sadequi (ed. and transl.), *Baybars I of Egypt* (London: Oxford University Press, 1958). Nothing is known about this manuscript's circulation before its accession to the British Library collection. This at least was before 1846, when it appears in W. Cureton and Charles Rieu's catalogue of Arabic manuscripts: *Catalogus codicum manuscriptorum orientalium qui in Museo*

manuscript covers roughly the first third of the text. It is likely missing only one folio at the start but is cut off early in the text's annalistic section. I have made little use of this edition, as it was superseded by ʿAbd al-ʿAzīz al-Khuwayṭir's full edition and translation of the text, in which he made use of both the British Library manuscript and a manuscript preserved in Istanbul's Süleymaniye library with call number Fatih 4366.[72] This manuscript is also incomplete: it is missing several folios at the start and has a few gaps due to incomplete quire preservation, but it contains nearly all of the text's annalistic section. It is cut off shortly after an account of Baybars' death, after which likely only a few folios would have been left in the text, perhaps containing a widely attested elegy for Baybars written by Ibn ʿAbd al-Ẓāhir (see the start of chapter two of this book). Al-Khuwayṭir first prepared his edition as part of a PhD dissertation at the London School of Oriental and African Studies, which consisted of three parts: a study of author and text as well as Baybars' life and actions, a full edition of the two manuscripts, and a full translation of the edition. The first two parts were published separately[73] but the translation has never been published outside of the PhD, although it is easily accessible in digital format. I have made extensive use of it below.[74]

Al-Khuwayṭir's edition initially comes across as a solid critical edition, but he in fact made a few questionable editorial choices. Where MS Fatih 4366 has gaps he tended to fill these gaps with whatever material he could find in later sources which was ostensibly lifted from the original *sīra*. In a few cases this information is in fact taken from Shāfiʿ b. ʿAlī's abridgement of that *sīra*, so the relationship between this material and the original text is sometimes tenuous. Below, in section 4.4.2. I will discuss a particularly problematic reconstruction. Additionally, al-Khuwayṭir published the text with the title *al-Rawḍ al-Zāhir fī Sīrat al-Malik al-Ẓāhir* ("The Radiant Garden: the Biography of al-Malik al-Ẓāhir"), which has as a result become commonly accepted as authentic. Because neither manuscript bears a title page and the text does not have any internal references to its title, al-Khuwayṭir took the title from Ḥajjī Khalīfa's (d. 1067/1657) famous bibliographical work *Kashf al-Ẓunūn ʿan Asāmī al-Kutub waʾl-Funūn*. In fact, there is little reliable evi-

---

Britannico asservantur : partem secundam codices Arabicos amplectentem (London: 1846–1871), 557–558.

72 Little is known about this manuscript's circulation. The flyleaf of the manuscript contains a seal of Ottoman Sultan Maḥmūd I (r. 1143–1168/1730–1754), as well as note referring to him.

73 Abdul-Aziz Khowaiter, *Baibars the First: His Endeavours and Achievements* (London: Green Mountain Press, 1978). ʿAbd al-ʿAzīz al-Khuwayṭir, *al-Rawḍ al-Zāhir fī Sīrat al-Malik al-Ẓāhir*, ed. ʿAbd al-ʿAzīz al-Khuwayṭir (Riyadh: n.p., 1976).

74 Abdul Aziz al-Khowayter, "A Critical Edition of an Unknown Source for the Life of al-Malik al-Ẓāhir Baibars, with Introduction, Translation, and Notes", 3 vols. (Unpublished PhD thesis, School of Oriental and African Studies, University of London, 1960).

dence for this title being correctly attributed in this case. Ḥajjī Khalīfa for example consistently misidentifies the authorship of the two other *sīras* written by Ibn ʿAbd al-Ẓāhir. Despite listing them immediately following the *sīra* of Baybars, for which his authorship designation is correct, he lists these two later works as written by Saladin's secretary al-Qāḍī al-Fāḍīl. This is chronologically impossible of course.[75] When semi-contemporary authors use this title at all, they tend to refer not to Ibn ʿAbd al-Ẓāhir's *sīra* of Baybars, but ʿIzz al-Dīn b. Shaddād's *sīra* of the same sultan. Another title for Ibn ʿAbd al-Ẓāhir's *sīra* is attested as *al-Faḍl al-bāhir fī sīrat (aw akhbār) al-sulṭān al-Malik al-Ẓāhir* ("The brilliant favour in the *sīra* (or: in the reports) of the sultan al-Malik al-Ẓāhir").

Even the act of attributing the text as we have it to Ibn ʿAbd al-Ẓāhir is not without problems. Scholars have noted that there is some variation between the text and material cited from it by later historians and that there are a number of self-designations in the text which imply the involvement of other authors, notably a certain Ibn al-Qaysarānī who identifies himself at one point as *mukhtaṣir* of the *sīra*. Ṣafwān Ṭāhā Ḥassan al-Nāṣir suggests that this may be rooted in Shāfi b. ʿAlī''s claim that Ibn ʿAbd al-Ẓāhir presented parts of his ongoing work on the *sīra* to the sultan and that these parts may then have been compiled or started to lead a life of their own before being finalised in a monograph, with Ibn al-Qaysarānī serving as an amanuensis to our author. As an alternative solution, he suggests that the text as we have it may in fact be a *mukhtaṣar* of the original work.[76]

While the appearance of these references to the author and scribe are certainly noteworthy and the possibility of different versions of the text having circulated historically would not be out of the ordinary, the text as we have it does remain the only substantial version of the *sīra* in existence.[77] While Ulrich Haarmann suggested that the current text was not the final version of the text ("nicht der Schlußfassung"), it seems to me more likely to me that the version as we have it in fact represents a stage following the *Schlußfassung*—if there ever even was a final version—when scribes in Ibn ʿAbd al-Ẓāhir's circles set about editing the text through abridging and compilation.[78] Without access to other versions of the text this

75 The confusiong arises possibly from the fact that Ibn ʿAbd al-Ẓāhir was often given the same honorary title. Ḥajjī Khalīfa, *Kashf al-Ẓunūn*, 2:1016.

76 For a thorough discussion of the available evidence, see: Ṣafwān Ṭaha Ḥasan al-Nāṣir, "'Sīrat al-Malik al-Ẓāhir Baybars' li-Muḥyī al-Dīn b. ʿAbd al-Ẓāhir (t. 692/1293): Dirāsa naqdiyya fī taḥqīq al-kitāb," *Majallat al-tarbiya waʾl-ʿilm*, 17, no. 3 (2010), 80–99. Al-Khuwayṭir in his editorial introduction suggests that these notes were possibly originally marginal notes which were included in the body text during copying. *Rawḍ*, 17–21.

77 For a good example of such a case close in time and space to our authors, see Thomas Bauer's discussion of a text by Ibn Nubāta in "Mamluk Literature as a Means of Communication," 27–29.

78 Haarmann, *Quellenstudien*, 100.

must remain a hypothesis, but as we shall see below in chapter four (section 4.4.2.), there is at least one case where we can see a process of editing at work due to the lucky survival of a variant version of a section of the *sīra*. The text as it has come down to us likely contains other such layers of revision. At the same time, large chunks of the text, including its introduction, come across as authentically related to Ibn ʿAbd al-Ẓāhir's historiographical project. As such, I follow al-Khuwayṭir and accept the text as an authentic if complex part of the corpus studied here. However, I refrain from employing the title *al-Rawḍ al-zāhir fī sīrat al-Malik al-Ẓāhir* in the body text of this book. For ease of reference, the footnotes do use *Rawḍ* to refer to the published edition. For the same reason I also retained the name when creating a digital version of the text in 2020.[79]

1.1.2 *Tashrīf al-Ayyām*

The two remaining *sīra* texts written by Ibn ʿAbd al-Ẓāhir exist in single manuscripts. The first, *Tashrīf al-Ayyām wa'l-ʿUṣūr bi-Sīrat al-Malik al-Manṣūr* deals with the sultanate of Qalāwūn. Only the second and most of the third volume of three original volumes have been preserved. These two volumes cover events from the year 680/1281 up to the death of Qalāwūn, although unevenly and with barely any coverage of events after 686/1287 (see 3.4. for a more extensive discussion of the contents). The two volumes are currently bound into a single large volume, BnF MS Arabe 1704, held by the Bibliothèque nationale de France in Paris.[80] Prior to the rebinding of the manuscript, some initial folios of the third volume, including its

79 I digitised the text with Google Drive's (Tesseract) OCR engine. It is filed in the OpenITI corpus with the URI (Uniform Resource Identifier) 0692IbnCabdZahir.RawdZahir.GVDB20200120-ara1. The digital text is of fairly high quality but was not precisely post-corrected, so it does contain some errors still. These and following URIs consist of the following parts: the first part of the filename is an author name in simplified transcription preceded by the author's death date in the *hijrī* calendar. The second part is a shortened version of the title, again in simplified transcription. The third part is a unique code to designate individual text files. In this and following instances GVDB stand for my initials (because I generated, annotated and post-corrected the file), while the string of numbers is the date at which I submitted the text to the OpenITI. The final part "-ara1" identifies it as an Arabic text, because the OpenITI in principle also accommodates texts in other Islamicate languages as well as different versions of the same text (which would be designated with -ara2, -ara3, and so on)

80 Before ending up in that library, it was part of the collections of the Abbey of Saint-Germain-des-Prés as is evident from a Latin note mentioning it being bequeathed to that library by Henri-Charles du Cambout, the duke of Coislin upon his death in 1732. De Camboust himself had inherited the manuscript along with several others (including BnF MS Arabe 1705, discussed in 1.2.3. below) from his great-grandfather Pierre Séguier (d. 1672). A description of the text's contents

likely title page, have gotten lost.[81] The manuscript is clearly a presentation copy: it features a decorated title page for volume two (see Figure 11 in appendix) and is written in a clear hand in seven widely spaced lines per page. The title page does not explicitly note its author, so the authorship of the text has been ascribed based on a designation introducing one of the poems in the text as "*qawl al-mamlūk ʿAbdallāh b. ʿAbd al-Ẓāhir.*"[82] This self-designation as "slave" is unlikely to refer to anyone else than the text's author. As we shall see below, two of the other manuscripts in the corpus—both also presentation copies—use the same designation on their title pages.

The manuscript was edited and published by Murād Kāmil. He prefaced the edition with extracts from the universal chronicle of Ibn al-Furāt to cover the years of Qalāwūn's sultanate not covered in *Tashrīf al-Ayyām.*[83] This is an odd choice as the historiographical style of those extracts is very different from Ibn ʿAbd al-Ẓāhir's. He also added an appendix of official documents dating to Qalāwūn's sultanate cited in a variety of sources.[84] Within the edition itself he did not make major interventions and presented the text mostly as it is found in the manuscript, although he did correct several Middle Arabic orthographic features and did not always provide information about some of the manuscript's distinctive layout features. In 2020 I created a digital copy of Murād Kāmil's edition for the OpenITI corpus with Google Drive's OCR engine.[85] Substantial portions of the text were translated by David Cook and published in a volume with other translations of texts from the same period.

---

by Dom Berthereau (d. 1794) can also be found on the manuscript's flyleaves. These must date from the time in which the text was held at Saint-Germain-des-Prés..

81 Considering that the third volume (which starts at BnF MS Arabe 1704, 148a) is already more voluminous than the second, my hypothesis is that only a limited number of folios would be missing, perhaps as little as one folio. Unfortunately, due to the codex having been rebound after its move to Europe, I could not establish the situation of its quire preservation in a study of the physical manuscript undertaken in December 2019. Nevertheless, the first words on 148a follow something that has not been preserved and following the last word of 147b there should be something like "al-juzʾ al-thālith."

82 Ibn ʿAbd al-Ẓāhir, *Tashrīf al-Ayyām wa'l-ʿUṣūr bi-Sīrat al-Sulṭān al-Malik al-Manṣūr*, ed. Murad Kāmil (Cairo: n.p., 1961), 82.

83 Ibn ʿAbd al-Ẓāhir, *Tashrīf*, 54–90.

84 Ibn ʿAbd al-Ẓāhir, *Tashrīf*, 185–251.

85 It is filed in the OpenITI corpus with the URI 0692IbnCabdZahir.TashrifAyyam.GVDB20200720-ara1. Due to the typeset of the edition and the fact that I only had access to a scan of middling quality of it, the OCR was not of the highest quality. Some parts of the text were corrected in more detail, but most of it was not closely proofread. For purposes of text reuse this is not problematic, but for other operations on the text it creates issues of reliability.

I have not made use of this translation (or any of the others included in the volume) as it is marred by frequent misreading of technical terminology.[86]

1.1.3 *al-Alṭāf al-Khafiyya*

Only the third of originally at least four volumes of Ibn ʿAbd al-Ẓāhir's *sīra* of al-Ashraf Khalīl, *al-Alṭāf al-Khafiyya min al-Sīra al-Sharīfa al-Sulṭāniyya al-Malikiyya al-Ashrafiyya*, survives. It only contains accounts for the years 690–691/1291–1292. The single known manuscript of this text is held by the Bayerische Staatsbibliothek in Munich, under the call number Cod. Arab 405.[87] The manuscript is similar in execution to that of *Tashrīf al-Ayyām*: a large volume with a decorated title page and widely spaced lines of text. The title page explicitly mentions its author as *al-mamlūk* ʿAbdallāh b. ʿAbd al-Ẓāhir (reproduced as Figure 10 in appendix).[88]

The text was published partially by the Swedish scholar Axel Moberg in 1902 along with a translation and a study of text and author in Swedish.[89] He subsequently also published part of the remainder of the text—partially redacted versions of two of the four *waqf* documents on which the text concludes—in 1918.[90] As a result, a full edition of the text has so far not been available to scholars. The closest one can get to a full version of the text today is by consulting the manuscript or the digital edition of the text I prepared for the OpenITI corpus in 2022.[91] For this I stitched together OCR results of Moberg's two editions with the remainder of the text which I digitised on the basis of the manuscript scan available on the website of the Bayerische Staatsbib-

86 David Cook (transl.), *Chronicles of Qalawun and His Son al-Ashraf Khalil* (London-New York: Routledge, 2020), 46–186.

87 Before ending up in Munich, the manuscript was owned by Étienne Marc Quatremère who himself likely obtained it from Jean-Joseph Marcel. The latter specifically mentioned the manuscript as one of the choice pieces he obtained in Egypt while serving in Napoleon's occupation force. J.-J. Marcel, *Histoire de l'égypte depuis la conquête des Arabes jusqu'à celle des Français* (Paris: H. Dupuy, 1834), xiv-xv. On the acquisition of Quatremère's library by the then royal library of Munich, see T. Seidensticker, "How Arabic Manuscripts Moved to German Libraries", in *Manuscript Cultures*, 10 (2017), 76–77. 73–82.

88 The panel with this identification, on the bottom left of the page, reads *khidmat al-mamlūk ʿAbdallāh b. ʿAbd al-Ẓāhir al-kātib al-Ashrafī*.

89 Axel Moberg (ed. and transl.), *Ur ʿAbd Allah B. ʿAbd eẓ-Ẓâhir's biografi over sultanen el-malik al-Aśraf Halîl*, ed. Axel Moberg (Lund: Gleerupska Univ.-Bokhandelen, 1902). Henceforth I designate this edition as *Alṭāf*. A new full edition of the text has been prepared by Tarek Sabraa but not published yet. Personal communication.

90 Axel Moberg, "Zwei ägyptische Waqf-Urkunden aus dem Jahre 691/1292," *Le monde oriental* 12 (1918), 1–64.

91 It has the URI 0692IbnCabdZahir.AltafKhafiyya.GVDB20220302-ara1.

liothek through HTR (Handwritten Text Recognition). I used the eScriptorium environment which allows for easier post-correction than Google Drive.[92] Like *Tashrīf al-Ayyām*, portions of this text were translated by David Cook in the same volume, but I have not made use of these translations in the present book.[93]

1.2 Shāfiʿ b. ʿAlī

Ibn ʿAbd al-Ẓāhir's nephew Shāfiʿ b. ʿAlī was born on the 25th of Dhū l-Ḥijja in 649 / March 27th 1252 and died, as noted above, on the the 17th of Shaʿbān 730 / June 5th 1330.[94] He was related to Ibn ʿAbd al-Ẓāhir through his mother—of whom we know nothing more than that she was Ibn ʿAbd al-Ẓāhir's sister—and hence his maternal grandfather Rashīd al-Dīn b. ʿAbd al-Ẓāhir, of whom he is consistently named *sibṭ* by biographers. The three biographers who met him personally—al-Ṣafadī, al-Nuwayrī, and al-Jazarī—also give him the family name Ibn ʿAsākir. The Banū ʿAsākir were a family who had a prominent role in Damascene intellectual life from the late 5th/11th century until the latter half of the 7th/13th century.[95] While the Ibn ʿAsākir name indicates that Shāfiʿ may have had ties to that famous Syrian dynasty I have not been able to match any of his ancestors to individuals discussed by Muḥammad Muṭīʿ al-Ḥāfiẓ in his overview of persons with family relations to the famous traditionist and historian Abū al-Qāsim ʿAlī b. ʿAsākir.[96] The fact that Shāfiʿ's date of birth more or less coincided with the waning of that great Syrian family's importance may explain why some of its members did not make it into the voluminous biographical literature on Syrian prominent figures. In any case, the marriage of a daughter of Rashīd al-Dīn b.

---

92 eScriptorium is a collaborative project and has been developed in a number of instances dependent on the target languages and type of material to be digitised. The environment I have use was developed together with the OpenITI project. It is currently only available on request, but general information can be accessed at: https://escriptorium.openiti.org/

93 Cook (transl.), *Chronicles of Qalawun*, 187–202.

94 His birth date is only mentioned by al-Nuwayrī (d. 733/1333) and al-Jazarī (d. 739/1338), the first of whom mentions a slightly later death date (the 24th of Shaʿbān/June 12) than the one cited from al-Ṣafadī at the outset of the introduction of this book. Al-Nuwayrī, *Nihāyat*, 33:239. Al-Jazarī, *Ḥawādith*, 2:428. Another semi-contemporary biographer, al-Fayyūmī (d. after 770/1368), provides the death date as the 14th of Shāʿbān, *Nathr al-Jumān fī Tarājim al-Aʿyān*, MS Chester Beatty Ar. 4113, 258b. I am grateful to Tarek Sabraa for providing me with this last reference.

95 Nikita Elisséeff, "Ibn ʿAsākir," *EI2*.

96 Muḥammad Muṭīʿ al-Ḥāfiẓ, *Al-Ḥāfiẓ Ibn ʿAsākir: Muḥaddith al-Shām wa-Muʾarrikhhā al-Kabīr* (Damascus: Dār al-Qalam, s.d.), 66–83. I am grateful to Muhammad Maslouh for pointing me to this publication. None of the ancestors match with the family members discussed by Suleiman Mourad in *Ibn ʿAsakir of Damascus* (London: OneWorld, 2021), chapter five: "The ʿAsakir extended family."

ʿAbd al-Ẓāhir, a respected Cairene scholar, to a person who claimed to be related to one of the most renowned Syrian scholarly families does appear significant. Al-Jazarī accords the (possibly only honorary) titles *mawlā* and *qāḍī* to his father Nūr al-Dīn ʿAlī and notes that his grandfather ʿImād al-Dīn Abū l-Faḍl ʿAbbās had been a preacher (*khaṭīb*) at the Cairo Citadel and *nāʾib* at the *dār al-ʿadl* in the days of al-Ṣāliḥ Ayyūb.[97] This information makes a direct link to ʿAsqalān less likely. The much later historian Ibn Ḥajar al-ʿAsqalānī (d. 852/1449) includes a *nasab* (genealogy), which he claims to have taken from the *Muʿjam* written by Ibn Rāfiʿ al-Salāmī (d. 774/1372), in which Shāfiʿ traces back his ancestry to pre-Islamic times to the legendary Kināna.[98] Only one author mentions a son of Shāfiʿ named ʿAlī but does not provide any further details.[99]

We do not know exactly how Shāfiʿ ended up working in the chancery either, but he does provide a number of personal comments from which we can infer that he was trained by his uncle. He started working as a *kātib* in the service of two important amirs at the very end of Baybars' reign. Afterwards he served Baybars' successor al-Saʿīd Baraka Qān directly (see chapters four and six for more thorough discussions of some of the material attesting to this). He remained active in the chancery under Qalāwūn. As noted above, biographers describe him as becoming blind due to injury sustained in the Battle of Homs. Al-Jazarī transmits the following eyewitness account directly from Shāfiʿ:

> فسألته عن سبب عماه فقال: في وقعة حمص سنة ثمانين دخلتُ أنا وشمس الدين ابن قريش رفيقي أحد كتاب الإنشاء إلى بستان وجمعة كبيرة، فما كان إلا ساعة والتتر قد دخلوا إلينا، فوقع في رأسي سهم نشّاب فاختلط دماغي ووقعت بين القتلى وقتل كل من كان في البستان. لما كان في الليل قمت ومشيت ووقع لي من أوصلني إلى العسكر ومرضت وعميت، وأبقا عليّ السلطان الشهيد الملك المنصور جامكيتي التي كانت لي في الديوان والراتب فأنا أتناوله إلى الآن.

> I asked him about the cause of his blindness, to which he replied: 'During the Battle of Homs in the year [6]80, I and Shams al-Dīn b. Quraysh,[100] my friend (*rafīqī*), one of the *kuttāb* of the *inshāʾ*, entered a garden with a large group, where an hour later the Tatars came upon us.

---

97 Al-Jazarī, *Ḥawādith*, 2:428

98 Ibn Ḥajar al-ʿAsqalānī, *Durar*, 2:283. On Ibn Rāfiʿ, see Eliyahu Ashtor, "Some Unpublished Sources for the Baḥrī Period," in *Studies in Islamic History and Civilization*, ed. U. Heyd (Jerusalem: The Magnes Press, 1961), 24–27. It should be noted that many persons with the *nisba* al-ʿAsqalānī also bore the *nisba* al-Kinānī, which suggests that there was an especially strong tribal connection to the city. This connection was also pronounced for much of Egypt and is still today sometimes invoked, especially in Jihādī Salafī circles.

99 Shihāb al-Dīn b. Faḍl Allāh al-ʿUmarī does so by giving our author the *kunya* Abū ʿAlī. *Masālik al-Abṣār fī Mamālik al-Amṣār*, 27 vols., ed. Kāmil Salmān al-Jubūrī & Mahdī al-Najm (Beirut: Dār al-kutub al-ʿilmiyya, 2010), 19:221.

100 Al-Ṣafadī tells us this man was about seventy years old at the time, that he was a *kātib al-darj* (like Shāfiʿ) and that he had served continuously in the chancery since the days of al-Ṣāliḥ Ayyūb. *Wāfī*, 29:34.

> A bowman's arrow entered my head and hit my brain, and I fell [as if I were] among those killed–everyone else who was in that garden was killed. When night fell, I stood up and walked away. Then someone who came across me took me to the army, ailing and blinded. The martyred sultan al-Malik al-Manṣūr maintained my monthly pay (*jāmakiyya*) which I had in the *dīwān*, and the ration (*rātib*) which I still receive now.'[101]

As noted above, this presentation and that in other capsule biographies is at odds with Shāfiʿ's self-presentation in his *sīra*s, where he implies that he continued working in the chancery afterwards, especially during the later years of Qalāwūn's sultanate. In this anecdote, by contrast, he tells us that he was given some sort of pension and sent home.

In any case, it is certain that he continued to live for quite a long time, and that he wrote several books and a great deal of poetry during his retirement. As far as I am aware, only four of these books have survived, three more or less in full and one only partially. Three of these are the *sīra* texts I will discuss below, while a fourth is a work in the *adab al-kātib* tradition, providing notes on various points of grammar and a host of poetical and epistolary examples from which an aspiring chancery scribe might take inspiration.[102] There is some evidence for a work not mentioned in his auto-bibliography but cited a few times by the historian Ibn al-Furāt, called *Naẓm al-Sulūk fī Tawārīkh al-Khulafāʾ waʾl-Mulūk*. It appears to have been a universal history, but Ibn al-Furāt only cites it for the Fatimid period.[103] This latter text is the only text of his that was cited by later historians. In general, Shāfiʿ's fame as a littérateur diminished dramatically after his death. Later biographers do mention him but mostly reproduce information found in the works of contemporary authors and focus nearly exclusively on his poetical writing. None of his *sīra*s seem to have been cited by later authors, although as we shall see one of them was consulted by a major historian of the 9th/15th century.

101 al-Jazarī, *Ḥawādith*, 2:429.

102 I discovered the existence of a manuscript of this text, *al-Raʾy al-Ṣāʾib fī Thibāt mā lā Budda minhu liʾl-Kātib*, only after finalising the main research project on which this book is based and have thus only made sparing use of it here. Unlike the *sīra* texts, this chancery work does not offer much specific information about its author. The text is preserved in the manuscript Topkapı Sarayı Müzesi Kütüphanesi Ahmet III 2583. The manuscript was copied in 1116/1705.

103 Fozia Bora, *Writing History in the Medieval Islamic World: The Value of Chronicles as Archives* (London: I.B. Tauris, 2019), 78, 124. The extracts from this text published by Bora are written in a rather plain style compared to Shāfiʿ's other known works.

1.2.1 *al-Faḍl al-Maʾthūr*

Shāfiʿ b. ʿAlī's biography of Qalāwūn, *al-Faḍl al-Maʾthūr min Sīrat al-Sulṭān al-Malik al-Manṣūr*, is likely the first *sīra* work he wrote. The single known manuscript of this text is held by the Bodleian Library in Oxford, under the call number Marsh 424.[104] The identification of *al-Faḍl al-Maʾthūr* as a work writen by Shāfiʿ b. ʿAlī stands beyond doubt given the author's identification on the title page.[105] While this manuscript bears no colophon, there are a number of features of the text and its materiality which suggest that it was offered to a patron sometime in the 690s/1290s (see chapter six for a more thorough discussion of this). The text covers all of Qalāwūn's reign but its chronological organisation is inconsistent.

The text has been known to scholars as a valuable source for the period for decades, especially for its inclusion of several official documents. This explains why no less than three scholars worked on an edition of it around the same time in the late 1990s, two of which were published nearly simultaneously.[106] The most widely available edition was prepared by ʿUmar Tadmurī in 1999. It has also been the primary edition on which I rely in this book and of which I created a digital edition in 2020 using Google Drive.[107] I have however also consulted Paulina Lewicka's edition, which was published in 2000. While both are based on a single manuscript, they do present several divergent readings of the text. For important passages, I have compared both editions as well as a scan of the manuscript. Selections of the text were translated by David Cook and published in the same volume as his

104 As that call number indicates, the manuscript was owned by the Irish bishop Narcissus Marsh (d. 1713) before being acquired by the Bodleian. The text's title page contains Marsh's ex-libris in Greek as well as a brief note, likely also written by him, identifying the text's contents in Latin, both on the top of the page. I am grateful to the staff at the Marsh Library in Dublin for confirming this. It is unclear who owned the text before Marsh, but much of his collection had been part of the Dutch orientalist Jacobus Golius' personal collection. However, I was not able to identify the text in a catalogue listing of Golius' collection which was distributed to potential sellers.

105 He is identified as the author in golden cloud bands to the left of the library (*bi-rasm*) designation, on the left of the page. It reads: *khidmat al-mamlūk al-Manṣūrī Shāfiʿ b. ʿAlī al-kātib.* Oxford Bodleian MS Marsh 424, 1a. Note the similarity of the phrasing (especially the use of *khidma*) with the panel identifying Ibn ʿAbd al-Ẓāhir's authorship on BSB Munich, MS Cod. Arab 407. Shāfiʿ also mentions a *sīra* of Qalāwūn in his autobibliography. Al-Ṣafadī, *Wāfī*, 16:80; al-Ṣafadī, *Aʿyān al-aṣr*, 2:507. He notes there that it consisted of a single volume which is consistent with the manuscript.

106 A third edition project which never came to be published is mentioned by Tahar Mansouri, who notes that he abandoned his publication after noticing the publication of the other editions. "Le portrait du sultan," 87.

107 It has the URI 0730ShaficIbnCali.FadlMathur.GVDB20200701-ara1. The digital text was quite closely post-corrected but most certainly still contains some errors.

translations of material from Ibn ʿAbd al-Ẓāhir's two later *sīras*.[108] As with the material translated from Ibn ʿAbd al-Ẓāhir, the translation is problematic and misreads several technical terms, so I have not made use of it in this book.

1.2.2 *Ḥusn al-Manāqib*

Shāfiʿ b. ʿAlī's second and until recently only other work known to scholarship is *Ḥusn al-Manāqib al-Sirriyya l-Muntazaʿa min al-Sīra l-Ẓāhiriyya*. Like most other texts in the corpus, it exists in a single manuscript, currently held by the Bibliothèque nationale de France under the call number BnF MS Arabe 1707.[109] This manuscript is the only one in our corpus bearing a dated colophon, situating the copying of the work in 2 Jumādā I 716 / 23 July 1316, that is, well within the lifetime of our author. This date has received some attention by P.M. Holt who used it to interpret why the contents of the text are markedly more critical of Baybars than his uncle's earlier work. Holt noted that its copying date fell within the third sultanate of al-Nāṣir Muḥammad, well after Baybars' lifetime and at a time when the heritage of Qalāwūn was firmly established in dynastic form.[110] Whether or not the original composition of *Ḥusn al-Manāqib* should be dated to this same period is not clear, although it for sure postdates the sultanate of Qalāwūn given that information is given on the conquest of Acre. Shāfiʿ also notes that he waited until his uncle had passed away before composing his abridgement (*mukhtaṣar*) of his uncle's original *sīra*, so it cannot have been finalised before 692/1293. As will become clear in the next two chapters of this book, a close reading of the text's introduction and its contents more broadly elucidates some of the dynamics of abridgement that governed *Ḥusn al-Manāqib*'s textual logic.

That the manuscript of *Ḥusn al-Manāqib* might not be the original holograph of the text is suggested by the fact it differs notably from most of the other manuscripts of the corpus in its materiality. It is a rather plainly produced volume and bears no decorated title page. The plain title page does note the title and its authorship.[111] One wonders whether it might be an authorised copy of the original text,

108 David Cook (transl.), *Chronicles of Qalawun*, 210–246. The translation is based on Paulina Lewicka's edition. Cook seems to have been unaware of Tadmurī's edition.

109 Unlike for MSS BnF MS Arabe 1704 and Arabe 1705, we do not know much about the manuscript's whereabouts before the 19th century, when a Latin description of the text's contents was appended to the codex, presumably when it had already entered the collections of the Bibliothèque nationale.

110 Holt, "Three Biographies," 26–27.

111 This authorship designation in fact differs from the two preceding designations on BSB Cod. Arab 407 and Bodleian Marsh 424. Here the identification reads: *taʾlīf al-ʿabd al-faqīr ilā Allāh*

overseen or commissioned by Shāfiʿ himself but intended for a more casual readership than the other manuscripts of his texts. As with *al-Faḍl al-Maʾthūr* our author also mentions the work in his autobibliography, where he even provides nearly the same title as the title found on the manuscript.[112]

An edition of the text was prepared and published by ʿAbd al-ʿAzīz al-Khuwayṭir in 1976, the same year he published his edition of Ibn ʿAbd al-Ẓāhir's *sīra* of Baybars. As noted above, al-Khuwayṭir had made use of passages from *Ḥusn al-Manāqib* to replace gaps in Ibn ʿAbd al-Ẓāhir's *sīra*, but he did not do so the other way around. As we shall see, there is an unexplained gap in the text of *Ḥusn al-Manāqib* where the author skips five years ahead. There is no noticeable physical gap in the manuscript here.[113] Al-Khuwayṭir did not add material to address this gap and in general his edition is a faithful rendering of the manuscript, even though it does correct middle Arabic orthographic features. The edition was reprinted in 1989. This later reprint is today more widely available, so I have used it for the present book as well as for a digital version prepared for the OpenITI corpus.[114] It should be noted, however, that the reprint used a different layout and hence pagination between the two editions is incompatible.

---

taʿālā al-kātib al-Nāṣirī | Shāfiʿ b. ʿAlī b. ʿAbbās al-kātib ʿafā Allāh ʿan-humā | wa-ghafara li-man duʿā li-humā biʾl-ʿafw waʾl-riḍwān. Note that there is no mention of *khidma* (service, offering) or a self-designation as *mamlūk* here. Instead, the authorial action is described with *taʾlīf*. The self-designation as *kātib* is consistent however, and in one of its two instances it is even qualified as being *kātib al-Nāṣirī*, that is, in the service of al-Nāṣir Muḥammad (again consistent with the designations above which refer to al-Manṣūr [Qalāwūn] and al-Ashraf [Khalīl]). However, in this case it is a somewhat ambiguous designation as it could also refer to Shāfiʿ's *laqab* Nāṣir al-Dīn. The second instance of *kātib* in this phrase may also refer to ʿAbbās's status, although I have come across no evidence of him having been a scribe. It is notable that Shāfiʿ does not employ either this family name or the Ibn ʿAbd al-Ẓāhir family name on these two contemporary title pages of his manuscripts. On the much later manuscript of *al-Raʾy al-Ṣāʾib* (Topkapı Sarayı Müzesi Kütüphanesi MS Ahmet III 2583, 1a) he is identified as *Nāṣir al-Dīn Abī al-Faḍl Shāfiʿ b. ʿAlī Abī al-Ḥasan ʿAlī b. al-ʿImād al-kātib.*

112 In the autobibliography the title is given without the first word *Ḥusn*. Al-Ṣafadī, *Wāfī*, 16:80; al-Ṣafadī, *Aʿyān al-aṣr*, 2:507.

113 *Ḥusn*, 312 (start of the year 672, while the previous page dealt with events in the year 667 (*Ḥusn*, 291–311)). It is possible that this is a copyist's mistake or can be attributed to a lacuna in an earlier manuscript of the text.

114 The URI of this file is 0730ShaficIbnCali.HusnManaqib.LMN20200820-ara1. This edition was digitised and post-corrected by Lorenz Nigst (hence the LMN initials in the URI) with eScriptorium, with additional post-correction and annotation by myself. Of all the digital versions used here it is one of the more reliable ones given that two people worked on it.

1.2.3 The *sīra* of al-Nāṣir Muḥammad

The final text of our corpus was until recently almost unknown among scholars. A few scholars had made use of the manuscript in which it is found, but they referred to it as an anonymous text and designated it by one of two titles added later to its title page—in fact a cover sheet, the original title page is lost.[115] In the course of researching the known texts of Shāfiʿ b. ʿAlī and Ibn ʿAbd al-Ẓāhir I consulted the catalogue descriptions of the manuscripts BnF MS Arabe 1704 (*Tashrīf al-ayyām*) and BnF MS Arabe 1707 (*Ḥusn al-Manāqib*) and noticed that a text filed within the same range of call numbers was noted as being similar in style to these two works.[116] Upon consultation of the manuscript, it struck me as stylistically especially similar to Shāfiʿ's works, and on closer study I could identify him as the author of the text beyond doubt. Within the manuscript the author cites an epigram he wrote about Ibn Taymiyya which is also cited by al-Ṣafadī as the final poem in the longer version of his *tarjama* of Shāfiʿ.[117] Frédéric Bauden had come to the same conclusion independently. Further confirmation came from Shāfiʿ's autobibliography, where the text is listed, although without a specific title. The author does note that it consisted of several volumes (*ajzāʾ mutaʿaddida*), so the preserved part—an acephalous manuscript lacking both its opening and ending folios—likely formed only a fraction of the original text. This is also suggested by its coverage, which amounts to only a handful of years (see 3.6) covering part of al-Nāṣir Muḥammad's second sultanate followed by his abdication and return to power in 709/1309. The manuscript itself was likely part of the original literary offering, as its layout is similar to BSB Cod. Arab 405 and BnF MS Arabe 1704 with widely spaced lines.

An edition of the text has been prepared by Frédéric Bauden. I have collaborated with him on the publication of this text, which is nearly complete. Because no published edition of the text exists as of yet, this is also the one text which I have not digitised for the OpenITI corpus, although a text file was available to me for word searches courtesy of Frédéric Bauden.

---

115 Michael Chamberlain, *Knowledge and Social Practice in Medieval Damascus, 1190–1350* (Cambridge: Cambridge University Press, 1994), 181; Hayat Nasser Al-Hajji, *The Internal Affairs in Egypt during the Reign of Sultan al-Nāṣir Muḥammad b. Qalāwūn (709–741/1309–1341)* (Kuwait: Kuwait University, 1978), 205–206. I am grateful to Mustafa Banister for alerting me to the Al-Hajji's use of the text. Since my discovery of the text Mohamad El-Merheb has also made use of it in his study *Political Thought in the Mamluk Period*, 78.

116 M. le Baron de Slane, *Catalogue des manuscrits arabes* (Paris: Imprimerie nationale, 1883–1895), 317.

117 Al-Ṣafadī, *Aʿyān al-aṣr*, 2:512. It is not included in the shorter version of the *tarjama* found in *Wāfī*. In the manuscript this poem is found at BnF MS Arabe 1705, 67b.

1.3 Other family members

Ibn ʿAbd al-Ẓāhir's son Fatḥ al-Dīn b. ʿAbd al-Ẓāhir and his grandson ʿAlāʾ al-Dīn b. ʿAbd al-Ẓāhir followed him into the chancery. Fatḥ al-Dīn b. ʿAbd al-Ẓāhir was born in 638/1240 or 1241 and died in Damascus in 691/1292,[118] while on the journey back to Cairo from al-Ashraf Khalīl's conquest of Qalʿat al-Rūm. He was buried in Damascus, at an age of about 52 years.[119] He thus preceded his own father in death, and a few short poems have been transmitted which appear to speak to Ibn ʿAbd al-Ẓāhir's grief as a parent.[120] Before his death he had become a powerful agent in the chancery by associating himself with al-Ashraf Khalīl's influential vizier Ibn al-Salʿūs (d. 693/1294). As noted, he took over the leading role in the chancery after his father retreated from that role, evidently early in Qalāwūn's reign. Some important official documents have been attributed to him in addition to poems cited in biographical dictionaries. Aside from these, however, no works have come to light that were authored by him. There is however a tantalising reference in a work by his son ʿAlāʾ al-Dīn in which it is suggested that Fatḥ al-Dīn may have written a *sīra* as well. This statement is worth citing in full as it speaks to the ways in which this later scion of the family dynasty perceived the literary achievements of his family:

> لأنّني حقيق بتسطير مناقب مولانا السلطان خلد الله ملكه وترصيف محامده * ووارث ولاء هذا البيت الشريف عن أبٍ شرُف بخدمته، ولا غَرو أن يحذو الفتى حذوَ والده * ولم يزل والد المملوك وجدّه ناظمي سير هذا البيت الشريف حتى صارت محاسنه كالمثل السائر * واصفي عزائمه المظفّرة في الحروب بشهادة ألسنة الأقلام وصدور الصُحف وأفواه المحابر *

> I am worthy of drawing up the virtues of our lord the sultan—may God sustain his kingship—and conjoining his praises, [for I am] the inheritor of the loyalty of this noble house, being born of a father who distinguished himself by his service (*khidma*)—no wonder that the youth takes after the example of his father! The father of the servant (*al-mamlūk*, that is, the author) and his grandfather continuously composed biographies of this noble house so that its merits became like a shining example (*al-mathal al-sāʾir*), and its victorious resolutions in warfare became clear, through the testimonial of the pens, the body texts, and the aromatic scents of inkwells.[121]

---

118 Nuwayrī, *Nihāyat*, 31:154–155; al-Ṣafadī, *Wāfī*, 3:366–369: Ibn al-Ṣuqāʿī, *Tālī*, 119–120 (same lemma as his father). A brief lemma for him is also attested in the Baghdadi historian Ibn al-Fuwaṭī's *Talkhīṣ Majmaʿ al-Ādāb fī Muʿjam al-Alqāb*, 6 vols, ed. Muḥammad al-Kāẓim, Tehran: Muʾassasat al-Ṭibāʿa wa-l-Nashr, Wizārat al-Thaqāfa wa-l-Irshād al-Islāmī, 1416/1995–1996), 2:502. The lemma cites a brief passage from him on "consolation" (*taʿziyya*).

119 Al-Ṣafadī, *Wāfī*, 3:290.

120 Al-Ṣafadī, *Wāfī*, 3:367.

121 ʿAlāʾ al-Dīn b. ʿAbd al-Ẓāhir, *al-Rawḍ al-Zāhir fī Ghazwat al-Malik al-Nāṣir, wa-bi-Dhaylihi: al-Manāqib al-Muẓaffarīya*, ed. ʿUmar Tadmurī (Ṣaydā: al-Maktaba al-ʿAṣrīya, 2005), 41–42. I am grateful to Frédéric Bauden for alerting me to the existence of this manuscript and this passage, as

In this self-assessment ʿAlāʾ al-Dīn saw himself as inheritor of a great writerly legacy, and as a result the worthiest literary chronicler of his age. We will see that this kind of discourse is in keeping with what we find in the introductions of the *sīra* texts.

ʿAlāʾ al-Dīn was born in 676/1276 or 1277 and passed away in 717/1317.[122] By the time he wrote the above quoted lines, around 702/1303, he was already widely considered a leading litterateur of his age. He is said to have become a member of the chancery at the tender age of eleven—that is, somewhere around 687/1288—and he subsequently rose through the ranks to gain a position of substantial influence. He fell from grace at the start of al-Nāṣir Muḥammad's third sultanate because of his association with the amir Sallār, but he seems to have gotten lucky and was able to continue working in the chancery.

The one text of ʿAlāʾ al-Dīn currently known to be attested in manuscript form—in addition to shorter texts cited in biographical dictionaries—is the one from which I have cited above. This text is a relatively short panegyric text entitled *al-Rawḍ al-Zāhir fī Ghazwat al-Malik al-Nāṣir* ("The Radiant Garden: the Battle of al-Malik al-Nāṣir"), which celebrates al-Nāṣir Muḥammad's victory over the Mongols lead by Ghāzān (r. 694–703/1295–1304) at the battle of Marj al-Suffar (702/1303). It is preserved in a fragmentary but luxuriously produced manuscript in St. Petersburg and in extensive quotations by al-Nuwayrī and al-Maqrīzī. Notably, neither of the quoted versions include the lines I have cited.[123] It was dedicated to al-Muẓaffar Mūsā, the son of al-Nāṣir Muḥammad's older brother al-Ṣāliḥ ʿAlī. A short praise is addressed to this Mūsā at the end of the manuscript. While not technically a *sīra*, ʿAlāʾ al-Dīn's text showcases important thematic and especially discursive continuities with the *sīra* corpus—which should already be clear from the extract cited above—and will thus be considered alongside the main texts.

Other members of the family are only mentioned in passing: two further sons of Ibn ʿAbd al-Ẓāhir are mentioned by ʿIzz al-Dīn b. Shaddād, one of whom is

---

well as for sharing a copy of the edition with me. A digital version of the text has been included in the OpenITI with the URI: 0717CalaDinIbnCabdZahir.RawdZahir.GVDB20200607-ara1

122 Nuwayrī, *Nihāyat*, 32:279–280; al-Ṣafadī, *Wāfī*, 22:52–61; al-Birzālī, *al-Muqtafī ʿalā Kitāb al-Rawḍatayn al-Maʿrūf bi-Tārīkh al-Birzālī*, 4 vols., ed. ʿUmar Tadmurī (Ṣaydā/Beirut: al-Maktaba al-ʿAṣriyya, 2006), 4:283–284.

123 I have only seen a few images of the manuscript: four images reproduced in black and white in Tadmurī's edition (the first and last folios of the main text and the first and last folios of the panegyric to al-Muẓaffar Mūsā) and a black and white scan of the title page reproduced by L.A. Mayer in *Saracenic Heraldry: A Survey* (Oxford: Clarendon Press, 1933), plate XIV. Tadmurī evidently relied on outdated information as he notes that the manuscript is currently in Berlin. Its current actual location in St. Petersburgh suggests this is one of several manuscripts that were transported to Poland and the Soviet Union after the Second World War.

identified as Zayn al-Dīn.[124] Ibn al-Furāt also mentions a daughter of Fatḥ al-Dīn named Ruqayya alongside her mother: a slave girl whom Fatḥ al-Dīn manumitted in 681/1282.[125] Ibn al-Furāt also mentions a wife of Ibn ʿAbd al-Ẓāhir, who was the sister of the Christian convert scribe Badr al-Dīn b. Hilāl al-Dawla.[126] There is also a possible indication that ʿAlāʾ al-Dīn had a son named Ḥasan.[127]

1.4 Conclusion

When Sirāj al-Dīn al-Warrāq appealed to Shāfiʿ b. ʿAlī to mediate with Fatḥ al-Dīn b. ʿAbd al-Ẓāhir, he appealed both to his literary sensibilities and to his familial network. Around the time he must have written these lines, members of the Banū ʿAbd al-Ẓāhir dominated the chancery and the literary landscape of the Cairo sultanate and, no doubt, they were unavoidable for anyone trying to make their way into the chancery. At least part of this revered status had been thanks to the *sīra* texts they had written. In the following chapters I will expand on this argument that the *sīra* texts themselves functioned as performative texts, to be understood within the context of a competitive chancery and literary environment.

124 ʿIzz al-Dīn b. Shaddād, *Taʾrīkh al-Malik al-Ẓāhir,* 238–239 (see for a translation and discussion of its context section 3.1. of this book)

125 Ibn al-Furāt, *Taʾrīkh Duwal al-Mulūk, volume 7,* ed. Q. Zurayq (Beirut: al-Maṭbaʿa l-Amīrikāniyya, 1942), 249–250. Ibn al-Furāt transmits the information on this manumission on the authority of Muḥammad b. al-Mukarram, who claims to have been a witness at the conclusion of the manumission contract.

126 Ibn al-Furāt, *Tārīkh,* 7:258. I am grateful to Frédéric Bauden for notifying me of this as well as the information about Fatḥ al-Dīn's daughter. For a brief discussion of Ibn Hilāl al-Dawla's career, see Donald P. Little, "The Recovery of a Lost Source for Bāḥrī Mamlūk History: Al-Yūsufī's Nuzhat Al-Nāẓir Fī Sīrat Al-Malik Al-Nāṣir," *JAOS* 94, vol. 1 (1974), 49–50.

127 Al-Nuwayrī accords him the *kunya* Abū al-Ḥasan. *Nihāyat,* 32:279

Chapter 2
The discourse of *Sīra*: Historiography, memory, and performance

قالت لك القلم الذي كم طرّزت   سِيَرٌ به وقصائد وترسلُ
ناديتُها لا شيء من ذا نافع   قلم البليغِ بغير حظٍّ مُغزَل

She said: 'Yours is the pen by which you have fashioned
so many sīras, odes, and letters'
I cried out in response: 'What's the use of all of that?!
Without fate's assistance the eloquent's pen is but a spindle!'[128]

These lines are part of a long elegy for al-Ẓāhir Baybars written by Ibn ʿAbd al-Ẓāhir. After several lines lamenting the death of the great sultan in general terms, Ibn ʿAbd al-Ẓāhir transitions here to an expression of his own experience of that loss. In a stage-sharing between poet and dedicatee typical for panegyric poetry, he foregrounds the poet's personal despair at the death of his patron because the loss of a patron also implies the loss of literary inspiration. In other words, Ibn ʿAbd al-Ẓāhir's livelihood itself is potentially brought into jeopardy and he fears losing fate's (*ḥaẓẓ*) assistance. It is a crucial transitional point in the poem, and its resolution is implied through an extended praise of Baybars' heir al-Saʿīd Baraka Qān (r. 676–678/1277–1279), whose patronage is desired so that the author may continue to compose inspired prose and poetry. Aside from the insight the poem provides into the logic of patronage, these lines are also notable for explicitly identifying three kinds of literary output as central to the author's identity: *sīras*, odes (*qaṣāʾid*), and letters (*tarassul*). *Sīra* is thus added to the two most time-honoured

128 The poem in which this line appears is not recorded by Ibn ʿAbd al-Ẓāhir himself, although it may have formed part of the lost closing folios of his *sīra* of Baybars. The longest attested version of it—77 lines—is quoted by ʿIzz al-Dīn b. Shaddād as the first poem in a section on "Choice elegies written for Baybars." ʿIzz al-Dīn b. Shaddād, *Tārīkh*, 243–248, quoted lines at 248. The poem is widely attested in versions of differing length, but only one other version includes these lines: a 39-line abridgement given by Ibn al-Furāt, *Tārīkh*, 7:90–92, in which *kam* ("how") is substituted for *qad*, and the verb *nādaytuhā* ("I cried out to her") for *fa-ajabtuhā* ("so I answered her"). An abridged 54-line version without these lines is quoted in Ibn al-Dawādārī, *Kanz al-Durar wa-Jāmiʿ al-Ghurar*, 9 vols., eds. Ulrich Haarmann e.a. (Freiburg: Schwarz, 1971), 8:214–217. The lines are also not included in a 22-line abridgement given by Shāfiʿ b. ʿAlī in *Ḥusn*, 336–338, nor in the most widely attested ten-line version given by Baybars al-Manṣūrī, *Zubdat al-Fikra fī Taʾrīkh al-Hijra*, ed. D.S. Richards (Beirut: Dār al-nashr, 1998), 161; al-ʿAynī, *ʿIqd al-Jumān fī Taʾrīkh Ahl al-Zamān*, 5 vols., ed. Maḥmūd Rizq Maḥmūd (Cairo: Maṭbaʿat Dār al-Kutub, 2009), 2:183–184; Ibn Iyās, *Badāʾiʿ al-Zuhūr fī Waqāʾiʿ al-Duhūr*, 2 vols., ed. Muḥammad Muṣṭafā (Wiesbaden: Franz Steiner, 1975), 1:339.

https://doi.org/10.1515/9783110753028-003

and prestigious forms of writing for a *kātib*. In the literary purview of Ibn ʿAbd al-Ẓāhir and his direct audience, *sīra* had gained a prestigious status on par with the two textual forms most directly associated with eloquence and penmanship.[129]

But what exactly were these *sīra*s, and why did Ibn ʿAbd al-Ẓāhir accord them such importance in his self-presentation? In this chapter I explore the polyvalence of the term *sīra* and situate our authors' understanding and usage of it in its historical, lexical, and discursive development. Following Tzvetan Todorov's definition of genres as "classes of texts that have been historically perceived as such," I argue that *sīra* was presented within a "discourse of genre" as a textual category distinct from other categories, that is, these authors perceived *sīra* to be a genre related to but distinct from the broader genre of history, *taʾrīkh*. This discourse is largely implicit. Our authors did not write down a definition of *sīra* but they did foreground some of its features which allows us to assess how *sīra* became a socially generated, codified and at least temporarily stable textual norm.[130] As such, this chapter studies how Ibn ʿAbd al-Ẓāhir and Shāfiʿ b. ʿAlī conceptualised history and the position of their own works in relation to this tradition.

Because of the profound interweaving of historiography and literary registers in the *sīra* corpus, this chapter will start with addressing an ongoing debate about the literarised nature of historiography in the late medieval period. Following this, I discuss some different usages of the term *sīra* in the work of contemporaries which I compare to Ibn ʿAbd al-Ẓāhir and Shāfiʿ b. ʿAlī. In the third section I move on to an evaluation of our authors' presentation of what *sīra* meant to them by parsing the surviving titles and introductions from the *sīra* corpus. I look at the rhetorical build-up of the three preserved introductions to texts from the *sīra* corpus. From these introductions common ideas emerge. To start, Ibn ʿAbd al-Ẓāhir and Shāfiʿ both defined *sīra* as a historical undertaking preoccupied with time, the rendering of the past, and the preservation of memory. They associated these historical goals

---

129 Note that the last word, *mughzal*, which I have translated as "spindle," is derived from the root letters *gh-z-l*, as is *ghazal*, which designates a popular form of poetry. Ibn ʿAbd al-Ẓāhir wrote several *ghazals* (see his *Dīwān*, 2–15). The last line may thus also imply that the author considered his *sīras*, *qaṣīdas* and letters to be of greater importance than his popular *ghazal* poetry, as the former types of literature gained their status by the assistance of fate, that is, the association with a sultan, whereas *ghazal* poetry were more of a casual pursuit for poets.

130 "In a given society, the recurrence of certain discursive properties is institutionalized, and individual texts are produced and perceived in relation to the norm constituted by that codification. A genre, whether literary or not, is nothing other than the codification of discursive properties." From Tzvetan Todorov's *Les genres du discours* (Paris, 1978), translated by Catherine Porter, included in David Duff (ed.), *Modern Genre Theory* (London: Routledge, 1999) (eBook). This interpretation will also be relevant for my thinking about the chancery and the court as institutions in chapters four and six of this book.

specifically with the memory of a sultan's life and glory, as well as, crucially, to the memory of their own contributions to that sultan's political project (*dawla*). Rather than histories in general, these are works that take the life and the reign of one sultan as primary point of reference. I argue that such a conceptualisation must be seen in a continuum with other genres of courtly and panegyrical discourse, that is, the odes and letter-writing referred to by Ibn ʿAbd al-Ẓāhir. All three of these textual forms created space for author and patron to join one another in a project of glorification and memorialisation within the remit of the text. Implicitly posited in these introductions is also the claim to superiority by our authors, performed through mastery of Arabic poetical and *inshā'* practices. On a rhetorical level, these introductions, as well as the titles of the text, provide a formidable prelude to the spectacle to be found in the body texts.

2.1 Historiography: Literarisierung, narrative, meaning

By the second half of the 7th/13th century historiography was a well-established textual practice in Arabic. The annalistic format which had established its dominance already early on remained the most convenient way of organising information in this period, along with a vigorous tradition of prosopography. For Chase Robinson, these two approaches of chronography and prosopography constitute the two main ideal types of historiography in Arabic, in addition to a third type, that of the biography proper, that is, *sīra*. Although this last ideal type shares many aspects with chronography and prosopography, biography differs from both these types in its sustained focus on the life of one person and their actions, which are presented in exemplary fashion.[131] Among the developments he discusses in how these ideal types were applied by late medieval historians, there is a notably increased presence of literary registers in the texts.[132]

For Robinson, then, late medieval historiography is distinct from earlier historiography on the levels of presentation and content matter. Already in the late 1960s and early 1970s, similar ideas were presented specifically on late medieval Syro-Egyptian historiography by Ulrich Haarmann. First in his doctoral dissertation *Quellenstudien zur frühen Mamlukenzeit* and then in a short but influential article, he advanced the thesis that historians of this period made increased use of narrative techniques in structuring historical works, populating them profusely with miraculous stories, topoi and clichés, as well as extensive citations of poetry.

131 Robinson, *Islamic Historiography* (Cambridge: Cambridge University Press, 2003), xxiv–xxv.
132 Robinson, *Islamic Historiography*, 100–101.

These new developments amounted to a "literarisation of the inner form."[133] For Haarmann, literature was to be equated with stories, with the anecdotal and the marvellous. Although these elements were not without value, they should be distinguished from actual history, which was about facts and data which could be mined from the sources. Haarmann's ideas can be compared to those of his contemporary Albrecht Noth, who wrote a dissertation on literary motifs in early Islamic texts, which was later translated and substantially revised in collaboration with Lawrence Conrad.[134] Both these works suggested that simply being aware of the "literary" nature of many accounts would help researchers distinguish between the information of historical value on the one hand and the literary embellishment on the other hand.

Comparing the studies of Noth and Haarmann already highlights the most important problem with Haarmann's thesis: literary elements had been present in Islamic historiography from early on.[135] Haarmann would in the following decades be challenged repeatedly by Bernd Radtke, who took issue especially with Haarmann's proposition of a strict dichotomy between history as a science (*ʿilm*) which he believed had been the norm in the classical period and history as *adab* as it emerged in the late medieval period. Radtke argued that Haarmann's evaluation of history as an objective science and literature as a subjective practice was a major anachronism because such a distinction never existed as such among contemporary authors. He furthermore highlighted that even the appearance of more entertaining elements in historiography was hardly a new development, as it had precedents at least as far back as al-Masʿūdī (d. 345/956). A much more thorough

---

133 Ulrich Haarmann, "Auflösung und Bewahrung der klassischen Formen arabischer Geschichtsschreibung in der Zeit der Mamluken," *ZDMG*, 121, no. 1 (1971), 46–60. It should be noted that a more general idea of "Literarisierung" was already present in early 20th-century German scholarship on the Islamic Middle Period, specifically in the work of Gustav Richter, Gustav von Grunebaum (who at one point speaks of a "literarization of ideas and rhetoricization of style" as a dominant cultural phenomenon in *Medieval Islam: A Study in Cultural Orientation* (Chicago-London: The University of Chicago Press, 1953), 229), and Götz Schregle. Bernd Radtke sees Haarmann's article as building on that foundation, *Weltgeschichte und Weltbeschreibung im mittelalterlichen Islam* (Beirut-Stuttgart: Orient Institut-Franz Steiner, 1992), 186.

134 Albrecht Noth, *Quellenkritische Studien zu Themen, Formen und Tendenzen frühislamischer Geschichtsüberlieferung* (Bonn: Orientalisches Seminar der Universität, 1973); Noth & Lawrence I. Conrad, *The Early Arabic Historical Tradition: A Source-Critical Study* (London: Darwin Press, 1994).

135 For a more recent evaluation of the distinctive characteristics of Middle Period historiography compared to earlier periods, see Konrad Hirschler, "Islam: The Arabic and Persian Traditions," in: *The Oxford History of Historical Writing*, eds. Sarah Foot and Chase Robinson (Oxford: Oxford University Press, 2012), 267–286.

diachronic evaluation of the intersection of historiographical and literary practices would be necessary before any such claims about "literarisation" could be made.[136]

Beyond German academia, scholars took Haarmann's evaluation of "Literarisierung" more or less at face value. This has bearing on the *sīras* because scholars have used the literarised designation in tandem with evaluations of legitimisation. Received knowledge in the field is that the *sīras* contain much unique and important material, but that one should be wary of taking this too literally. Rather, it comes down to filtering out the panegyrical, propagandistic, indeed, literarised layers and retaining only those facts that can be confirmed in other, less biased sources.[137] In a related way, Tarif Khalidi's evaluation of later Middle Period historians as working under the "epistemic" umbrella of *siyāsa*, that is, "politics" has been deeply influential as well. He argued that in this period writing texts in which "historical knowledge is all knowledge that bears a direct or indirect relationship to the governance of *mamalik*, or feudal principalities," and in which "the connection between power and knowledge [. . .] was pronounced."[138] Khalidi's evaluation of consecutive epistemic categories informing historical thought has rightly been criticised for being too sweeping,[139] but the idea that there was a far-reaching entanglement of rulers and historians and that historians' growing focus on contemporary

---

136 Radtke first developed his criticism in his "Einleitung" to his edition of the first volume of Ibn al-Dawādārī's *Kanz, Erster Teil: Kosmographie,* ed. B. Radtke (Cairo-Wiesbaden: Franz Steiner, 1982), 23–27. His most extensive treatment of the issue can be found in his diachronic study of universal histories *Weltgeschichte*, esp. 186–195. Radtke here engages with Haarmann's first article, Haarmann's response to Radtke's criticism formulated in the introduction to his edition of the first volume of Ibn al-Dawādārī's *Kanz* as well as with points raised by Barbara Langner in *Untersuchungen zur historischen Volkskunde Ägyptens nach mamlukischen Quellen* (Freiburg: Klaus Schwartz, 1983). He also revisited the topic in later articles, most prominently: "Zur 'Literarisierten Volkschronik' Der Mamlukenzeit," *Saeculum* 41, no. 1 (1990), 44–52. He eventually changed his mind slightly in "Die Literarisierung der mamlukischen Historiografie: Versuch einer Selbstkritik," in *O ye Gentlemen: Arabic Studies on Science and Literary Culture. In Honour of Remke Kruk,* eds. Arnoud Vrolijk & Jan P. Hogendijk (Leiden: Brill, 2007), 263–274. This last article still argues that historiographical "fictionality" was not a Mamluk innovation, but Radtke acknowledges that some changes in its uses may have taken place in the period. For a much fuller reconstruction of the debate, see now Van Steenbergen, "History Writing."

137 For two early insightful critiques of this separation of content and form also visible in much other 20th century scholarship on historiography, see: Hartmut E. Fähndrich, "The Wafayāt al-Aʿyān of Ibn Khallikān: A New Approach," *JAOS* 93, vol. 4 (1973), 432–445; Fedwa Malti-Douglas, "Dreams, the Blind, and the Semiotics of the Biographical Notice," *Studia Islamica* 51 (1980), 137–162. I am grateful to one of the peer reviewers of this book for reminding me of the former article.

138 Tarif Khalidi, *Arabic Historical Thought in the Classical Period* (Cambridge: Cambridge University Press, 1994), 184–188. See also Robinson, *Islamic Historiography,* 100–102.

139 Julie Scott Meisami, "Review of *Arabic Historical Thought in the Classical Period,*" *JAOS* 116, no. 2 (1996), 309–313.

events was a direct result of it, has held wide currency.[140] The idea that the *sīras* formulated legitimising or propagandistic presentations of the past is deeply influenced by such an evaluation.[141]

Khalidi's conceptualisation is relevant for our purposes insofar as it rightly identifies the importance of contexts in which our authors were active—especially those of the chancery and the court—as defining for the specific narratives of rulership they constructed. I argue that it is rewarding to consider the multifocal nature of interactions within those contexts. Literarisierung in this approach, then, can be a useful focus if we identify it as working within a matrix of literary communication, in which historiographical discourses interacted with discourses of (among others) poetry and correspondence writing.[142]

2.2 Defining *sīra*

The lexicographer Ibn Manẓūr (d. 711/1311 or 1312), a direct peer of our authors, provided the primary signification of the root letter *s-y-r*, from which the noun *sīra* is derived, as "going," "*al-dhahāb*,"[143] while *sīra* itself had a primary meaning of "*ṭarīqa*," "a way of going," or even "a road."[144] The later lexicographer Muḥammad Murtaḍā al-Zabīdī (d. 1205/1791) starts out similarly in his definition but adds the

---

140 See for example Meisami's own "Rulers and the Writing of History" in *Writers and Rulers: Perspectives on Their Relationship from Abbasid to Safavid Times*, eds. Beatrice Gruendler & Louise Marlow (Wiesbaden: Reichert Verlag, 2004), 73–96; Robinson, *Islamic Historiography*, 114–123.

141 Interestingly, in his own evaluation of the period's sources, Haarmann made an exception for the *sīras*: these were texts that followed in the footsteps of an older chancery tradition and thus fell outside of the influence of new historiographical tendencies. Haarmann, "Auflösung," 54. Haarmann does not explain which chancery tradition our authors would be following then, but he likely referred to the Ayyubid works about Ṣalāḥ al-Dīn written by Bahāʾ al-Dīn b. Shaddād and ʿImād al-Dīn al-Iṣfahānī, and possibly the *Taʾrīkh al-Yamīnī* by the Ghaznavid historian Abū Naṣr al-ʿUtbī (d. 427/1036 or 1040), which is often cited as an important precedent for rhetoricised historical writing. On this latter text, see Robinson, *Islamic Historiography*, 98–99.

142 On the idea of a "Mamluk cultural matrix," see Jo Van Steenbergen, "Qalāwūnid Discourse," which builds on ideas put forward by Jonathan P. Berkey in "Culture and Society during the Late Middle Ages," in *The Cambridge History of Egypt, vol. 1, Islamic Egypt, 640–1517*, ed. Carl F. Petry (Cambridge: Cambridge University Press, 1998), 386–411. On literary communication, see Thomas Bauer, "Mamluk Literature: Misunderstandings and New Approaches," *MSR* 9, no. 2 (2005), 105–130.

143 Muḥammad b. Mukarram b. Manẓūr, *Lisān al-ʿArab*, 2169, in https://ejtaal.net/aa/ On the identification of Ibn Manẓūr as the *kātib* Ibn al-Mukarram who was active in Qalāwūn's chancery and whom we will come across a few more times, see Johann W. Fück, "Ibn Manẓūr," *EI2*.

144 Ibn Manẓūr, *Lisān al-ʿarab*, 2170. It should be noted that Ibn Manẓūr compiled information from earlier dictionaries and usually did not offer new lexicographical definitions.

important derived meaning of *ṭarīqa* as a specific person's way of going, that is, a way of doing things, with the connotation of being exemplary. He also gives *sunna* as a metaphorical synonym (*min al-majāz*).[145] We can see in these specifications the origins of the derived meanings "behaviour" and "conduct," and a suggestion of the common idea of *sīra* as a record of history as it relates to a particular person's "paradigmatic behaviour or conduct."[146]

The term became already early on associated with historical reports (*akhbār*), specifically those dealing with the life and actions of the Prophet Muḥammad—especially his battles, or *maghāzī*. Prophetic *sīra* came to be a genre that remained intimately linked to the collection and transmission of hadith.[147] As a genre, it remained continuously popular. One of its most famous specimens was even written by a contemporary and direct acquaintance of our authors.[148] In the early period already the term was also used to designate the lives of kings and great men, *siyar al-mulūk*.[149] Gradually, the term would in some cases also come to be equated to *tarjama*, the term otherwise used for capsule biographies in prosopographical works. Arguing for this continuity, a team of scholars working with Dwight Reynolds rendered *sīra* as "exemplary life story."[150] Finally, in the centuries following the lives of our authors, the term would also grow to great significance because of its use to denote popular epics that were predominantly performed orally, most obviously the *Sīrat Baybars*.[151]

---

145 Murtaḍā al-Zabīdī, *Tāj al-ʿArūs min Jawhar al-Qāmūs*, 40 vols., ed. Ḍāḥī ʿAbd al-Bāqī e.a. (Kuwait: Muʾassasat al-Kuwayt li'l-taqaddum al-ʿilmiyya, 2001), 12:116–117.

146 Robinson, *Islamic Historiography*, xiii.

147 Wim Raven, "Biography of the Prophet," *EI3*.

148 Ibn Sayyid al-Nās (d. 734/1334), who according to al-Ṣafadī studied with Ibn ʿAbd al-Ẓāhir, wrote an exceedingly popular such *sīra* called *ʿUyūn al-Athar fī Funūn al-Maghāzī wa'l-Shamāʾil wa'l-Siyyar*. On the author, see Franz Rosenthal, "Ibn Sayyid al-Nās," *EI2*.

149 Wim Raven, "Sīra," *EI2*. By the 4th/10th century, when Ibn al-Nadīm compiled his famed *Fihrist*, the term appears to have been widely used already. In addition to works of Prophetic *sīra*, he lists *sīra*s of Muʿāwiyya (in one case also extended to further reports of the Umayyad dynasty), of the Persian ruler Anūshirwān (one of which is attributed to Ibn al-Muqaffaʿ) and Ardashīr, of the Banū al-Jarrāḥ, of "the imams," and of the early caliphs Abū Bakr and ʿUmar. Results of a word search in the OpenITI file 0385IbnNadim.Fihrist.Shia003355-ara1.mARkdown, 27 August 2021. Lorenz Nigst e.a. "OpenITI: a Machine-Readable Corpus of Islamicate Texts (2021.2.5)" [Data set] *Zenodo* (2021), https://doi.org/10.5281/zenodo.5550338

150 Dwight F. Reynolds e.a., *Interpreting the Self: Autobiography in the Arabic Literary Tradition* (Berkeley-Los Angeles-London: University of California Press, 2001), 39.

151 On the latter, see various studies by Thomas Herzog, especially his monograph *Geschichte und Imaginaire: Entstehung, Überlieferung und Bedeutung der Sirat Baibars in ihrem sozio-politischen Kontext* (Wiesbaden: Harrassowitz, 2007).

Given this distinctive evolution of the term's usage, it is not surprising that for Ibn ʿAbd al-Ẓāhir and Shāfiʿ, *sīra* was not fully interchangeable with *taʾrīkh*, a concept they only rarely referred to in internal references to their works.[152] This is not to say that *sīra* and *taʾrīkh* were completely separate endeavours: in line with the above-noted historiographical developments of the Middle Period the *sīra*s too were intensely preoccupied with recent events and accorded the relationship between the author and the ruling elites a central place in the work. Moreover, while the *sīra*s contain remarkable amounts of compiled documents, prose texts and poetry, many semi-contemporary works of explicitly chronographic or prosopographical inclination also contain great amounts of such material. Yet, I argue that, when studied closely, the approach to historiography found in the six *sīra*s showcases distinctive features and a discursive self-awareness. To refer to Todorov again, the fact authors denoted their works as *sīra* is in itself a speech act by which they embedded their work in a perceived genre tradition and designated it as distinct from other genres.

This distinctiveness can be brought out by comparing the six *sīra*s written by Ibn ʿAbd al-Ẓāhir and Shāfiʿ b. ʿAlī to the closely related and contemporaneous biography of Baybars written by ʿIzz al-Dīn b Shaddād. The latter moved in similar circles as our authors: he was a courtier in the retinue of Baybars' vizier Ibn Ḥinnā (d. 677/1278) and had earlier served the Ayyubid ruler of Damascus and Aleppo al-Nāṣir Yūsuf (r. 634–659/1238–1260).[153] The second volume of this text—the only extant part of the text in manuscript form—is explicitly denoted by the title *Taʾrīkh al-Malik al-Ẓāhir* on its title page. In one internal reference the text is also referred to as a *taʾrīkh*.[154] On the simple level of designating the text, ʿIzz al-Dīn b. Shaddād's text is thus already distinct from those of Ibn ʿAbd al-Ẓāhir and Shāfiʿ b. ʿAlī. This has repercussions for the contents, especially on how it takes the life and rule of a sultan as the chronological ordering principle of his work. While the bulk of ʿIzz al-Dīn b. Shaddād's subject matter is directly related to actions of the sultan or his agents, he also includes much seemingly unrelated material, including lengthy

---

152 Ibn ʿAbd al-Ẓāhir does indirectly refer to his duty as that of a *muʾarrikh* once in his *sīra* of Baybars. All further internal references to the text denote it as *sīra* and its author as *muʾallif* (author) or, at only one point, *kātib*. See for an overview of these instances: al-Nāṣir, "'Sīrat al-Malik al-Ẓāhir," 90–92.
153 Zayde Antrim, "Ibn Shaddād, ʿIzz al-Dīn," *EI3*. Note that Baybars himself served this sultan before becoming sultan of Egypt.
154 Edirne Selimiye Kütüphanesi MS 2306, 1a. For the internal reference, see: *Taʾrīkh al-Malik al-Ẓāhir*, 88. As noted above, later historians often referred to the text by the same title as that ascribed to Ibn ʿAbd al-Ẓāhir's *sīra* by Ḥajjī Khalīfa, *al-Rawḍ al-zāhir fī sīrat al-Malik al-Ẓāhir*, but this is not supported by the manuscript. I believe the fact that these later authors referred to Ibn Shaddād's text as a *sīra* is the result of changing conceptualisations of the distinction between *sīra* and *taʾrīkh* in generations following those of our authors.

obituaries of various personalities, many of whom did not have any link to the sultan. He also includes a long account of the life and actions of the Ḥafṣid ruler of Tunis, Muḥammad b. Abī Zakariyā (d. 675/1277), which he notably introduces as a *sīra*.[155] In general, the format of his text is much more closely related to the "obituary chronicles" tradition which had an influential representative in Sibṭ b. al-Jawzī's earlier noted *Mirʾat al-Zamān* which generated several continuations in early 8th/14th century Syria.[156] An even closer cognate to Ibn Shaddād's text is the dynastic chronicle *Mufarrij al-Kurūb fī Akhbār Banī Ayyūb* ("The Dissipator of Anxieties: Reports about the Ayyubids") written by another contemporary of our authors, Ibn Wāṣil (d. 697/1298). This author moved in some of the same circles as Ibn ʿAbd al-Ẓāhir before returning to his hometown Hama shortly after Baybars' ascent of the throne.[157] While his text includes several obituaries, Ibn Wāṣil also includes several sections denoted as *sīra* in his text. These in fact amount to obituaries for Ayyubid rulers in which the focus lies on their ideal qualities. These sections also feature poetry composed in relation to them.[158]

It is this approach to *sīra* which we do find in the final section of Ibn Shaddād's text, which is set apart by a specific title: *Dhikr mā Yazhū ʿalā Zahr al-Khamīla min Jumal Sīratihi al-Jamīla* ("A report of what blossoms into luxuriant flowers from the totality of his beautiful actions").[159] Its construction in fourteen chapters also relinquishes the text's otherwise dominant annalistic framework and instead zooms in on anecdotes exemplifying the sultan's virtues and deeds. Here, Ibn Shaddād's text can most meaningfully be compared to the corpus of *sīras* written by Ibn ʿAbd al-Ẓāhir and Shāfiʿ b. ʿAlī. Ibn ʿAbd al-Ẓāhir's *sīra* of Baybars even includes a similar

155 ʿIzz al-Dīn b. Shaddād, *Taʾrīkh al-Malik al-Ẓāhir*, 188–200. There may be an element of symmetry at play here, considering the placement of this short "life" of a ruler who died in the same year as the text's primary subject, Baybars. The reason to include this life may also be related to that ruler's proclaiming himself caliph, a fact Ibn Shaddād notes at one other point. ʿIzz al-Dīn b. Shaddād, *Taʾrīkh al-Malik al-Ẓāhir*, 220–221.

156 Jozsef Somogyi, "Ibn al-Jauzī's School of Historiography," *Acta Orientalia Academiae Scientiarum Hungaricae* 6 no. 1/3 (1956), 207–214. See also Van Steenbergen, "History Writing," 8. Van Steenbergen references in particular Li Guo's research into early 8th/14th century Syrian historiography, *Early Mamluk Syrian historiography: Al-Yūnīnī's* Dhayl mirʾat al-zamān (Leiden: Brill 1998).

157 For a detailed account of Ibn Wāṣil's peregrinations, see Konrad Hirschler, *Medieval Arabic Historiography: Authors as Actors* (London: Routledge, 2006), 20–28.

158 Ibn Wāṣil, *Mufarrij al-Kurūb fī Akhbār Banī Ayyūb*, 5 vols., eds. Jamāl al-Dīn Shayyāl, Ḥasanayn Muḥammad Rabīʿ and Saʿīd ʿAbd al-Fattāḥ ʿĀshūr (Cairo: Dār al-Kutub wa'l-Wathāʾiq al-Qawmiyya, 1957). Examples of such *sīras* in vol. 1:27, 100–106, 116–117, 189–190, 230; vol. 2:107.

159 I have translated *sīra* here with the more basic meaning "actions," though of course the polyvalence with "biography" is intended. Actions works better here due to the section's lack of chronology and focus on anecdotal examples of ideal rule and comportment.

virtues section which separates its pre-sultanate accounts from the annals devoted to Baybars' sultanate.

Exemplarity and "ideal rule" were thus crucial for both Ibn Shaddād and Ibn Wāṣil to denote something as *sīra*. For them, it was as it were a sub-discourse of the broader discourse of history, appropriate for talking about the exemplarity of great men in history. The conceptual framework of Ibn ʿAbd al-Ẓāhir and Shāfiʿ b. ʿAlī is not altogether very different in its interpretation of *sīra* as an exemplary record of history, but their foregrounding of it as their texts' primary focus is notable. In some cases, the temporal nature of the reports included in these texts is only of secondary importance to the fact that they are somehow related to the sultan; almost every account is included for the specific reason of highlighting one or more qualities of the ruler or for constructing an appropriate narrative rendering of some aspect of his rule. While digressions do appear, they always perform a particular narrative function in strengthening the meanings of the primary *akhbār*. Most of all, both authors foregrounded their own position *vis-à-vis* the events through the prism of the *dīwān al-inshāʾ*. In the texts' logic this institution held a central position in the ruler's *dawla*, responsible as it was for the linguistic articulation of the sultan's claim to authority. The panegyrical content many previous researchers have highlighted as an obstacle is in fact central to how the authors conceived of *sīra*.

This is not to say that our authors did not have precedents and successors of sorts in conceiving of *sīra* in this way. Other authors, too, named their works *sīra*, but conceptualised its role somewhat differently. The most direct precedent of our authors is Bahāʾ al-Dīn b. Shaddād's biography of Ṣalāḥ al-Dīn, which is on many manuscripts denoted explicitly as *sīra*. It has furthermore been highlighted as a direct inspiration for Ibn ʿAbd al-Ẓāhir's *sīra* of Baybars.[160] The dynamics of this text, however, play out rather differently due to the author's relationship as a close companion and confidant of Ṣalāḥ al-Dīn. Rather than a relationship of literary service and praise, Bahāʾ al-Dīn b. Shaddād portrays the sultan and himself almost nostalgically as companions in military, political and personal struggle. The pervasive focus on the *dīwān al-inshāʾ* is not found here, though it is paralleled in ʿImād al-Dīn al-Iṣfahānī's texts on Ṣalāḥ al-Dīn. These, however, are again distinct from those of our authors by their approach to historical time: in one case only focussing on the final few years of Ṣalāḥ al-Dīn's life, and in the other case a thorough interweaving of personal memoirs with the life of Ṣalāḥ al-Dīn, sometimes digressing substantially from the focus on the sultan's life. By contrast, our authors only come to the foreground as agents in their texts insofar as they performed a role in

160 Holt, "The Sultan as Ideal Ruler," 129. See also Van Den Bossche, "Narrative Construction," 136–137.

sultans' political projects. Al-Iṣfahānī's use of *saj*ʿ has also been parsed in detail by Lutz Richter-Bernburg, who argued that it was highly idiosyncratic.[161] In comparison, Ibn ʿAbd al-Ẓāhir presents a somewhat more sober and balanced style, even regularly relinquishing *saj*ʿ and writing in straightforward prose. Shāfiʿ b. ʿAlī tends to use *saj*ʿ much more profusely, but even in his texts we find him regularly scaling back to unadorned prose.

As a notable successor, we can highlight Ibn al-Dawādārī (d. after 740/1340) who accorded the final volume of his nine-volume universal history *Kanz al-Durar* the status of *sīra* in its title: *al-Durr al-Fākhir fī Sīrat al-Malik al-Nāṣir* ("The Outstanding Pearl: The Biography of al-Malik al-Nāṣir"). This volume is devoted entirely to the second and third reign of al-Nāṣir Muḥammad. Despite this title, Ibn al-Dawādārī generally follows ʿIzz al-Dīn b. Shaddād's approach to regnal history as a structural chronological phenomenon. Most of the work is strictly divided into years and much of the material included is not directly related to the life and rule of the sultan.[162] He also includes obituaries, although more haphazardly than Ibn Shaddād. In the mid-8th/14th century Ibrāhīm b. al-Qaysarānī (d. 753/1352) also referred to his panegyric of al-Ṣāliḥ Ismāʿīl (r. 743–746/1342–1345) *Al-Nūr al-Lāʾiḥ waʾl-Durr al-Ṣādiḥ fī ṣṭifāʾ Mawlāna l-Sulṭān al-Malik al-Ṣāliḥ* ("The Brilliant Light and the necklace of Pearls, demonstrating that our lord the sultan al-Malik al-Ṣāliḥ enjoys divine favour")[163] as a *sīra* at one point. It is notable however that he did not use the term in his title for the work. The contents also demonstrate that *sīra* is here used to refer to the paradigmatic qualities of a life and not as guiding principle for the text, which does not contain much in the way of biographical information.[164]

What emerges thus, is that *sīra* was a concept in flux, and that important differences in approach emerge even in the relatively short period between the early 7th/13th up to the mid-8th/14th century. Rather than a fixed lexeme denoting "biography," the term designated a web of associations related to biographical practice,

161 Lutz Richter-Bernburg, *Der Syrische Blitz: Saladins Sekretär zwischen Selbstdarstellung und Geschichtsschreibung* (Stuttgart: Steiner, 1998).

162 It is however significant that the sultan's first reign is not related in this part but in the eighth volume, together with (among others) the reigns of al-Nāṣir Muḥammad's brother al-Ashraf Khalīl, father Qalāwūn, and that of Baybars. In his introduction, Ibn al-Dawādārī claims that he devoted a single volume to this ruler mostly because there was not enough space to do so adequately in the preceding volume. However, the introduction does also include a panegyric to al-Nāṣir Muḥammad replete with celestial metaphors, linking it to the work's general historical-cosmological approach. *Kanz*, 9:2–4 (the panegyric), 5–6 (the argument for a separate volume). The titles of the preceding eight volumes do not use the term *sīra*, but opt for *akhbār*, even for the volume devoted to the life of the Prophet and the Rāshidūn caliphs.

163 Translation of the title by Van Steenbergen, "Qalāwūnid Discourse," 3.

164 Van Steenbergen, "Qalāwūnid Discourse," 21.

paradigmatic comportment, and ideal rule. Authors picked up on these valances and sometimes developed them in idiosyncratic ways. Ibn ʿAbd al-Ẓāhir in particular appropriated a malleable *sīra* form and redesigned it according to his purposes. His nephew Shāfiʿ took up his uncle's example and constructed works in similar fashion.

2.3 The arguments for *sīra*: Titles and introductions

Neither Ibn ʿAbd al-Ẓāhir nor Shāfiʿ b. ʿAlī explain their choice for the term *sīra*, but they did write rhetorically complex introductions to their texts which lay out their reasons for writing them. Three of these introductions have been preserved but we can safely assume the other texts had such introductions as well, given their near universal presence in historical and literary writing of the period. Peter Freimark has conducted a meta-study of such introductions which I have used to highlight where our authors fall in line with common discourses and where they diverge.[165] However, while Freimark considered rhetoric introductions to be mostly irrelevant for the ensuing contents and found their value to be mostly literary, I take them to be important statements of intent.[166] The introductions to the *sīra*s have been parsed by P.M. Holt and Anne Troadec, but I argue that their readings contain a number of misinterpretations with significant consequences for their general interpretation of these texts. In the following I present a detailed and analytical study of the three preserved introductions, in which I focus especially on the logical trajectory of the argument. I will also suggest a few ways in which we can read these introductions in relation to the body text following them and in relation to the titles of the works.

---

165 Peter Freimark, "Das Vorwort als literarische Form in der arabischen Literatur" (Unpublished PhD thesis, Westfälische Wilhelms-Universität zu Münster, 1967).

166 "In vielen Fällen könnte man [das Vorwort] bei der Lektüre des Werkes übergehen und sich diesem sofort zuwenden, man würde das Werk dennoch in allen Einzelheiten verstehen." Freimark, "Das Vorwort," 12. Freimark does argue for the value of these sections as an expression of authors' contemporary anxieties and experiences. For more recent ideas about the relationship between introductions and the works they precede, see, among others: Aboubakr Chraïbi, "L'émergence du genre 'muqaddima' dans la littérature arabe" in *Entrer en matière: les prologues*, eds. Jean-Daniel Dubois & Bernard Roussel (Paris: Cerf, 1998), 89–101; James E. Montgomery, "Serendipity, Resistance, and Multivalency: Ibn Khurradadhbih and his Kitāb al-Masālik wal-Mamālik," in *On fiction and adab in medieval Arabic literature*, ed. Philip F. Kennedy (Wiesbaden: Harrassowitz, 2005), 177–232; see also James E. Montgomery, *Al-Jāḥiẓ; In Praise of Books* (Edinburgh: Edinburgh University Press, 2013).

In these introductions, the authors bring together three main elements to posit their undertaking, two of which are common to all three texts—the remaining third element is specific to Shāfiʿ's aim to abridge his uncle's *sīra* of Baybars and is thus understandably absent from the other texts.

- The importance of history writing, specifically in the form of *sīra*, as a medium to edify later generations.
- The exemplarity of this specific sultan's life and reign, amounting to panegyric framed in the context of historical writing.
- The author's own presence as an eyewitness and participant in the events discussed in the *sīra* as a claim for superiority. In Shāfiʿ's case of abridging his uncle's *sīra*, it is the personal relationship between the author and his uncle which is stressed.[167]

In these three introductions it is thus argued that the texts gain their relevance as historical exempla – essential to the concept of history and *sīra* especially – not only through the exemplarity of a specific sultan's deeds, but also through the exemplarity of the author who recorded these deeds.

Aside from the introductions, I also touch on the titles of the *sīras*, securely preserved for four of the six texts, and their relationship to the body texts. From the 4th/10th century onwards Arabic texts were often given a title in two rhyming parts. A. Ambros has designated these two parts respectively as literary "guiding phrase" (*Leitphrase*) and "thematic phrase" (*Themaphrase*).[168] As George Wickens notes, however, many modern researchers have tended to treat titles in a "rather casual, not to say cavalier" way, and often translated them somewhat freely.[169] Some have also not always paid close attention to the precise grammatical function of the con-

167 Note that these differ from the three main aspects distinguished for the *sīra* corpus by Anne Troadec ("Les Mamelouks" 226–227): 1. "datation," that is "un travail de datation et de mise en ordre chronologique d'une série d'événements," 2. "référence au passé" or "la recherche de validation des figures de leur temps par la référence à des modèles éprouvés du passé," and 3. "souci d'édification morale," i.e. as an advice text. She notes the fact that the *sīras* often contain a personal vision of history but does not evaluate it as a crucial building block of their general writerly project. While Troadec's first and third aspects are reflected in mine, her second aspect is not as important across the whole corpus and is only really pronounced in Ibn ʿAbd al-Ẓāhir's biography of Baybars. It can furthermore be subsumed under the idea of exemplarity.

168 Arne A. Ambros, "Beobachtungen zu Aufbau und Funktion des gereimten klassisch-arabischen Buchtitels," *Wiener Zeitschrift für die Kunde des Morgenlandes* 80 (1990), 13–57. I borrow the translations of these terms from Hirschler, *Medieval Arabic Historiography*, 66.

169 George M Wickens, "Notional Significance in Conventional Arabic "Book" Titles: Some Unregarded Potentialities" in *The Islamic World From Classical to Modern Times: Essays in Honor of Bernard Lewis*, eds. Clifford E. Bosworth e.a. (Princeton: The Darwin Press, 1989), 369–388.

necting prepositions—most often *fī*, but as we shall see, for our corpus, there are meaningful divergences from this.[170] By contrast, Wickens and Konrad Hirschler have noted that in many cases titles were one of several domains in which one may see authorial agency at work. In Hirschler's view, titles were "markers for modes of emplotment and were intended to prepare the reader for the following narrative structure."[171]

There is an important caveat here: neither of our authors made internal references to their texts by using these titles. When they do refer to their texts, they do so by simply referring to "the/this *sīra.*" Neither do our authors refer to their titles in the preserved introductions.[172] Finally, in two cases the works' titles have not unambiguously come down to us. Unfortunately, this is also the case for one of the works for which we do have a meaningful if only partially preserved introduction. As such, we must make do with the titles as rendered on four of the six manuscript title pages and establish a hypothetical direct relation with the contents of the works.

2.3.1 Ibn ʿAbd al-Ẓāhir's *sīra* of Baybars

At least one initial folio is missing from the British Library manuscript of Ibn ʿAbd al-Ẓāhir's *sīra* of Baybars, and its first extant folio has its lower part cut off.[173] The fact that this first folio starts with the introduction's *wa-baʿd* indicates that likely only one folio is missing at the start: its recto would likely have been the text's title page while its verso would have contained the introduction's *basmallah* and *taḥmīd.* As noted above, doubts have been raised about Ibn ʿAbd al-Ẓāhir's exact role in the composition of the present text, but considering the contents of the

---

170 Alfonso Carmona has lamented that scholars often translate titles too literally and interpret their two parts as grammatically dependent on each other. He sees the *fī* preposition in most cases as a separator between a main title and a subtitle and argues that they have "an independent significance." He does acknowledge, however, that when other connecting prepositions are used, the titles tend to function more cohesively. Carmona, "Sobre la estructura convencional del título en los libros árabes," *al-Qantara* 21, no. 1 (2000), 85–96.

171 Hirschler, *Medieval Arabic Historiography*, 67.

172 Several earlier and later works of a similar nature to the *sīra*s do explain or at least mention their title in their introductions. See among others: Bahāʾ al-Dīn b. Shaddād, *al-Nawādir al-Sulṭāniyya wa'l-Maḥāsin al-Yūsufiyya, aw Sīrat Ṣalāḥ al-Dīn*, ed. Jamāl al-Dīn al-Shayyāl (Cairo: Maktabat al-Khānjī, second edition, 1994), 26; ʿImād al-Dīn al-Iṣfahānī, *al-Fatḥ*, 11–12; Ibn al-Dawādāri, *Kanz*, 9:5; Ibn al-Shiḥna, *al-Badr al-Zāhir fī Nuṣrat al-Malik al-Nāṣir Qāyitbāy*, ed. ʿUmar Tadmurī (Beirut: Dār al-Kitāb al-ʿArabī, 1983), 31.

173 The Süleymaniye manuscript does not preserve the introduction at all.

preserved introduction and its immediate relevance for Ibn ʿAbd al-Ẓāhir's project of writing a *sīra* of a sultan whom he directly served, it strikes me as unlikely that this particular part of the text has come down to us in a substantially altered version. Whether or not the later parts of the text exist in a similarly unaltered state remains unclear, but I will consider them to be at least closely related to Ibn ʿAbd al-Ẓāhir's original text.

Despite the lacunae, a substantial part of the introduction has still been preserved. Its first lines run as follows:

> وبعد فإنه لما كانت السيرة طراز الدول * ومرآةً يرى الناظر فيها أحوال الملوك الأول * وشهادةً على ما يحسن كل منهم أو يسيء فيه من قول وعمل * وبها يعلم الناس كيف تصرّمت الأيام وتصرّفت * وبماذا جرت وتوقفت * وعلى ماذا أقبلت عليه من خير وشرّ (. . .)[174] * فلم تخل دولة من الدول من مؤرخ يسطر أخبارها * ويودع الصحف آثارها *
>
> Now then, given that [the genre of] *sīra* has served as a model for states (*duwal*, s. *dawla*), a mirror in which the spectator may see the power of the first kings, and a testimony of the benefactions and evils each of them committed in words and deeds—by way of which people may be informed about how the days elapsed and turned about, how [events] were brought about or averted, and why the [days] were filled with good and bad [. . .]—[it follows that] no state can take its place among other states without a chronicler to write down its accounts and entrust its traces to paper.[175]

In this opening statement Ibn ʿAbd al-Ẓāhir connects two of the main elements of his discourse: on the one hand the oft-repeated notion of history as a model (*ṭirāz*)[176] for later generations and a mirror in which the reader may ponder the past, from

---

174 The editor of the text reads *aqaffat* here and translates it as "ended," which seems to make sense in the translation but is problematic grammatically. On consulting the manuscript (BL Or. Add 2333A 1a), it turns out this word is largely blotted out due to the folio being damaged. Only the final letter *tā'* is discernible (that is, the female ending of the verb *-at*), and its first letter might be an *ʿayn*. The rhyming pattern would indeed suggest that this is a verb ending on *afat* (with *tashdid* on the radical preceding *fā'* rather than on *fā'* itself).

175 *Rawḍ*, 45. My translations from this text here and throughout this book are based on the translation of the text included in ʿAbd al-ʿAzīz al-Khuwayṭir's unpublished PhD dissertation, although I have substantially revised these translations. Perhaps the most important difference here is that I have chosen to translate *lammā* as "since" and not as an introductory statement (rendered by al-Khuwayṭir as "as it were"). I understand the *lammā* to introduce a conditional sentence—especially as it is preceded by *fa-innahu*. The condition is then resolved by the *fa-lam takhalla dawla*^{tun} on the last line. While the difference in translation is subtle, it highlights the connection between these statements. Abdul Aziz al-Khowayter, "A Critical Edition", 3:311.

176 Rendered by Khuwayṭir as "adornment." I have translated a verbal form of this root similarly in the poem at the start of this chapter. However, here I have chosen a translation that resonates more with the following statements. Of course, the polyvalence is likely intentional. For stimulating perspectives on the interpenetration of discourses on garments and visual literary effect, see Karjoo-Ravary, "Adorning the King of Islam."

which I have derived the conceptualisation of *sīra* as spectacle, and on the other hand the idea that the history of a *dawla* can only exist by the grace of a historian (notably here: *mu'arrikh*) who writes down what should be remembered.[177] The historian is the one who fashions the mirror from the raw materials of history. This last part of the statement will prove to be crucial for the text's construction. Ibn ʿAbd al-Ẓāhir in the following lines praises the sultanate of Baybars but following from this opening claim this reign can only achieve its rightful greatness if its achievements are committed to paper by a chronicler and hence saved from the abyss of forgetfulness. Ibn ʿAbd al-Ẓāhir thus lays out the three main elements of his argument in one powerful programmatic sentence: the exemplarity of history in general, the specific exemplarity of this sultan's life and deeds, and the role of the historian as guardian of historical merit. The remainder of the introduction may be seen as an elaboration of this three-sided argument for the superiority of his biographical project.

The directly following part of the introduction explicitly connects the opening claims to the subject matter of the *sīra* in a lengthy praise of the exceptionality of Baybars' state. The factor of *dawla* introduced in the opening sentence and the edifying function of *sīra* are directly associated with Baybars' sultanship. There is a part missing after the first lines of this praise due to the cut off part of the first folio, but the narrative picks up again with a specific comparison: an unidentified ruler (likely either Baybars' direct predecessor Quṭuz or Tūrān Shāh—according to Ibn ʿAbd al-Ẓāhir, Baybars had a hand in both their assassinations) is portrayed as unwilling to fight and quick to flee. Baybars' ascension is praised as a resolution of this problem. This contrasting of good and bad practice and the sultan's ascension as resolution for a problematic situation will continue to be the driving narrative force for the first part of the *sīra*.

In concluding his praise of Baybars' victorious rule, Ibn ʿAbd al-Ẓāhir claims that:

> وكان ما سيذكر في مكانه * ويستقصى في بيانه * وجب أن تُسطّر سيرتها لتبقى على ممرّ الأيام * وتكتب حسناتها وإن كانت قد كتبتها الملائكة الكرام * وكان المملوك الأصغر مشاهدها سفراً وحضراً * ومعايناً لا خبراً * والمطلّع على غوامض أسرارها * وتسطر مبارها*

> [As such,] things which will be mentioned and clearly explained in their proper place, necessitated that a *sīra* of [the sultan's victories and achievements] should be written so that [the memory of them] may remain [known] throughout the passage of time, and so that its good works may be recorded—though the noble angels have already listed them.[178] This humble servant [i.e. Ibn ʿAbd al-Ẓāhir] was an eyewitness of these events, traveling and attending

177 Compare this to the classical Greek notion of "fama." Aleida Assmann, *Cultural Memory and Western Civilization* (Cambridge: Cambridge University Press, 2011), 28–29.

178 Compare Qur'ān 43:80, 50:17–18, 68:1; 80:15–16, 82:10–12, 86:4.

> [at court], beholding them himself and not being told about them. He is acquainted with its innermost secrets and the recording of its good work.[179]

This passage immediately follows an enumeration of Baybars' heroic qualities and establishes a chain of necessities that will prove to be crucial in the *sīra*'s grand construction. As the sultan's achievements were so important, writing them down becomes a necessity according to the edifying and commemorative logic of the introduction—here again repeated as the fundamental goal of a *sīra*. While the initial lines stated that this necessitated a chronicler (*mu'arrikh*) for every self-respecting *dawla*, this is taken a crucial step further here: Ibn ʿAbd al-Ẓāhir nominates himself as the ideal chronicler, for he has unparalleled inside knowledge of the history and the workings of the sultanate.[180] If Baybars' idealised sultanate requires the writing of an ideal history, then Ibn ʿAbd al-Ẓāhir is the ideal historian to undertake this task. Ibn ʿAbd al-Ẓāhir sets the tone for a *sīra* that would not only showcase the exemplarity of a specific sultan, but also join the loftiest group of exemplary historical works because of the author's right credentials.

Parts of this idea are also reflected in the titles of the two other *sīras* written by Ibn ʿAbd al-Ẓāhir, neither of which have preserved their introduction. *Tashrīf al-Ayyām wa'l-ʿUṣūr bi-Sīrat al-Sulṭān al-Malik al-Manṣūr*, the title of Ibn ʿAbd al-Ẓāhir's biography of Qalāwūn, may be rendered as "The exaltation of days and epochs by way of the *sīra* of the sultan al-Malik al-Manṣūr."[181] *Tashrīf* is a significant word choice, denoting both a verbal and ritual form of honouring, with the latter being a sultanic prerogative in the form of the granting of robes of honour.[182] *Ayyām* was often used as a denominator for the temporal aspect of a period of rule, similar but with a less wide ranging signification as *dawla*. As a phrase *Tashrīf al-Ayyām* thus has strong significations of the rituals of power and ideal sultanic rule: *tashrīf* as the gifting of robes of honour which was a sultanic prerogative and an integral part of power's ritual performance, as well as the more abstract meaning of the conveying of honour on a

---

179 *Rawḍ*, 46. Translation again substantially emended from "A Critical Edition," 312. There might an ambiguous play on words here between *malā'ika* (angels) and *mamlūk* (here rendered as servant), both of which derive from the root letters *m-l-k* which also generate *mulk* (kingship), *malik* (king) and *milk* (possession).

180 Note also that whereas every state needs a chronicler (*mu'arrikh*), Baybars' exceptional state requires the writing of a *sīra*, which perhaps speaks to an idea of distinctiveness attached to the *sīra* genre by Ibn ʿAbd al-Ẓāhir.

181 Only present on the manuscript's title page. The only internal reference that is more extensive than just "this *sīra*" is the general title "al-sīra l-sulṭāniyya l-Malakiyya l-Manṣūriyya." *Tashrīf*, 75.

182 Werner Diem, *Ehrendes Kleid und ehrendes Wort: Studien zu Tašrīf in mamlūkischer und vormamlūkischer Zeit*, (Würzburg, 2002), esp. 135–170 on various stylistic examples (*tajnīs*, metaphor, metonymy, paradoxon) of the use of this term.

beneficiary and of integrating that beneficiary in the benefactor's circle, while *ayyām* denotes the temporal aspect of power itself as well as the beneficiary of that honour. Returning to the arguments for a historiographical undertaking that matched historical time and sultanic exaltedness to the personal literary project of the author, this title may be said to convey a similar idea: *tashrīf* denotes the sultan's power, *ayyām* and *ʿuṣūr* connect it to time as historiography's major concern, and the following connecting word to *sīra* stresses the authorial agency of Ibn ʿAbd al-Ẓāhir.

This connection is more pronounced than in many other titles because Ibn ʿAbd al-Ẓāhir uses the prefix *bi-* (with) instead of the much more commonly used preposition *fī* (in) to link the guiding and thematic phrases here—as we shall see shortly, the three other known titles from the corpus do not use *fī* either and resort to the standalone word *min*. The shift in meaning is significant: *bi-* establishes an instrumental relation between the guiding and thematic phrases which *fī* merely suggests. Common translations for this prefix are "with" and "by," but there is also a strong connotation of "by means of." The days and eras/epochs are thus exalted exactly because of or by way of the *sīra*. Whether the focus should be on *sīra* or the sultan here remains debatable, but considering that *tashrīf* already alludes to the sultan's powerful position, one may perhaps see *sīra* as powerful in its own right, while "al-sulṭān al-Malik al-Manṣūr" adds the specification of this *sīra*'s subject matter.

This idea is echoed in Ibn ʿAbd al-Ẓāhir's final *sīra*, *al-Alṭāf al-Khafiyya min al-Sīra al-Sharīfa al-Sulṭāniyya al-Malakiyya al-Ashrafiyya*. The title of this text has usually been rendered with an equivalent of "hidden" or "concealed" for the adjective *khafiyya*.[183] The term actually has significations both of being hidden and of its opposite, of something that appears, or which becomes perceptible or manifest.[184] Furthermore, there is a related phrase *khafī al-luṭf* which is still widely used as a designation for God in supplication prayers (*duʿāʾ*) and poetry. The connotation in

---

183 See among others: Bauden, "Ibn ʿAbd al-Ẓāhir," *EI3;* Donald P. Little, "Historiography of the Ayyubid and Mamluk epochs" in *The Cambridge History of Egypt, Volume One: Islamic Egypt, 640–1517,* ed. C.F. Petry (Cambridge: Cambridge University Press, 1998), 422; Willem Flinterman, "The Cult of Qalāwūn: *Waqf,* Commemoration, and Dynasty in early Mamluk Cairo, ca. 1280–1340" (Unpublished PhD thesis, Universiteit Amsterdam, 2017), 26.

184 Edward W. Lane, *An Arabic-English Lexicon* (Beirut: Librairie du Liban, 1863–1893), 776. For Kazimirski, the primary meaning of the verb *khafā* is even "faire paraître au grand jour," while *khafiya* bears the meanings of hiddenness. It should be noted that both Lane and Kazimirski only note these meanings of "appearance" for the verbal forms, and not for the adjective. For the adjective they both enumerate a number of meanings linked to concealedness, conspicuousness and faintness, although Kazimirski defines *khafī* in the first place as "latent." Albert de Biberstein Kazimirski, *Dictionnaire arabe-français: contenant toutes les racines de la langue arabe, leurs dérivés, tant dans l'idiome vulgaire que dans l'idiome littéral, ainsi que les dialectes d'Alger et de Maroc*, 2 vols. (Paris: Maisonneuve et Cie, 1860), 1:604–605.

that sense is that God is not so much the concealer of grace (*luṭf*), but the keeper of it, the one who may dispense it to who addresses Him in supplication. The phrase *al-alṭāf al-khafiyya* itself seems to have been less common however.[185] In any case, Ibn ʿAbd al-Ẓāhir likely intentionally used this phrase for its slightly ambiguous and semiotically wide ranging meanings.[186] Considering the titles of other works by Ibn ʿAbd al-Ẓāhir and Shāfiʿ b. ʿAlī, I choose to render the title as "The benevolences manifest through the noble *sīra* of the sultan al-Malik al-Ashraf," as I believe Ibn ʿAbd al-Ẓāhir wanted to convey the idea that this *sīra* would convey benevolences, and not actually conceal them. The use of the preposition *min* as connection between the guiding and thematic phrases again establishes a connection that is stronger than one with *fī*, as it not only stresses that the sultan's "benevolences" will be reflected *in* the work, but also *through* or *by way* of the work. The work itself becomes once more instrumental in achieving the manifestation of grace.

Another notable word used in this title is *sharīfa*, which I have here rendered as "noble." Its basic meaning is related to genealogical distinction: Ibn Manẓūr for example typifies the basic meaning of the term *sharaf* as "nobility through parentage" (*al-ḥasab bi'l-ābāʾ*).[187] This connotation is particularly meaningful for this title, as this is the only *sīra* written by this author about a sultan who, as the son of Qalāwūn, ascended the throne by inheritance. Unfortunately, the only surviving part of this text deals with events that took place when the sultan was already firmly in power, so we have no way of ascertaining how our author translated this idea in a possible narrative arch of rightful position through inheritance, perhaps engaging with the powerful signifiers *ḥasab* ("distinction," "merit") and *nasab* ("descent," "genealogy").[188] Of course, *sharīf* and *ashraf* as used in the sultan's royal title al-Ashraf derive from the same root, a resonance that was surely intended as well.

2.3.2 *al-Faḍl al-Maʾthūr*

Two full introductions composed by Shāfiʿ have come down to us from the *sīra* corpus, plus another one if we include his chancery manual *al-Raʾy al-Ṣāʾib*. Both

---

185 Ḥajjī Khalīfa lists one work that is similarly entitled *al-Alṭāf al-Khafiyya fī Ashrāf al-Ḥanafiyya* by a certain Majd al-Dīn al-Fīrūzabādī. *Kashf al-Ẓunūn*, 1:149. It must have been either a work of Ḥanafī *fiqh* or a biographical dictionary of Ḥanafī *fuqahāʾ*

186 This is what al-Nabulsī would consider to be *kināya*, or "concomitance" (metonymy). See ʿAbd al-Ghānī al-Nābulsī, *The Arch Rhetorician, or, The Schemer's Skimmer: A Handbook of Late Arabic badīʿ*, ed. and transl. Pierre Cachia (Wiesbaden: Harrassowitz, 1998), 64.

187 Ibn Manẓūr, *Lisān al-ʿarab*, 2241.

188 On this issue, see: Asma Afsaruddin, *Excellence and Precedence: Medieval Discourse on Legitimate Leadership* (Leiden: Brill, 2002) and Louise Marlow, "Ḥasab o Nasab," *EIr.*

sīra texts have also preserved their title pages, so we can explore their meanings more in detail. I start with the likely earlier text *al-Faḍl al-Maʾthūr.* Like nearly every Islamic text, *Faḍl* starts with a *taḥmīd* (laudatory preamble) in which God is praised. Authors in the Middle Period increasingly expanded on this phrase and used it as a first part of their introductions' literary communicative project.[189] In this case, the praise is interwoven with gratitude for God's gift of a good king to the Islamic community. As both editions of this text contain reading errors, I have newly edited the Arabic by comparing the manuscript to the editions and will note deviations in footnotes.

الحمد لله الذي أعزّ الإسلام وأهله بأعزّ سلطان * وجباهم[190] منه بمن وقف عند أمر الله فلم يتجاوز في حكمه العدل وفي إقتداره الإحسان * وخوّلهم خير مَلِك يكبره العيان * ويتنزه في منظره ويتمتع بمخبره كل إنسان * وأراد بهم خيرًا فولي عليهم خيارهم فقرن الإقتيان من جميل خَلقِه وخُلقه بالإقتان[191] * وجعلهم رَعية لخير راع لم يزالوا من عنايته بأعزّ مكان * وعمّهم بفيض إنعامه حتى غدى المُقِلّ بسوابغها وهو ذو إمكان * ونحمده على جزيل الامتنان *

Praise be to God, Who has strengthened Islam and its people by [appointing over them] the mightiest of sultans; and Who selected for them in him someone who occupied himself with God's decree and who did not overstep justice in his judgment and beneficence in his potency; [praise be to Him who] bestowed on them the benefit of a king whom any onlooker extolled; whose outward appearance proves a delight and whose inner nature proves a blessing for everyone; [He] who, having the best of designs for them, appointed over them the best of them, thus bringing about a flourishing of a beautiful physical constitution (*khalq*) adorned by his character (*khulq*); [He] who has made them into a herd to the best of shepherds, without them hereby falling from His own utmost care; and who has showered them with His abundant kindness, so that even the destitute one is amply taken care for, for He is endowed with great power. Him we praise with the most plentiful gratitude![192]

---

189 Aziz K. Qutbuddin, "A Literary Analysis of *Taḥmīd*: A Relational Approach for Studying the Arabic-Islamic Laudatory Preamble," in *Reflections on Knowledge and Language in Middle Eastern Societies*, eds. Hussain Qutbuddin, Yonatan Mendel & Bruno De Nicola (Newcastle: Cambridge Scholars Publishing, 2010), 63–89.

190 Tadmurī (*Faḍl*, 23) reads *"jabalahum"* ("to create, to mould") and Lewicka (*Šāfiʿ Ibn ʿAlī's Biography*, 195) "*ḥabāhum*" ("he awarded them"), both of which do not follow the manuscript's orthography which reads *"jabāhum."*

191 These last two words are partly covered by a piece of paper in the manuscript. Tadmurī reads *wa-khalqathu bi'l-iqtān* (*Faḍl*, 23) and Lewicka (*Šāfiʿ Ibn ʿAlī's Biography*, 195) *khulqahu l-iqtitān*, both of which either add or omit letters from the manuscript's orthography. I instead read it as *wa-khulqahu bi'l-iqtān*, also a tentative reading and translation, but following the manuscript's phrasing and the logic of paronomasia in which an author would not use the exact same word twice in a row unless different meanings are intended. I derive the meaning of *iqtān* as "adornment" from the root letters *q-y-n*, as in *Tāj al-ʿarūs*, vol. 36:34–35.

192 Bodleian MS Marsh 424, 1b.

The immediate start of the *sīra* is framed in laudatory language: not only towards God, but also towards the sultan whose life and actions will be the main subject of the text. The linguistic and rhetorical dexterity shown here by Shāfiʿ can be seen as a first taster of the literary spectacle to follow throughout the rest of the text, the majority of which is written in cadenced rhyming prose. It is as if he interweaves three types of praise here: of God, of the sultan, and, implicitly, of language itself.

This last observation is only implicit in the *taḥmīd*, but it is underlined by what follows: Shāfiʿ goes on to write three lines as a variation of the Islamic proclamation of faith (*shahāda*). While staying close to the standard form of this obligatory part of any introduction, his variation adds one interesting detail by expressing the wish that the prayers for the Prophet "may remain [couched in] the sweetness of the tongue" (*lā tazāla ḥilyatu l-lisāni*). The preceding lines' association of praise for God with praise for the sultan in a language so dense with rhetorical flourishes that the text almost automatically becomes a performative literary text, is here more explicitly framed in terms that connect this discourse to the language register and the *sīra*'s stylistic objectives.[193]

Before the author has even delved into the specific subject matter of the text, he has already signposted the two central stakes of his project: the text as laudatory portrait of the sultan and as a display of Shāfiʿ's command of the Arabic language. The rest of the introduction develops these stakes in further detail, adding to it the specific notion of the importance of *sīra*

وبعد فإن سير الملوك الصيد نزهة من <سمر>[194] * وذكرى مَن أذكر * وعبرة لمَن اعتبر * و أعوذ (. . .) مثاله * ودليل على سداد الملك في أقواله وأفعاله * وهي[195] عنوان سطور علاه ودَرَج لا بل دُرج مودع ثمين حلاه وشاهد بحزمه * ومُوضِح قوة عزمه * وسمير يؤنَس بحديثه * وجليس يستفهم منه كنه قديم عز سلطانه وحديثه * لا سيما إذا كان ملكًا همامًا * وسلطانًا فضلت أيامه بالعدل والإحسان أيامًا فأيامًا * وخوادًا إن استمطر كفّه كان غمامًا * وإن اعتبرت قلائد مِننه اتّسقت نظامًا * وإن ذُكّرَت[196]

193 The phrase *ḥilyatu l-lisāni* is directly invoked as a quality of poets by the early scholar of Arabic literature Khalīl b. Aḥmad (d. between 160/776 and 175/791) as cited by the North African literary scholar Abū Isḥāq al-Ḥuṣrī (d. 453/1022) in *Zahr al-Ādāb wa-Thamar al-Albāb*, 4 vols., ed. Muḥammad Muḥyī al-Dīn ʿAbd al-Ḥamīd (Beirut: Dār al-Jīl, 2011), 3:687. The phrase is also used in al-Ḥarīrī's *al-Maqāmāt*, ed. Yūsuf al-Biqāʿī (Beirut: Dār al-Kutub al-Lubnānī, 1981), 131.

194 Tentative filling of a gap in the manuscript by the verb *samara*, which would work in the rhyme pattern of the following phrases. Shāfiʿ often uses this verb and uses the derived form *samīr* a few lines below. I have not been able to come up with a plausible filling for the next line where probably about two words are obscured due to this gap.

195 Reading *hiya* instead of *huwa* as Tadmurī does (*Faḍl*, 23). Perhaps he corrected this to a male form because the following word is male, but I believe the female form denotes the two directly preceding plural forms. The text then, perhaps rather unusually, makes a singular male word the predicate of these plural forms. Lewicka adheres to the manuscript's female form.

196 Tadmurī reads this as *dhukirat* (*Faḍl*, 23) and Lewicka as *dh-k-rta* (*Šāfiʿ Ibn ʿAlī's Biography*, 196, only the last consonant vocalised), both of which do not agree with the manuscript's orthography

فروسيته * كانت أعلا نت عنتر وعبسيتة * ومن البطال وفروسيته * وإن تلمحت أراؤه ألفي الصواب مكتنفًا بجوانبها * والسداد محيطًا بمذاهبها * كمولانا السلطان الملك المنصور[197]

> Now then: *Sīras* of strong-willed kings[198] are a diversion to who [passes the night in listening], a reminder to who bears in mind [the examples offered by history], and an admonition to who takes warnings; they place [he who takes inspiration from?] his example under God's protection; they are a proof of the king's apposite sayings and deeds; they are a model for the lines of writing dealing with his exaltedness; a scroll, nay, a casket in which his precious sweetness is deposited; a testimony to his resoluteness; a clarification of the strength of his determination; an intimate conversation partner telling [delightful stories]; and a table companion who inquires in detail about the greatness of [the ruler's] power both in the past and in the present. [And this is] especially the case for a magnanimous king, a sultan whose days were blessed with justice and beneficence for a long time [*ayyāman fa-ayyāman*]; so generous that if his open hand would ask for rain, a cloud [would appear]; [a sultan,] the necklace of whose graces would be found to be of a well-ordered system upon consideration; whose horsemanship [*furūsiyya*], if it were to be mentioned, would be found to be greater than that of ʿAntar and his ʿAbsiyya [tribe] as well as Baṭṭāl and his heroism; [a sultan,] whose opinions, if they were to be glanced at, would be found to include the correct one, enclosing all its aspects, and the proper [opinion], encompassing all of its views; such a [ruler is] our lord the sultan, al-Malik al-Manṣūr.

The web of significations spun here is intricate and dense: Qur'ānic concepts (*dhikr*, *ʿibra*), terms central to descriptions of ideal rule (*ʿadl, iḥsān, quwwa, ʿazm*), expressions related to the contexts of literary performance (*jalīs, samīr*), and references to great literary heroes (ʿAntar and Baṭṭāl) are associatively bound together. But there is a logical build-up here. Whereas the first lines of the section deal with the idea that biographies of kings (*siyar al-mulūk*) communicate exemplarity, closely related to concepts of remembrance and forbearance, this gradually makes way for their value as entertaining reading material, and eventually concludes with a panegyric to a still unnamed king. The following section continues in the same vein but explicitly names Qalāwūn as an example of such a king. This is done via the prefix *ka-* ("like," "such as"), which establishes the relationship between these two subjects within a continuous discourse, considering the necessary usage of *ka-* between two things that may be compared.[199] After a dividing mark, a short poem of three lines building upon themes set forth in the preceding lines follows—the sultan as

---

which has a clear *shadda* on the *kāf*, and a *fatḥa* on the *rāʾ*. I thus read it as a second form third person singular female.

197 Bodleian MS Marsh 424, 1b-2a.

198 *Siyar al-mulūk al-ṣīd*: in which the last word denotes the "fixedness of the face of a king, so that it does not turn aside to the right or left, by reason of pride." Lane, *An Arabic-English Lexicon*, 1753.

199 Tadmurī (*Faḍl*, 24) misleadingly starts a new paragraph with this *ka-*, but the dividing space present in the manuscript suggests only a change in rhyme pattern while the discourse is continuous.

receiver of Godly sent rain, the duality of time,[200] and the sultan being admired by his flock. To conclude, in the last section Shāfiʿ wraps up the discourse by looping back towards the author himself and his writing as one of the two central nodes of the *sīra*:

وكنت قد باشرتُ خدمته كاتب إنشاء سفرًا وحضرًا * ووردًا وصدرًا * ومعاني وصُوَرًا * وآياتٍ وسُوَرًا * وخُبرًا وخَبرًا * وتأثيرًا وأثرًا * وكتبتُ عنه سرًّ وجهرًا * وشهدتُ وقائه برًا وبحرًا * وأطلعتُ على ما لم يَطلع عليه غيري بمشافهته * وعلمتُ من أحواله ما ام يعلمه إلا كاتب سره بوساطة مشاركته * وحضرت مهادنته وموادعته * وكتبت بما استقر منها وحررت نسخ الإيمان له وعليه * وأوضحت من شكوكها مُبهمها عند المثول بين يديه[201] * فأوجب على ذلك أن أسطره محاسن أيامه الزاهرة * وأن أثبّتها لتغدو على ألسِنة الأقلام الدوام والاستمرار سائرة * وأنا أشرع بالله التوفيق

> I have served him as *kātib of inshāʾ*, while travelling and at home, arriving and leaving [with him]; [composing writings appropriate] in meanings[202] and in form, [which are embellished] with Qurʾānic verses and chapters, relying on knowledge and reporting; by exerting my influence and by my writings; writing for him confidentially and publicly; witnessing his battles on land and at sea. I was informed of things that nobody else but me has seen because he told them to me personally. I was informed about his situations such as no-one knew except his confidential secretary (*kātib sirrihi*) [who knows these things] by means of his partnership [with the sultan]. I was present at his settlements of peace and reconciliations. I wrote down what he decided in these matters, and accurately rendered the copies of oaths he gave or received, and I clarified what was ambiguous in their uncertainties during audiences [I had] in his presence. Because of that I was obliged to write down on paper the merits of his radiant days and to establish these things so that they may be permanently and enduringly fed to the tongues of the pens. By the aid of God, I commence.[203]

This passage has received some attention, notably from Anne Troadec, who also translated it into French.[204] However, in her translation she followed Tadmurī's edition, which contains a crucial reading mistake concerning a marginal insertion which adds "during the audiences [I had] in his presence" (*ʿinda l-muthūli bayna yadayhi*) after Shāfiʿ's claim of having been obliged to write the *sīra*. In accordance with the text's rhyming patterns and following a clearly noted *signe-de-renvoi* in the manuscript, the insertion in fact needs to be added earlier where Shāfiʿ is still writing

---

200 Here focusing on the classic duality of sun and moon, a salient feature of the Qurʾānic discourse on time. See among other instances Qurʾān 39:5.

201 This is a marginal addition which Tadmurī (*Faḍl* 23) adds after فأوجب على ذلك أن أسطّره, as the insertion seems to immediately follow the end of the line in the manuscript. Thus he implies that Shāfiʿ wrote the text and then presented it in audiences. However, this is incorrect, it should be inserted after وأوضحت من شكوكها مبهمه, considering the *signe-de-renvoi* in the manuscript as well as the text's rhyming patterns (*yadayhi*; *ʿalayhi*). Lewicka renders this correctly. *Šāfiʿ Ibn ʿAlī's Biography*, 198

202 This is the important concept *maʿnā*, central to Arabic literary theory. I will return to this concept in more detail in chapter five.

203 Bodleian MS Marsh 424, 2b–3a; *Faḍl*, 24; Lewicka, *Šāfiʿ Ibn ʿAlī's Biography*, 197–198.

204 Troadec, "Les Mamelouks," 80–81.

about his professional interaction with the sultan. He only claims that he clarified the contents of oaths in audiences. The following argument of necessity or obligation is thus comparable to the one made by Ibn ʿAbd al-Ẓāhir and certainly not proof that this was "a commissioned work."[205] The necessity to compose this text derives from Shāfiʿ's claim to a unique insider perspective on the happenings due to his close professional relation to the sultan. While Shāfiʿ will at one point in this text note that he offered a part of it to the sultanic library, he never writes that he performed it in the sultan's presence. Shāfiʿ's claim to historiographic superiority does not arise from such a literal sense of performance, but from the fact that the text performs his centrality to the sultan's political project as scribe, and for that his language ability is the primary tool. As we shall see, what may at first sight appear to be a small correction to the reading of this text in fact has important ramifications for the remainder of this book as it shifts the agency from the sultan to the historian.

The introduction's ideas are echoed in the title of the text, which may be rendered as "The merit transmitted through the *sīra* of al-Malik al-Manṣūr." The first word *faḍl* covers a rich semantic field that is not easily rendered into English. The broad meaning is evident from the extensive use of the related plural form *faḍāʾil* (singular, *faḍīla*) to denote a genre of texts which, in Rudolf Sellheim's words, "exposes the excellences of things, individuals, groups, places, regions and such for the purpose of a *laudatio*."[206] The association with *maʾthūr* draws it into a different construction. *Maʾthūr* is derived from the root letters *ʾ-th-r* with a basic meaning of "transmission," and a pronounced link to traces of time past. The use of this signification in Shāfiʿ's title lends it a claim to the authority of transmitted knowledge. This authority is actively used as a connector between *faḍl*, that is, "benefit" or "merit," and the *sīra*, by way of which this transmission is achieved. This connotation is then strengthened by use of the preposition *min*. In this case it is again grammatically possible to read this as a single phrase communicating the idea of merit transmitted (to the reader) by way of this *sīra*.

2.3.3 *Ḥusn al-Manāqib*

To reiterate, Shāfiʿ's second *sīra*, *Ḥusn al-Manāqib*, is a reworking of the earlier *sīra* of Baybars written by his uncle Ibn ʿAbd al-Ẓāhir. It is noteworthy that Shāfiʿ entirely excised his uncle's original introduction from the *sīra* and wrote a completely new one which is still firmly embedded within the stakes set by the two

205 "L'ouvrage apparaît clairement comme une commande." Troadec, "Les Mamelouks," 81.
206 Rudolf Sellheim, "Faḍīla," *EI2*.

previous introductions. Only in the final lines does he explicitly note the text's origins as an abridgement of an earlier text.

In *Faḍl*, Shāfiʿ used the *taḥmīd* to praise the sultan, but here he foregrounds the practice of history. The focus on history is already obvious in the introduction's *taḥmīd*, in which Shāfiʿ embeds a praise of historical narration or remembrance (*dhikr*).[207]

الحمد لله الذي احيا ذكر الملوك بأيامهم الزاهرة * وسيرهم التي هي بتفاصيل أحوالهم سائرة * وأشهد حلية أحوالهم التي هي بمناقبهم حالية * وطرّز حلل معاليهم بإثبات هممهم العالية * نحمده على وافر نعمه * ونستزيده من مواد كرمه *

Praise be to God, who has allowed kings to be remembered (*dhikr*) through their resplendent deeds, and through their biographies (*siyarhum*) as these unfold the details of their conditions and testify of their delightful conditions, graced with their virtues (*bi-manāqibihim*); who has embroidered[208] the vestments of their exalted qualities with the fixtures of their exalted endeavours. We praise Him for his abundant blessings, and we ask Him to give more plentiful of the affection of his generosity.[209]

Shāfiʿ's choice to start his book with these lines suggests that his appraisal of the work's topic is, even more than in *Faḍl*, not so much about the sultan, as it is about the writing of *sīra* itself. The functions of informing and remembering are praised here, but not directly related to the memory of the sultan himself, he is not even specifically mentioned. Shāfiʿ's start of the introduction proper continues in the same unspecific vein.

وبعد فإن في إثبات سير الملوك ما يشهد الغائب * ويعيد الذاهب * ويوقف على أحوال المعاصر وغير المُعاصر * ويمتع بحسن المسامرة بما للوقائع من الموارد والمصادر * وكان السلطان السعيد الشهيد الملك الظاهر * ركن الدين بيبرس الصالحي قد ملك فأسجح * وسعي في ذات الله فأنجح * وقام بأعباء السلطنة أيما قيام * وسهر في إقامة منار الإسلام * والناس نيام *

Now then, in establishing the *sīras* of kings there is what allows the absent one to witness first-hand [what transpired], which makes the one who departed return, what allows one to contemplate the conditions of one's own age and one's past, and which carries away the one who listens in nightly conversation to the excellence of what is in the happenings along roads and starting points. The sultan al-Malik al-Ẓāhir Rukn al-Dīn Baybars al-Ṣāliḥī, the blissful martyr, was possessed of power and acted with goodness, proceeded in accordance with God['s decree] and was given success. He took up the burdens of sultanship in whichever circumstances and passed the night in erecting the light tower of Islam while the people slept [. . .][210]

207 Excerpts of this introduction have been translated before by P.M. Holt in "Some Observations," 124–125. I have used his translations as an initial reference, but my rendering differs substantially.
208 Note the use of the verb *ṭaraza* and its connotations of being a "model" (see the introduction to Ibn ʿAbd al-Ẓāhir's *sīra* above).
209 *Ḥusn*, 53.
210 *Ḥusn*, 53–54. Slight edits of the Arabic text based on BnF MS Arabe 1707, 2b–3a. The praise for Baybars continues for several more lines.

The qualities of *sīra* here are rather harmonious with those expressed in *al-Faḍl al-ma'thūr* and Ibn ʿAbd al-Ẓāhir's *sīra* of Baybars. The earlier used metaphor of *sīra* as a nightly conversation partner is even recycled. But there is an important difference: while the text implies a connection between the general statement at the outset and the specific praise of Baybars, it is not explicitly stated so. When Shāfiʿ praised Qalāwūn, he established a connection between the characteristics of an ideal ruler and the ways in which this specific sultan personified these virtues. Here, the ideal virtues are not separately discussed but exemplified by Baybars.

While P.M. Holt argued that Shāfiʿ could get away with writing more critically about Baybars because he did so during the third reign of al-Nāṣir Muḥammad when the image of Baybars did not loom large anymore, perhaps a more important reason for his different perspective lies in the literary context in which he wrote about this sultan.[211] It was not so much about writing a laudatory *sīra* anymore but about abridging an already well received *sīra*, an exercise in conciseness and selection. Of course, as the source text from which Shāfiʿ b. ʿAlī constructed his own variation was a laudatory *sīra*, Shāfiʿ's own text could not simply excise such subject matter. It is certainly true that our author is a lot more critical of Baybars in this text than he is of Qalāwūn in *al-Faḍl al-ma'thūr* or of al-Nāṣir Muḥammad in his *sīra* of that sultan, but the presentation of Baybars remains generally laudatory. In this introductory praise a characterisation of the sultan as a great warrior predominates. Gradually the martial language is enriched with terminology that will make the subject transition towards a focus on the written word. He writes how the sultan "publicly elevated the word of faith" (*wa-aʿlā kalimat al-īmān ʿalā ru'ūs al-ashhād*) and uses the second form verb *addaba* ("disciplined" or "edified", related to *adab*) to denote how the sultan set deviators back on the right path. The following lines further develop this intersection of martial and writerly terminology, but also finally introduces Shāfiʿ's position with respect to his predecessor Ibn ʿAbd al-Ẓāhir:

وكان كاتب سره البليغ محيي الدين ابو الفضل عبد الله ابن شيخ الإسلام رشيد الدين عبد الظاهر قد افتتح أيامه بنظم سيرة رتل فيها سور محاسنه صورةً صورةً * وأرخ وقائعه التي هي في صحائف حسناته مسطورة * فأطال وأطاب * وخطب بأمتع خطاب * وأتى على مجموع أيامه يومًا يومًا وصرح بمناقبه وإلى إبداعها أومى * لكل إقتضى الحال أن يثبت منها الغث والسمين * وإن[212] يكرر ما يشافه به سمع سلطانه من أطرا وإن كان فيه صادق لا يمين *

And his confidential secretary [*kātib sirrihi*] was the eloquent Muḥyī al-Dīn Abū l-Faḍl ʿAbdallāh b. *shaykh al-islām* Rashīd al-Dīn ʿAbd al-Ẓāhir, had inaugurated his days by composing a *sīra* in which he eloquently constructed chapters on his good qualities [*suwaru maḥāsin-*

211 Holt, "Three Biographies," 26–27.
212 The edition reads this as "an," but the manuscript (BnF MS Arabe 1707, folio 4a) does not provide vocalization here. I believe "in" makes more grammatical sense here.

> *ihi*] in various ways, and he chronicled [*arrakha*] its happenings which are drawn up on the pages of his excellent actions, and he extended [these accounts] and made them agreeable, he uttered the most delightful of orations, presented the totality of his reign (*ayyāmihi*) day-to-day, clarified his virtues [*ṣaraḥa bi-manāqibihi*] and indicated their uniqueness. However, the situation demanded [of him] that he register of these accounts [both] the lean and the fat, and if [in doing so] he reiterated what he had uttered orally, [it is because] his sultan gave ear to eulogisers [*man aṭrā*],[213] and though he was truthful in this, he was not under oath.[214]

This is the lead-up to the crux of the introduction, the point at which Shāfiʿ wraps up the earlier discourse and creates a gap to be addressed in the last part of the section. One can see how he reuses several powerful terms that had been present in the earlier lines and in the title of the work: *ḥusn*, *manāqib*, and *sirr*. Shāfiʿ once more intensifies the semantic breadth as he edges closer towards the critical point in which his personal stake in the project will be explained. This happens in the last sentence translated in the above excerpt, in which he argues how and why Ibn ʿAbd al-Ẓāhir's *sīra*, while a praiseworthy effort, was inevitably flawed. Shāfiʿ employs a complex understanding of truth and truthfulness here, strengthened by usage of the idiomatic expression of registering "the leanness and fatness," which was widely used both in terms of evaluation of good and bad practice, but also in establishing truth and falsehood.[215] Truth here is bound to the context in which that truth is performed or written down, partly dependent on whether or not any accompanying oaths were employed. As such, truth needs to be re-evaluated if the circumstances change in which a certain truth was expressed.

As it turns out, Shāfiʿ is just the man to do such a re-evaluation. Here he makes a different type of claim to fitness for this task than he did in *Faḍl*.

> وكان–رحمه الله–قد تحدث معي في إختصارها فلم يتقف في حياته * ولم يقع تأدّبًا معه في إثبات نفيه ونفي إثباته * وقد إختصرتها رغبةً في الإيجاز الذي هو عين البلاغة * وعذوبة مياه الفصاحة المساغة * وذكرت منها الأهم المقدم لتلذّ مطالعها * وتروق مراجعتها * وبالله التوفيق

213 The manuscript has a *kasra* below the *ṭāʾ* here and al-Khuwayṭir thus read this as the substantive form *iṭrā[ʾ]*, reading further also من as *min* and not *man*. I instead read this as the verbal form *aṭrā* ("to praise"), which makes a lot more sense in the context. If we do take the *kasra* into account, we can read it as the passive verbal form *uṭira* (which would then need to be followed by *aw* ("or") and not *wa-* ("and")), and the phrase would mean something along the lines of "his sultan listened to who had been bent." This seems to make metaphorical sense in English, but I have not found lexicographical attestation for such a use in Arabic.

214 *Ḥusn*, 55–56. Slight emendations based on BnF MS Arabe 1707, 4a.

215 Compare usage by Nāṣir b. ʿAbd al-Sayyid al-Muṭarrazī (d. 610/1213), as translated by Matthew L. Keegan in "Throwing the Reins to the Reader: Hierarchy, Jurjānian Poetics, and al-Muṭarrizī's Commentary on the *Maqāmāt*," *Journal of Abbasid Studies* 5, vol. 1–2 (2018), 109.

> And he—may God have mercy on him—had talked to me about abridging his *sīra*, but this did not take place during his lifetime; it did not occur out of courteousness for him, acknowledging that he might reject it as well as rejecting that he might acknowledge it. I have abridged it desiring brevity—which is the goal of eloquence—and the sweetness of fluency's freely flowing water. I have mentioned of [the original text] the most important parts, giving precedence to the gratification of its perusal and making clear[216] its examining. I trust in God.[217]

Shāfiʿ's claim to authority is once more related to intimate connection, but this time not to the sultan whom he does not claim to have served, but to his uncle who suggested that his nephew abridge his work. Most importantly, our author also tells us how he went about abridging the *sīra*. The fact that his statement to have done so "desiring brevity" is of course a major recurring topos of Arabic introductions in general, but that does not mean it is a meaningless phrase.[218] Rather, by using this topos embedded in his signature rhetorical play with metaphors and rhyme, he is once more able to draw attention to the essence of his project: the literary reworking of a well-known work in the specific form of a *mukhtaṣar*. More specifically, it draws attention to the agency of Shāfiʿ himself as the abridger (*mukhtaṣir*).

Returning to the work's title, the idea of the centrality of *sīra* is taken even further than in the previous titles. We may render the title as "The excellence of the confidential virtues derived (or extracted) from the *sīra* of al-Ẓāhir [Baybars]." This title, which contains an exceptionally long thematic phrase,[219] is built around powerful terms. *Manāqib* is often taken as a genre of "biographical works of a laudatory nature, which have eventually become a part of hagiographical literature."[220] Charles Pellat notes that in the early Islamic period the term would often be used interchangeably with such terms as *faḍāʾil*, *mafākhir* and *maʾāthir*–note the similarity to *maʾthūr* just above. That (variants of) two of these terms, as well as *manāqib* appear in the titles of our *sīras*—with *sīra* itself a term often found in conjunction with these signifiers—is important: the idea that such terms highlighted the exemplary nature of the contents resonated with our authors. *Ḥusn* itself is less intimately related to a genre or a set of discourses but reappears extremely often (as does the derived form "*iḥsān*," "beneficence") throughout the *sīra* corpus, especially as a signifier in descriptions praising the sultan's performance of ideal rule.

---

216 This verb is related to the clearing of drink "without pressing it." The verb choice is thus intimately related to the earlier noted metaphor of fluency as freely flowing water. Lane, *An Arabic-English Lexicon*, 1191.

217 *Ḥusn*, 56–57.

218 Freimark, "Vorwort," 34.

219 Ambros counted only nine titles which contained two adjectives in their guiding phrases. "Beobachtungen," 34.

220 Charles Pellat "Manāḳib," *EI2*.

While the two first terms of the title are recognisable and unsurprising in this text, the two next terms are more peculiar. The use of *sirriyya*, or "secret" may seem strange but in the context of *inshāʾ* writing it is a powerful signifier denoting a particular type of *inshāʾ* writing. It is most famous from the office of *kātib al-sirr*, or "confidential secretary," referred to in this introduction to denote Ibn ʿAbd al-Ẓāhir's relationship to Baybars—though note that Shāfiʿ writes *kātib sirrihi* both here and in the introduction to *Faḍl*, implying more of a relationship than a formal state function.[221] Considering that Shāfiʿ here abridged a *sīra* written by a renowned *kātib* from a previous generation, one may interpret the *manāqib al-sirriyya* as denoting the virtues of *inshāʾ* as written by a *kātib al-sirr* – if not one who held that specific title, at least one who fulfilled the same functions. However, while this could then be read as a title praising Ibn ʿAbd al-Ẓāhir's undertaking, Shāfiʿ adds a crucial word to highlight his own agency: these virtues are not inherent to the original *sīra*, they are "derived from," even "extracted from" (*muntazaʿa min*, see my remarks above about the use of *min* in these titles) the *sīra al-Ẓāhiriyya*. Shāfiʿ has brought out their full potential by the act of composing a *mukhtaṣar* of the original work.

2.4 Conclusion

A close reading of the surviving introductions to these works yields a wealth of information about how our authors conceptualised the writing of *sīra*. In the following chapters I will argue that these discourses should not be seen as self-contained rhetorical exercises but that the approach to history writing they posit is reflected in the remainder of their textual constructions. Similar ideas may also be found in the texts for which no introductions have survived. To compose such an introduction, authors made use of common tropes of introductory discourse, but that does not mean that they had only limited direct meaning. Rather, such tropes were instrumentalised in the larger arguments formulated in the introductions, which embedded the discourse in literary continuities. Our authors tried to make a cohesive argument for their work and at the same time participated in discursive traditions on the stakes of history. This may be seen as an interplay between what Paul Ricoeur calls "innovation" and "sedimentation."[222] Considering that our authors

221 I will return to this issue in chapter four, section 4.1.

222 Ricoeur, *Temps et récit* 1:132–134. At 134 he writes: "les paradigmes constituent seulement la grammaire qui règle la composition d'oeuvres nouvelles – nouvelles avant de devenir typiques." He returns to this argument a number of times, as it is an important component of his mimetic theory. For example, he interprets Hayden White's "types" of historiography as (rather too rigidly conceived) "paradigms," *Temps et récit*, 1:296.

were not the first to write about the value of writing history, or even of a *sīra* specifically devoted to a contemporary ruler, they could build upon "sedimented" textual forms: received paradigms about historical value, common notions of history as exemplum and as a way of rendering the past accessible. But at the same time, as authors they "innovated," adding something of what Ricoeur calls "déviance calculée" to those paradigms, flexing their formal characteristics or, in this case, their recurrent discursive markers to say something subtly new about the importance of history writing and their own role in doing so. It is this understanding of a delimited newness which is necessary if we want to evaluate the discursive webs post-classical authors constructed.

Chapter 3
Sīra as an act of narrative construction

> *Here is the past and all its inhabitants miraculously sealed as in a magic tank; all we have to do is to look and to listen and to listen and to look and soon the little figures—for they are rather under life size—will begin to move and to speak, and as they move we shall arrange them in all sorts of patterns of which they were ignorant, for they thought when they were alive that they could go where they liked; and as they speak we shall read into their sayings all kinds of meanings which never struck them, for they believed when they were alive that they said straight off whatever came into their heads. But once you are in a biography all is different.*[223]

Virginia Woolf was an outspoken critic of the great amount of biographical writing produced in late nineteenth and early twentieth century Great Britain. Having lampooned the self-serious pompousness of the genre in two time-, genre- and genderbending biographies herself (*Orlando* and *Flush*, both subtitled *A Biography*), she also expressed her dismay in the essay "'I Am Christina Rossetti'," published in 1930. In this essay she lamented her contemporaries' habit of reading too much into poets' biographies when evaluating their poetry. She stated that "it is poetry that matters."[224] That is, authors should be judged by their works and not by how it ties into whatever was going on in their lives. In a way, she effectively foreshadowed debates that would rage in 1960s criticism in the wake of Roland Barthes' *The Death of the Author*. Like Woolf, Barthes criticised the over-reliance on authorial subjectivities in informing the understanding of text and argued for a text's multiple meanings through readers' engagements with it in addition to that of the author.[225]

The times of Virginia Woolf and those of our authors were obviously fundamentally different, and so is her perspective from Roland Barthes'. Yet her observation highlights a central problematic of this book: a *sīra*, in its capacity as a reconstruction of the actions and deeds of a specific person, is essentially an author's interpretation of that past, his (or in Woolf's case, her) selection of actions and deeds. Some of this reconstruction may be of tenuous historicity and all of it is meaningful foremost within the context of the textual whole. It is in that sense important to understand a text within the remit of its internal logic, but, and this is where much of the pushback against Barthes has concentrated itself, authors

223 Virginia Woolf, "'I Am Christina Rossetti'," in *The Common Reader, Second Series* (London: The Hogarth Press, 1965), 237.

224 Virginia Woolf, "'I Am Christina Rossetti'," 241.

225 An overview of these debates is beyond the scope of this book, but see for one classic discussion: Seán Burke, *The Death and Return of the Author: Criticism and Subjectivity in Barthes, Foucault and Derrida* (Edinburgh: Edinburgh University Press, 1992).

https://doi.org/10.1515/9783110753028-004

do not operate in a historical vacuum: it remains of central importance to include some of an author's context and background in any analysis to assess how their text speaks to other texts and contemporary concerns. For our concerns this means that while the contexts in which our authors worked deeply influenced how they wrote their texts, we also cannot read them exclusively from the perspective of the court, the chancery or the literary field. To try to understand what they were communicating, we need to read the texts on their own terms, attentive to the multitudes of meaning they contain.

Having outlined in the previous chapter how our authors presented their endeavours in programmatic introductions and titles, in this chapter I will explore how they executed their biographical projects, how they made "the past and all its inhabitants" speak and act in their literary spectacles of sultanship. While in the following chapters I will highlight formal literary aspects of these projects, here I want to maintain a macro view of each text and examine how authors created narrative cohesion in their texts. To paraphrase Ricoeur, I will investigate how they reconfigured the cognitive remnants of lived experience into narrative history.

The textual cohesiveness I will be arguing for is partly in response to the idea that the *sīras* were compiled texts consisting of information written at various points throughout their authors' years of service to the sultan.[226] This is not to say that compilation was not an important part of our authors' undertaking, nor do I want to challenge the idea that these texts came together over prolonged periods of time. The importance of compilation is not only evident from the inclusion of much quoted material, but also by Shāfiʿ's repeated self-designation as *"jāmiʿ hādhihi l-sīra,"* that is, "the one who *compiled* this *sīra*" (my emphasis) when introducing a text to be quoted.[227] And it is indeed the case that most of the texts were finished only after their subjects' deaths—the exception being Ibn ʿAbd al-Ẓāhir's *sīra* of al-Ashraf Khalīl and Shāfiʿ's *sīra* of al-Nāṣir Muḥammad, as both sultans outlived the respective authors. However, even if we allow for a text's gradual genesis and final compilation only after the sultan's death, this does not mean that there is no overarching textual construction to be discerned. In the following I will argue how our authors consciously integrated material in a *sīra* with a comprehensive argument and compelling image of a sultan's life and reign. I will discuss the texts in order of chronology of the events they depict.

226 Holt identified especially *Faḍl* as such a text, writing that "this is an assemblage of biographical pieces, written at different times, rather than a single work conceived as a whole." *Early Mamluk Diplomacy*, 3. Haarmann also evaluated *Tashrīf* as such. *Quellenstudien*, 99.

227 *Faḍl*, 128, 143, 156; BnF MS Arabe 1705, 27r, 48r, 67r, 96r. The texts quoted are both prose and poetry. Ibn ʿAbd al-Ẓāhir only does so once, when introducing a poem in *Rawḍ*, 243: *"fa-naẓẓama l-qāḍī Muḥyī l-Dīn jāmiʿ al-sīra."*

3.1 Ibn ʿAbd al-Ẓāhir's *sīra* of Baybars

While the *sīra* of Baybars is by far the most studied text in our corpus, most scholars have followed P.M. Holt's evaluation of it as a legitimising panegyric. Linked to this evaluation, several scholars have focussed on Ibn ʿAbd al-Ẓāhir's narrative use of re-enactment. Claims about the greatness of a sultan are advanced through favourable comparisons with illustrious rulers of the past, and these claims drive the historical representation of the works in general.[228] Ibn ʿAbd al-Ẓāhir and other historians constructed a historical vision in which the past was instrumentalised to serve the present. Scholars have also seen links between this biography of Baybars and the sultan's architectural endeavours, especially in newly conquered areas of Syria.[229]

It is true that in Ibn ʿAbd al-Ẓāhir's *sīra*, Baybars is repeatedly compared to earlier rulers and mythical figures, among others the pre-Islamic rulers Solomon[230] and Alexander,[231] the caliph ʿUmar b. al-Khaṭṭāb,[232] sultan Ṣalāḥ al-Dīn,[233] and even the Prophet Muḥammad. The latter's influence is especially clear from several instances in which Baybars is said to have acted in line with behaviour commended in hadith or where Ibn ʿAbd al-Ẓāhir inserts citations from hadith into the narra-

---

228 This process of referencing the past has been defined as "historicisation" by Konrad Hirschler. He argued that for the two historians Abū Shāma and Ibn Wāṣil this was an important mode of emplotment in which authors placed "[their] protagonists into specific historical continuities or discontinuities [which] evoked particular associations among audiences." Hirschler, *Medieval Arabic Historiography*, 77. This type of evaluation was introduced in studies of western medieval historiography and narrative much earlier, most prominently by Gabrielle M. Spiegel, whose *Romancing the Past* evaluated historical writing from the vantage point of aristocratic ideology. She argues, for example, that "both history *and* prose performed critical social functions in the life of the French aristocracy, which sought to embed its ideology in history and thereby endow that ideology with the prestige and imprescriptible character that the past was able to confer in medieval society," Gabrielle M. Spiegel, *Romancing the Past: The Rise of Vernacular Prose Historiography in Thirteenth-Century France* (Berkeley: University of California Press, 1993), 2. Italics from the original.

229 Yehoshua Frenkel, "Baybars and the Sacred Geography of Bilād al-Shām: A Chapter in the Islamization of Syria's Landscape," *Jerusalem Studies in Arabic and Islam* 25 (2001), 153–170; Anne Troadec, "Baybars and the Cultural Memory of Bilād al-Shām: The Construction of Legitimacy," *MSR* 18 (2014), 113–147; Hanna Taragan, "Sign of the Times: Reusing the Past in Baybars's Architecture in Palestine," in *Mamluks and Ottomans: Studies in Honour of Michael Winter*, ed. David J. Wasserstein and Ami Ayalon (London-New York: Routledge, 2006), 54–66.

230 *Rawḍ*, 272. The sultan is also called the "Solomon of the age" (*Sulaymān al-zamān*) in a poem written by the amir Jamāl al-Dīn b. al-Imām al-Ḥājib, quoted by Ibn ʿAbd al-Ẓāhir in *Rawḍ*, 219.

231 *Rawḍ*, 193, 448. The associations are both made in contexts that are linked to the city of Alexandria: the renewal of the Alexandarian canal in 662/1263 or 1264, and the repair of the lighthouse in 673/1275.

232 *Rawḍ*, 325.

233 *Rawḍ*, 120, 474. See also *Tashrīf*, 179.

tive to comment upon one of the sultan's actions.[234] While most such references are relatively isolated instances in the *sīra* and can often be understood easily due to contingent associations, there are also more extended comparisons.[235] The best example is that with Sayf al-Dawla in the last part of the text to which I will return in detail in chapter five (section 5.2.1.), and where I will show the comparison must be read as a complex amalgam of historical comparison and authorial performance. While these are important practical aspects of how Ibn ʿAbd al-Ẓāhir wrote history, it does not capture the cohesiveness of the entire work. In the following, I will reconsider the broader construction of this most studied *sīra*, especially in the light of how the author himself presented the rationale for writing in in his introduction.

P.M. Holt has observed that the text consists of a tripartite structure. He asserts this was inspired by Bahāʾ l-Dīn b. Shaddād's earlier *sīra* of Ṣalāḥ al-Dīn, *al-Nawādir al-Sulṭānīya.* The shared three-part construction—excluding introductions—consists of a first part which details the sultans' deeds before he ascended the throne; a second is an enumeration of various virtues in respectively eight (Ṣalāḥ al-Dīn) and seventeen (Baybars) subsections; and a third, constituting by far the bulk of each text, dealing extensively with the events of the sultanate in a dominantly annalistic framework. Whereas Bahāʾ l-Dīn b. Shaddād's biography races through Ṣalāḥ al-Dīn's first years and only becomes more detailed for the period in which he himself was a companion of the ruler, Ibn ʿAbd al-Ẓāhir's account is more chronologically balanced.

Because the pre-sultanate chapter in Ibn Shaddād's *sīra* is much shorter than Ibn ʿAbd al-Ẓāhir's, Holt remarks that Ibn ʿAbd al-Ẓāhir's copying of this construction was a "clumsy interpolation which breaks the flow of the narrative."[236] At the same time, he underlined the "critical importance" of the first part, that is, the accounts of Baybars' pre-sultanate years: by far the majority of his discussion of the *sīra* deals with this part in conjunction with the virtue chapters, because it is in the first part that the important events of Baybars' two regicides, his exile in Syria and the Battle of ʿAyn Jālūt are mentioned.[237] Unlike Bahāʾ l-Dīn b. Shaddād, for whom only Ṣalāḥ al-Dīn's later achievements really counted in his depiction of an ideal ruler, Ibn ʿAbd al-Ẓāhir considered Baybars' pre-sultanate years as crucial. Holt argues that this is the case because of the need to legitimise Baybars' origins and usurpation, but there is more at play in the narrative logic of the section. Why did Baybars

234 *Rawḍ,* 200–201, 222, 227, 231–232, 239, 275–276, 282, 287, 293, 301–302.

235 By contrast, Shāfiʿ only makes use of such isolated references. His writing of history can thus most certainly not be understood as profoundly influenced by ideas of re-enactment.

236 Holt, "The Virtuous Ruler," 28. See also, Holt, "The Sultan as Ideal Ruler," 123, 129.

237 Holt, "Three Biographies," 26.

not take power immediately after killing Tūrān Shāh instead of rambling about in Egypt and Syria for another ten years before actually ascending the throne, for example? If Baybars was indeed the predestined successor to al-Ṣāliḥ Ayyūb, why did he not take power immediately, sparing Egypt and Syria the unstable intervening decade? Ibn ʿAbd al-Ẓāhir found a way to explain these questions by emplotting the sultan's early life as a narrative of heroic development.

To put it schematically, Baybars moves from a position of stability and prosperity under al-Ṣāliḥ Ayyūb, whose reign is described in terms of ideal rule, to great instability under his successors Tūrān Shāh and al-Muʿizz Aybak. While Tūrān Shāh is killed by Baybars and his companions, resulting in a short return to political stability, al-Muʿizz Aybak then conspires against Baybars and eventually has his companion Fāris al-Dīn Aqṭāy killed, whereupon Baybars and his remaining companions flee to Syria. From there, Baybars goes through a series of trials in local politics and leads failed attacks against the Egyptian forces of al-Muʿizz Aybak.[238] When the Mongols appear as a great exogenous enemy, Baybars unites his forces with the Egyptian ones under al-Muẓaffar Quṭuz, who has by now taken over the reins of the Egyptian sultanate. With these united forces Baybars heroically defeats the enemy at the battle of ʿAyn Jālūt, where he is presented as the foremost hero who even leads further attacks on fleeing bands of Mongols. During the return journey of the Mamluk troops to Egypt, Quṭuz, who is framed as developing unjust and incompetent tendencies, is murdered. Baybars is now finally able to claim his rightful place as sultan, as the legitimate heir of al-Ṣāliḥ Ayyūb.

Ibn ʿAbd al-Ẓāhir does not seem to have aimed at presenting a strictly annalistic presentation of Baybars' life here. Instead, he used the events as a basis to tell a captivating story of growth and heroism about Baybars' early years. He conceptualised the decade between al-Ṣāliḥ Ayyūb's death and Baybars' own ascension to the throne as political growth through a series of trials, in which he had to wait for the right moment to claim the throne. Early in this section Ibn ʿAbd al-Ẓāhir praises the sultan as being eager to learn from al-Ṣāliḥ Ayyūb's example: "his soul directed itself to the ascent of the way-stations of kingship (*manāzil al-mulk*)." This signals the idea that the ascension of the sultanate could only come about following a journey of growth and learning.[239]

In presenting this tale of growth and rightful ascendancy, Ibn ʿAbd al-Ẓāhir used a mode of narration found throughout many cultures' mythologies and narratives. This first part of the *sīra* aligns with several of the stages in the "monomyth"

238 Ibn ʿAbd al-Ẓāhir cites Baybars' explanation of the failure of one of these attacks as due to impure intentions among his followers. *Rawḍ*, 59–60.
239 *Rawḍ*, 47

posited by Joseph Campbell, as well as the structuralist plot sections of the folk tale distinguished by Vladimir Propp, and with Northrop Frye's "archetype" of "the journey."[240] Although the theorisation of these grand constructions has been mostly based on myths and stories from Western Christian culture, they are not alien to Arabic-Islamic literature. The structure can for example be found in early Islamic panegyrics in the form of the theme of the *raḥīl,* the wandering poet faced with many hardships and trials in the desert in the second part of the traditional tripartite *qaṣīda.*[241] Furthermore, there is a striking parallel to this storyline in the prophetic *hijra,* when the Prophet Muḥammad had to leave Mecca due to external pressure and then garner strength in Medina before eventually returning victoriously to his hometown.[242] It also appears in a later period as an essential feature of how Turco-Mongol rulers matured into rightful sovereignty after spending periods of time as political vagabonds.[243]

In Ibn ʿAbd al-Ẓāhir's presentation Baybars is forced to abandon his position as well and has to flee to distant lands before he can regain his rightful status. This "crossing of the threshold" is a central part in heroic narratives, the journey to a place where the hero can garner strength to regain his predestined position. While in the traditional stories upon which Propp and Campbell based their ideas, the retrieval of stasis is the endpoint of the journey, here it sets the stage for the later heroic acts of Baybars' sultanship, to be narrated in the third part of the text.

Of course, Ibn ʿAbd al-Ẓāhir did not invent Baybars' pre-sultanate experiences to fit his narrative. Seeing the potential of these early events, however, he emplotted his version of the events in existing paradigms that strengthened the narrative and performative qualities of the text. Moreover, by mixing well known events with

---

240 Joseph Campbell, *The Hero with a Thousand Faces* (Princeton, NJ: Princeton University Press, 1968); Vladimir Propp, *Morphology of the Folktale,* transl. Laurence Scott (Austin, TX: University of Texas Press, 1968); Northrop Frye, *Anatomy of Criticism: Four Essays* (Princeton, NJ: Princeton University Press, 1957).

241 Stefan Sperl, "Islamic Kingship and Arabic Panegyric Poetry in the Early 9th Century," in *JAL* 8 (1977), 25, 28.

242 On the narrative pacing of the prophetic *sīra,* though not explicitly linked to any narrative theories, see: Uri Rubin, *The Eye of the Beholder: The Life of Muhammad as Viewed by the Early Muslims (A Textual Analysis)* (Princeton: The Darwin Press, 1995).

243 This is the so called *Qazaqlïq*. In Joo-Yup Lee's words "the term *qazaq* was used to refer to these political refugees who ventured into the steppes or some remote places of refuge and resorted to brigandage, while the term *qazaqlïq* was used to describe the period of political vagabondage or the way of life such *qazaqs* experienced." *Qazaqlïq*, or *Ambitious Brigandage, and the Formation of the Qazaqs: State and Identity in Post-Mongol Central Eurasia* (Leiden and Boston: Brill, 2016), 21 and 29–30 for a discussion of Babur and precedents. I am grateful to Mustafa Banister for pointing this out to me and for providing me with this reference. One wonders whether a similar perception of brigandage was already known among Qipchaq Turkish *mamlūks* in $7^{th}/13^{th}$ century Syro-Egypt.

a recognisable story arch, and sprinkling it with references to figures, events and concepts derived from the shared cultural background of author and audience, he aimed to pull along his audience in a richly poetic and spectacular universe that made narrative sense of the remarkable ascendancy of Baybars.

There is some evidence that our author was not the only contemporary observer to observe Baybars' early years as suffused with wondrous events. The surviving annalistic part of 'Izz al-Dīn b. Shaddād's *sīra* does not cover these early years, but its lyrical appendix (that is, the section of the text designated as *sīra*, see chapter two, section 2.2.) in which the author deals with Baybars' virtues does explicitly frame the importance of these events. Not only does he categorise several of the events in this period as *'ajīb(a)* ("marvellous"), he also writes about Baybars' departure from and eventual return to Egypt and explicitly compares it to the Prophet's *Hijra*:

> وخرج من مصر لما قتل الأمير فارس الدين أقطاي الجامدار فارًّا بنفسه * في شرذمةٍ من أبناء جنسه * فقضى الله في عوده إليها مالكًا أسوة نبيّه حيث أُخرج من مكة دار أُسرته * فأعاده إليها وقد أناله بملكها فوق ما تمنّاه في حال عسرته *

> He left Egypt when the amir Fāris al-Dīn Aqṭāy al-Jāmdār was killed, fleeing himself with a small group of the sons of his race. Then God decreed for his return to Egypt, in accordance with the example set by His Prophet (*uswat nabiyyihi*) who left Mecca, the land of his family, allowed him to return there and obtain its rule, beyond what he desired in his condition of destitution.[244]

It is significant that here 'Izz al-Dīn b. Shaddād evaluates these events in a register and in conceptual terms akin to Ibn 'Abd al-Ẓāhir's. It is possible that 'Izz al-Dīn b. Shaddād read Ibn 'Abd al-Ẓāhir's text by this point, but he may also have been expressing a common discourse espoused in courtly circles around the time.

While the first section of Ibn 'Abd al-Ẓāhir's *sīra* only takes up a relatively small part of the whole, it is important for the text's further development. As noted, the account of Baybars' ascension is immediately followed by a discussion of various virtues, which Holt argued was directly inspired by Bahā' al-Dīn b. Shaddād, although it is a common enough feature of medieval discourses on rulership in general.[245] If we consider the book's construction on its own terms it makes a lot

---

244 Ibn Shaddād, *Ta'rīkh al-Malik al-Ẓāhir*, 268.

245 In addition to 'Izz al-Dīn b. Shaddād's just noted *Ta'rīkh*, compare Ibn 'Aqīl's literary offering to al-Ẓāhir Barqūq, *al-Durr al-Naḍīḍ fī Manāqib al-Malik al-Ẓāhir Abī Sa'īd*, which ends on such a virtue section. Staatsbibliothek zu Berlin, MS Wetzstein I 38a–44b. Ibn 'Arabshāh also interwove ideal virtues in the form of a mirror for princes with examples of how al-Ẓāhir Jaqmaq personified these virtues in *al-Ta'līf al-Ṭāhir fī Shiyam al-Malik al-Ẓāhir*, British Library MS Or. 3026. See Mustafa Banister, "Professional Mobility in Ibn 'Arabshāh's Fifteenth-Century Panegyric Dedicated to Sultan al-Ẓāhir Jaqmaq," *MSR* 23 (2021), 133–164.

of sense: where the first part deals with heroic development and the eventual attainment of the protagonist's rightful position, the second part on virtues presents a sampling of material on how the sultan's ascension initiated a time of justice and prosperity, much of which later reappears in the annalistic third section of the book. Although this may give the impression of a neatly divided text, there is in fact some overlapping evolution: note for example that the first meticulously dated event of the text is part of the sultan's ascension ceremony which concludes the first part as the climax of the sultan's journey, namely the point at which he "rode out with the emblems (*shaʿāʾir*) of the sultanate."[246] This event is followed by the virtue chapters, and only after the text transitions again into annalistic narrative our author picks up the chronological thread again. In the remainder of the text dating becomes prominent and the manuscripts clearly highlight the changes in years.[247] It generally becomes a much more traditional historiographical text. This is not to say that the third part of the manuscript is entirely devoid of heroic elements and explicit associations of the sultan to the great examples of preceding rulers, but these are firmly embedded in the annalistic framework.

The virtues section is not an interpolation then, but a bridge between the heroic time scale utilised in the first part and the historically specific annalistic section. As an overview of the sultan's good qualities taken from various moments in his life it underlines how the sultan's heroic promise was regularly delivered on in virtuous deeds throughout the rest of his life. By conveniently grouping these accounts in the virtues section, and having them precede the annalistic section, the reader may be informed both about—in Ibn ʿAbd al-Ẓāhir's own words from his introductory discourse—"the benefactions and evils each of [the kings] committed in words and deeds" and "about how the days elapsed and turned about, by which [causes events] were brought about or averted."

The historical exceptionality of Baybars' reign is underlined by a distinctive feature of the text's third annalistic part: digressive historicisations. All but one of these are found in reports about Baybars' many conquests and raids in Syria.[248] Here the author provides an overview of a conquered city or castle's preceding

246 *Rawḍ*, 71.

247 The Istanbul manuscript highlights the year changes with prominent headings, although it only picks up doing so from the year 663/1264 onwards: MS Fatih 4366, 62b, 75b, 98a, 123a, 136b, 143a, 153a, 160a, 166b, 172b, 182b, 192b. The British Library manuscript is cut off during this particular year, which is prominently highlighted on 95r. This is preceded by a specifically and prominently dated event on 73a.

248 The remaining case details the founding of the al-Azhar Mosque and its subsequent history following a short account about the Friday prayer at that mosque in the year 665/1266 when the mosque received a new endowment (*waqf*) from an amir. *Rawḍ*, 277–280.

history, sometimes augmented by more broadly geographical information. Ibn ʿAbd al-Ẓāhir provides such digressions for Caesarea, Jaffa, Shaqīf Arnūn, Tripoli (which was not actually conquered by Baybars, he only undertook some raids on its hinterland), Antioch, Baghrās, Balāṭunus, the Ismāʿīlī strongholds in northwestern Syria, Ḥisn al-Akrād (Crac des Chevaliers), Ḥisn ʿAkkār, Ḥisn al-Kaff, Kaynūk, and a number of Cilician castles.[249] Ibn ʿAbd al-Ẓāhir's digressions are usually introduced as information gained from other historians (in rare cases attributed to earlier historians such as al-Balādhurī and Ibn Munqidh),[250] from books (*dhukira fī al-kutub*), or as authorial interventions by way of the phrase "the author of the *sīra* says" (*qāla mu'allif al-sīra*). One can see the logic of *adab* compilations in these digressions, as an author showcasing his broad knowledge and entertaining his reader by giving information related in broad terms to the book's general topic.[251]

Ibn ʿAbd al-Ẓāhir's authorial process of historicisation is nicely encapsulated by the following excerpt from the *sīra* of Baybars found at the end of the account of the sultan's death:

> وكان مدة مرضه–قدس الله روحه–ثلاثة عشر يومًا وهي مدة مرض الشهيد صلاح الدين–رحمه الله تعالى. وأول ما فتحه السلطان بنفسه قيسارية وآخر ما فتحه قيسارية، وأول جلوسه مرتبة السلطنة يوم الجمعة سابع عشر ذي القعدة وآخر جلوسه في تخت السلطنة آل سلجوق بقيسارية الروم الجمعة سابع عشر ذي القعدة، وأوّل من بنى أنطاكية – على ما تقدم ذكره – اسمه بالعربية الملك الظاهر وآخر من ملكها وأخربها هذا الملك الظاهر، وكان القائم بدولة التركية السلجوقية السلطان ركن الدين طغرلبك وهذا السلطان ركن الدين هو الذي أقام الدولة التركية من حين المنصورة، وركن الدين ذاك هو الذي رد الخلافة لبني العباس نوبة البساسيرى وركن الدين هذا رد الخلافة لبني العباس–رضي الله عنهم–بإقامة الخليفين وهما المستنصر والإمام الحاكم بأمر الله أمير المؤمنين، والخطبة لهذا الظاهر بعد الحاكم أمير المؤمنين. وهذا من عجيب الاتفاق.

> The length of his sickness—may God hallow his soul—was thirteen days, and this is [equal to] the length of the martyr Ṣalāḥ al-Dīn's sickness—may God have mercy on him. The sultan's first conquest was Caesarea [in Palestine] and his last conquest was [also named] Caesarea [Kayseri in Anatolia]; the first time he ascended the seat of the sultanate was on Friday the 17th of Dhī al-Qaʿda, and his final ascent of the throne of the Saljuq sultanate in Kayseri

---

249 *Rawḍ*, 232–233, 294–295, 295–296, 301–304, 313–323, 326–327, 348–349, 365–370 (in fact a brief history of the Ismāʿīlī sect), 377–378, 382, 413, 417–418, 438–440, 443–445 (more interwoven with the narrative than in the other accounts). Not every conquest receives such a treatment. No such information is given for the early conquests of Arsūf and Safad. Although that may suggest Ibn ʿAbd al-Ẓāhir only took up the practice later, the fact that it is present for Baybars' earliest conquest of Caesarea gainsays that idea.

250 *Rawḍ*, 316, 377.

251 About the literary uses of digression, or *istiṭrād*, see, among others: Everett K. Rowson, "An Alexandrian Age in 14th-Century Damascus: Twin Commentaries on Two Celebrated Arabic Epistles," *MSR* 7, no. 1 (2003) 107–109; Otto Weintritt, *Formen spätmittelalterlicher islamischer Geschichtsdarstellung: Untersuchungen zu an-Nuwairī al-Iskandarānīs* Kitāb al-ilmām *und verwandten zeitgenössischen Texten* (Beirut-Stuttgart: Orient Institut-Franz Steiner, 1992), 87–92 (and 92–101 for examples).

> (*Qaysariyyat al-Rūm*) was [also] on Friday the 17th of Dhī al-Qaʿda; the Arabic name of the first who built Antioch—as has been reported above—was "al-Malik al-Ẓāhir" (i.e. the resplendent king),[252] and the last who took it into his possession and devastated it was this al-Malik al-Ẓāhir [Baybars]; the one who established the Turkish Saljuq *dawla* was sultan Rukn al-Dīn Tughril-bek [d. 455/1063] and this sultan Rukn al-Dīn [i.e. Baybars] elevated the Turkish *dawla* at the time of [the Battle of] Manṣūra; that Rukn al-Dīn restored the caliphate to the Abbasids in the time of al-Basāsīrī [d. 451/1060, a Buyid amir who briefly ruled Baghdad in the name of the Fatimids], and this Rukn al-Dīn restored the caliphate to the Abbasids—may God be pleased with them—by appointing the two caliphs, and they are al-Mustanṣir, and the imam al-Ḥākim bi-Amr Allāh, the commander of the believers; and the *khuṭba* in the Egyptian [Fatimid] *dawla* was [delivered in the name of] al-Ẓāhir [d. 427/1036] after al-Ḥākim [d. 411/1021] the commander of the faithful, [as was] the *khuṭba* for this al-Ẓāhir after al-Ḥākim the commander of the faithful. And this is among the wonders of coincidence (*min ʿajāʾib al-ittifāq*).[253]

It is these kinds of associations that most scholars have highlighted for the *sīra* of Baybars, but they gain in meaning when evaluated in the light of Ibn ʿAbd al-Ẓāhir's stated intentions and within the larger narrative framework of the text. Ibn ʿAbd al-Ẓāhir had a keen eye for such "coincidences" of names and dates, but he embedded them in a larger narrative presentation of the sultan that would withstand the forgetfulness of time. Compare how historians in thirteenth-century France wrote about contemporary events as an effort, in Gabrielle Spiegel's words, "to endow the discrete, concrete, and particular elements of contemporary reality with the same sense of moment and significance that medieval society normally accorded to an already valorized, traditional past."[254] Ibn ʿAbd al-Ẓāhir's approach was informed by similar ideas. By explicitly associating the contemporary or recent events with those of the distant past which had already been sanctioned by the tradition, he ensured that the connection between those past events and the present was made explicit.

The *sīra* of Baybars thus situates itself in a rich historiographical continuum, while at the same time underlining the exceptionality of the times to which it is devoted. Ibn ʿAbd al-Ẓāhir envisioned a work of high literary stature, which would ensure that the memory of this sultan would stand the test of time and underline its author's literary credentials.

---

252 The earlier report (*Rawḍ*, 313) names this king as "Asūkhsh" (no vocalisation, so this is a tentative reading), possibly a (corrupt) rendering of the name of its actual founder Seleucus I Nicator. "Seleukos" in Greek (Σέλευκος) is likely related to a meaning of "bright, white."

253 *Rawḍ*, 474. Translation emended from Khowayter, "A Critical Edition," 875.

254 Spiegel, *Romancing*, 215.

3.2 *Ḥusn al-Manāqib*

Shāfiʿ's take on a *sīra* of Baybars is governed by its aim to abridge his uncle's *sīra*, but we have already seen that Shāfiʿ did not just abridge the text. He added an entirely new introduction in which he shifted the stakes of the project considerably to one that celebrates the practice of abridging. This results in a text that at times feels rather truncated—Holt found the text to be "inartistically constructed"[255]—in which Shāfiʿ often glosses over historical information but leaves intact quoted documents and poems.[256] In general, the original text's tripartite division is more or less retained. Shāfiʿ does not fully excise the virtue chapters, although he does pick and choose from them and gives alternate versions for some of its claims. He also only starts dating events more thoroughly after Baybars' ascension of the throne.[257] A puzzling aspect of the text is that it skips five years without explanation.[258]

As P.M. Holt has noted, Shāfiʿ's abridgement often explicitly corrects the claims of its source text or adds a perspective that sheds different light on the events. For the heroic narrative found in Ibn ʿAbd al-Ẓāhir's first section, this has rather important consequences, because Shāfiʿ regularly undermines his uncle's claims, for example by correcting Ibn ʿAbd al-Ẓāhir's claim that Baybars was initially acquired by al-Ṣāliḥ Ayyūb. He notes that, in fact, Baybars was bought by the amir ʿAlāʾ al-Dīn Aydīkīn al-Bunduqdārī first, which explains Baybars' *nisba* al-Bunduqdārī. Most notably, he provides a different, less auspicious version of the episode of Baybars' regicide of his predecessor Quṭuz. In this version Baybars' ascension of the sultanate is presented as an agreement among the prominent amirs and not as divinely ordained.[259]

Those criticisms and interventions in the narrative are doubtlessly the most conspicuous element of the abridgement. Additionally, Shāfiʿ also stresses a com-

---

255 Holt, "Some Observations," 124.

256 See chapter four, section 4.4., Table 1 for an overview of the amount of documentary material in each text. As is clear from the discrepancy between the two Baybars biographies in that overview, Shāfiʿ did not retain all the documents included in his uncle's biography. Nevertheless, for those he did retain he did not tamper with their contents.

257 *Ḥusn,* 70 (riding out with the emblems of the sultanate). The next dated event is on p. 79 (the caliph's investiture). The manuscript of the text does at some points highlight the changes in years: BnF MS Arabe 1707 *(Ḥusn),* 38a, 79a, 144a, all dealing with post-ascension events. On 126a a *dhikr* is also specified as taking place in a specific year. Furthermore, many events are introduced with a visually pronounced *wa-fīhā*, "and in this [year]."

258 *Ḥusn,* 312 (start of the year 672, while the previous page dealt with events in the year 667 (*Ḥusn,* 291–311)). It is of course possible that this is a copyist's mistake or can be attributed to a lacuna in an earlier manuscript of the text.

259 Holt, "Some Observations," 125–126.

pletely different set of historical continuities than Ibn ʿAbd al-Ẓāhir by excising most of his uncle's historical digressions. Instead, he adds his own digressions which follow a different approach from Ibn ʿAbd al-Ẓāhir's in the sense that they are mostly flash-forwards to events that took place after Baybars' death. Shāfiʿ was too young to have served Baybars directly for most of his reign, but in these digressions he is able to present himself as an important agent. These narratives often overlap in content with accounts also included in his *sīra* of Qalāwūn, but they differ in form and in some details. One long digression for example follows a discussion of Baybars' dealings with Tripoli, when our author skips forward to Qalāwūn's dealings with the same city. In these later events Shāfiʿ himself is a crucial agent for the narrative's development through setting straight a Frankish ambassador.[260] A similar episode is found slightly later in the text, in a digression from Baybars' dealings with Acre, when Shāfiʿ details his crucial role in finding a loophole in the peace treaty with the last remaining Frankish stronghold near the end of Qalāwūn's reign.[261] In the manuscript these interventions are marked in pronounced orthography by the verbal form "*aqūl*" ("I say").[262] They were meant to be easily visible, so that even a quick glance would get the idea across that this was not merely an abridgement, but also a sort of running commentary.

While Ibn ʿAbd al-Ẓāhir valorised the recent past of Baybars' sultanate by explicitly linking it to the already meaningful distant past, Shāfiʿ in *Ḥusn al-Manāqib* linked the events of Baybars' sultanate to continuities with the more recent past, showing later developments following on Baybars' actions. A good illustration of how this works is found when he details a raid of Baybars against Acre and adds:

أقول، لم يتهيأ للملك الظاهر فتح هذه عكا وأخرجها ليفرغ عن فتح ما هو أهم منها. ولما أفضت نوبة الملك للسلطان الملك المنصور رشيد الدين قلاوون الصالحي في سنة ثمان وسبعين وستمئة حضر رسل بيوت عكا وسألوا مهادنتهم على حكم هدنة الملك الظاهر. فأجيبوا وكتبت أنا هدنتها ولم تزل الهدنة مستمرة إلى سنة تسع وتسعين وستمئة ففسحت.

> I say: it was not possible for al-Malik al-Ẓāhir [Baybars] to conquer this Acre, and he let it be so he could conclude the conquest of a more important [place]. When the rotation of kingship (*nawbat al-mulk*) settled on the sultan al-Malik al-Manṣūr Rashīd al-Dīn (sic, should be Sayf al-Dīn) Qalāwūn al-Ṣāliḥī in the year 678, messengers of the noble houses of Acre (*buyūt ʿAkkā*) came for an audience (*ḥaḍara*), and they asked for a truce according to the [earlier] ruling of

260 *Ḥusn*, 271–277. See Holt, *Early Mamluk Diplomacy*, 58–68 for a translation of this episode, a translation of a variant episode given in *Faḍl*, as well as a translation of the truce which is quoted by Baybars al-Manṣūrī.

261 *Ḥusn*, 284–286.

262 BnF MS Arabe 1707, 32b, 34a, 78a, 78b, 84b, 85a, 96a, 112a, 135a, 138a, 139a, 143a. It should be noted that forms of the verb *qāla* (to say) are in general written in a distinctive eye-catching orthography by the manuscript's copyist. These personal interventions by the author are nonetheless clearly discernible.

> the truce of al-Malik al-Ẓāhir. Their request was acceded so I wrote its truce which would have remained in force until the year 699, but it was invalidated [before that].[263]

Shāfiʿ next goes on to detail the reasons for the invalidation, which have been discussed at length by P.M. Holt. Suffice it here to highlight this excerpt as an example of Shāfiʿ's flash-forward digressions, in which he also always details his own role in the narrative—in this case by noting that he wrote the renewed truce himself.[264] This section is also concluded by quoting the same lengthy felicitation poem for the conquest of Acre which Shāfiʿ quotes at the end of *al-Faḍl al-Ma'thūr*.[265]

The result of this parallel construction results in a complex text that may have seemed "inartistic" to Holt but which is effective in performing the textual pre-eminence of the abridger. The complex timeline associates the abridger not only with the important original author and his subject, but also with a claim to historical truth, exemplified through this "corrected" narrative. In that sense, it resonates in interesting ways with the other *sīras* written by our author, as we shall see.

3.3 *al-Faḍl al-Ma'thūr*

According to P.M. Holt *al-Faḍl al-Ma'thūr* was "largely composed as an encomium of Qalāwūn in his lifetime," but "not finally put together until after the murder of his son and successor, al-Ashraf Khalīl."[266] Although Holt has discussed several of its anecdotes and documents, the most thorough analysis of its overall structure was made by Tahar Mansouri. He divides *Faḍl* into three main parts: "the context of Qalāwūn's taking over of power," "the pacification of the sultanate," and lastly "the daily administration of power," which according to him is "the most important part of the text."[267] This last section is however quite heterogeneous. I will single out some of its parts more precisely below.

The first sections of *al-Faḍl al-Ma'thūr* appear similar to the *sīra of* Baybars. They showcase a structure that can also be understood as a "monomyth." This is then followed by a more or less chronological presentation of events and related documents following the sultan's ascension of the throne (Mansouri's "pacification

263 *Ḥusn*, 120.

264 P.M. Holt, "Qalāwūn's treaty with Acre in 1283," *The English Historical Review* 81, vol. 361 (1976), 802–812.

265 In *Faḍl*, 181–183 the poem is 50 lines long; in *Ḥusn*, 122–127 the poem is 48 lines long.

266 P.M. Holt, "The Presentation of Qalāwūn by Shāfiʿ ibn 'Alī," 143, 148; Holt, "A Chancery Clerk in Medieval Egypt," 673. Lewicka subscribes to Holt's interpretation, calling it a "compilation of biographical pieces." *Šāfiʿ Ibn ʿAlī's Biography*, 97.

267 Mansouri, "Le Portrait," §4.

du sultanat")—a notable contrast to Ibn ʿAbd al-Ẓāhir's bridging of pre-sultanate events and sultanate annals through virtue chapters. In the first section Qalāwūn is portrayed as being personally selected by al-Ṣāliḥ Ayyūb to join his elite corps because of his excellent physique. Shāfiʿ does not develop Qalāwūn's relationship to this sultan in much detail, however. Nor do we get much information about Qalāwūn's actions in the decade between al-Ṣāliḥ's death and the ascension of Quṭuz—interestingly, the episodes in which Tūrān Shāh and Quṭuz are murdered are both omitted, although the second is alluded to. Qalāwūn's importance as an advisor to Quṭuz is stressed and it is implied that he was the one amir whom Quṭuz could not gainsay.

The narrative only really picks up when describing Baybars' reign. Shāfiʿ does not discuss Qalāwūn's relation to Baybars chronologically, but rather singles out a few important examples of Qalāwūn's importance to Baybars' *dawla*. The most important of these is the marriage of Baybars' son and successor al-Saʿīd Baraka Qān to Qalāwūn's daughter, for which Ibn ʿAbd al-Ẓāhir (noted as *khālī*, "my maternal uncle") composed the ceremonial *khuṭba* (introduced as a *kitāb al-ṣadāqi*). This text is quoted in full and followed by a response document written by Shāfiʿ himself—the earliest text he attributes to himself. It is here explicitly noted as being an example of a type of variation of official documents his uncle made him write, presumably as part of his scribal training.[268] Shāfiʿ then returns to detailing Qalāwūn's importance during Baybars' *dawla*, now by stressing his martial abilities and his advisory role in the management of political affairs, concluding that "all this was according to the view of our lord the sultan [Qalāwūn] who unfailingly advised [Baybars]."[269] The result is an extended section of narrative "stasis," in which Qalāwūn is presented as having harmonious relations with the sultans he served and acquiring the necessary traits of an ideal ruler by participating in the rule of his predecessors. It is probably precisely for that reason that all the troublesome reigns of sultans preceding Baybars are not dealt with in much detail, as this would put too much stress on Baybars' responsibility in bringing stability after his ascension.

The real challenge to this harmonious state comes with the ascension of al-Saʿīd Baraka Qān to the throne after Baybars' death.[270] Immediately after his ascension

268 *Faḍl*, 28 and 32–35 (Shāfiʿs variation). Another one of Qalāwūn's close associations with Baybars is his brokerage of the marriage between Baybars himself and the daughter of the Mongol amir Karmūn, which is related on p. 27.

269 *Faḍl*, 36.

270 See now also Kühn, *Sultan Baibars*, 371–379, which compares Shāfiʿ's accounts of this period with those of other historians and argues that the author made a conscious choice to foreground Qalāwūn.

of the throne, news arrived about Mongol plans to invade Syria. The sultan decides to set out for Syria to prepare, but it is Qalāwūn who shows himself to be the real leader, "covering [Baraka] with the wing of his fatherhood." As Tahar Mansouri notes, Baraka is presented as "a misguided youngster" who is surrounded by bad advisors.[271] This is evident from the following quote:

> وأما العدو فإنهم أحجموا * وفشلوا وما أقدموا * وخافوا وما حافوا * إلا أن الملك السعيد وافق من حوله من ذوى اللهو * وأرباب الزهو * فانعكف وما اعتكف * واستمطر سحاب المكرم الأكرم وقد وكف * وما كف في تناوله ساعدًا ولا كفت * واحتجب عن الرأي وصوابه * والقول وجوابه *

> And concerning the enemy, they recoiled, lost courage and were not bold, they were scared and impaired. Al-Malik al-Saʿīd [Baraka], however, sanctioned people of amusement (*dhawā l-lahw*) and masters of vanity in his surroundings, and he withdrew and did not apply himself [to matters of state], invoking the most honourable clouds and they dripped. He did not renounce his unceasing eating and became fat. He withdrew from judgement and reason and from speaking and answering.[272]

This portrayal adheres to a classic narrative portrayal of rulerly incompetence: the indulging in poetry, music, food and drinking at a time of crisis is reminiscent of stories told about the Abbasid caliph al-Amīn (r. 193–198/809–813) and closer in time Tūrān Shāh.[273] One anecdote tells of a drunken poet who offends Qalāwūn at the foot of the Citadel of Damascus by his insolent behaviour, which leads to a tense exchange between Baraka and Qalāwūn. To defuse the situation, Qalāwūn suggests that he go out to raid the lands of Sīs together with another amir. Things do not improve after Qalāwūn's departure, however, and Baraka proves his unfitness at several points. This makes Shāfiʿ conclude that he engendered *fitna* and *miḥna* among the amirs. These are two powerful terms to stress discord considering their associations with periods of major political turmoil in early Islamic history.[274] In these troubled times, Qalāwūn is presented as wanting the best for the sultanate, negotiating with Baraka, and at one point even with his mother,[275] but resistance from Baybars' old amirs results in more *fitna*. In the end Baraka finally abdicates

---

271 Mansouri, "Le Portrait," §16.

272 *Faḍl*, 38.

273 For the former, see Tayeb El-Hibri, *Reinterpreting Islamic Historiography: Hārūn al-Rashīd and the Narrative of the ʿAbbāsid Caliphate* (Cambridge: Cambridge University Press, 1999), 61–66. For Tūrān Shāh, see the grotesque portrayal of him by al-Kutubī paraphrased in Herzog, "Romans populaires," 99–100.

274 *Faḍl*, 41, 43. See now also the discussion of these terms for a later period, Onimus, *Les maîtres du jeu*, 273–276.

275 *Faḍl*, 44–45.

in favour of his infant brother al-ʿĀdil Sulāmish, but the amirs are then presented as showing a preference for Qalāwūn's personal ascension of the throne, which he reluctantly accepts after deposing Sulāmish.[276]

Where one would now expect the installation of the sultan's harmonious rule as in Ibn ʿAbd al-Ẓāhir's narrative, Shāfiʿ instead continues detailing the internal and external troubles of the sultanate: Baraka Qān remains a nuisance until he dies shortly after Qalāwūn's ascension, the Mongols prepare new attacks, and the powerful amir Shams al-Dīn Sunqur al-Ashqar establishes a counter-sultanate in Damascus. Finally, after the description of the Battle of Homs, the work all but loses its chronological focus, and becomes much more compilatory, starting with a text on the "good tidings" (*bushrā*) about the victory at Homs, which Shāfiʿ himself acknowledges to have been a stand-alone text both at the beginning and the end of the section.[277] The remainder of the book is an assortment of various sections:

- A section on further dealings with Sunqur al-Ashqar and the amir Sayf al-Din Aytmish, including a letter written by Shāfiʿ.[278]
- An important cohesive section on the diplomatic exchange with the Mongol ruler Aḥmad Tegüder, including two letters.[279]
- Three related "memoranda" (*tadhkira*, pl. *tadhākir*) for Qalāwūn's heirs written respectively by Ibn ʿAbd al-Ẓāhir, his son Fatḥ al-Dīn, and Shāfiʿ himself.[280]
- A short section on the sultan's dealings with Khiḍr, the youngest son of Baybars, including a letter written by Shāfiʿ.[281]
- A longer section on various dealings with the Frankish lordships of Acre, Marqab, Tripoli, including several documents, some of which written by Shāfiʿ.[282]
- Three short sections on the co-sultanship and death of Qalāwūn's son al-Ṣāliḥ ʿAlī, including an elegy written by the author.[283]
- A section on the construction of the sultan's madrasa and *bīmaristān*.[284]
- A short section on the sultan's virtues.[285]
- A relatively long and diverse but internally cohesive section on the preparations for the conquest of Acre during which Qalāwūn died and which was eventually achieved by his successor al-Ashraf Khalīl. This includes an elegy for

---

276 *Faḍl*, 51.
277 *Faḍl*, 77–85
278 *Faḍl*, 85–92.
279 *Faḍl*, 92–118. See section 4.4.1. below.
280 *Faḍl*, 118–134. See section 5.2.3. below.
281 *Faḍl*, 134–140.
282 *Faḍl*, 140–162.
283 *Faḍl*, 162–166.
284 *Faḍl*, 166–170.
285 *Faḍl*, 170–173. Not announced as a virtues section as in *Rawḍ*.

Qalāwūn and a congratulatory ode for al-Ashraf Khalīl's conquest, which closes off the text. Both were written by Shāfiʿ himself.[286]

The narrative construction is much less streamlined than Ibn ʿAbd al-Ẓāhir's *sīra* of Baybars. The set-piece qualities found in the first section are not sustained in the later parts. If there is any resolve of the breach of stasis, then it is only after the Battle of Homs, in what Mansouri has named "the daily administration of power": the variety of anecdotes and documents exemplifying in non-chronological fashion how the sultan ruled his domains. Unlike Baybars, whose growth was situated in the decade between al-Ṣāliḥ Ayyūb's rule and the start of his own, Qalāwūn's growth continues throughout the first years of his sultanate. Once pacification of the lands is achieved, the desired harmoniousness is reached, but it is not represented in narrative but in compilation. It is hence perhaps not surprising that the text never really picks up regular dating. Giving a meticulous overview of the events was not our author's primary concern here. The few dates given are significant, such as the death of the sultan's rival and predecessor al-Saʿīd Baraka or the exact date at which the army set out to confront the Mongols at the Battle of Homs.[287] The attainment of ideal rule is articulated in the form of *inshāʾ* and *adab* discourses on power, especially through the various documents and poems written by Shāfiʿ and his colleagues.

As I have suggested in my analysis of the introduction (see 2.3.3.), it was Shāfiʿ's intention to construct a textual edifice of praise both to the sultan *and* to the practice of *inshāʾ* as fundamentally constitutive to his *dawla*. The comparatively high amount of compiled text already shows the crucial importance attached to text produced in service of or in direct relation to the sultan. It is telling that of the manuscript's first eleven pages, five are taken up in large part by a *khuṭba* written by Shāfiʿ's uncle and a response document to this *khuṭba* written by Shāfiʿ himself.[288] This sets the scene for several such response documents to follow further on (I will return to this in section 5.2.3. of this book). Already early on then, the importance of scribal activity for the sultan's state is foregrounded. One of the most important turning points for Qalāwūn's sovereignty, the return to obedience by the breakaway viceroy Sunqur al-Ashqar, is even discussed immediately following the citation

---

286 *Faḍl*, 173–183.

287 *Faḍl*, 58, 71.

288 For tabulated overviews of the types of quoted official material per text, see 4.4. *Faḍl* contains 21 quoted pieces spread over about 130 folios in MS Marsh 424. Compare *Rawḍ:* 20 pieces for about 250 folios (almost 100 pages in the British Library Manuscript, almost 200 in the Istanbul manuscript, the first part of which overlaps with the BL Manuscript); *Tashrīf*, 15 pieces for 376 folios (but only 7 lines per page). For a tabulated overview of poetry in the *sīras*, see 5.2.1.

of a letter written by Shāfiʿ, which creates the impression that this letter was crucial in convincing Sunqur to return to the fold.

The role of the *dīwān* is not only stressed by way of the compiled texts, but also in anecdotes directly involving the *dīwān*. These anecdotes, some of which overlap with accounts discussing the same events in *Ḥusn al-Manāqib*, usually also feature Shāfiʿ in an essential role—in Holt's words: "the man with the bright conclusive idea."[289] These instances often involve a change in register as well, including some direct speech, at two points even portraying Qalāwūn speaking colloquial Arabic.[290] The first such episodes are situated during al-Saʿīd Baraka's reign. An important one is when our author refuses to write to the Ismāʿīlīs of northern Syria—who had only recently, during Baybars' reign, been eliminated as an exogeneous threat and integrated into the sultanate—to help Baraka, followed by his switching sides to Qalāwūn.[291] Qalāwūn's reign itself also starts with such an episode, when Shāfiʿ relates how he was called upon to provide the sultan's regnal title but refused to do so without the proper ceremonial.[292] Another early example involves the important *kuttāb* Fakhr al-Din b. Luqmān and Shāfiʿ's cousin Fatḥ al-Dīn b. ʿAbd al-Ẓāhir being unsure about how to write a specific document, upon which our author provides the necessary perspective for a breakthrough.[293] There are several more such instances throughout the text.[294]

These interventions are of course interesting for Shāfiʿ's self-presentation, especially in the light of what we are told by other sources concerning his early retirement,[295] but they also contribute to a pervasive presence of the workings of the *dīwān* throughout the text. The regular occurrence of a common phrase further underlines this: the verbal forms *rasama*, meaning "he prescribed," or *amara*, meaning "he ordered," referring to the ruler's decisions, used in direct association with the first-person plural *fa-katabnā* or the first-person singular *katabtu*, meaning respectively "so we wrote" or "so I wrote." Sometimes these phrases precede a full

---

289 P.M. Holt, "The Īlkhān Aḥmad's Embassies to Qalāwūn: Two Contemporary Accounts," *BSOAS* 49, no. 1 (1986), 129.
290 *Faḍl*, 52, 169.
291 *Faḍl*, 49.
292 *Faḍl*, 51.
293 *Faḍl*, 61.
294 *Faḍl*, 67, 71, 76, 83, 102, 146–148, 163, 172.
295 The lack of chronology is suggestive in this sense, one feels as if the author did not want his readers to situate these events either before or after the event that blinded him. Notably, he only refers ambiguously to the event of his blinding in this text, despite devoting substantial space to the Battle of Homs.

or paraphrased rendering of a document,[296] but they are also regularly used in the same instances where our author talks extensively about his own involvement.[297] I have not come across similar phrases in Ibn ʿAbd al-Ẓāhir's work, and it only appears once in *Ḥusn al-Manāqib* and twice in the *sīra* of al-Nāṣir Muḥammad, so it is a peculiar choice to use this phrase so often in *Faḍl*.[298] Yet it makes perfect sense in Shāfiʿ's general approach, as the participative and performative qualities of such a statement are significant. The process of political decision making is here effectively broadened to include not just the sultan as the maker of decisions, but also the *dīwān al-inshāʾ* who translate the sultan's decision into an eloquently written prose letter, edict, or another appropriate document before it becomes effective.

By contrast, the kind of historicisations that are so prominent in Ibn ʿAbd al-Ẓāhir's *sīra* of Baybars, and which Anne Troadec underlined as a common feature of the whole corpus, are not prominent at all in *al-Faḍl al-Maʾthūr*. When they do appear, they are much less developed than Ibn ʿAbd al-Ẓāhir's.[299] The greatness of this sultan, in Shāfiʿ's view, is not to be situated in his historical lineage then, but in his management of the state, and especially through the service of the *dīwān*.

It will become clear from my general analysis in this book that this focus on the *dīwān* is not unique to *al-Faḍl al-Maʾthūr*, but it is by far the most explicit in positing this narrative predominance. As I will argue, this is an idea that came to the foreground during Qalāwūn's rule, as it is also much more pronounced in Ibn ʿAbd al-Ẓāhir's later *sīras*. There may also have been other reasons for its foregrounding in this text, however: the manuscript of this text is the only one in our corpus which allows us to tentatively identify its patron. This is notably not a sultan but Shihāb al-Dīn Maḥmūd al-Ḥalabī (d. 725/1325), the leading chancery official of the 690s/1290s (see 6.4. for a more extensive discussion). Shāfiʿ's creative resume of his own work embedded in a *sīra* and the extended praise of the workings of the *dīwān al-inshāʾ* offered in *al-Faḍl al-Maʾthūr* surely appears as appropriate for the eyes of the person leading the chancery at the time of Shāfiʿ's finalisation of the text, perhaps also a moment when his direct connections to the chancery and court were

296 As in *Faḍl*, 40, 46 (peculiar, because the phrase is broken up by quotation of the text), 56, 68 (excluding *rasama* or *amara* but with a clear statement that these were the sultan's words, "*kalām*"), 76, 85, 87, 137, 141.

297 *Faḍl*, 42, 52, 55, 65, 89, 101–102 (narratively spread out, detailing the various stages of composition in the *dīwān* after the sultan's request), 172.

298 *Ḥusn*, 322; *Arabe 1705*, 48a, 103b.

299 There are some exceptions, such as *Faḍl*, 169–170, where the author traces events back to Shajar al-Durr. He also provides some background to the conquests of Marqab and Tripoli, without however demarcating it as clearly nor going into as much detail as his uncle. Most references to the deep past in this text are like the brief references to ʿAntar and Baṭṭāl in the extract from the introduction cited in chapter two (section 2.3.2.), that is, they are literary references without historical contextualisation.

more complicated, following the deaths of Fatḥ al-Dīn b. ʿAbd al-Ẓāhir in 691/1292 and Ibn ʿAbd al-Ẓāhir himself a year later.

3.4 *Tashrīf al-Ayyām*

With this text we arrive at the three incompletely preserved *sīra* texts. Assessing their narrative construction thus becomes more hypothetical. The preserved part of Ibn ʿAbd al-Ẓāhir's *sīra* of Qalāwūn—the second volume and likely most of its third volume—starts in the middle of the year 680/1281, the second year of Qalāwūn's sultanate. Considering that the combined manuscript of the second and third volume consists of 376 folios, it is likely that even a volume of half that size would have contained ample space for a discussion of Qalāwūn's early life and early sultanate, perhaps culminating in the important Battle of Homs, of which we have no preserved account by Ibn ʿAbd al-Ẓāhir.

Like *al-Faḍl al-Maʾthūr*, *Tashrīf al-Ayyām* has been evaluated as essentially a text built around compiled materials.[300] Yet, strict chronology is an essential part of the text's organisation: the second volume of the text starts chronographically and follows an annalistic format in which most accounts are precisely dated.[301] The manuscript of it is also the only text in our main corpus to consistently highlight the changes in years. The lavishly executed manuscript of *Tashrīf al-Ayyām* renders all but one of these year changes in a larger script than the regular text, thus making them easily retrievable for a reader.[302] However, the last year explicitly noted in the text is 686/1287, well before the death of Qalāwūn. In fact, the book then peters out, although it does include an account of the sultan's death. Notably, there is no account of the Conquest of Tripoli in 688/1289. It is clear from other sources that

300 Ulrich Haarmann notes that "man [*Tashrīf al-Ayyām*] eher als eine wohlgeordnete Materialsammlung denn als Chronik bezeichnen möchte." *Quellenstudien*, 99. The predominance of quoted materials even pushed Robert Irwin to designate *Tashrīf* with characteristic hyperbole as "not much more than a collection of Ibn ʿAbd al-Ẓāhir's choice pieces of chancery draftsmanship joined to one another with linking narrative." Robert Irwin, "Mamluk History and Historians," *The Cambridge History of Arabic Literature: Arabic Literature in the Post-Classical Period*, ed. R. Allen & D.S. Richards (Cambridge: Cambridge University Press, 2006), 163.

301 E.g.: *Tashrīf*, 17, 18, 20–21, 24, 43, 44, 52, 68, 91, 92, 112, 126.

302 *Arabe 1704 (Tashrīf)*, 1b, 46b, 108b, 258b, 296a. The one change that is not noted in larger script is found at the top of a page (108b) immediately above a *dhikr* in larger script and is thus still easily visible. ʿIzz al-Dīn b. Shaddād also highlights the changes in years in his biography of Baybars: Selimiye 2306, 14b, 27b, 51b, 68b, 93b, 152b. All these headings are situated on the verso page (as are all other major subdivisions, such as the yearly obituaries and the virtues section at the end of the manuscript), a dominant page position in Arabic books.

this conquest was at least as widely celebrated textually as was that of Marqab, which Ibn ʿAbd al-Ẓāhir discusses in various textual forms.[303]

The manuscript layout of *Tashrīf* highlights a topic that is familiar from my discussion of *Faḍl*: the importance of the *dīwān*, here especially focused on compiled documents. In the entirety of the manuscript of *Tashrīf*, by far the most eye-catching headings are those which signal the letters that were part of the diplomatic correspondence between Qalāwūn and the Ilkhanid ruler Aḥmad Tegüder, which I will discuss more extensively in chapter four (4.4.1.). The visual prominence some of these texts were allocated in the manuscripts is visible in Figure 3 (as well as Figure 4 further in this book).[304]

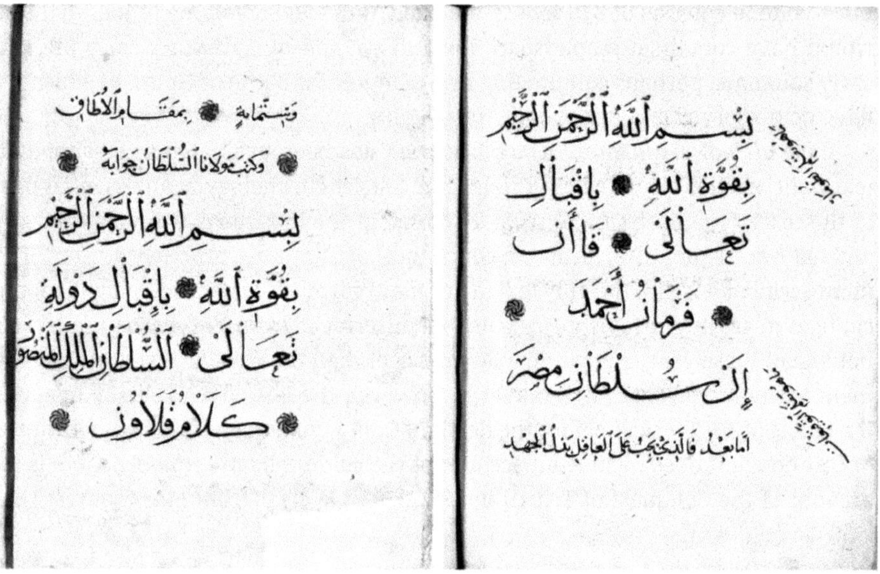

Figure 3: BnF MS Arabe 1704 folios 18b (Qalāwūn's reply to Tegüder's first letter) and 135b (Tegüder's second letter). Note that the letters sent by Tegüder were designated by the Persian term *firmān*, whereas Qalāwūn's single included answer is called "*kalām Qalāwūn*" ("Qalāwūn's discourse").

Due to this prominence of compiled material and the text's general interest in activities related to the *dīwān*, similar ideas appear to have been at work in the textual

---

303 See for example a letter sent to Yemen about the Tripoli conquest written by Tāj al-Dīn b. al-Athīr quoted in al-ʿUmarī, *Masālik*, 12:267–268. The same author also wrote a letter celebrating the conquest of Marqab to al-Ashraf Khalīl. al-ʿUmarī, *Masālik*, 12:266–267.

304 BnF MS Arabe 1704 *(Tashrīf)*, 9a, 18b, 135b. For a reproduction of folios 8b–9a, see Figure 4 in section 4.4.1. of this book.

construction of this text as in *Faḍl.* Ibn ʿAbd al-Ẓāhir also makes much less use of historicisations here than in his *sīra* of Baybars. The most notable case where he does digress into a historical overview of a newly conquered place is in the section dealing with Qalāwūn's conquest of the castle of Marqab, which was also the occasion for quoting a great deal of poetry and a piece of *inshāʾ* writing.[305] He also does this for the earlier conquest of the castle of Kakhkhuta.[306] In general, however, such material is not as pervasive as it is in Ibn ʿAbd al-Ẓāhir's *sīra* of Baybars.[307] The topos of sultanic excellence is also less pronounced. In similar fashion to his accounts in the *sīra* of Baybars, Ibn ʿAbd al-Ẓāhir's account of Qalāwūn's building of a *qubba* in the Citadel of Karak, contains a reference to it being "a wonder among buildings, the like of which has not been built by a king in a kingdom among the kingdoms."[308] He also makes claims about the unique excellence of Qalāwūn's conquest of Marqab: "[to conquer] it had been impossible for kings, none of whom were able to get near to it, much less besiege it. [. . .] God had preserved it for our lord the sultan so that it could be one of his brilliant conquests, and so that the most excellent *sīra* may be crowned by it."[309] Ibn ʿAbd al-Ẓāhir's first poem celebrating this conquest includes a line that communicates a similar idea:

حصن عظيم القدر في سيرة   لمن مضى قبلك لم يكتب

> None of the *sīras* of your predecessors
> record [the conquest] of a castle of such might.[310]

It is interesting to note that in both these comments the sultan's achievement is directly linked to the composition of his *sīra*, which by necessity also excels other biographical writings. In fact, this last poem has a strong stress on the importance of writing and books to celebrate and solidify the sultan's achievement. Roughly a decade after Ibn ʿAbd al-Ẓāhir's first take on the *sīra* format, the stakes of such a project had shifted and the role of the *dīwān* in state building and preservation

---

305 *Tashrīf*, 85–87.
306 *Tashrīf*, 28–29.
307 It is of course true that Qalāwūn simply conquered a good deal less than his predecessor.
308 *Tashrīf*, 139: فجاءت من عجائب الأبنية التى ما عمّر مثلها ملك في مملكة من الممالك
309 *Tashrīf*, 77. See for another, but in my opinion incorrect, translation, Gabrieli, *Arab Historians of the Crusades*, transl. E.J. Costello (London: Routledge, 2010), 199.
وخبأه الله لمولانا السلطان ليكون من فتوحاته[. . .]لأنه كان قد أعجز الملوك ولم يقدر أحد منهم على التقرّب منه فكيف النزول عليه المنيرة * ولتطرّز به أحسن سيرة *
310 *Tashrīf*, 82.

needed to be underlined more forcefully. That said, it is unclear when Ibn ʿAbd al-Ẓāhir finalised *Tashrīf al-Ayyām*. It appears that he briefly abandoned writing it—hence the omission of important events, such as the conquest of Tripoli and the death of Qalāwūn's eldest son and initial heir al-Ṣāliḥ ʿAlī—or that he had been writing it retrospectively, and quickly finished it after the death of Qalāwūn, perhaps so he could offer it to the new sultan al-Ashraf Khalīl or someone in his entourage. It may thus have preceded Shāfiʿ's *al-Faḍl al-Maʾthūr* which was completed only after al-Ashraf Khalīl conquered Acre. Given this likely order of composition–that is, *Tashrīf al-Ayyām* preceding *al-Faḍl al-Maʾthūr*–it is not unlikely that the relative innovation of focussing more squarely on the *dīwān* in the *sīra* format was Ibn ʿAbd al-Ẓāhir's rather than Shāfiʿ's, even if the latter took it further. Unfortunately, neither manuscript is dated, so this cannot be ascertained.

3.5 *al-Alṭāf al-Khafiyya*

Because only one of originally at least four volumes of this survive, and since no later text quotes directly from Ibn ʿAbd al-Ẓāhir's third *sīra* it is difficult to assess the original scope of the text. Based on what is contained in the other *sīras* we can make a few guesses, however. Since al-Ashraf Khalīl only ascended the throne in 689/1290, the first volume likely would have contained information about his pre-sultanate activities and his ascension of the throne. The text also certainly included some description, and most likely also extensive literary celebrations of the conquest of Acre and the ensuing conquest of all remaining Crusader strongholds on the coast which took place early in his reign. This event is referred to near the end of the extant volume as something that has been mentioned before.[311] On the occasion of this conquest several praise poems were written that can be found in other texts—two such poems are found at the end of Shāfiʿ's *al-Faḍl al-Maʾthūr*, one of which is attributed there to Ibn ʿAbd al-Ẓāhir. There is also some evidence of historical material on the conquest of Acre written by Ibn ʿAbd al-Ẓāhir, in a single quotation by Ibn al-Furāt: a marvellous anecdote (*min gharīb al-ittifāq*, "of strange happenings") about a dream of the Sufi shaykh and poet Sharaf al-Dīn al-Būṣīrī (d. 686/1294), in which the conquest is predestined in a short poem. Immediately following this anecdote, Ibn al-Furāt quotes three lines from a poem by Ibn ʿAbd al-Ẓāhir, which is unrelated to the poem quoted by Shāfiʿ in *al-Faḍl al-Maʾthūr*.[312]

311 *Alṭāf*, 69: على ما تقدم شرحه في هذه السيرة الفضيلة

312 Ibn al-Furāt, *Taʾrīkh Ibn al-Furāt [= Taʾrīkh duwal al-mulūk], volume 8*, Q. Zurayq & N. ʿIzz al-Dīn (Beirut: al-Maṭbaʿa al-Amīrikāniyya, 1939), 113.

A short description of al-Ashraf Khalīl's qualities (*ṣifāt*) attributed to Ibn ʿAbd al-Ẓāhir, but not to a particular text, is also cited in al-Maqrīzī's biographical dictionary *al-Muqaffā*.[313] Finally, a truce document with the Crown of Aragon dated to just after the conquest is also attested both in documentary form (preserved in the Archives of the Crown of Aragon in Barcelona) and in a later quotation by al-Qalqashandī, which may have been included in one of the volumes of the text.[314]

As far as its surviving volume is concerned, the *sīra* follows a chronological order. It provides several exact dates, although it does not highlight the changes in years.[315] Rather than a narrow focus on the sultan's virtues, I would suggest that the text is rather broadly organised around courtly practices, somewhat in line with what Tahar Mansouri called Qalāwūn's "daily administration of power." There is a pervasive focus on the rituals of power undertaken by the sultan and the caliph, who has an unusually strong presence in the text, even if it is only for a handful of sections at the start of the volume. In fact, this is confirmed by other historiographical texts: it has been suggested that al-Ashraf Khalīl strengthened the relationship between caliphate and sultanate after it had fallen into relative disuse since the early years of Baybars' sultanate. He is thought to have done so out of concerns for his position on the throne which remained volatile because he did not command the full support of his father's amirs.[316]

This is not to say that ritual does not figure extensively in the other texts, nor that *Alṭāf* is substantially different from the presentation of power in *Tashrīf*, however. Essentially, ideas about the centrality of the pen to the sultan's *dawla* are here embedded in a somewhat broader courtly focus, which remains difficult to assess at scale because of the short length of the text. Uniquely for this text, however, there is one aspect which does implicitly stress the importance of administration: the fact that nearly half of the manuscript (80 folios of the manuscript's total 182) is taken up by four *waqf* (endowment) deeds.[317] These related *waqf* deeds detail the endowment of Qalāwūn's mausoleum by his son al-Ashraf Khalīl and al-Ashraf Khalīl's own funerary complex in the Qarāfa. Willem Flinterman has discussed the contents of these documents at length and presumed that they were written by Ibn

---

313 al-Maqrīzī, *al-Muqaffā*, 3:456.

314 Interestingly, Frédéric Bauden has observed that the text overlaps substantially with the earlier truce document with Acre quoted in *Tashrīf*. "Mamluk Diplomatics: The Present State of Research," in *Mamluk Cairo, a Crossroads for Embassies: Studies on Diplomacy and Diplomatics*, eds. Frédéric Bauden and Malika Dekkiche (Leiden: Brill, 2019), 11–12.

315 *Alṭāf*, 6, 15, 24, 39, 54, 59, 64.

316 Banister, *Abbasid Caliphate*, 41.

317 As noted in 1.1.3., these *waqf* documents have only been edited and published in part in Moberg, "Zwei ägyptische waqf-urkunden."

ʿAbd al-Ẓāhir himself. He suggests that the inclusion of these documents in the *sīra* "completed the codex as a royal memorabilium and an example for posterity." He sees them "as vehicles of royal representation."[318] Indeed, the *waqf* document itself starts with a rather lengthy list of the sultan's titles. However, it is noteworthy that this list is preceded by an explicit note that "[the sultan] ordered it to be written, accurately drawn up, elucidated, and recorded."[319] This type of claim is hardly unusual and fits in perfectly with the legal register used for such documents, but the phrase does draw the attention for at least a little while to the crucial contribution of the *kātib* in creating this document. Hence, the inclusion of the *waqf* documents function not just as "royal representation" as Flinterman argues, but like all other compiled documents in this text it stresses the close and crucial association between the sultan and his eloquent servant, whose role is exemplified through his writing. I will discuss a strong example of this discourse taken from this text in the next chapter, section 4.3.

3.6 *Sīrat al-Malik al-Naṣīr*

The original extent of Shāfiʿ's *sīra* of al-Nāṣir Muḥammad is unknown, but in the *ijāza* he accorded to al-Ṣafadī where he lists his books, he notes that it amounted to multiple volumes (*ajzāʾ mutaʿaddida*).[320] We do not know how many volumes preceded the surviving volume nor how much material may have followed but given that the text starts a few years into the sultan's second reign, certainly a substantial part of the text has been lost. In addition to accounts of the sultan's two preceding ascensions of the throne, one would also expect accounts of the battle of Wādī al-Khaznadār in 699/1299, when the Mongols humiliatingly defeated al-Nāṣir Muḥammad's armies, and even more certainly an account of the Battle of Marj al-Suffar/Shaqḥab in 702/1303, when al-Nāṣir Muḥammad's armies defeated the Mongols triumphantly, putting an end to their incursions into Syria. Above I have briefly discussed the laudatory battle treatise composed by Shāfiʿ's cousin once removed ʿAlāʾ al-Dīn b. ʿAbd al-Ẓāhir about this event. One could imagine Shāfiʿ including a similar kind of text into his *sīra*.

---

318 Flinterman, "Cult," 162–163.

319 BSB Munich MS Cod. arab 405, 102b. I have added "the sultan," but it should be noted that in the Arabic original the subject of these verbs only follows the quoted string of verbs.

320 This section contains some material also found in my essay "Literarisierung Reconsidered in the Context of Sultanic Biography: The Case of Shāfiʿ b. ʿAlī's *Sīrat al-Nāṣir Muḥammad* (BnF MS Arabe 1705)," in *New Readings in Arabic Historiography*, 466–489. In the essay I go into more detail and provide more quotes from the section.

While an assessment of its general construction is thus impossible, the surviving part of the text does cover a period of substantial interest. It starts in the middle of al-Nāṣir Muḥammad's second reign but spends substantial space on the period between his abdication and return to the throne nine months later. The first two-thirds of the text are reminiscent of Ibn ʿAbd al-Ẓāhir's *Tashrīf* and *Alṭāf*: like in those texts, we find here a strong focus on the sultan's administration of power. A distinctive feature of the present *sīra* is a relative prevalence of material dealing with diplomatic relations with the Mongols (both the Ilkhanids and the Golden Horde, though much more extensively on the former), Armenians of Cilicia (Sīs), Venetian "Franks," Aragon ("Alfūnsh"), the Byzantines, the Nubians, and Yemen. Additionally, it contains several accounts about dealings between members of the military elites, as well as, uniquely for this *sīra*, accounts dealing with the management of orthodoxy and heterodoxy, including a brief account about Ibn Taymiyya's first trials in Damascus and several accounts that are not corroborated in any other historical source of the period. While that would suggest the *sīra* to be the most wide-ranging of the corpus in contents, the author does continuously frame all its contents as contributing to the glory of the sultan. In the sections on heterodoxy, for example, the author always reverts to praise of the sultan for handling these situations in exemplary fashion.

Shāfiʿ had to deal with the fact that during this period al-Nāṣir Muḥammad did not exercise power directly but was dominated by the two amirs Sallār and Baybars al-Jāshnikīr. The tensions this generated come to a head in the final third of the preserved manuscript, but it is also implicitly noticeable in the first two-thirds of the text. This observation together with the fact there is a gap in the historical coverage between the year 706 and 708 indicates that Shāfiʿ may have been writing relatively close to the events and was caught by surprise by the sultan's abdication.[321] On the sultan's return to power Shāfiʿ may have hastened to produce an account of these recent tribulations and appended them to his work in progress without substantially revising what he had already written. The fact that the section on al-Nāṣir Muḥammad's abdication and return is written almost entirely in *sajʿ* whereas the text otherwise oscillates between registers also contributes to the cohesiveness. Additionally, in the first two thirds of the *sīra* the author concludes the majority of accounts with a statement along the lines of an event having taken place "in this way" (*ʿalā hādhihi al-ṣūra*) but he abandons doing so entirely in the final third of the

321 There is no noticeable gap in the manuscript between the two sections, and the title of the new section is even spread across a verso and recto page, so if it is a gap, it must be a copyist's mistake. As noted above, *Ḥusn* also contains a gap of five years.

text.[322] Despite this shift in framework and tone, the section was integrated in the context of the *sīra* considering that Shāfiʿ refers to things he has mentioned earlier.

Like Baybars and his father Qalāwūn before him, al-Nāṣir Muḥammad's ascension of the throne was not straightforward: he was first put on the throne as an infant but quickly dethroned again, only to be reinstalled a few years later. When al-Nāṣir Muḥammad abdicated at the end of this second reign, Baybars al-Jāshnikīr became sultan with the regnal title al-Muẓaffar. The section deals with this abdication, the sultan's installation at Karak, and his eventual return to power as both a reaction against bad management of the state by al-Muẓaffar Baybars and a claim of his rightful inheritance. It concludes on a unique *taqlīd* (diploma of investiture) written by Shāfiʿ himself in name of the Caliph for al-Naṣir Muḥammad's return to the throne. This is the culmination point of this narrative section, after which the annalistic account of the sultan's reign is picked up again and the elevated register of the preceding section is toned down. This only continues for a few more pages however, as the manuscript is cut off on folio 107b.

In contrast to the relatively heterogeneous first two-thirds of the text, the closing section of the manuscript reads as a thematic whole and recalls the monomyth structure of Ibn ʿAbd al-Ẓāhir's *sīra* of Baybars. The section starts with a laudatory introduction which highlights a number of important features to follow: the sultan's being chosen by God (later on more abstractly referred to as being favoured by fate), the accusatory tone against Qalāwūn's *mamlūk*s who dominated al-Nāṣir's first two reigns, and the suggestion that al-Nāṣir overcame his difficulties and established his divinely ordained authority.[323] While the text to follow contains a fair amount of narrative suspense, the sultan's return is thus already announced and is also evident from the first chapter heading which reads "An account of the third time kingship returned to our lord the sultan" (*dhikr ʿawd al-mulk li-mawlānā al-sulṭān marra thālithā*).

The departure-return structure results in strong symmetrical qualities with several elements that are directly mirrored. Particularly notable is the location of the first resting station on the way from Cairo to Syria, the Pond of the Well (Birkat al-Jubb), where two important developments take place. Shortly after the sultan's installation in Karak, his harem followed him. Uniquely, Shāfiʿ describes how al-Nāṣir Muḥammad's son behaved like a worthy successor at a banquet held at the same Pond and that courtly ceremonial was performed in honour of the young

322 Bnf MS Arabe 1705, 9a, 13a, 15a, 18a, 22b, 23b, 35a, 46a, 49a, 57a, 65b, 67a. While not an unusual phrase per se (Ibn ʿAbd al-Ẓāhir also uses it three times in *Tashrīf*, 29, 88), it does seem to have been a mannerism of Shāfiʿ to use it so extensively. He also uses variations of it several times in *Faḍl* (28, 38, 59, 69, 100, 114, 118, 139, 140, 150, 156, 162) and *Ḥusn* (66, 113, 118, 172, 264, 321).
323 See for a translation Van Den Bossche, "Literarisierung Reconsidered," 475.

son.[324] This scene is mirrored at the end of the section when al-Nāṣir Muḥammad returns to Cairo together with the Syrian armies which had flocked to him. Here, before re-ascending the throne he chooses Birkat al-Jubb as the location for celebrating the Feast of Sacrifice. The sultan's departure and his return are thus both accompanied by a rich banquet and extensive ceremonial, including the distribution of robes of honour "according to habit."[325] The situation is not just one of repetition but of a reversal of fortunes: whereas in the son's banquet the amirs Baybars and Sallār are portrayed as humbling themselves before the sultan's infant child but arguably in a context that is insincere and haughty, now Baybars is on the run after abdicating and Sallār comes before the sultan "frightened and fearful, searching for a way out of his [imminent] destruction, entreating that he had not left obedience [to the sultan] and had not taken off its noose from his neck." Shāfiʿ uses this symmetrical construction to stress the narrative growth of the sultan's glory. If in the first instance ʿAlāʾ al-Dīn takes over his father's duties, in the second excerpt the sultan himself, at this point a fully grown man, is presented as a paragon of ideal rule. Shāfiʿ implies that it is the sultan's coming of age which allows him to finally triumph over his oppressors and to come into his own as ideal ruler. While his departure is framed in glorious language but with several comments denoting the impure intentions of his companions, upon his return, any trace of doubt is erased and the sultan re-ascends the throne gloriously, as is evident from the laudatory description of his ascension of the Citadel:

وكان قد عزم على الإقامة يوم عيده * والطلوع إلى القلعة ثانيه بمقتضى يُمن الطالع وسعيده * ثم بدى له أنّه لا طالع أسعد من رقية إلى منبر مُلكه وطلوعه * وعوده والعَوْد أحمد إلى منبر سلطنته ورجوعه * فركب في موكِبه وَالشَّمسُ في قبّة شرفها * ودائرة آنفتها وأنفها * والنجوم قد قارنته سعودها * وتنازل دون علوّ ركابه صعودها * وقد استغنى ببيض الصفائح عن سود الصحائف النجومية ووثق بمتونها في جلاء الشك الريب عملًا ونية وبات ليلته ببعض قاعاتها وأصبح جالسًا بايوان ملكه العالي الرواق الباهر الإشراق * الحسن النطاق *

He had decided to celebrate the day of his Feast [of Breaking the Fast at the Pond of the Well] and to ascend the Citadel on the following day as decreed by the good fortune of the ascendant

324 The son was likely the infant al-Manṣūr ʿAlāʾ al-Dīn ʿAlī (d. 710/1310), who was only five or six years old at the time, based on Frédéric Bauden's "The Qalawūnids: A Pedigree" in: http://mamluk.uchicago.edu/qalawunids/qalawunid-pedigree.pdf In the manuscript his name is consistently blotted out (three mentions on 75r, 75v, and 76r), perhaps because he died shortly after the events depicted in this account. This would suggest that this part was written before 709/1310, but the manuscript only finished later. The much later historian Ibn Ḥajar al-ʿAsqalānī notes that this son came to al-Nāṣir Muḥammad from Karak when the latter returned to Cairo (which would mean that the son joined his father before the sultan's re-ascension) and was loved by his father because he was his only child at that point. He died while his father was hunting. Ibn Ḥajar al-ʿAsqalānī, *Durar*, 3:190.

325 Arabe 1705, 90b–91b.

> and its auspicious [sign]. Then it appeared to him that no ascendant had been more auspicious than his mounting and his ascent of the dais of kingship, and his return to the pulpit of his sultanate and his restitution—for finishing what one started is commendable! So he rode triumphantly as the sun in in the dome of its elevated place and [in] the sphere of its pride and freshness. And the stars had aligned their good fortune to him, so that he dismounted [to attain on foot], without the greatness of his mounts, the insurmountable difficulty, and he could dispense with the draft pages in favour of the clean copies of the stars,[326] trusting in action and intention in [those pages'] contents [in his struggle] against the manifest doubt and the suspicion.[327]

The astronomical metaphors and the sultan's following of good fortune underline that this was an action of excelling, an attainment of a predestined position by way of overcoming the doubts and uncertainties of his second reign. This is even further underlined by a mixing of astronomical metaphors with terminology of manuscript reproduction, in which al-Nāṣir Muḥammad's third ascent of the throne is as it were a move from a "draft copy" of sultanship (that is, his second reign) to a clean copy (that is, his third reign).

Other elements of symmetry are used as contrast: the most obvious of these is the respective portrayal of al-Nāṣir Muḥammad (and by extension his son) and Baybars al-Jāshnikīr who reigned as sultan for nine months while al-Nāṣir Muḥammad was in Syria. While the first is portrayed as having fortune and fate by his side the latter is portrayed as an incompetent ruler who only sits on the throne by the grace of his supporters. Once those supporters start switching sides to al-Nāṣir Muḥammad's camp, Baybars's authority starts to crumble. This crumbling support is also symbolically refracted: when the news reaches him of al-Nāṣir Muḥammad moving towards Cairo with growing military support, he is depicted as throwing his turban on the ground in anger.[328] Considering the importance attached to headgear by sultans of the Cairo Sultanate, this can be understood as a symbolical relinquishment of authority.[329] Baybars is generally defined as having destiny against him while al-Nāṣir Muḥammad is basically flying on the wings of fortune. Following a speech in *sajʿ* by the sultan situated at the point where he is about to enter the

326 Literally the "white of the pages" and the "black of the pages," derived from terms related to clean copies (*mubayyaḍa)* and draft copies (*musawwada*) common to manuscript reproduction.

327 Arabe 1705, 91b.

328 Arabe 1705, 86b. Note also that Baybars is never named by his regnal title but always by a reference such as "the aforementioned" (*al-mushār ilayhi*) or by his personal name "Baybars," whereas al-Nāṣir Muḥammad is either called by his regnal title or by the reverential *mawlānā al-sulṭān* (our lord the sultan).

329 Albrecht Fuess, "Sultan with Horns: The Political Significance of Headgear in the Mamluk Empire," *MSR* 12, no. 2 (2008), 71–94.

Egyptian lands, the author concludes that "there is no doubt that Egypt['s future] is auspicious and this good omen is a confirmation [of that]."[330]

Conspicuously absent from this narrative and from much of the *sīra* in general is Shāfiʿ himself as the *kātib* whose presence was so crucial in *al-Faḍl al-Maʾthūr* and the able abridger who constructed *Ḥusn al-Manāqib*. It is likely that our author at this point did not enjoy the same position towards the sultan as he did a few decades earlier. Yet he is not entirely absent, and he does make his presence felt at a crucial point at the end of this section, as the author of the Caliph's *taqlīd*. This document is introduced as follows:

> وأنشا المملوك جامع هذه السيرة التي هي في الحقيقة عنوان السيّر والمتضمنة ما أرى به ملكها على من عبر من الملوك وغير تقليدًا مناصبًا للواقعة ترتاح إليه كل أذن سامعه وضمنه صورة العهد المجدّد من أمير المؤمنين لمولانا السلطان خلد الله ملكه
>
> The *mamlūk* who compiled this *sīra*—which, in truth, is the epitome of *sīras*, the contents of which show its king surpassing [the deeds of those] kings who passed and [whose days have] elapsed—composed the diploma of investiture to be declared for the occasion, which satisfied every ear that heard it, and its contents are a copy of the renewed contract from the Commander of the Faithful for our Lord the Sultan—may God perpetuate his kingship.[331]

The statement is of course significant in the context of Shāfiʿ's claims to historiographical authority, but it is also contextually significant because of its relation to the preceding part and the text of the *taqlīd* itself. However, we need to read beyond the pages of the *sīra* itself to evaluate the full weight of this statement. When Baybars al-Jāshnikīr ascended the throne, he too had a *taqlīd* written for his ceremonial investiture, and al-Ṣafadī and others tell us that this *taqlīd* was written by Shāfiʿ's relative ʿAlāʾ al-Dīn b. ʿAbd al-Ẓāhir. This is said to be one of the reasons why al-Nāṣir Muḥammad "hated" him.[332] Shāfiʿ's claim (not confirmed by any historian) to have written al-Nāṣir Muḥammad's own *taqlīd* may be seen in the light of the competition between him and his relatives that is also discernible in *al-Faḍl al-Maʾthūr*. The present *taqlīd* suggests something along these lines when it reads "this contract dispenses with any other contract for anyone other than the sultan,"[333] thus positioning the diploma itself as a reaction against a former contract, which we can contextually surmise to have been ʿAlāʾ al-Dīn b. ʿAbd al-Ẓāhir's diploma for Baybars.

---

330 Arabe 1705, 90a.
331 Arabe 1705, 96r.
332 Al-Ṣafadī, *Wāfī*, 15:349 (lemma for caliph al-Mustakfī (Sulaymān), in which ʿAlāʾ al-Dīn's authorship is noted), 22:53 (lemma for ʿAlāʾ al-Dīn in which mention is made of al-Nāṣir Muḥammad "hating him" because of his association with Sallār and his writing of the document). See also al-Maqrīzī, *al-Sulūk li-Maʿrifat Duwal al-Mulūk*, 4 vols., ed. Muḥammad M. Ziyāda and Saʿīd ʿAbd al-Fattāḥ ʿAšūr (Cairo: Lajna al-taʾlīf waʾl-nashr, 1939–1972), 2:48.
333 Arabe 1705, 96b. هذا عهد ناقص من سواه لمن سواه من العهود

In the end, Shāfiʿ is once more able to steer the attention at least for some time back to himself. Of course, as in his other texts, he had been present all along by way of the intricate prose that dominates the *sīra* as well as through an earlier quoted document and poetry, but here he comes to the foreground again as an active participant in history. The question whether this *taqlīd* written by Shāfiʿ was also effectively used in the sultan's ceremonial third investiture, or if it was only composed as a textual exercise of variation, in line with other documents quoted by the author in *Faḍl* must remain unresolved until further evidence emerges. Within the *sīra*, however, the *taqlīd* serves to refract the preceding discourse in the elevated stylistic register of *inshāʾ* writing, and not the relatively toned-down register usually employed in writing history.

3.7 Conclusion

"Here is the past," wrote Virginia Woolf, and although she meant it ironically, our authors may be thought of as similarly stating, as it were: "here is the sultan, and here are his deeds." Their *sīras* were explicitly announced in their introductions as historical works preoccupied with presenting a picture of a ruler's life and reign. But at the same time, the authors also posited their own crucial role as the ones who made sense of that life and those deeds. Because of their privileged position as prominent scribes, they believed they were the ones who could most meaningfully turn a narrative of a sultan's life into an exemplum of ideal rule. They invite us to think about how they went about presenting that life and what meanings they intended to convey by their narrative choices. Earlier scholars have regularly noted that because of their panegyric proclivities we should always take our authors' words with a pinch of salt and interpret them within the workings of patronage and praise. I hope to have highlighted the important layer of authorial agency *within* such panegyrical language and within historical narrative more generally. These authors did not just present a picture of the sultan and his life that stretched the possibilities of historical truth, it was also an illustration of the authors' performance of their own role as ideal *kuttāb* alongside the depicted sultans. The masterfully composed texts in which these narratives were embedded highlight their continuing claims to literary pre-eminence.

Chapter 4
Sīra as chancery practice: Composition and compilation

أما تسمية الكتابة كتابة: فلما نُقل عن الأصمعي أنه قال إنما سميَت كتابة لأنه يجمع بها يعض الحروف الى بعض كما يجمع الشيء الى الشيء وهو مأخوذ من الكتيبة وهي الخيل لمجموعة ولهذا اسمى الكاتب كاتبًا لضمّه الحروف بعضها الى بعض

> *On why writing is called kitāba: it is transmitted about [the early Islamic grammarian Ibn Qurayb] al-Aṣmaʿī [d. 216/831] that he said: "writing is called kitāba because it gathers letters, similar to how a thing is gathered with other things. It is derived from* katība *which means a herd of horses. And because of this a writer is called* kātib *because he joins letters to other letters."*[334]

These lines are taken from the beginning of *al-Raʾy al-Ṣāʾib*, a chancery manual written by Shāfiʿ b. ʿAlī. The pole position of these lines in the text suggests that this definition of writing as "gathering letters" was a fundamental one for a discussion of writing in general. The etymological explanation he cites is limited to the gathering of letters of the alphabet as a basic prerequisite for the act of writing words and sentences, but in his *sīras* he also frequently uses the derived form *jāmiʿ* ("compiler, gatherer") to denote his own agency. Notably, such statements almost always precede the citation of a document or poem he has written himself.[335] The *kātib* is thus not just a gatherer of letters of the alphabet, but also one who compiles poems, documents, and other materials, inserting them in their appropriate textual context. Simply gathering alphabetical letters into words and sentences will not automatically lead to a *kitāb* ("book"). To attain the more advanced stage of writing one needs the talent or at least the education to gather letters into meaningful wholes, one needs to be familiar with the rules of eloquent composition to craft worthwhile sentences and texts. A similar rationale appears in al-Nuwayrī's vast encyclopaedia *Nihāyat al-Arab*, at the outset of his discussion of the importance of scribes to a ruler.[336] Al-Nuwayrī's placement of this etymology draws attention not just to the practical side of writing, as Shāfiʿ does in his chancery manual, but also to its political importance. Like our authors, al-Nuwayrī assigns to *kuttāb* the crucial role of gathering the necessary linguistic prerequisites for the sultan's claim to power.

334 Shāfiʿ b. ʿAlī, *al-Raʾy al-Ṣāʾib*, MS Ahmet III 2583, 2b.
335 *Faḍl*, 127, 143, 156; Arabe 1705, 48a. He also uses it to refer to his uncle in *Ḥusn*, 164, 216.
336 This leads off the long final (14th) subchapter of his fourth chapter about what and whom a ruler should rely on. Al-Nuwayrī, *Nihāyat*, 7:3; *The Ultimate Ambition in the Arts of Erudition*, transl. Elias Muhanna (New York City: Penguin Books, 2016), 103.

https://doi.org/10.1515/9783110753028-005

While the *sīras* are essentially historical-biographical works—hence why I have foregrounded that aspect in my organisation of chapters—the primary official function of both our authors was as chancery agents working in the *dīwān al-inshāʾ*. Scholars have acknowledged the importance of this background extensively. Already early on, the European reception of some of these texts was focussed on the fact that they contain valuable diplomatic material. The early interest in this material can for example be seen on the manuscript of *Tashrīf al-Ayyām* (BnF MS Arabe 1704): preceding its title page there is a French note detailing the text's contents, one part of which is especially appreciative of the diplomatic material.[337] This note was written by the Benedictine monk and early orientalist Dom Berthereau (d. 1794), presumably when the manuscript was still preserved at the Abbey of Saint-Germain-des-Prés. The manuscript also has several marginal notes in Latin identifying the start of such letters. These possibly even predate Berthereau's note. In the next century, when the manuscript had moved to the French national library, the orientalist Marc-Étienne Quatremère edited and translated some of these diplomatic documents as an appendix to the third volume of his widely read *Histoire des sultans mamlouks*, a partial translation of al-Maqrīzī's *al-Sulūk*, published between 1837 and 1845.[338] This interest continued in the 20th century and culminated in P.M. Holt's translation of several treaties concluded between Baybars and Qalāwūn and Latin states, many of which are found in the *sīra* corpus. As we have already seen, Holt also pioneered the influential evaluation of these texts as emanating from a propagandistic chancery institution. Diplomacy and historical writing were seen as part of a legitimising continuum, even if it had the opposite effect on the perception of these texts' reliability: whereas the inclusion of diplomatic material made them important sources in the absence of preserved archival documents,[339] the legitimising aspect of their historiographical contents was problematic for a reconstruction of the historical events.

---

337 This part of the note reads (I have not updated the French spelling): "Cette vie est tres detaillée et ce que je nai vu dans aucune autre historie, on y trouve tout au long des diplomes ou traités de paix et de commerces avec des remarques de lauteur sur la singularité des scrivants et des signatures, scavoir avec les templiers et hospitaliers, les francs de s. jean dacre, la reine de saide les rois de chipre, de sicile et darragon; plus des letters apportées par des ambassadeurs et les reponses." MS Arabe 1704, unfoliated flyleaf.

338 Taki-Eddin-Ahmed-Makrizi, *Histoire des sultan mamlouks*, 4 tomes, transl. Marc-Étienne Quatremère (Paris: Oriental Translation Fund of Great Britain and Ireland, 1837–1845), tome 2 volume 1:158–235.

339 See now for criticisms of the idea that few physical documents have been preserved: Frédéric Bauden, "Mamluk Diplomatics"; Marina Rustow, *The Lost Archive: Traces of a Caliphate in a Cairo Synagogue* (Princeton: Princeton University Press, 2020).

In this chapter I re-evaluate the position of the chancery and its importance to the historiographical endeavour. Much of the material discussed in chapters two and three has already underlined the centrality of this kind of thinking to how our authors conceived of *sīra*. In the present chapter I expand on this discourse about the centrality of the chancery. I argue that the sultanic biography was a textual genre that functioned within the linguistic, stylistic, and topical idioms common to the *dīwān al-inshā'*. To better understand the position of this discourse of the *dīwān*, I argue that we must more closely evaluate the function of *inshā'* discourses and documents within the texts, paying attention to matters of compilation and wholeness. The "gathering" of letters of the alphabet which Shāfiʿ uses to explain the etymology of writing, may be taken a little further then, and we can understand composition (*inshā'*) as a larger gathering of discourses and documents. These practices of compilation will be the focus of section 4.4. of this chapter. Two subsections here serve as case studies of how documents came to be integrated into the *sīras*.

Understanding how such compilatory and discursive practices function with respect to the chancery, it is however important to first gain an understanding of how the chancery worked in this time and place. Hence, this chapter start with a re-evaluation of the chancery and its workings itself in section 4.1. An image of the chancery as a rather well-defined institution is still common in the field, largely based on extensive information taken from the monumental chancery manuals composed about a century after our authors. As will become clear, however, the normative representation of these manuals cannot always be applied wholesale to the late 7th/13th century context. I will highlight how the representation of the chancery in the *sīra* corpus suggests rather an institution in the sense of Bourdieu's view of fields of interaction and the operation of a habitus within such fields. That is, the chancery, like the literary field, was a circumscribed field of action in which a set of normative practices were continuously produced and reproduced by agents claiming membership of the field. Its appearance as an institution should be considered in conjunction with the appearance of the court, discussed at length in chapter six of this book, and revolves around the power dynamics particular to a sultan's reign. I develop this line of thinking especially in the chapter's first section on the chancery's formal organisation and the second section, where I look at how our authors came to work in the chancery. Section 4.3. considers how the chancery appears in the *sīra* corpus discursively, that is, as an idea informing how authors wrote about the sultanate. The fourth section then moves on to textual practices common in the chancery field as reflected in the *sīra* corpus.

4.1 Chancery

The practices and functions of the chancery in the late medieval period are detailed at considerable length in a few chancery manuals.[340] The best-known author of such a work is Shihāb al-Dīn al-Qalqashandī (821/1418) who wrote an encyclopaedic multi-volume work entitled *Ṣubḥ al-Aʿshā fī Ṣināʿat al-Inshāʾ*.[341] This text deals extensively with all the types of knowledge deemed appropriate for an aspiring *kātib* to study. It is especially concerned with discussing and quoting at considerable length the various types of texts he should be able to write or interpret. Many letters and documents by earlier masters—including our authors—were reproduced whole or in part to illustrate the various forms such texts could take and the evolution they had gone through before al-Qalqashandī's own time. He also included a great amount of historical information on the roles and make-ups of the chancery in earlier times. As such, while presenting a normative vision of the chancery of his own time, al-Qalqashandī also explicitly posits an institution that had evolved in significant ways throughout the centuries. Similar large-scale synthetic works, which are somewhat less exclusively focused on the chancery, such as al-Nuwayrī's *Nihāyat al-Arab fī Funūn al-Adab,* and some of the works of Shihāb al-Dīn b. Faḍl Allāh al-ʿUmarī (d. 749/1349), further add to our understanding of the workings of the chancery.[342] From a slightly earlier period, there are also a few works more narrowly focussed on *inshāʾ* as a stylistic concern, such as *Ḥusn al-Tawassul fī Ṣināʿat al-Tarassul* (Achieving Excellence in the Art of Epistolography), written by our authors' contemporary and direct peer Shihāb al-Dīn Maḥmūd b. Fahd al-Ḥalabī.[343] Shāfiʿ b. ʿAlī's own *al-Raʾy al-ṣāʾib,* from which I have cited above is more akin to this latter work than to the later chancery manuals.

340 For a general overview of the evolution of the chancery throughout pre-modern Islamic history, see Maaike L.M. van Berkel, "Archives and Chanceries: pre-1500, in Arabic," *EI3.*

341 An early study of this work, specifically focussed on how it describes the formal operation of the chancery and its history over time, is Walter Björkman's *Beiträge zur Geschichte der Staatskanzlei im islamischen Ägypten* (Hamburg: Friedrichsen, De Gruyter & co., 1928). Björkman also provides an extensive annotated overview of its contents, pp. 75–177. A more literary study of al-Qalqashandī's work has recently been undertaken by Rebecca Sauer in her habilitation thesis "Towards a Pragmatic Aesthetics of the Written Word: al-Qalqashandī (d. 821/1418) between Balāgha and Materiality" (Unpublished habilitation thesis, Heidelberg University, 2018) (non vidi). I am grateful to one of the peer reviewers of the present book for directing my attention to these works.

342 He composed a chancery manual proper *al-Taʿrīf biʾl-Muṣṭalaḥ al-Sharīf* as well as the more wide-ranging encyclopaedic text *Masālik al-Abṣār fī Mamālik al-Amṣār.*

343 Shihāb al-Dīn Maḥmūd's text remained popular and was published already in the late 19th century. *Ḥusn al-Tawassul ilā Ṣināʿat al-Tarassul* (Cairo: Maṭbaʿat Amīn Afandī Hindīyah, 1315 [1897]). It was a major source for al-Qalqashandī's *Ṣubḥ al-aʿshā*. Björkman, *Beiträge*, 77. On these works in general, see: Elias Muhanna, "Why was the 14th century a century of Arabic encyclopaedism?"

These chancery manuals present the chancery as entailing a variety of *dīwāns*, or "bureaus." Among others, there was a financial bureau, a bureau dealing with army matters (*dīwān al-jaysh*), and most importantly for our purposes, a bureau invested with official communication, the *dīwān al-inshāʾ*. These were mirrored at smaller scale in provincial governorates and in the personal *dīwāns* of highly placed amirs. Ibn ʿAbd al-Ẓāhir and Shāfiʿ b. ʿAlī are both best known as *kuttāb* in the *dīwān al-inshāʾ*, but they both appear to have worked in regional and/or amiral bureaus before joining the Cairo chancery. Such trajectories appear to have been common (see below, section 4.2.). The *dīwān al-inshāʾ* dealt with high profile correspondence and public discourse in documents such as diplomas of investiture (*taqlīd*, pl. *taqālīd*) and contracts (*ʿahd*, pl. *ʿuhūd*). Leading this bureau also sometimes entailed the responsibility of advising the sultan in political decisions. This was especially pronounced under Ṣalāḥ al-Dīn, two of whose closest advisors, al-Qāḍī al-Fāḍil and ʿImād al-Dīn al-Iṣfahānī, served him in the first place as *kuttāb*—the former had started working in the Fatimid chancery before eventually being promoted to vizier (*wazīr*). By the second half of the 7th/13th century, however, this hierarchy had taken on a different form: now the vizier and the *dawādār* (bearer of the royal inkwell) dominated this position of closely advising the sultan and overseeing the chancery. Neither of these two positions were innovations, but the specific functions they fulfilled are distinct from those occupied by predecessors under the Fatimids and Ayyubids. They were furthermore more often occupied by members of the military elites.[344] As we shall see, some of the *kuttāb* in our purview were directly linked to these agents through patronage.

The actual *kuttāb* were led by a *ṣāḥib dīwān al-inshāʾ* (master of the composition bureau). Various sources tell us that this function was transformed into that of *kātib al-sirr* (confidential secretary) during the reign of al-Manṣūr Qalāwūn, but both terms continued to be used interchangeably for a while or were ambiguous even to later authors.[345] Most sources tell us that the first person to hold the title of

---

in *Encyclopaedism from Antiquity to the Renaissance*, eds. Jason König & Greg Woolf (Cambridge: Cambridge University Press, 2013), 343–356. This article was later revised as the first chapter of *The World in a Book: al-Nuwayrī and the Islamic Encyclopedic Tradition* (Princeton, NJ: Princeton University Press, 2017).

344 Maaike van Berkel has argued that this shows "a growing influence of the sword over the pen." M. van Berkel, "The People of the Pen: Self-Perceptions of Status and Role in the Administration of Empires and Polities," in *Prince, Pen, and Sword: Eurasian Perspectives*, eds. Maaike van Berkel and Jeroen Duindam (Leiden: Brill, 2018), 402.

345 Consider for example the fact that Shihāb al-Dīn b. Faḍl Allāh al-ʿUmarī is denoted as *ṣāḥib dawāwīn al-inshāʾ* on a manuscript (Danmarks Kongelige Bibliotek, MS Cod. Arab 294) dedicated to his library by al-Ṣafadī, despite al-ʿUmarī being active only around the second quarter of the 8th/14th century. The text is a holograph of al-Ṣafadī's own *Kashf al-Ḥāl fī Waṣf al-Khāl* (Revealing the Situation

kātib al-sirr was Fatḥ al-Dīn b. ʿAbd al-Ẓāhir, who took over his father's leading role in the *dīwān al-inshāʾ* when he became too old to actively lead the bureau.[346] When al-Nāṣir Muḥammad later abolished the post of vizier itself, the *kātib al-sirr* was assigned a number of his duties and was significantly boosted in importance.[347] At the same time, however, the title *wazīr* was sometimes liberally applied as an honorary title, similarly to the title *qāḍī*, "judge." Ibn ʿAbd al-Ẓāhir was often designated with the latter title by later writers even though there is no indication he had any legal expertise, let alone held the position of judge,[348] and Shāfiʿ repeatedly designates him as *wazīr* in *Ḥusn al-Manāqib*.[349]

These transformations and liberal usages of terminology already highlight that the seemingly stable institution as described in normative manuals like al-Qalqashandī's *Ṣubḥ al-Aʿshā* were still in flux in the 7th/13th century. Unfortunately, the earlier *adab al-kātib* manuals by Shāfiʿ b. ʿAlī, Shihāb al-Dīn Maḥmūd and even Ibn Faḍl Allāh al-ʿUmarī are overwhelmingly focussed on *inshāʾ* as a textual practice and do not provide much clarification about the institutional make-up of the chancery in their own day. Some material may however be taken from them as well as from our authors' own references to their activities in the *sīras*.

A division of labour in the *dīwān al-inshaʾ* has been foregrounded in scholarly research, with scribes working as either *kuttāb al-dast* (scribes of the bench)[350] and

about Describing Beauty Marks). See for a reproduction and a discussion of the manuscript and other holographs of al-Ṣafadī's work: Élise Franssen, "al-Ṣafadī: The Scholar as a Reader," 137.

346 The anecdote usually given as triggering Qalāwūn's rationale for instating a *kātib al-sirr* involves Ibn ʿAbd al-Ẓāhir miswriting an appointment given to him by the *dawādār*, so that it was incomprehensible. Baybars then complained to Ibn ʿAbd al-Ẓāhir who claimed that he wrote it exactly as the *dawādār* had spelled it out, upon which Baybars exclaimed that the sultan should have a private *kātib al-sirr* to whom the sultan could dictate directly. Qalāwūn apparently overheard this and would go on to establish the position when he became sultan. Al-Ṣafadī, *Wāfī*, 10:178–179.

347 Bernadette Martel-Thoumian, *Les civils et l'administration dans l'état militaire mamelouke (IXe/XVe siècle)* (Damascus: Institut français, 1992), 41; Eychenne, *Liens personnels*, 68. Shāfiʿ usually refers to his cousin Fatḥ al-Dīn as *ṣāḥib dīwān al-inshāʾ* and only once calls him *kātib sirrihi*, which I argue below does not denote an actual function in this phrasing. *Faḍl*, 61. He uses the same form for his uncle in the introduction of *Ḥusn*, 55. Al-Ṣafadī (who related the anecdote referred to above) and even Ibn Taghrī-Birdī still referred to Fatḥ al-Dīn b. ʿAbd al-Ẓāhir as *ṣāḥib dīwān al-inshāʾ*. Al-Ṣafadī, *Wāfī*, 17:135; Ibn Taghrī-Birdī, *Manhal*, 7:99.

348 Al-Qalqashandī denotes him consistently with that title in *Ṣubḥ*, 1:137,176; 6:310; 7:353, 357, 360, 366; 8:40, 120, 299; 9:270, 407; 11:7, 116, 166, 179.

349 *Ḥusn*, 155, 164, 186.

350 The *dast* refers to the "platform" or "place of honor" on which they were seated during sessions in the *dār al-ʿadl* (court of justice). I follow al-Musawi's translation of it as "bench" which feels more idiomatic. Muhsin Al-Musawi, "Pre-Modern Belletristic Prose," in *Arabic Literature in the Post-Classical Period*, eds. Roger Allen and Donald S. Richards (Cambridge: Cambridge University Press, 2008), 101.

kuttāb al-darj (scribes of the scroll).[351] While both functions entailed the composition of chancery documents overseen or commissioned by the *ṣāḥib* and later the *kātib al-sirr*, they did so largely in different contexts. The role of the *kuttāb al-dast* was that of intermediaries between petitioners and the sultan in the *dār al-ʿadl*: they read out the petitions and applied the sultan's verdict (*tawqīʿ*) to them.[352] By contrast, *kuttāb al-darj* mostly occupied themselves with composing correspondence and royal discourse: they formulated or copied texts commissioned by the *ṣāḥib* (or later, the *kātib al-sirr*), the *dawādār*, or the *wazīr*.

In the *sīras* this division of labour does not appear at all. A certain distinction is however suggested by the fact that they sometimes specify the appearance of scribes of the *darj*. By contrast, they never even mention the *dast*, despite relatively regular discussion of sessions in the *dār al-ʿadl*.[353] When examining all the explicit mentions of *darj* in the *sīras* a suggestive pattern emerges, however. Shāfiʿ only uses it twice: first to identify his presence in the sultan's service as *kātib darj* in a discussion of Qalāwūn's work on a canal connecting the Nile to the Buḥayra region.[354] Shāfiʿ mentions this to stress the fact that he observed Qalāwūn himself participating in the digging. He thus implies that a *kātib darj* was to be understood as a title for a scribe who personally accompanied the dignitary he served. This idea is reinforced by the second case where Shāfiʿ uses the phrase *kātib darj*—again without defining particle—in *Ḥusn al-Manāqib*. Here he mentions how after the ceremonial of the inauguration of and pledge of allegiance to the Abbasid caliph in Cairo under Baybars, al-Ḥākim bi-Amr Allāh, the caliph was allowed to go around as he pleased, and was even assigned a secretary, that is, a *kātib darj*—named as Sharaf al-Dīn b. al-Maqdisī al-Dimashqī—before Baybars became concerned about his potential power and forbade him to leave the Citadel.[355] The idea here is again

351 This division of labour appears to have already existed in the Fatimid period. Björkman, *Beiträge*, 22. However, even in al-Qalqashandī's time this theoretical division was not necessarily followed strictly, as he commented that in his time, the 130 *kuttāb al-darj* employed in the *dīwān* were incapable, and that most of their work was done by more able *kuttāb al-dast*. Al-Musawi, "Pre-Modern Belletristic Prose," 110.

352 Martel-Thoumian, *Les civils*, 44. See also Jorgen S. Nielsen, *Secular Justice in an Islamic State: Maẓālim Under the Baḥrī Mamlūks (662/1264–789/1387)* (Istanbul: Nederlands Historisch-Archeologisch Instituut, 1985), 85–87.

353 *Rawḍ*, 176, 188, 197, 249; *Tashrīf*, 32; *Ḥusn*, 75–77, 142, 157–158, 202–204, 219–221.

354 *Wa-kuntu fī khidmatihi kātib darj*, "I was a scribe of the scroll in his service." *Faḍl*, 172. Note that he uses an *iḍāfa* without defining particle. Like most of the accounts in *Faḍl*, Shāfʿ provides no date here. Amalia Levanoni notes that work on the Ṭayriyya canal was undertaken in 682/1283. Levanoni, *Turning Point*, 258.

355 *Ḥusn*, 114. This information is confirmed by other historians. See for a digest: Mustafa Banister, "The *ʿĀlim*-caliph: Reimagining the Caliph as a Man of Learning in Eighth/Fourteenth and

that a *kātib darj* is a personally assigned scribe rather than someone representing a particular institutional affiliation.

Ibn ʿAbd al-Ẓāhir at first glance appears to have understood *kātib al-darj* more in line with al-Qalqashandī's definition. He uses the singular form *kātib al-darj al-sharīf*—"scribe of the noble scroll"—three times in the specific context of identifying scribes who would go out to secure oaths from Frankish principalities.[356] In a fourth case he uses *kuttāb al-darj al-sharīf* to refer to seven scribes who were summoned to be present at a ceremonial occasion following Baybars' destruction of a Christian church in the hinterland of Acre in the year 661/1262, early in Baybars' reign. The scribes listed here were part of a larger gathering of the sultan's various servants, including also the *kuttāb al-jaysh* (scribes of the army bureau) and the treasurers, to witness the honouring and promotion of various members of the sultan's military retinue. In the list of *kuttāb al-darj*, he mentions Fakhr al-Dīn b. Luqmān, whom he also just identified as "*wazīr al-ṣuḥba*," Badr al-Dīn al-Mawṣilī, Shihāb al-Dīn b. ʿUbayd Allāh, a certain Burhān al-Dīn, Kamāl al-Dīn b. al-ʿAjamī, and Fatḥ al-Dīn b. al-Qaysarānī.[357] The fact that he does not mention himself here is notable. He may not have done so simply because he was not actually present.

While Ibn ʿAbd al-Ẓāhir thus appears to use the phrase *darj al-sharīf* more precisely in these instances, the fact that he always does so with a specific designation of who exactly represented it indicates that he did in fact use it similarly to Shāfiʿ. Taking all these instances together, the *darj* appears not so much as a title one holds at all times, but as a status of being invested with the authority to represent the sultan's textual authority in a particular time and place. This does not mean the status was entirely unstable. The right to represent the sultan's authority would only be given to scribes from the inner circle of the chancery, that is, experienced scribes who were trusted to act as personal secretaries to the sultan. This is how Ibn ʿAbd al-Ẓāhir's and Shāfiʿ's presentation of the *darj* can be made to agree: as personal secretaryship writ large. Not so much a clearly defined institution or title then, but a recognition of status dependent on context, where the *darj* was a recognition of an agent's privileged personal position vis-à-vis the sultan and an investment of the sultan's textual authority to someone who can formulate it linguistically.

Ninth/Fifteenth-Century Egypt," in *Knowledge and Education in Classical Islam: Religious Learning Between Continuity and Change*, ed. Sebastian Günther (Leiden: Brill, 2020), 745.

356 *Rawḍ*, 283 (naming Shams al-Dīn b. Quraysh), 329 and 398 (naming Fatḥ al-Dīn b. al-Qaysarānī in both cases). These scribes will reappear below.

357 *Rawḍ*, 160–161. See preceding footnote for this Fatḥ al-Dīn b. al-Qaysarānī.

The idea that the division of labour between *darj* and *dast* was not clearly established yet in the 7th/13th century is also suggested by an important list of scribes of Baybars' *dīwān al-inshā'* given by ʿIzz al-Dīn b. Shaddād in his biography of Baybars—it forms part of a section where he provides such lists for various different offices in the sultanate.[358] Ibn Shaddād had intimate knowledge of the organisation of Baybars' state, as he himself worked as a secretary to Baybars' vizier Bahā' al-Dīn b. Ḥinnā.

ملك–رحمه الله–وفي ديوان الإنشاء من الكتّاب القاضي فخر الدين إبراهيم ابن لقمان الأسعدي، والقاضي محيي الدين عبيد الله بن الشيخ رشيد الدين عبد الظاهر، وشمس الدين يوسف بن قريش وبدر الدين حسن بن علي الموصلي، وأخوه جمال الدين حسين بن علي، وولدا عبيد الله زين الدين وأخوه. ثم استكتب في أيامه كمال الدين أحمد بن عز الدين عبد العزيز بن أبي جعفر محمد بن العجمي الحلبي، وفتح الدين عبد الله بن القيسراني الحلبي. ثم استدعى الصدر الكبير العالم الفاضل تاج الدين أحمد بن الصدر شرف الدين أبي البركات سعيد بن شمس الدين أبي جعفر محمد بن الأثير من دمشق، وفوض إليه أمر المترجم على عادته في الأيام الناصرية، وسعد الدين سعد الله بن مروان الفارقي، وفتح الدين محمد بن القاضي محيي الدين عبيد الله بن عبد الظاهر، وعلاء الدين أحمد بن قاضي القضاة زكي الدين المعروف بابن الزكي قاضي القضاة دمشق، ثم صرف، وعز الدين عبد العزيز بن كمال الدين أحمد العجمي بحكم وفاة والده.

[When Baybars] came to power—God have mercy on him—the *kuttāb* in the *dīwān al-inshā'* were:

- the *qāḍī* Fakhr al-Dīn Ibrāhīm b. Luqmān al-Asʿadī
- the *qāḍī* Muḥyī al-Dīn ʿUbayd Allāh b. al-Shaykh Rashīd al-Dīn ʿAbd al-Ẓāhir
- Shams al-Dīn Yūsuf b. Quraysh
- Badr al-Dīn Ḥasan b. ʿAlī al-Mawṣilī
- and his brother Jamāl al-Dīn Ḥusayn b. ʿAlī
- and the two sons of ʿUbayd Allāh: Zayn al-Dīn
- and his brother.

Then were appointed as *kuttāb* (*thumma staktaba*) during his reign:

- Kamāl al-Dīn Aḥmad b. ʿIzz al-Dīn ʿAbd al-ʿAzīz b. Abī Jaʿfar Muḥammad b. al-ʿAjamī al-Ḥalabī
- Fatḥ al-Dīn ʿAbd Allāh b. al-Qaysarānī al-Ḥalabī
- Then the honourable (*al-ṣadr*), the great, the knowledgeable, the excellent Tāj al-Dīn Aḥmad, son of the honourable Sharaf al-Dīn Abī l-Barakāt Saʿīd b. Shams al-Dīn Abī Jaʿfar Muḥammad b. al-Athīr was summoned from Damascus, and he was entrusted with overseeing espionage (*amr al-mutarjim*) as he had been used to in the days of al-Nāṣir [Yūsuf].

[Were also appointed] (*wa-*):

- Saʿd al-Dīn Saʿd Allāh b. Marwān al-Fāriqī
- Fatḥ al-Dīn, son of the *qāḍī* Muḥyī al-Dīn ʿUbayd Allāh b. ʿAbd al-Ẓāhir

358 He provides similar lists for the office of vizier, *dawādār*, judges, as well as a range of military officials. He does not, however, discuss any of the other chancery bureaus.

- ʿAlāʾ al-Dīn Aḥmad, son of the chief *qāḍī* Muḥyī al-Dīn Yaḥyā, son of the chief *qāḍī* Zakī al-Dīn, known as Ibn al-Zakī, the chief *qāḍī* of Damascus, who was later dismissed (*thumma ṣurifa*)
- ʿIzz al-Dīn ʿAbd al-ʿAzīz b. Kamāl al-Dīn Aḥmad b. al-ʿAjamī by virtue of the death of his father [mentioned above].[359]

Written from the vantage point of Baybars already being dead, this list serves as an assessment of how the personnel of the chancery evolved during his reign. Six of the seven names given by Ibn ʿAbd al-Ẓāhir for the group of scribes present at Acre also appear here, five of them as being in the chancery at the start of Baybars' reign (so presumably they were already in their position during Quṭuz's short reign), and the other two as joining after he came to power—the only one not represented here is the Burhān al-Dīn mentioned by Ibn ʿAbd al-Ẓāhir.[360] Given that most of these names are also mentioned in Ibn ʿAbd al-Ẓāhir's 661/1262 list or are known to us from elsewhere, Ibn Shaddād's presentation of the *dīwān al-inshāʾ* here appears comparable to Ibn ʿAbd al-Ẓāhir's interpretation of the *darj*. Rather than presenting a large institution involving dozens of officials, both historians present the *dīwān* as essentially being represented by an inner circle of scribes who could be invested with the authority of representing the sultan's textual presence.

Ibn Shaddād's list also highlights the importance of scribal families, with several agents following their fathers into the chancery—note in that sense the appearance of not just one but three sons of Ibn ʿAbd al-Ẓāhir.[361] A close reading of the list also changes our perception of the hierarchy in the chancery given in other sources. No leader is explicitly identified here. We know that Fakhr al-Dīn b. Luqmān was the leader of the chancery in Baybars' early reign and that at some

---

359 ʿIzz al-Dīn b. Shaddād, *Taʾrīkh al-Malik al-Ẓāhir*, 238–239.

360 By the middle of the 8th/14th century, the great scribe Shihāb al-Dīn b. Faḍl Allāh al-ʿUmarī only included two of the scribes listed here in his overview of important Egyptian scribes: Tāj al-Dīn b. al-Athīr and Kamāl al-Dīn b. al-ʿAjamī. He also included Fatḥ al-Dīn b. al-Qaysarānī's son Sharaf al-Dīn in this list. It is remarkable that he omitted Ibn ʿAbd al-Ẓāhir. *Masālik*, 12: 260–269 (lemma about Tāj al-Dīn [b. al-Athīr]), 269–271 (lemma about Kamāl al-Dīn b. al-ʿAjamī), 290–293 (lemma about Sharaf al-Dīn b. al-Qaysarānī).

361 I have not come across other mentions of a Zayn al-Dīn b. ʿAbd al-Ẓāhir, and it appears to me unlikely that "his brother" denotes Fatḥ al-Dīn b. ʿAbd al-Ẓāhir (the only son of Ibn ʿAbd al-Ẓāhir mentioned by other authors) as he is named in full a few lines below. The fact that Ibn ʿAbd al-Ẓāhir is named ʿUbayd Allāh here (unlike ʿAbd Allāh by most other historians) is also notable. Ibn Shaddad is consistent in doing so: he also introduces him as such when reproducing his elegy for Baybars. ʿIzz al-Dīn b. Shaddād, *Taʾrīkh al-Malik al-Ẓāhir*, 244. I presume these two sons died long before Ibn ʿAbd al-Ẓāhir himself died, and that they faded from the historical record. The likely younger Fatḥ al-Dīn as a result gained in status and eclipsed the memory of his older brothers.

point Ibn ʿAbd al-Ẓāhir took over this role, but from this list we do not actually get the impression of a change of roles.

This is not to say that such hierarchies did not exist and were not influential at certain times, but that we must be careful in interpreting them as defining an institution for the whole of a reign. If we can conceive of the chancery as an institution, then it is much like a smaller version of the state at this time: a household formation defined by interpersonal dynamics, and especially by the relationship of these individuals to the sultan himself or to his representatives the vizier and the *dawādārs*. The chancery as such was continuously recreated and renegotiated by those agents amongst each other. The textual evidence given by authors so far removed in time as al-Qalqashandī should not be taken at face value but must be carefully compared and aligned with the contemporary evidence. A similar impression emerges when we consider how authors ended up working in the chancery, to which we will turn now.

4.2 Career paths and patronage

As the list of scribes given by Ibn Shaddād indicates, Ibn ʿAbd al-Ẓāhir was already a member of the *dīwān al-inshāʾ* at the start of Baybars' sultanate. For a long time I believed he must have accessed the chancery after gaining a position of some fame in Cairene literary circles. One of his most famous texts, a *risāla* (epistle) in which he denounced an unnamed Shīʿī criticiser, is dated to 653/1255 or 1256. This dating is given by al-Ṣafadī who claimed to have copied it in full "from [Ibn ʿAbd al-Ẓāhir's] handwriting."[362] In his biographical lemma on Ibn ʿAbd al-Ẓāhir, al-Ṣafadī also includes another *risāla* (epistle) "presented as a gift to a number of high-ranking *kuttāb* in the days of al-Muʿizz [Aybak, d. 655/1257]," which starts off by praising the importance of their writing.[363] Considering that Ibn ʿAbd al-Ẓāhir did not have any known association with the *dīwān*, I assumed that he used this work to gain a position there by currying favour from a patron. His sudden appearance in a high position in the *dīwān* some years later suggests that this strategy worked.

The discovery of the Sofia manuscript compiling various types of correspondence by or addressed to Ibn ʿAbd al-Ẓāhir changes the picture significantly. Most importantly, the text includes specimens of official letters written for the Ayyubid ruler of Damascus al-Malik al-Ṣāliḥ Ismāʿīl b. al-ʿĀdil (r. 634–643/1237–1245, with an

362 See the introduction to chapter five for references, a partial translation, and more details on this text.
363 al-Ṣafadī, *Wāfī*, 17:141. أهداها إلى جماعة من الكتاب في الأيام المعزية الأقدار

interruption, d. 648/1250).[364] Rather than debuting in Cairo, our author thus first appears on the scene in Damascus, only to reappear about a decade later in Cairo. The letter addressed to scribes serving al-Muʿizz Aybak was thus more likely meant to secure a *new* position in Cairo after having left Damascus. In any case, it is likely that he had a function under Quṭuz, given ʿIzz al-Dīn b. Shaddād's listing him as a *kātib* at the start of Baybars' reign.[365]

The first piece of chancery writing Ibn ʿAbd al-Ẓāhir quotes himself dates from Baybars' early years as sultan: a diploma of investiture (*taqlīd*) for the first Abbasid caliph of Cairo al-Mustanṣir in 659/1261. It was written not by our author but by Fakhr al-Dīn b. Luqmān (d. 693/1293) whom he at this point specifically refers to as *ṣāḥib dīwān al-inshāʾ*.[366] Ibn ʿAbd al-Ẓāhir continues to refer to Ibn Luqmān as *ṣāḥib* throughout the first quarter of his *sīra* of Baybars.[367] By the time the second Cairene Abbasid caliph al-Ḥākim (d. 701/1302) was instated in 660/1262, the prestigious

---

364 Sofia MS Or. 2026, 95a. This letter is addressed to a certain al-Malik al-Saʿīd from al-Malik al-Ṣāliḥ Abī al-Khaysh. While the compilation provides no further information on them, they are likely al-Saʿīd Ḥasan who ruled Banyās from 630 to 644 and al-Malik al-Ṣāliḥ Ismāʿīl b. al-ʿĀdil who ruled Damascus from 637 to 643 and died in 648. The same manuscript also contains a letter sent by al-Malik al-Ṣāliḥ—either the same as above, or the Egyptian sultan al-Ṣāliḥ Ayyūb (d. 647/1249)—to al-Malik al-Manṣūr of Hama (d. 683, ruled there from 642) informing him about the purchase of a falcon. Sofia MS Or. 2026, 95a. For the reigns of Ayyubid princes, I rely on R. Stephen Humphreys, *From Saladin to the Mongols: The Ayyubids of Damascus, 1193–1260* (Albany: State University of New York Press, 1977), 381–386.

365 Al-Qalqashandī quotes a diplomatic letter written to Yemen during Quṭuz's reign which he "thinks" was written by Ibn ʿAbd al-Ẓāhir, but Eliyahu Ashtor has argued convincingly that this is a case of mistaken royal identities: the letter was not sent from al-Muẓaffar Quṭuz to a Yemeni ruler with the regnal title al-Manṣūr, as no such ruler is known for that time, but from al-Manṣūr Qalāwūn to al-Muẓaffar Yūsuf, two decades later. Al-Qalqashandī, *Ṣubḥ*, 7:360–362; Strauß (Ashtor), "Muḥyî'ddîn b. ʿAbdaẓẓâhir," 198. There is another moment where al-Qalqashandī is clearly mistaken when ascribing a text to Ibn ʿAbd al-Ẓāhir: a short diploma of investiture for al-Nāṣir Muḥammad dating to 717/1317 cannot have been written by him as our author died even before al-Nāṣir Muḥammad's first ascension of the throne. One wonders whether maybe it was written by Shāfiʿ who was sometimes denoted with the family name Ibn ʿAbd al-Ẓāhir as well.

366 *Rawḍ*, 101. Identical in Shāfiʿ, *Ḥusn*, 81; al-Qalqashandī, *Ṣubḥ*, 11:111.

367 *Rawḍ*, 161, 163. Ibn Luqmān's own career path is a bit better known due to a lemma devoted to him in Ibn al-Ṣuqāʿī's *Tālī Kitāb Wafayāt al-Aʿyān*, a work that is unusually informative about the career paths of *kuttāb*, due to Ibn al-Ṣuqāʿī's own background as a scribe. Ibn al-Ṣuqāʿī tells us that Ibn Luqmān served in Āmid before its conquest by the Ayyubid sultan al-Malik al-Kāmil (d. 635/1238), upon which he was taken in by his vizier Bahāʾ al-Dīn b. Zuhayr, who would continue to serve al-Ṣāliḥ Ayyūb as vizier. The famous historian Ibn Wāṣil was active in the same circles and enjoyed a similar *ṣuḥba/mulāzama* relation with the vizier (see Hirschler, *Medieval Arabic Historiography*, 19–20, 23) before transferring to the service of Ibn Ḥinnā. It is not known what Ibn Luqmān did in the decade between al-Ṣāliḥ Ayyūb's death and Baybars' ascension when he appears again as leader of the *dīwān* and according to Ibn al-Ṣuqāʿī would go on to "ascend [the hierarchy] until he became *wazīr*" himself

khuṭba (Friday sermon) delivered in the presence of Mongol messengers from the Golden Horde was according to Shāfiʿ written by his uncle. This suggests that only a year later, the "competition" that some later historians allege existed between Ibn ʿAbd al-Ẓāhir and Fakhr al-Dīn b. Luqmān may have turned out in favour of the former.[368]

Earlier studies of the chancery and scribes have shown that gaining a position based on personal merit was rare. J.H. Escovitz has argued that heredity, clientelism and venality were the more common ways into the chancery.[369] The rise of Ibn ʿAbd al-Ẓāhir's son Fatḥ al-Dīn into the chancery was doubtlessly at least in part through heredity. ʿIzz al-Dīn b. Shaddād lists him as one of the *kuttāb* who joined the *dīwān al-inshāʾ* during Baybars' sultanate,[370] and Ibn ʿAbd al-Ẓāhir himself refers to letters composed by his son in the year 670/1271.[371] We have more information about how he eventually became *ṣāhib* and reportedly the first *kātib al-sirr* during Qalāwūn's reign. Al-Ṣafadī notes that "he became master [of the *dīwān al-inshāʾ*] in the *dawla* of al-Manṣūr [Qalāwūn] because of his insight (*ʿaql*), his vision (*raʾy*), his ambition (*himma*), and the closeness (*taqaddum*) to his father, the *qāḍī* Muḥyī al-Dīn [b. ʿAbd al-Ẓāhir]." This suggests a mixture of merit and heredity. Further on, however, he mentions that it was Ibn Luqmān who chose Fatḥ al-Dīn as his successor when he was asked to name a substitute upon being appointed vizier by Qalāwūn.[372] Al-Ṣafadī, al-Nuwayrī and Ibn al-Ṣuqāʿī all mention that he attained a position of influence (*tamakkana*) under Qalāwūn and al-Ashraf Khalīl.[373] Al-Nuwayrī adds that after his death in mid-Ramaḍān

in Qalāwūn's days. Ibn al-Ṣuqāʿī, *Tālī*, 9. On whether either Ibn Luqmān or Ibn ʿAbd al-Ẓāhir effectively led Baybars' chancery, see the comments by Holt, "A Chancery Clerk," 671.

368 Shāfiʿ, *Ḥusn*, 108. Ibn ʿAbd al-Ẓāhir includes the same sermon, but does not mention its author: *Rawḍ*, 142–143. Shāfiʿ's claim is corroborated by al-ʿUmarī, *al-Taʿrīf biʾl-Muṣṭalaḥ al-Sharīf*, ed. Muḥammad Ḥusayn Shams al-Dīn (Beirut: Dār al-Kutub al-ʿIlmiyya, 1988), 121 and several later historians. For the claim of "competition," see Kühn, *Sultan Baibars*, 240 n. 268.

369 Escovitz, "Vocational Patterns of the Scribes of the Mamlūk Chancery," *Arabica* 23, no. 1 (1976), 42–62. For the 9th/15th century, see Martel-Thoumian, *Civils*, 82–92. For a wider diachronic discussion of backgrounds and social status of people working in chanceries of the Middle Period, see Adrian Gully, *The Culture of Letter Writing in Pre-Modern Islamic Society* (Edinburgh: Edinburgh University Press, 2008), 72–101. The best study of social relations behind gaining a position in the chancery is Matthieu Eychenne's *Liens personnels*, which throws light on the individual trajectories several scribes with data gathered from biographical dictionaries.

370 *Taʾrīkh al-Malik al-Ẓāhir*, 239 (see 4.1. above for translation).

371 *Rawḍ*, 392. Fatḥ al-Dīn is not mentioned by name, however, so it is possible one of his two other sons is meant here.

372 Al-Ṣafadī, *Wāfī*, 3:290.

373 Ibn al-Ṣuqāʿī even notes that "he travelled a road not travelled by any other vizier or scribe." *Tālī*, 119.

691/August 1292, "the sultan al-Malik al-Ashraf [Khalīl] bestowed his salary (*jāmikiyya*), daily food rations (*jirāya*), and his pay (*rātib*) to his son, the *qāḍī* 'Alā' al-Dīn 'Alī and he remained among the *kuttāb al-inshā'*."[374] The position of *kātib al-sirr* was however not given to 'Alā' al-Dīn at that time, according to Baybars al-Manṣūrī because he was too young.[375] His entry into the chancery when he was only eleven years old in 686/1287 is undoubtedly once more a marker of the strength of heredity as a road to the *dīwān*. Later on, he cast his lot with the powerful amir Sallār (d. 710/1310), who, as we have seen, dominated politics during al-Nāṣir Muḥammad's second reign in consort with Baybars al-Jāshnikīr. This move backfired when al-Nāṣir Muḥammad reasserted his personal authority upon his return to the sultanate.[376] In the end 'Alā' al-Dīn was lucky, however. He escaped the purges that al-Nāṣir Muḥammad undertook in the years following his return. He was also lucky to only be held back from attaining the highest point of the hierarchy and not being shifted around from department to department like many of his peers.

Aside from this last association of 'Alā' al-Dīn to Sallār and Fatḥ al-Dīn's association with Ibn Luqmān, explicit mentions of patronage are largely absent from the accounts about the Banū 'Abd al-Ẓāhir. This contrasts with what we know about many other *kuttāb* for whom patronage was crucial in attaining a position of some importance in the chancery. As noted, Ibn Luqmān himself owed his position to a vizier recruiting him, and Ibn 'Abd al-Ẓāhir's contemporary 'Izz al-Dīn b. Shaddād, often specifically stresses that he served the vizier Bahā' al-Dīn b. Ḥinnā and reserves laudatory language in large part for praising this vizier.[377] Considering his position as vizier, Ibn Ḥinnā was of course also a powerful agent to whom Ibn 'Abd al-Ẓāhir owed allegiance, and judging from how he addresses Ibn Ḥinnā in a letter sent to update the vizier on what happened during Baybars' expedition in Anatolia there was certainly a sense of hierarchy here.[378]

The distinctive autobiographical touch of Shāfi''s writings allows us to better assess his early career in the chancery. He tells us that his uncle had him write "responses" or "variations" (*mithāl*) to texts Ibn 'Abd al-Ẓāhir had written. He provides an example of this in the form of his response to the marriage contract drawn

374 Al-Nuwayrī, *Nihāyat*, 31:154–155. This is also reproduced in two separate accounts by Ibn al-Furāt, *Ta'rīkh*, 8:144, 150; and by Baybars al-Manṣūrī, *Zubdat*, 291. I wonder whether the fact that this information was relatively widely reproduced means that it was seen as unusual.

375 Baybars al-Manṣūrī, *Zubdat*, 291

376 Al-Ṣafadī, *Wāfī*, 22:53.

377 'Izz al-Dīn b. Shaddād, *Ta'rīkh al-Malik al-Ẓāhir*, 79–83 (especially 81–82), 168, 225, 234. Ibn al-Ṣuqā'ī confirms that Ibn Shaddād's "importance" during Baybars' sultanate was due to his *mulāzama* bond with the vizier. *Tālī*, 135.

378 *Rawḍ*, 454. On this letter, see section 3.4.2. below.

up for Baybars' son al-Saʿīd Baraka Qān and Qalāwūn's daughter, not long before Baybars' death. This does not mean that he was already a member of the chancery but suggests rather how his uncle trained him for this career.[379] His earliest claim to having written an official document is a letter announcing the death of Baybars to al-Saʿīd Baraka Qān in the name of Baybars' Syrian viceroy Badr al-Dīn Baylīk al-Khāzindār. This text is included at the end of *Ḥusn al-Manāqib*.[380] While he does not tell us anything about how he ended up working there, he does provide some information in his *sīra* of Qalāwūn about his ascension of the ranks in the chancery under al-Saʿīd Baraka. Near the end of this sultan's short and ill-fated reign he provides us with the following account:

> كنت مع الملك السعيد في هذه الكَرّة وكان له دواداران، أحدهما الأمير الإسفهلار سيف الدين بلبان الرومي الظاهري والآخر دونه في الرتبة وهو الأمير عز الدين أيدمر الدوادار. وكان حظّي من الأمير سيف الدين الحظ الأوفى الأوفر * ومحلّي من تقدمته المحلّ الأعلى الأكبر * فإنه هو الذي ندبني بخدمة السلطان وعول عليّ في سر المكاتبات وجهرها على صغر سنّي وكِبَر قدر وسنّ من في الديوان

> I was [serving] with al-Malik al-Saʿīd [Baraka] at this time, when he had two *dawādārs*. One of them was the *amīr al-isfahlār* Sayf al-Dīn Balābān al-Rūmī al-Ẓāhirī. The other, ʿIzz al-Dīn Aydamur al-Dawādār, was below him in rank.[381] I received the greatest and most abundant favour (*al-ḥaẓẓ al-awfā wa-l-awfar*) from the amir Sayf al-Dīn [Balābān] and the fact that I took up the highest and most exalted position was his doing (*min taqdimatihi*). For he was the one who appointed me to serve the sultan, and he relied on me for both secret and public correspondence (*sirr al-mukātabāt wa-jahruhā*) despite my young age and the greatness of the capacity and age of those who were [already] in the *dīwān*.[382]

The anecdote continues to detail how Shāfiʿ decided not to write a letter to the Ismāʿīlīs to request their help in Baraka's struggles with Qalāwūn, despite Baraka

---

379 *Faḍl*, 32, document on pp. 32–35, preceded by Ibn ʿAbd al-Ẓāhir's text on 28–32. Shāfiʿ uses the term *ṣila* here to denote the relationship to his uncle. This term usually implies a form of patronage relationship but may have been used with a more familiar connotation here.

380 *Ḥusn*, 342–348. Given the relatively lively information he provides about sessions in the *dār al-ʿadl* during Baybars' reign in the same text (for example, 202–207), I wonder whether he may have worked as a *kātib al-dast* before moving up in the ranks in the later years of Baybars' sultanate. This must remain entirely hypothetical however, as he provides no information about this and never even mentions the *dast*.

381 On the fact that there were two *dawādārs*, note this information given by al-Ṣafadī about a predecessor of this ʿIzz al-Dīn, Ḥusām al-Dīn Lājīn al-Aydamurī al-Darfīl (d. 672/1273 or 1274): "the sultan had appointed this Ḥusām al-Dīn and Sayf al-Dīn Balābān al-Rūmī to the post of *dawādār*. When Balābān al-Rūmī travelled around as envoy, this Ḥusām al-Dīn would take over the duties of *dawādār*." Al-Ṣafadī next cites two elegiac epigrams for him written by Ibn ʿAbd al-Ẓāhir and a longer elegy by Sirāj al-Dīn al-Warrāq. *Wāfī*, 24:391. Both of Ibn ʿAbd al-Ẓāhir's poems are also found in his *Dīwān*, 52–53, 66.

382 *Faḍl*, 49.

requesting Shāfiʿ to do so. Instead, Shāfiʿ defected to Qalāwūn's camp. The historicity of the account may be doubtful, as no other author mentions Shāfiʿ's actions, which are here effectively portrayed as part of the *coup de grâce* for Baraka's sultanate, but it is insightful for the relation between *dawādār* and *kātib*. Balābān's importance to the *dīwān* is clear here: Shāfiʿ claims that he was the one who could appoint *kuttāb* to high positions and deal directly with them, even when they served the sultan. However, we also know that Balābān's loyalty towards Baybars cost him his position when Qalāwūn took power. The new sultan shifted responsibilities between offices and in the process curtailed the wide-ranging duties of the *dawādār*.[383]

The fact that Shāfiʿ explicitly names Balābān al-Rūmī as his patron is interesting because one might have expected his uncle Ibn ʿAbd al-Ẓāhir in that role. Beyond the reference to his uncle having him write responses, Shāfiʿ never implies that his position in the chancery was dependent on his uncle's influence.[384] At a later point he claims to have been "a *kātib* of *inshāʾ* [...] in the *ṣuḥba* of [al-Manṣūr Qalāwūn],"[385] only to add a few pages later that he accompanied Balabān al-Rūmī, also using the same term "*ṣuḥba*."[386] This term, which is related to a meaning of companionship, was an oft-used denominator in conjunction with, or more or less synonymous to the term *mulāzama*, for a variety of close personal relationships between individuals.[387] The fact that Shāfiʿ could use the term interchangeably to refer to either the *dawādār* or the sultan implies that his *ṣuḥba* to Balabān was indirectly also a *ṣuḥba* to the sultan, as Balabān himself enjoyed a *ṣuḥba* relationship to Baybars, being an amir from his own Ẓāhirī *mamlūk* corps.[388] Furthermore, this relationship was apparently flexible

383 Northrup, *From Slave to Sultan*, 241.

384 At one point he does reproduce a suggestive little part of direct colloquial speech from Qalāwūn ordering Ibn ʿAbd al-Ẓāhir to write a number of documents, in which Qalāwūn says "take your two children" (*khudh waladayak*). Considering the context, I assume these two "children" are Fatḥ al-Dīn and Shāfiʿ. *Faḍl*, 52.

385 *Ḥusn*, 271. The sultan is not explicitly mentioned in this sentence, but it is contextually clear that he is the only likely candidate for this *ṣuḥba* relationship.

386 *Ḥusn*, 275.

387 Hirschler, *Medieval Arabic Historiography*, 19–20; Eychenne, *Liens personnels*, 43–45.

388 Other sources suggest that Balabān was not an easy patron. Ibn al-Ṣuqāʿī and al-Yūnīnī both relate how he harshly reprimanded two Damascene *kuttāb* who had neglected to send him their accounts for seven years. When they were not able to produce the totality of the accounts on the day after his arrival to Damascus—he was passing through upon a return journey from Tripoli where he had just visited as envoy (*tawajjaha rasūlān ilā Ṭarābulus*)—he had them beaten and their noses and beards cut off. Eychenne, *Liens personnels*, 65–66. Balabān al-Rūmī's centrality to Baybars' *dawla* would remain well known in later periods. The much later historian Ibn Taghrī-Birdī (d. 874/1470) for example writes that after the death of Ḥusām al-Dīn Lājīn al-Aydamurī

(or it was conceivable to present it as flexible), for at another point our author claims to have refused to oblige the sultan's order to accompany Balabān on a mission to Tripoli because he did not want to affront his cousin Fatḥ al-Dīn and because he had doubts about the effectiveness of the mission. Here, apparently, Shāfiʿ's *ṣuḥba* relationship was overridden by family loyalties.[389] Coincidentally, Balabān al-Rūmī died during the same Battle of Homs in which Shāfiʿ himself was blinded. In his own account of this event, cited in chapter one (1.2.), Shāfiʿ makes no mention of Balabān and notes instead that he was in the company of Shams al-Dīn b. Quraysh, one of the scribes also noted by Ibn ʿAbd al-Ẓāhir and ʿIzz al-Dīn b. Shaddād in their lists above.

There is an interesting occurrence of a note written by Balabān al-Rūmī (and another one by his otherwise unattested son) on an important manuscript of Bahāʾ al-Dīn b. Shaddād's biography of Ṣalāḥ al-Dīn, now held in Berlin, dated to the early years of Qalāwūn's reign but praising Baybars.[390] This note not only makes Balabān's relationship to Qalāwūn even more interesting, it also shows that someone in the highest echelons of power had an interest in sultanic biographies. This may help to explain why three of the scribes he worked with wrote their own such biographies of the sultans they served. It suggests a historiographic reading culture in the courtly orbit, which may have been conducive to the relative boom of *sīra* writing observable at this time. Note in that sense also that the 8th/14th century historian Ibn al-Dawādārī continuously stresses his father's connections to Balabān al-Rūmī on the title pages of the nine volumes of his universal chronicle *Kanz al-Durar*. While Balabān's interest in history is tantalising, with the evidence currently available it can be no more than hypothetical. In the remainder of this chapter I will discuss more substantial evidence for the ways in which the chancery influenced the composition of the *sīras*.

---

he took over the management of state affairs by himself, and that there was as such no need for a vizier. Although this assessment is incorrect, considering the contemporary information we have about Baybars' powerful vizier Bahāʾ al-Dīn b. Ḥinnā, it does show the posterior image of Balabān's towering influence. Ibn Taghrī-Birdī, *al-Nujūm al-Zāhira fī Mulūk Miṣr waʾl-Qāhira,*16 vols., ed. Muḥammad Ḥusayn Shams al-Dīn (Beirut: Dār al-Kutub al-ʿIlmiyya, 1992), 7:296.

389 *Faḍl*, 148. This mission to Tripoli may be the same as the one from the anecdote in the preceding footnote.

390 Staatsbibliothek zu Berlin, MS Wetzstein II 1893, fols 233b–235a. See chapter six for a transcription and translation of this note.

4.3 *Sīra* as expression of *inshāʾ* identity

Muhsin al-Musawi refers to the *sīras* as "a genre which, almost *ipso facto*, sits at the very centre of the tradition of belles-lettres."[391] This assessment is doubtlessly due to the kind of material they compile extensively—artful letters, poems—but also due to the fact that the language register employed even for the writing of history was so thoroughly related to *inshāʾ* practices. The term *inshāʾ* had already earlier become a stand-in for both the practice of epistolography and the specific language register used in letter writing. This register is marked by an artful and complex interweaving of prose and poetry, often famous one-liners that were apposite to the subject at hand. In Jo Van Steenbergen's words this register was "part of the increasing social importance of literature, having become a wide-ranging skill that was a defining aspect of elite identities and a predominant channel for verbal elite communications."[392]

A defining feature of *inshāʾ* is its reliance on cadenced rhyming prose (*sajʿ*). This stylistic had become the norm in chancery writing in preceding centuries, but it also gained a prominent presence in texts unrelated to correspondence writing around the turn of the (common era) millennium. One of the greatest writers to extensively use the stylistic, Badīʿ al-Zamān al-Hamadhānī (d. 395/1109), made it a defining characteristic of an innovative and widely influential new genre, the *maqāma*, which was further perfected by his student al-Ḥarīrī (d. 516/1122). The latter's *maqāmāt* continued to be extensively copied and commented upon during our authors' times.[393] The genre remained hugely popular and is of direct relevance to our authors: one of Ibn ʿAbd al-Ẓāhir's most celebrated writings was a *maqāma*[394] and Shāfiʿ lists a collection of *maqāmāt* among his writings in the *ijāza* given to al-Ṣafadī.[395] One of the most well-known examples of the period is a *maqāma* on

391 Muhsin al-Musawi, "Pre-Modern Belletristic Prose," 123–124.

392 Van Steenbergen, "Qalāwūnid Discourse," 19.

393 Al-Musawi, "Pre-Modern Belletristic Prose," 114–117; Matthew L. Keegan, "Commentators, Collators, and Copyists: Interpreting Manuscript Variation in the Exordium of Al-Ḥarīrī's Maqāmāt," in *Arabic Humanities, Islamic Thought: Essays in Honor of Everett K. Rowson*, ed. Joseph Lowry & Shawkat Toorawa (Leiden: Brill, 2017), 307–308. Al-Ṣafadī produced an exquisite manuscript copy of his own commentary on al-Ḥarīrī's *maqāmāt* in 720/1320–1321 (Royal Danish Library, ms Cod. Arab. Add. 83). For two reproductions and a discussion of the manuscript, see: Franssen, "al-Ṣafadī: The Scholar as a Reader," 128–131.

394 Quoted in full by al-Ṣafadī in *Wāfī*, 17:137–141.

395 Named simply *al-Maqāmāt al-Nāṣiriyya*, in which the latter term probably refers to his *kunya* Nāṣir al-Dīn. Al-Ṣafadī, *Aʿyān*, 507.

the art of *kitāba*, that is, official writing, and a term often more or less synonymous with *inshā'*, written by al-Qalqashandī.[396]

Despite its contemporary stylistic ubiquity, scholars of medieval Islamic history have tended to look down on the florid style of writing, especially in the context of historiography, suggesting it is something one needs to wade through rather than appreciate in itself.[397] The tension between a so-called "simple style" and an "artificial" or "ornate style" has been explored in the context of Persian historiography, but the rhetorical qualities of Arabic historical writing have received less attention.[398] Admittedly, the style often makes for difficult reading due to its predilection for rare words and rhetorical flourishes. However, as Henri Massé has rightly noted, in ʿImād al-Dīn al-Iṣfahānī's *al-Fatḥ al-Qussī*, a notably successful Arabic historical text with about two dozen known manuscript copies, the use of rhyme does not necessarily complicate the reading and the historical narrative often remains easy to follow. This is especially the case for a reader who is well acquainted with the stylistic qualities to which the text adheres.[399] The corpus of *sīra*s represents an interesting set of texts in which these qualities and their textual functions may also be evaluated. While not per se representative of Arabic historical writing of the period at large, it does form a cohesive set of texts that is at least representative of a distinctive type of history writing. A careful evaluation of the stylistics used by Ibn ʿAbd al-Ẓāhir and Shāfiʿ respectively would be interesting to pursue as well, as generally it would seem the former had a less convoluted style than the latter. The

---

396 Clifford E. Bosworth, "A 'maqāma' on Secretaryship: al-Qalqashandī's 'al-Kawākib al-durriyya fī'l-manāqib al-Badriyya'," *BSOAS*, 27 no. 2 (1964), 291–298; Muhsin J. al-Musawi, "Vindicating a Profession or a Personal Career? Al-Qalqashandī's *Maqāmah* in Context," *MSR* 7, no. 1 (2003), 111–135; Rebecca Sauer, "Al-Qalqašandī's maqāma *al-Kawākib ad-durrīya:* A Re-Consideration Within the Framework of Ego-Document," in *Islamische Selbstbilder: Festschrift für Susanne Enderwitz*, ed. Sarah Kiyanrad, Rebecca Sauer & Jan Scholz (Heidelberg: Heidelberg University Publishing, 2020), 253–269. In the latter article, Sauer argues that al-Qalqashandī's *maqāma* is not just an ego-document but also expresses a "scribal 'esprit de corps'."

397 For a classic derogatory attitude towards rhymed prose, see Franz Rosenthal, *A History of Muslim Historiography* (Leiden: Brill, 1968), 176–179. He concludes: "All in all, whatever attractiveness the use of rhymed prose may have added to historical literature in the eyes of the cultured reader, it made no contribution to a deepening of the historical understanding, nor did it produce an essentially new form of historical presentation."

398 Julie S. Meisami, "History as Literature," in *A History of Persian Literature X: Persian Historiography*, ed. Charles Melville & Ehsan Yarshater, (New York: I.B. Tauris, 2012), 19–34. Lutz Richter-Bernburg has evaluated the rhetorics of excerpts from ʿImād al-Dīn al-Iṣfahānī's *al-Barq al-Shāmī* and compared them to earlier artfully written historical texts by al-Ṣābī, al-ʿUtbī, and al-Qāḍī l-Fāḍil that are commonly cited as having been his inspirations in *Der Syrische Blitz*, 137–189.

399 ʿImād al-Dīn al-Iṣfahānī, *La conquête de la Syrie et de la Palestine*, transl. Henri Massé, ed. Charles Pellat (Paris: Paul Geuthner, 1972), x.

fact that Shāfiʿ's prose was designated as "dull" by at least one pre-modern reader is notable in that sense.[400] Understanding why pre-modern readers make such assessments remains difficult however, even if recent research has done much to understand the modalities behind Arabic literary criticism.[401]

One of the few scholars who has devoted somewhat more extensive attention to the stylistics of *inshāʾ* writing in the *sīras* and its influence on the historiographical form used by our authors is Anne Troadec. She rightly claims that such language use has a performative aspect to it. However, she limits this performative layer to the actual staging of a text's contents in the context of oral communication, linked to the idea of the text serving a legitimising end. Authors would embed sultanic feats into a timeless narration of the Islamic past ("the past in service of the present") and perform it in a public courtly setting by reading their texts out loud.[402] While this may indeed have been the case, this is a rather reductive interpretation of performance. It can be argued that *sajʿ* is highly performative as a display of prowess in a style of writing held to be the ultimate form of written expression in secretarial milieus. I argue that these texts were performative in the sense that they perform a *kātib*'s mastery of specific stylistic forms and textual genres of high literary technicality, and not because they were literally performed at court.[403]

As we shall see below, letters and other official documents which originated from or were at least related to the professional practice of *inshāʾ* took up important positions in the *sīras*, and although these were often demarcated and signposted in their textual surroundings, the section boundaries do not divide the language registers, which work rather according to an internal logic across the texts. One example of how such language even bleeds into how sections are signposted is found in Ibn ʿAbd al-Ẓāhir's *sīra* of al-Ashraf Khalīl. The section that follows it is also particularly illuminating for ideas of what kinds of writing he considered appropriate for a *kātib* of his stature. Its introductory *dhikr* refers to the ensuing contents in *sajʿ*:[404]

---

400 al-ʿUmarī, *Masālik*, 19:224.

401 On the nature of how pre-modern authors evaluated literary quality, see Adam Talib, "Al-Ṣafadī, His Critics, and the Drag of Philological Time," *Philological Encounters* 4 (2019), 109–134.

402 Troadec, "Les Mamelouks" 82–84.

403 For a similar argument, see Erez Naaman, *Literature and the Islamic Court: Cultural Life Under al-Ṣāḥib b. ʿAbbād* (London: Routledge, 2016), 26. Naaman claims that al-Qāḍī al-Jurjānī's writing in the ornate *inshāʾ* style in his *Tahdhīb al-Taʾrīkh* was "valued not only for its historical content but equally for its rhetorical merits. [His introduction] aimed at illustrating his excellent prose style, and hence it is a manifestation, or position-taking in the terms of Pierre Bourdieu, in the literary field."

404 Of *Alṭāf*'s twenty *dhikr* headings, only one other has a similar "non-informative" construction, while a second one is both informative and "literary" (by using rhyme). *Alṭāf*, 41, 49.

ذكر تدبير ملوكي
أعاد هجته * وأراح مهجه * وأوضح محجه

Report of a royal measure
which restored [the sultan's] gaiety, gladdened his soul, and elucidated his method.[405]

This header introduces a report about al-Ashraf Khalīl's reorganisation of sultanic correspondence: the viceroy Badr al-Dīn Baydarā and vizier Shams al-Dīn [b. al-Salʿūs] would take care of minor correspondence. The bulk of this chapter then discusses the loftiness of sultanic correspondence, starting with a discussion of how it had been of the greatest importance since time immemorial but had been corrupted by al-Muʿizz Aybak and his successors. It was finally duly reinstated by al-Ashraf Khalīl, who is praised for this action.[406] Ibn ʿAbd al-Ẓāhir uses the format of the *dhikr* heading not just to signal what is to follow but as a variation of its central message: the praise of the mutually reinforcing bond between sultan and scribe, for the actions described are said to have gladdened the sultan. These are the first lines immediately following the header:

المكاتبات السلطانية كانت لها حرمة في قديم الزمان * وإنها لا يظفر بها الا ذو حظ عظيم من الملوك الأكابر وأعيان الأعيان*

There was a sacredness to sultanic correspondence in the old times, and only the most auspicious of rulers[407] and the most eminent of the elite would take care of it.[408]

The fact that Ibn ʿAbd al-Ẓāhir spent a considerable amount of space singing the praises of this policy decision is telling about what he thought to be important in the management of the state. In his view, proper organisation of correspondence was crucial for the smooth running of the sultan's *dawla*. It is notable that the section ends on a praise poem that employs themes and motifs from the genre of debates between the pen and the sword.[409] This was a well-established genre going back to ancient Near Eastern literary practice of textual debates.[410] By the time of

405 *Alṭāf*, 36. For the layout, see BSB Cod. arab 405, 51b.

406 This type of argument is of course something of a scribal trope. See for example the paraphrase of our author's colleague Ibn al-Mukarram's praise of Qalāwūn's lavish endowment of the medical sciences cited in Muhanna, *The World in a Book*, 65.

407 Note that the term *ḥaẓẓ* used here also appears in the lines I quoted from Ibn ʿAbd al-Ẓāhir's elegy for Baybars at the start of chapter two. There it was associated with the status of a great scribe who would compose odes, letters and *sīras*.

408 *Alṭāf*, 36.

409 *Alṭāf*, 38–39.

410 For a historical overview and discussion of some typical examples of the genre, see Geert-Jan van Gelder, "The Conceit of Pen and Sword: On an Arabic Literary Debate," *Journal of Semitic Studies*, 22, no. 2 (1987), 329–360; Jaakko Hämeen-Anttila, "The essay and debate (al-risāla and al-munāẓara)," in *Arabic Literature in the Post-Classical Period*, eds. R. Allen and D.S. Richards

our authors, many great earlier authors had participated in this debate form, in which they often argued directly or indirectly for the primacy of the pen: through a display of the advantages of language and writing and by being written in a virtuoso register that showcased the author's superior command of language.[411] Our authors at several points worked elements of the discursive tradition into their own works. Shāfiʿ b. ʿAlī told al-Ṣafadī that he wrote a work entitled *al-Durr al-Munaẓẓam fī Mufākharat al-Sayf waʾl-Qalam* ("The Systematised Pearls: the Boasting of the Sword and the Pen").[412] In ʿAbd al-Ẓāhir's take on the genre the poem starts out on a fairly equal tone, but throughout the following lines it is clear that the pen is associated with far more positive qualities than the sword, especially when the poet says how "by this one misfortunes (*ṣurūf*) are removed, while by that one they are caused."[413] This resonates with what Ibn ʿAbd al-Ẓāhir argues throughout this section, namely that there is an association of a sultan's political success to the correspondence written in his name. While detailing the sultan's initiatives to put the administration of the kingdom in order—he uses the term *tadbīr*, or "arrangement," a common term in Arabic Mirrors for Princes in the title—Ibn ʿAbd al-Ẓāhir takes this a step further in his composition, by claiming that the sultan's authority is not only established by the help of swords and manpower, but even more so by those that articulate his claim to power in eloquent prose.

The above example shows how Ibn ʿAbd al-Ẓāhir creatively reiterated the discourse on the importance of *inshāʾ* writing to the sultan's political project. In section 3.3. I have highlighted how Shāfiʿ similarly invoked the authority of the chancery repeatedly in his *sīra* of Qalāwūn. The most obvious way in which our authors foregrounded the importance of the chancery, however, was by including specimens of texts authored by chancery agents, especially themselves. In the next section I give an overview of this material and discuss two examples in more detail. Broadly speaking I argue that compiled documents need to be understood contextually: close attention needs to be paid to how authors embedded documents in their texts

(Cambridge: Cambridge University Press, 2008), 134–144. For a cross-cultural perspective, see van Berkel, "The People of the Pen," 440–446.

411 See for a description of such a text written by al-Ṣafadī: Gully, *The Culture of Letter Writing*, 54. See also chapter three of that work in general.

412 Al-Ṣafadī, *Aʿyān*, 2:507. Al-Ṣafadī also quotes and approves of the literary merit (*jawwadahā*) of a relatively short prose text by ʿAlāʾ al-Dīn b. ʿAbd al-Ẓāhir entitled *Risāla fī ʾl-Mufāḍala Bayna ʾl-Rumḥ waʾl-Sayf* ("Epistle on the comparison between the spear and the sword"), which is tangentially related to the topic. Al-Ṣafadī, *Wāfī*, 22:54–56.

413 *Alṭāf*, 39. Ibn ʿAbd al-Ẓāhir's poem uses plural forms to denote the pens, and a singular form to denote the sword in this poem, perhaps to highlight the collaborative effort of *kuttāb* as opposed to an idea of singular military power of the sultan.

and how they marshalled them for narrative ends. I argue that we need to try to understand the rhetorical depth of the *inshāʾ* discourses both within and without the documents to understand what authors were trying to communicate with this material.

4.4 Compiling documents

Diplomatic material as well as documentary texts related to the management of the sultanate are amply present in the *sīras* and have received extensive scholarly attention. However, few scholars have deeply considered the reasons behind such compilatory practices.[414] The quoting of correspondence, poetry, and other assorted material is simply seen as part of how historians wrote or compiled books since the beginning of the Islamic historiographical tradition.[415] While ideas of the archival function of chronicles, especially that of Ibn al-Furāt, have been put forward by Fozia Bora recently, she was ultimately not so much interested in documentary material, but in how historians preserve historical material from earlier sources.[416] While that is a worthwhile subject in itself, it runs the risk of making the term "archive" a simple stand-in for historical citation practices.[417] In the following I conceptualise of the compilatory practices not so much as archival in the first place, but as performative record-keeping.[418] That is, I look at how our authors embedded material they or, to a lesser degree, their peers had written in chancery contexts in their historical texts and how doing so contributed to a pervasive idea of memorialisation of the chancery as constitutive to the sultan's *dawla*. While I am interested in some of the formal features of document citation and compilation, an assessment of the possibly archival function of the recording of such formal

---

414 Konrad Hirschler explicitly leaves out this "very rich corpus" in his important study "From Archive to Archival Practices: Rethinking the Preservation of Mamluk Administrative Documents," *JAOS* 136, no. 1 (2016), 3.

415 See for example the exceedingly brief discussion of this kind of material in Yehoshua Frenkel, "Mamluk Historiography Revisited: Narratological Perspectives in Damascene Chronicles" in *Mamluk Historiography Revisited: Narratological Perspectives*, ed. S. Conermann (Bonn: V&R Unipress/ Bonn University Press, 2018), 40–41.

416 Bora, *Writing History*, 14–16 and passim.

417 Compare the concerns voiced about the use of "memory" instead of historiography in the study of early Islamic historical material. Sean W. Anthony, *Muhammad and the Empires of Faith: The Making of the Prophet of Islam* (Oakland: University of California Press, 2020), 8–10.

418 I have been inspired in this by Frederik Buylaert & Jelle Haemers, "Record-Keeping as Status Performance in the Early Modern Low Countries," *Past and Present* 230 (2016), 131–150.

features would require a much broader study involving other historical texts and preserved documents.[419]

I start with an assessment of the documentary coverage in the corpus. Documents are cited in full and in paraphrased form in the *sīras*.[420] The former tend to be announced by *wa-nuskhatuhu* ("and its transcript [runs as follows]") while the latter are usually signposted by *wa-maḍmūnuhu* ("and its content is"). I have listed the types of documents—broadly defined to include a few texts which are explicitly noted as *inshāʾ* writing, but which would not usually be filed under "documents," such as a prose *tahniʾa* ("congratulation")—in Table 1.

Table 1: Documents per sīra.

Document type	*Rawḍ*	*Tashrīf*	*Alṭāf*	*Faḍl*	*Ḥusn*	*Sīrat al-Nāṣir*
Fully quoted letters	7	6		11	3	1
Paraphrases or excerpts of letters	6	3	1	1		
Taqlīd (Diploma of investiture)	2	1	2	1 (*iqṭāʿ*)	2	1
Full *tadhkira* (memorandum)	1			2		
Paraphrased *tadhkira*	1			1		
Khuṭba (Friday sermon)	1		1	1	1	
Futuwwa investiture	1		1			
Truces/peaces		4				
Inscription	1					
Inshāʾ praise texts		1		4		
ʿAqd (marriage contract)					1	
Waqf			4			
Of which explicitly written by the author	3	2	1	11	2	2

419 A study along the lines of Marina Rustow's *The Lost Archive* focused on late medieval Egypt and Syria would be most desirable in that sense.

420 While a formal subdivision of *inshāʾ* writings into *ikhwāniyyāt* and *dīwāniyyāt*, respectively letters meant for communication between friends (*ikhwān* means brothers) and acquaintances on the one hand, and letters which were written in and for the official context of the chancery on the other hand, is often mentioned, this division is not really of relevance for the *sīra* corpus, as all epistolary texts included in them are *dīwāniyyāt*. Al-Musawi, "Pre-Modern Belletristic Prose," 111. On *ikhwāniyyāt* in earlier periods, see: Naaman, *Literature and the Islamic Court,* 146–147. For a discussion of the diplomatic formalities of *ikhwāniyyāt* letters applied to two specific examples, see Frédéric Bauden, "Maqriziana XIII: An Exchange of Correspondence between al-Maqrīzī and al-Qalqashandī," in *Developing Perspectives in Mamluk History: Essays in Honor of Amalia Levanoni,* ed. Yuval Ben-Bassat (Leiden: Brill, 2017), 207–210.

As can be seen in the table, there are important differences in the relative presence of such documents across the corpus. We must thus remain careful not to make blanket statements about these practices. *Waqf* documents and truces for example appear only in single texts, but they take up substantial space in both of those texts. The most common form of document found across the corpus is letters, found in all texts if we include paraphrased letters in our purview. *Taqlīd* documents are found in all texts, but not in large numbers.

In the following discussion I will limit myself to two specific clusters of examples—only the first cluster of which appears in the table above, for reasons that will become clear—as they throw light on the reasons for and logic behind the inclusion of documents in our texts. A few further documents will be discussed in chapter five, section 5.2.3. to evaluate the performative uses of such document quotations. The choice for the first cluster, the correspondence between Qalāwūn and the Ilkhanid ruler Tegüder, is due to its central position within two of our authors' texts, so we can explore the similarities and differences of how our authors dealt with these compiled documents. While this means that other documents are usually much less extensively framed or glossed, these documents and their contexts still speak to common compilatory processes. The second cluster is a unique example but important because it provides crucial insights into how compilation worked as an integral part of the composition of *sīra*.

4.4.1 The diplomatic correspondence between Aḥmad Tegüder and Qalāwūn

The documents deriving from the diplomatic exchange between Aḥmad Tegüder (reign 681–683/1282–1284) and Qalāwūn are perhaps the best studied documents found in the *sīra* corpus. Because the letters have been analysed extensively, I will here only broadly consider their contents and focus mostly on their textual embeddedness. The historical context has been perused in some detail before as well, so suffice it to note here that Tegüder came to power in a volatile succession crisis following the death of Abagha, which itself followed not long after the disastrous Mongol defeat at the Battle of Homs. Given that recent confrontation, and the preceding decades of hostilities, it is not surprising that when news reached Cairo that Abagha had been succeeded by Tegüder and that this new ruler had converted to Islam, the authorities in Cairo kept a wary eye on developments on the other side of the Euphrates. Soon after, a letter arrived in Cairo from Tegüder informing the sultanate officially of his conversion and proposing some form of co-operation. The scholars who have studied these letters before (predominantly P.M. Holt, Adel Allouche, Judith Pfeiffer, and Anne Broadbridge) disagree on the degree to which the Mongol letter was either a threat and call for submission or whether it was in fact a call for Islamic cooperation and to settle border disagreements.[421] I am most inclined to follow Pfeiffer's evaluation of the letter as a call for cooperation, considering Tegüder's contemporary political situation in which he was keen to establish an alliance that could strengthen his position of power. Nevertheless, there is a clear element of Mongol superiority expressed in the first letter which may be read in several ways—if the letter was indeed a call for cooperation, it was not framed as cooperation between equals, but rather as a call to establish a relationship of vassalage. In any case, the letter instigated the correspondence for which Ibn ʿAbd al-Ẓāhir's *Tashrīf al-Ayyām* and Shāfiʿ b. ʿAlī's *al-Faḍl al-Maʾthūr* provide some of the most important testimonies. The letters also appear in other sources, which I will not be considering here.

Ibn ʿAbd al-Ẓāhir's letters are spread over two sections of his *sīra* of Qalāwūn, both in the second of the text's three original volumes. He historicises the context of these letters by discussing the events that led to the ascension and conversion of Aḥmad Tegüder as well as the subsequent power struggles among the Mongol elites. He also includes a paraphrase of a letter sent by Aḥmad to Baghdād to communicate the good news (*bushrā*) of his conversion to the people of that city, and later a letter that is noted as a "*mutarjam*" "from those most informed about the hidden issues of the people," that is, a letter sent by an informant or spy in Mongol lands.[422] Ibn ʿAbd al-Ẓāhir then describes the concealed travel of the messengers who conveyed the letter and an oral message to Cairo. The first letter is introduced as follows, with strong visual emphasis in the manuscript.

In addition to this visual emphasis, which is echoed in the inclusion of the two later letters, this case also bears an interesting marginal insertion on the left side of the folio which is not rendered in the text's edition. It functions as a paratextual comment, likely included at the time of the text's original copying. At about the same height as what we may call the formal description of the text this note states *mā huwa bi-qalam al-ṭūmār*, or "what is [written] in *ṭūmār* script." This denotes the type of scribal hand in which the document was written and which is imitated to some extent in the manuscript, by the larger script of the *basmallah* and what

421 The letters are dealt with in these studies: P.M. Holt, "The Ilkhān Aḥmad," 128–132; Adel Allouche, "Teguder's Ultimatum to Qalawun," *IJMES*, 22 no. 4 (1990), 437–446; Judith Pfeiffer, "Aḥmad Tegüder's Second Letter to Qalā'ūn (682/1283)," in *History and Historiography of Post-Mongol Central Asia and the Middle East*, eds. Judith Pfeiffer & Sholeh A. Quinn (Wiesbaden: Harrassowitz, 2006), 167–202; Anne F. Broadbridge, *Kingship and Ideology*, 38–44. Pfeiffer's article contains an excellent unravelling of the various works which refer to or quote all this material.

422 *Tashrīf*, 63–66. من أكبر مطّلعين على بواطن القوم

In fact, the issue of espionage is a central one in Tegüder's first letter to Cairo: he accused Cairo of having sent out spies disguised as Sufis.

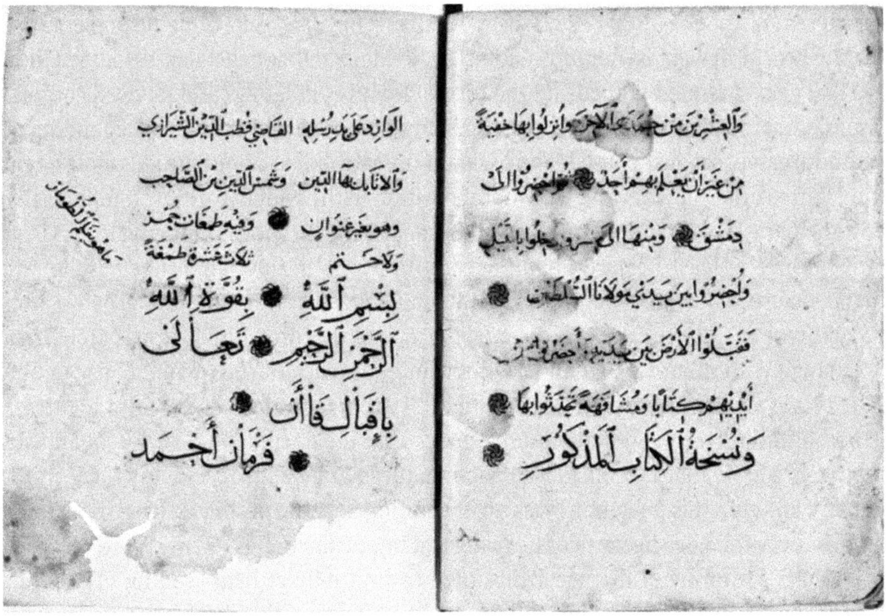

Figure 4: BnF MS Arabe 1704 folios 8b–9a.
(bottom line of 8b) The text of this aforementioned letter (9a) which arrived by the hand of its messengers—the *qāḍī* Quṭb al-Dīn al-Shīrāzī, the *atabek* Bahā' al-Dīn and Shams al-Dīn b. al-Ṣāḥib[423]—and [this text] is lacking a signature and a seal * and on it are red Mongol seals, [to be precise] thirteen seals. In the name of God, the merciful the compassionate. By the strength of God most high. By the fortune of the Khān, the *firmān* of Aḥmad.

follows.[424] The appearance of the second Mongol letter also contains such notes in this manuscript, but no formal description of the document – that is, no note about the lack of seals and signatures. Here the first lines are also noted as "by the pen of the scroll," but the start of the text is noted as *mā huwa bi-qalam al-tawqīʿāt*, or "what is [written] in *tawqīʿāt* script" (see Figure 3, section 3.4.). The reproduction of these letters in the manuscript of Shāfiʿ's *Faḍl* contain no such indications.

Ibn ʿAbd al-Ẓāhir thus exhibits a keen interest in the formal qualities of these letters. This should be understood in line with his general focus on the various guises of the chancery—note in that sense also the discussion of information gathered from spying activities. He does something similar when citing a letter from Tegüder's

423 These persons have been mentioned in more detail by Ibn ʿAbd al-Ẓāhir a page earlier.
424 The end of the first letter is also clear because it is followed immediately by Qalāwūn's answer, itself introduced as *wa-kataba mawlānā al-sulṭān jawābahu* and then a large script incipit, BnF MS Arabe 1704, 18b.

predecessor Abaghā (d. 680/1282) received during Baybars' reign, but the presentation in *Tashrīf al-Ayyām* is notably extensive.[425] Malika Dekkiche has discussed how scribal agents tended to focus on the formal features of letters and devised complex rules for composing letters with appropriate salutations and titulature depending on the addressee, because these features communicated ideas about the sultanate's relationship to other powers and its general position in the wider world.[426] It follows that letters themselves also speak to those relationships and that reproducing their visual appearance at least in part was important to assess in how far proper diplomatic norms were followed. Of course, the Ilkhanids were at this time the greatest military threat to Qalāwūn, so it is not surprising that this direct and formal diplomatic exchange with them was given such a prominent place in the textual construction. The relatively detailed description of the first document received can also be understood differently: Ibn ʿAbd al-Ẓāhir's remark that the document lacks a seal and signature suggests that he considered such features to be appropriate for high-profile letters, and that this document was an aberration, a badly produced letter which our author only includes because of its historical importance.

Shāfiʿ's framing of the letter makes my admittedly radical reading of Ibn ʿAbd al-Ẓāhir's remarks on the letters less tenuous. I argue that both authors provide glimpses into how the letters were received in the sultan's chancery, although they do so differently. Shāfiʿ only includes two letters from this diplomatic exchange: Aḥmad's first letter and Qalāwūn's response. He extensively contextualises the letters and their reception in Damascus and Cairo. One short comment he makes just before he cites the first letter is enlightening:

وقد قعقع فيه قعقعة الأعجام * وأراد ان يزيّنه بالإعراب فشانه بالإعجام *

> And in [this letter] the noises of the Persians clattered * and while [Jamāl al-Dīn b. ʿĪsā, the Mongol letter's author] was keen on embellishing it with [the markings for] inflectional endings, he disfigured it with diacritical points.[427]

In these lines Shāfiʿ disparages Jamāl al-Dīn b. ʿĪsā's prose: apparently, its use of vocalisation to signpost the correct pronunciation was erratic and the stylistic register was too Persian. To convey his feelings about the letter's prose, Shāfiʿ

425 *Rawḍ*, 339–441. Note that the manuscript here does not include visual emphasis. It is likely that neither of the two manuscripts of this text are original copies, however. Ibn al-Dawādārī includes the same description in his description of Tegüder's first letter: *Kanz*, 8:249.

426 Malika Dekkiche, "Diplomatics, or Another Way to See the World," in *Mamluk Diplomatics*, 185–213.

427 *Faḍl*, 94; Marsh 424, 68r. Neither form of اعجام is vocalised in the manuscript, so I am following Tadmurī's editorial choice here. P.M. Holt already drew attention to this comment in passing: "The Īlkhān Aḥmad," 128.

employs the rich ambiguities of the Arabic language. He employs the root letters for the term by which Persians (and non-Arabs in general) are designated, *ʿ-j-m*, in two forms: *aʿjām* as the plural of *ʿajam*, that is "foreigners" and more specifically "Persians," as well as *iʿjām*, that is, "diacritical points," but also denoting that something is unidiomatic or ungrammatical. Shāfiʿ pairs the latter form with *iʿrāb*, or "[the markings for] inflectional endings". This term is derived from the root letters *ʿ-r-b*, that is, "Arab." These terms thus establish a contrast between Persians and Arabs, which may be extrapolated to a contrast between Tegüder, who ruled predominantly Persian-speaking lands, and Qalāwūn, who ruled predominantly Arabic-speaking lands. There is even more: Shāfiʿ's choice for the verb *shāna*, meaning "to disfigure" has an association with the verb *qaʿqaʿa* found twice in the extract. This verb is also used in the expression *mā yuqaʿqaʿa lahu biʾl-shināni*, which means among other things that one does not let oneself be intimidated by imagined dangers.[428] Of course, this phrase does not literally appear, but the pairing of the verb *qaʿqaʿa* and another verb which is not etymologically related to *shinān* but looks similar to it would have triggered this association according to the stylistic figure of *al-jinās al-mudhayyal* or "tailed paronomasia" as distinguished by al-Nabulsī (and translated by Pierre Cachia).[429] Considering the intimidating tone of Aḥmad's letter and the belittling tone of Qalāwūn's response, Shāfiʿ's comment participates in the discourse in which the letter's threat is waved aside. The statement communicates the idea that Aḥmad's letter was perceived to be badly written and conveys the message that Cairo was not impressed by Tegüder's overtures.

Similar ideas are discernible in Shāfiʿ's narrative portrayal of the Mongol messengers. Shāfiʿ reports that upon receiving Qalāwūn's response,[430] Aḥmad Tegüder decided to send his shaykh ʿAbd al-Raḥmān, who had been named as the one responsible for Aḥmad's conversion in the first letter, to Cairo. The descriptions of the shaykh's journey tell of how Qalāwūn's agents humiliated the shaykh and his retinue, how he was covertly brought to Aleppo and had to wait until after the death

---

428 Kazimirski, *Dictionnaire arabe-français*, 2:784. Muʿāwiyya is said to have used this proverb when addressing a party from ʿAlī's camp during the Battle of Ṣiffīn, in the famous account given by al-Ṭabarī, *Taʾrīkh al-rusul wa-l-mulūk*, 11 vols., ed. Muḥammad Abū l-Faḍl Ibrāhīm (Cairo: Dār al-Maʿārif bi-Miṣr, 1960) 5:5. This association with narratives about a battle that looms large in the context of the Sunni-Shii divide may be intentional, as Tegüder's conversion to Islam was considered dodgy and, if not necessarily of a Shii nature, certainly as aberrant and heterodox.

429 Al-Nābulūsī, *The Arch Rhetorician*, 29. See also "(pseudo-)derivative paronomasia." Al-Nābulūsī, *The Arch Rhetorician*,. 29–30.

430 Note that Shāfiʿ claims that the authorship of Qalāwūn's answer to Aḥmad Tegüder's letter is the result of a collaborative effort between Fatḥ al-Dīn b. ʿAbd al-Ẓāhir's and himself (*Faḍl*, 102), but Ibn al-Dawādārī and other authors ascribe it to Ibn ʿAbd al-Ẓāhir alone. Al-Qalqashandī claims it was written by Shāfiʿ (*Ṣubḥ*, vol. 7:237).

of Aḥmad Tegüder before even being granted an audience—although Shāfiʿ and Ibn ʿAbd al-Ẓāhir disagree on this timing, as we shall see. In addition to providing us with this historical information, Shāfiʿ constructs a narrative set-up to strengthen the derogatory tone and inserts comments that can be read literally as well as symbolically. When describing how Aḥmad prepared "his shaykh, the one who guided him to Islam" (*shaykhihi wa'l-hādī lahu ilā 'l-islām*) to go to Cairo, he adds the afterthought "as he claimed" (*ka-mā zaʿama*).[431] As in Qalāwūn's letter, the earnestness of Aḥmad's conversion is not taken entirely seriously, and we can thus see how Shāfiʿ's narrative context for these letters interacts with the letter's contents.[432] In this same description, Shāfiʿ notes that during his travels the shaykh Aḥmad had "raised above his head the *jitr*, that is a leather cupola."[433] Soon after they crossed the Euphrates, the Mongol party was deprived of this symbol and was told that only the sultan could ride with the *jitr* in these lands. Shāfiʿ then adds this comment:

فحين عدى ما تعدّى وحطّ مرفوعه عن رأسه * وعرف منذ حلّ أرض مولانا السلطان قدر نفسه *

> And as soon as he abandoned that which was excessive (*ʿaddā mā taʿaddā*) and he took down that which was erected above his head (*wa-ḥaṭṭa marfūʿahu ʿan raʾsihi*), he became aware of his [appropriate] personal rank upon arrival in the territory of our lord the sultan.[434]

Here Shāfiʿ takes the symbolic deprivation of the envoys' magnitude as starting point for a rhetorical variation. In this statement he effectively inverts Aḥmad's bestowal of honour to his *shaykh* (*wa-rafaʿa ʿalā raʾsihi al-jitr*) by using related terminology for the opposite action (*wa-ḥaṭṭa marfūʿahu ʿan raʾsihi*). The choice of verbs in the first cola is furthermore telling, as *ʿaddā* and *taʿaddā* are respectively forms II and V of the radicals *ʿ-d-w*, the substantive form of which, *ʿadūw*, means "enemy," which was commonly used to describe the Mongols.[435] The substantive *ḥall* which I have here translated as "arrival" bears a wide range of meanings, but

---

431 *Faḍl*, 113. The editor adds the *sukūn* on the last letter of *zaʿama*, following the manuscript Marsh 424, 78b. I have chosen to disregard this.
432 See also, Broadbridge, *Kingship and Ideology*, 42.
433 *Faḍl*, 113. Ibn ʿAbd al-Ẓāhir confirms that the party rode with this *jitr* and adds some further descriptions of the shaykh's elaborate retinue, but his tone is much more straight-forward. *Tashrīf*, 49. The *jitr* was a kind of parasol which was carried over the ruler's head during ritual processions. In the Cairo Sultanate its closest cognate would have been the *qubba wa'l-ṭayr*, the palanquin carried above the Mamluk sultan when he rode out. Urbain Vermeulen, "Une note sur les insignes royaux des mamelouks," in *Egypt and Syria in the Fatimid, Ayyubid and Mamluk Eras*, eds. Urbain Vermeulen & Daniel De Smet (Leuven: Peeters, 1995), 356.
434 For example, *Faḍl*, 113.
435 As in *Faḍl*, 71, 92.

an important one of those is related to permissible and pure things, as in *ḥalāl*.[436] We could thus read this statement as a symbolic purification, the enemy's presence being made permissible by deprivation. This is pushed even further by the conclusion that the shaykh became aware (*ʿarafa*) of the rank/extent/worth (*qadr*) of his person (*nafs*) became known to all. Again, the choice of words is not random here: these three words have important connotations in Sufism. *Nafs* is the "soul" of a person, but also the "self" that needs to be overcome in the quest towards spiritual union with God, *qadr* has important connotations of "fate," and becoming aware by gaining knowledge (*ʿarafa*) is an important layer of the Sufi path.[437] Given that he has already underlined how this shaykh surrounded himself with Sufis, we may understand Shāfiʿ's comments here as ironic commentary on Sufi knowledge and its hypocrisy as it relates to asceticism and splendour. The knowledge dawning on this person is perhaps also a foreshadowing of the humiliating fate awaiting this Sufi shaykh. Unlike in Ibn ʿAbd al-Ẓāhir's account, however, at this point the reader does not yet know what will happen to the *shaykh*, so Shāfiʿ's comments are building up narrative tension.[438]

The shaykh's Sufi inclinations come to the front much more explicitly a little further in the text. After describing the shaykh's house arrest on his arrival in Aleppo, Shāfiʿ writes—notably not in *sajʿ*—that "an announcement was sent by the governor [Shams al-Dīn Sunqur al-Manṣūrī] of Aleppo about the number of persons accompanying the shaykh." He adds that "among the most remarkable things I saw in [this announcement] was the presence of four sufis (*fuqarāʾ*) intended for murmuring (*zamzama*) and listening (*samāʿ*)."[439] While *samāʿ* is a well-known ritual practice in Sufism, *zamzama* was a practice of murmuring prayers associated with Zoroastrianism.[440] Considering the Persian background of the shaykh, and Shāfiʿ's

436 The verbal form *ḥalla* is also used a little further to describe Qalāwūn's arrival in Damascus. *Faḍl*, 115.

437 Compare also the Sufi saying *man ʿarafa nafsaha fa-qad ʿarafa rabbahu* ("He who knows himself will come to know his Master", that is, God). This saying became the topic for a treatise by Jalāl al-Dīn al-Suyūṭī, *al-Qawl al-Ashbahu fī man ʿArafa Nafsahu faqad ʿArafa Rabbahu*, attested among others in BnF MS Arabe 773.

438 ʿIzz al-Dīn b. Shaddād's *Taʾrīkh al-Malik al-Ẓāhir*, 222 contains a cola that uses similar terminology when describing how Baybars became sick and eventually died: *wa-**taʿaddā al-qadru** ʾl-ladhī yaḥṣal liʾl-**nafsi** gharaḍahā* ("and fate overtook the one who is overtaken by the soul's intent"), which suggests that these terms were commonly used to describe fateful situations.

439 *Faḍl*, 115.

وسيّرت مطالعة من النائب المذكور بحلب بعدّة من معه ومن أعجب ما رأيتُ أربع فقراء برسم الزمزمة والسماع

440 See for a brief discussion of the practice and its associations in Arabic historiography: Charles E. Bosworth, "The Heritage of Rulership in Early Islamic Iran and the Search for Dynastic Connections with The Past" *Iranian Studies* 9 (1978), 11.

earlier quoted attitude towards Persians, our author here questions the shaykh's (and by extension the Mongol ruler's) Islamic credentials by suggesting that his Islam was tainted by a Persian form of heterodoxy.[441]

The disdain towards Sufi composure is also evident in Shāfiʿ's description of the *shaykh*'s audience with Qalāwūn in Damascus:

ودخل هذا الشيخ في هيئة الفُقراء مُعمَّمًا بفوطة مُرخاةٍ لها عَذَبة بدلقٍ قد طوى كُمَّية وجمجم.

> This shaykh entered in the guise of the Sufis wearing as a turban an Indian cloth from which the extremities [flowed down] with a Sufi robe which had enveloped and concealed his two sleeves.[442]

This statement has a symmetrical function, as it is flanked by detailed descriptions of Qalāwūn's own glorious presence on the throne (*kursī sulṭānihi*) in Damascus. The shaykh's unusual appearance establishes a contrast. But the statement is again layered, with Shāfiʿ making full use of Arabic ambiguities. The sentence describing his turban can be read as a variation of the proverb *arkhā ʿamāmatahu*, that is, "he has unwinded his turban," meaning that someone is at ease and without worries.[443] This is not just an ironic remark given what is to follow, but also a criticism considering the strictly organised nature of courtly audiences at the time, especially in an exchange as tense as that with the Mongol enemy. A relaxed, loose attitude towards protocol would have been perceived as extremely inappropriate. This point is strengthened in what follows: the noun *ʿadhaba* here denotes the extremities of the turban, but the root *ʿ-dh-b* also has a verbal connotation of "to hinder, handicap, impede, obstruct" and in form II of "to torment" and "to chastise."[444] Similarly, I have rendered the verb *jamjama* as "concealed," but it also has a strong connotation of "talking unintelligibly."[445] This section not only presents the *shaykh* as a visual aberration because of his distinctive Sufi clothes, but also as a nuisance to the courtly audience because of his bad speech and inappropriate

441 The disparaging attitude towards Persians is not uncommon in Arabic texts of the late medieval period. Christian Mauder has shown that they were frequently portrayed as antinomian and untrustworthy. "Being Persian in Late Mamluk Egypt: The Construction and Significance of Persian Ethnic Identity in the Salons of Sultan Qānișawh al-Ghawrī (r. 906–922/1501–1516)," *Al-ʿUṣūr al-Wusṭā* 28 (2020), 385–386.

442 *Faḍl*, 115. The edition incorrectly omits the word *qad* before *ṭawā* and is furthermore hindered by a number of confusingly places comma's, which I have disregarded in my reading. MS Marsh 424, 80a.

443 Kazimirski, *Dictionnaire arabe-français*, 1:842.

444 Hans Wehr, *Arabic-English Dictionary: The Hans Wehr Dictionary of Modern Written Arabic*, ed. J.M. Cowan (Ithaca, NY: Spoken Language Services, 1994), 701.

445 Kazimirski, *Dictionnaire arabe-français*, 1:323.

composure. The attentive reader would not be surprised to read a few lines further that the company's presents for the sultan were "found to be deficient" (*astanqaṣa hidiyyatahum*).[446]

When after this first audience the news reached Qalāwūn that Aḥmad had died, the shaykh was brought in front of the sultan again and informed of his patron's death. Hearing the news, the shaykh fainted and died a few days later. Shāfiʿ notes the fates of his two main companions in similarly derogatory fashion: Shams al-Dīn b. al-Tītī was locked away in the Citadel while the "rabble who came with him" (*raʿāʿ man jāʾa maʿahu*), that is, the sufis Shāfiʿ had earlier denigrated, were allowed to leave. Of this al-Tītī and another companion, however, Shāfiʿ tells us that "it would not have been more commendable (*aḥmad*) if they had been packed with what eluded them from their king Aḥmad," punning on the meaning of the Īlkhān's Islamic name and alluding to his violent death.[447]

Shāfiʿ's framing of the diplomatic exchange with Aḥmad Tegüder in *al-Faḍl al-Maʾthūr* functions as it were as a running commentary. The author picks up on certain themes found in the letters—the derogatory language of both letters, the accusation of employing Sufis as spies—and amplifies them in narrative form. This can be understood as an extension of the *inshāʾ* practice of responding to letters, which necessitated the responder to engage with the themes and topics set by the initial sender.[448] This practice is here taken further and applied to the narrative prose. The fact that Shāfiʿ's account of these letters and the historical happenings runs as a continuous, uninterrupted section in the *sīra*—concluded with the statement that "such was the situation concerning the case of the first and second Tatar envoy"—even indicates that he composed it as a cohesive whole.[449] He furthermore paid attention to narrative pacing and character development as well, which is evident from the fact that we get Shāfiʿ's description of the shaykh's audience before we are even told of Aḥmad's death, which results in a narrative suspense that is only resolved near the end of the section.

Ibn ʿAbd al-Ẓāhir's more straightforward account of this diplomacy works less as a cohesive whole, as it is situated in the general chronological framework of the text. As a result, the narrative development is divided into chronologically consec-

446 *Faḍl,* 116. On appropriate courtly gifts, see Doris Behrens-Abouseif, *Practising Diplomacy in the Mamluk Sultanate: Gifts and Material Culture in the Medieval Islamic World* (London and New York: IB Tauris, 2014).

447 *Faḍl,* 117. On some of these people, see Anne F. Broadbridge, "Careers in Diplomacy among Mamluks and Mongols, 658–741/1260–1341," in *Mamluk Cairo: A Crossroads,* 276–277.

448 Malika Dekkiche, "The Letter and Its Response: The Exchanges between the Qara Qoyunlu and the Mamluk Sultan: MS Arabe 4440 (BnF, Paris)," *Arabica,* 63, no. 6 (2016), 580–581.

449 The whole section runs from *Faḍl,* 92–118. As noted above (chapter three, section 3.3.), Shāfiʿ regularly concludes sections with this phrase in *Faḍl* and in his *sīra* of al-Nāṣir Muḥammad.

utive parts, and the reader knows already well before the account of the shaykh's audience that Aḥmad Tegüder has died. In his description of the audience Ibn ʿAbd al-Ẓāhir does not choose for the building up of tension and rhetorical play we see in his nephew's text—although several parts of Ibn ʿAbd al-Ẓāhir's narrative are also in *saj*ʿ—but tells us that "[shaykh ʿAbd al-Raḥmān] was ordered to kiss the ground, and he declined out of arrogance and haughtiness (*fa-abā kibran wa zahwan*)." We are next told that he was forced to the ground and that his limbs were broken, as were those of his companions. The harsh treatment makes sense here: the reader of *Tashrīf al-Ayyām* already knows that there was at this point no authority backing up the shaykh's misplaced arrogance. By contrast, Shāfiʿ's description is more aloof because he is holding back the crucial information that the Mongol ruler has by now died. This choice makes the actual unveiling of this information all the more effective.

Essentially, both our authors communicated a derogatory attitude towards this Mongol diplomatic exchange while at the same time performing the supremacy of Cairo's command of the proper diplomatic comportment. Although Shāfiʿ's account may be more effective on a narrative level, Ibn ʿAbd al-Ẓāhir's evaluation draws attention to the formal qualities (and defects) of the exchange. Generally, they both engaged with the letters' discursive matrix of derision and narratively amplified their meaning, using compilation as a powerful compositional tool.

4.4.2 Documents before history: the re-use of letters as historical narrative

While the letters discussed above are clearly identified by our authors as copies from original documents, there is suggestive evidence that other material in the *sīras* also descended from documents but was reworked to fit into the *sīras*. This was certainly the case for Shāfiʿ's description of the Battle of Homs, which was integrated into *al-Faḍl al-Maʾthūr*. We are only provided with the version of the text as presented in the *sīra* context and not with its earlier form, however. Fortunately, there is one case where we can actually evaluate the process of editing at work. When ʿAbd al-ʿAzīz al-Khuwayṭir set out to edit and publish Ibn ʿAbd al-Ẓāhir's *sīra* of Baybars, he was confronted with several lacunae in the Süleymaniye manuscript, presumably due to missing quires. For some of these lacunae al-Khuwayṭir made use of information quoted by other authors, or he copied the abridged accounts from Shāfiʿ b. ʿAlī's *Ḥusn al-Manāqib*. In one case he covered up a missing section in the Istanbul manuscript which presumably described the outset of Baybars' Anatolian campaign near the end of his reign by using a parallel text quoted by al-Qalqashandī in *Ṣubḥ al-Aʿshā*.[450] Al-Qalqashandī introduces this as a "battle letter" (*risālat al-ghazw*) sent by Ibn ʿAbd al-Ẓāhir to the vizier Bahāʾ al-Dīn b. Ḥinnā, whom we have come across before as a powerful agent during Baybars' reign and as the patron of ʿIzz al-Dīn b. Shaddād. Not only is this also a text written by Ibn ʿAbd al-Ẓāhir about the same subject, the letter itself is highly similar, but not entirely identical to the text included in the manuscript of the *sīra* of Baybars.[451] When comparing the text, one is struck by the fact that despite the overlapping subject matter and the largely similar textual structure, there is a significant degree of difference in phrasings and word choices. The text in al-Qalqashandī also includes even more poetry. As an illustration of the amount of divergence between the two recensions, Figure 5 shows the difference between the first lines shared

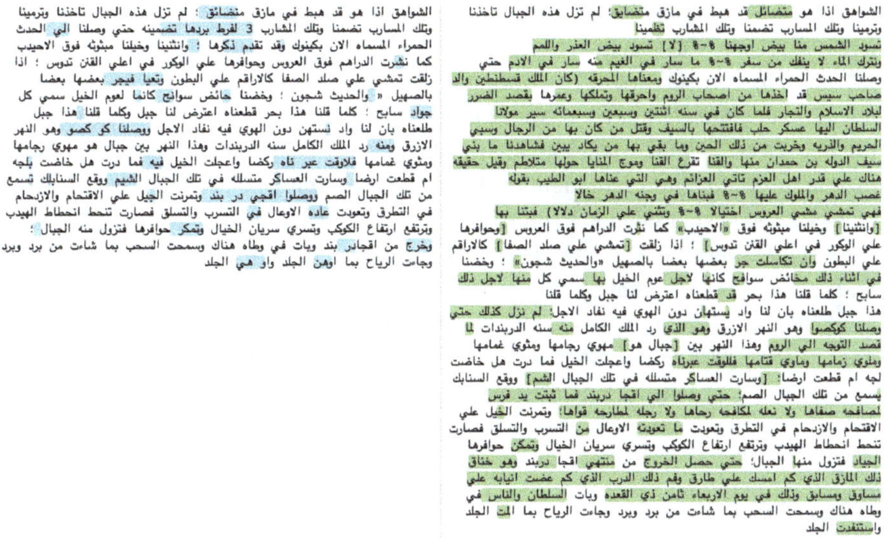

Figure 5: KITAB DiffViewer comparison of extract from *Rawḍ* to matching extract from *Ṣubḥ al-aʿshā*. Blue for text only found in the *sīra*, green for text only in *Ṣubḥ al-Aʿshā* and non-highlighted for text shared between the two. Image generated on 22 February 2022.

450 Anne Troadec has devoted some attention to this section and sees it as typical for the way Cilicia is represented in writing of the period. The Armenians are associated with the Byzantines of bygone eras, and the land is a place where the sultan could deploy his image as "sultan de guerre." She does not discuss the parallel text. Troadec, "Les Mamelouks," 140–143.

451 The section in *Rawḍ* runs from pp. 453–471. The corresponding part of the letter in *Ṣubḥ al-Aʿshā* 14:139–164. Al-Khuwayṭir does not note that the two texts showcase a significant degree of variance, and he does not reproduce the last two paragraphs of the letter as well as a poem at the end. The letter is briefly described by Muhsin al-Musawi in "Pre-Modern Belletristic Prose," 111–112.

between the *sīra* (left)[452] and the letter cited in *Ṣubḥ al-Aʿshā* (right),[453] generated by loading the digital texts of both sections into the KITAB DiffViewer developed by Peter Verkinderen.[454]

Without going into detail, one can see that the variation is significant and that the text given by al-Qalqashandī is more elaborate. This is not only true for these first lines, but continues for the remainder of the section, the totality of which runs for 2711 tokens in the *sīra* versus 5344 tokens in *Ṣubḥ al-aʿshā*, almost double that amount.[455]

Clearly, the version of the text copied by al-Qalqashandī constituted a different form of this text. While it apparently formed the basis from which the version included in the *sīra* was derived, thorough editing took place. For the extract highlighted in Figure 5, this means two lines of poetry are left out (marked by the %~% hemistich splitter in OpenITI mARkdown).[456] Additionally, a historical digression about Kaynūk which runs for several lines in the letter cited in *Ṣubḥ al-Aʿshā* is replaced by the statement "the account of this has already been given" (*wa-qad taqaddama dhikrahā*). If we retrace our steps in the *sīra*, we find a short account of the history of Kaynūk, some small parts of which are also found in the letter quoted in *Ṣubḥ al-Aʿshā*, but not in identical form.[457] When Ibn ʿAbd al-Ẓāhir reworked the letter he had earlier written to Bahāʾ al-Dīn b. Ḥinnā as historical narrative, he must have remembered that he had already earlier included an account about Kaynūk and referred back to that description.

The letter is not the same text then, but an earlier incarnation that was thoroughly reworked to fit into the *sīra*'s textual construction. It sheds some revealing light on our author's working method. It also provides an interesting perspective on the literary qualities of such a reworking– these are dealt with in

---

452 *Rawḍ*, 458. (OpenITI text file: 0692IbnCabdZahir.RawdZahir.GVDB20200120-ara1.mARkdown)

453 *Ṣubḥ al-aʿshā*, 14:142–143 (OpenITI text file: 0821Qalqashandi.SubhAcsha.Shamela0009429-ara1.mARkdown).

454 In Verkinderen's words: "This app displays the differences between two strings of characters. Contrary to most other diff viewers, it is geared towards comparing texts rather than code, especially texts from the OpenITI corpus and text reuse date created by passim for the KITAB project." https://github.com/kitab-project-org/diffViewer The actual application is accessible at: https://kitab-project.org/diffViewer/

455 A token signifies any string of letters separated from another string by a space. It is necessary to speak of tokens rather than words because Arabic is an agglutinating language. Token counts are based on the OpenITI versions of the text.

456 OpenITI mARkdown is a markup language developed by Maxim Romanov which allows for easy annotation of digital texts. For a brief explanation and further links see http://kitab-project.org/corpus/markdown

457 *Rawḍ*, 417–418.

more detail in chapter five. If Ibn ʿAbd al-Ẓāhir reused an earlier written letter to construct this part of the *sīra*, he possibly did so at other points as well, but unfortunately this is difficult to establish with certainty. We owe the fact that this specific letter survives in two redactions to al-Qalqashandī considering it a good stylistic example of a letter informing about martial activities.[458] No other similar letters or excerpts are quoted by al-Qalqashandī or other authors, nor do any survive independently, which would allow us to evaluate other examples of text reuse. Nevertheless, the earlier noted elements of discursive similarities between documents and narrative accounts suggests that the boundaries between the two were often not so strict.[459]

4.5 Conclusion

Writing is gathering letters of the alphabet, but it can also be understood as a gathering of letters in the sense of *belles-lettres*, and even in the sense of epistolary letters. The *sīra*s written by our authors included a good deal of compiled material, but that does not make them mere letter or poetry collections: the above sections have shown how texts of various kinds were all meaningfully integrated in their new contexts. This was mostly the case by an interaction between the narrative contexts and the compiled texts, or by reworking the original texts to function within the *sīra*. On a broader level, these compiled texts can also be argued to function within the performance of distinction in the literary field. The biographies showcase not only historiographical agency, but also significant literary and linguistic agency. The chancery environment defined a good deal of the terms for such a performance: the registers, textual forms, and stylistic expressions common to the chancery—and the mastery of which, as I have suggested, defined a person's membership of and status within it—were all called on to contribute to the literary spectacle of *sīra*. This resonates strongly with one of the common arguments presented by our authors as the rationale for writing their *sīra*s: the importance

458 It is in that sense notable that a much shorter version of the text is also included in BnF MS Arabe 4440, 30b–31b. On the importance of this manuscript, see Frédéric Bauden, "Les relations diplomatiques entre les sultans mamlouks circassiens et les autres pouvoirs du Dār al-islām: l'apport du ms. ar. 4440 (BNF, Paris)," *Annales Islamologiques* 41 (2007), 1–29; Dekkiche, "The Letter and Its Response."

459 One section in *Tashrīf* informing about the plight of envoys in Castile, is explicitly a paraphrase of a letter from these envoys, presumably sent when they were in Tunis and had already undertaken part of the return journey. The language register of the section suggests that Ibn ʿAbd al-Ẓāhir reworked the letter into historiography. However, as far as I am aware, the original letter is not attested elsewhere. *Tashrīf*, 112–114.

of the *kātib* to the sultan's *dawla*. This is a performative claim to necessity as it is only by the scribe's role in writing them down that the sultan's achievements would survive the forgetfulness of time. The compositional elements distinguished above highlight how this penetrated the entire works. The *sīra*s were written by prominent scribes, and their professional background informed not only what they chose to relay about the past, it also defined the formal qualities of their texts. The chancery's presence is felt implicitly (through excellent prose and poetry) and explicitly (through compilation) and supports claims of superior authorship. In the next chapter I will further explore this notion for the broader literary field.

Chapter 5
Sīra as literary communication

بلغني (. . .) أنّ فلانًا غضّ منّي كل غضّ الجنى * وأنه عبث بي عبث الأيام بالمنى * وأنّه ردّني إلى أر ذل العمر في الاطراح *
وغلق في وجه تنجيحي أبواب النجاح * وزعم أن إناء أناتى غير مُفعم * وبغاء مجدي غير مُحكم * وجواد إجادتي غير مُلجم *
وأنّ ميلاد مجدي حديث * وسبب سعدي رثيث * (. . .)
وإذ أتتك مذمتي من ناقص فهي الشهادة لي بأنّي كامل

Word has reached me [. . .] that someone detracted my reputation, wishing for the succulence of an entire harvest, and that he mocked me like time mocks death, opposing me so much that it would be like repudiating life if I neglected [to respond]; [as a result] he successfully closed the gates of accomplishment, for he [must have] believed that the vessel of my perseverance is not filled to the brim, that my desire for distinction was not sturdy, that my lavish output was not bridled, that the birth of my distinction is recent, and the tent rope of my good fortune shabby [. . .]

If me being blamed reached you,
then that serves me as proof of my perfection.[460]

When Ibn ʿAbd al-Ẓāhir was about 32 years old, he wrote the above quoted lines to introduce a letter (*risāla*). As the lines indicate, Ibn ʿAbd al-Ẓāhir had been told that a man whose name is now lost to time had criticised him behind his back. All we know is that this criticaster was a Shīʿī, and that he had called Ibn ʿAbd al-Ẓāhir out for, in Everett Rowson's words, "having shown himself excessively humble in a scholarly gathering."[461] In his response Ibn ʿAbd al-Ẓāhir showed just how well he could boast when necessary. After a rhyming cadenced prose set-up of the topic, a poetic line quoted from the notoriously arrogant poet al-Mutanabbī (d. 354/956) drives home the point.[462] The earliest attestation of this boastful letter is in al-Ṣafadī's extensive commentary on a famous Andalusian epistle, *Tamām al-Mutūn fī Sharḥ Risālat Ibn Zaydūn.* Al-Ṣafadī claimed to have copied it in full "from [Ibn ʿAbd al-Ẓāhir's] handwriting" and provides the date cited above. Versions of the letter are also included in at least one later anthology—the *inshāʾ* collection preserved

---

460 Al-Ṣafadī, *Tamām al-Mutūn fī Sharḥ Risālat Ibn Zaydūn,* ed. Muḥammad Abū l-Faḍl Ibrāhīm (Ṣaydā/Beirut: Manshūrāt al-Maktaba l-ʿAṣriyya, 1969), 404–405.
461 Rowson, "Alexandrian Age," 108–109.
462 The letter goes on in a similar fashion and cites, alongside more lines by al-Mutanabbī, a line by Abu al-ʿAlāʾ al-Maʿarrī and four scathing lines by an Umayyad era poet directed against the ʿAlid leader Muḥammad b. al-Ḥanafiyya. The letter also contains a section in which Ibn ʿAbd al-Ẓāhir boasts about his ancestors.

https://doi.org/10.1515/9783110753028-006

in the unique manuscript BnF MS Arabe 4440[463]—and in at least four independent codicological units.[464]

Muhsin al-Musawi has argued that "the large-scale and diverse cultural production in Arabic in the postclassical era (approximately the twelfth through the eighteenth centuries) was the outcome of an active sphere of discussion and disputation spanning the entire medieval Muslim World."[465] That is to say, the field of textual production in late medieval Egypt and Syria, and beyond, was deeply competitive and profoundly intertextual. Pierre Bourdieu argued that a literary field and the cultural expressions produced within its framework must adhere to a social logic, which generates and reproduces the stakes of literary discourse and performance. These are either followed (and thus conserved) or actively transformed by authors participating within its logic.[466] While Bourdieu tends to stress the centrality of "struggle" in such engagements, a field is essentially about agents' variegated interactions with one another. If writing did not require outright challenging of peers and predecessors, any text at least required a position taking in relationship to what had already been written and brought into circulation. Thomas Bauer captured that dynamic with the concept of "literary communication" which he borrowed from communication studies. He argued that literary texts of the late medieval period were meant to spark debate, to incite response, to engender dialogue. A text could lay implicit claim to be literary insofar as it was meant to live on beyond its initial pragmatic context and create new meanings with new readers.[467] Such types of literary communication and performance can be seen as engagements with the literary field and as position takings to negotiate social status by way of literary performance of the agent's mastery of cultural capital.

463 BnF MS Arabe 4440, ff. 26a–28b.

464 Three rather recent copies are in the Egyptian Dār al-kutub (MSS Adab 3911, Majāmiʿ 840, and Adab Taymūr 34) and another copy of unknown date, possibly based on a microfilm of one of the Egyptian copies, is included in a *majmūʿa* in Damascus (Maktabat al-Asad MS 9205, fols. 171b–181a). That it may be a microfilm was communicated to me by Tarek Sabraa.

465 Al-Musawi, *Medieval Islamic Republic of Letters*, 1.

466 Bourdieu, "Le champ littéraire," 4–5. Note that Bourdieu in this essay already compares his concept of literary field to the "Republic of Letters" in its Enlightenment era formulation by Pierre Bayle (d. 1706).

467 Bauer, "Mamluk Literature as a Means of Communication," 24–25. Literary communication understands literary texts in a continuum with ordinary, or pragmatic communication, but distinguished by "some sort of aesthetic benefit" and a "convention of polyvalence," that is, their possibility to speak to and engender disparate reactions with different audiences across time and space. Bauer adapted these conceptualisations of communication from the German philosopher and communication scientist Siegfried J. Schmidt.

The opening lines of Ibn ʿAbd al-Ẓāhir's *risāla* cited above fit these characteristics perfectly: these lines are openly in dialogue with an earlier text which sparked the response (that is, the Shīʿī's remarks and/or a letter informing him of the slander), they harnessed the literary canon—most obviously, the citation of a line originally written by al-Mutanabbī—and they proved to be of continued literary interest—the letter's anthologisation by al-Ṣafadī and the existence of independent copies. The same is true for much of Ibn ʿAbd al-Ẓāhir's other writing, including not in the least the *sīra*s. While these texts have traditionally been read from the perspective of an author negotiating his position vis-à-vis the sultan or the political authorities more generally, I argue that they were meant to have an impact beyond that immediate courtly context, even if they were not necessarily successful in this regard. The final chapter of this book will investigate this courtly context and its implications more closely, but before doing so the present chapter assesses the literary nature of the *sīra*s and their relationship with the literary field of the late 7th/13th and early 8th/14th centuries. I specifically consider the use of literary registers and forms within these texts, and their embeddedness in our authors' surviving oeuvres.

A first section of this chapter will present a picture of the literary field as it existed at the time of our authors by zooming in on evidence for exchanges between them and other literary agents. I start my evaluation of literary communication with those types of discourses that are unambiguously literary, that is, the poetical (and to a lesser degree prose) exchanges in which our authors were involved. The following section will focus on the literary materials included in the *sīra*s: poetry and prose. Building on the insights on prose from chapter four, I specifically discuss a practice that I consider to be essential to the literary field of Cairo in this time: *muʿāraḍa*, the direct engagement with earlier texts through imitation and amelioration of form and theme set by an earlier author. It will be shown how this was a crucial part of how Shāfiʿ b. ʿAlī wrote his *sīra*s.

5.1 The literary field

The production and consumption of literary works is a social phenomenon. Authors implied an audience that would read and respond to their texts. Poems or prose pieces may have been written for specific occasions but were regularly reproduced by later authors who compiled these exchanges, or they were recycled by the authors themselves, highlighting their polyvalence across time and space. Later compilers often provided some framing information to understand the meanings of poems and prose pieces, but in other cases such meanings would be self-evident from the figurative language used. Ideally, the framing information provides information about the instigator or the recipient of a particular piece, or it mentions the occasion for which it was written. By parsing such descriptions given in literary anthologies, biographical dictionaries, and obituaries sections in annalistic chronicles, some of the dynamics involved in these exchanges can be reconstructed. In Figure 6 I have visualized this in a network of literary exchange, taking our two authors as the central nodes and mapping their literary relations. While compilations of Ibn ʿAbd al-Ẓāhir's poetry and his correspondence are extant, for Shāfiʿ b. ʿAlī such material has largely survived only as discrete units, often without framing information. For pragmatic reasons I have here only looked at those pieces that were specifically attributed as being sent to or received by specific agents. I have limited myself only to those agents who are specifically named as exchanging poetry or, more rarely, prose with our authors or other relevant agents. It goes without saying, given the limited source base and the fact I did not follow up on every invidual, that this network is not exhaustive. In the first place, it provides some insight into the literary network of the Banū ʿAbd al-Ẓāhir as portrayed by later biographers, and not into the wider literary field.

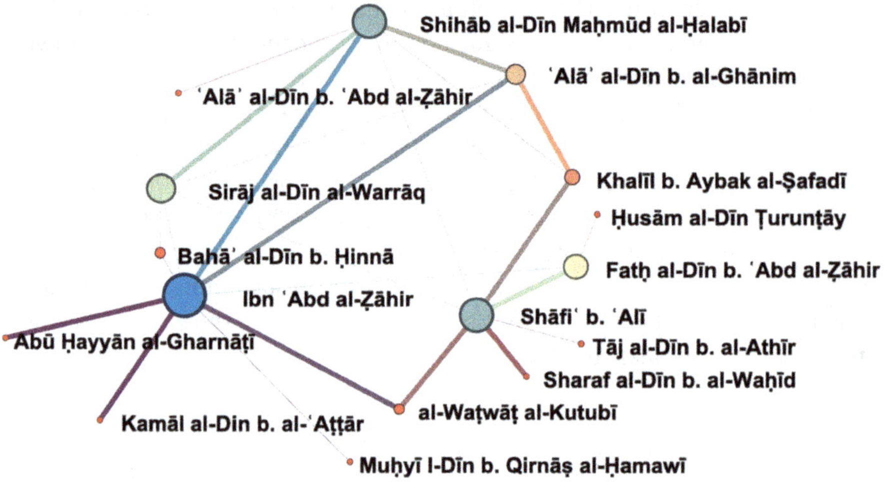

Figure 6: Literary communication of the Banū ʿAbd al-Ẓāhir and related agents. A thin edge means one-sided communication, a thick edge denotes reciprocal communication, that is, an actual exchange of poetry or prose by two authors. The size and colour of the nodes are defined by the number of edges they are connected to.

When looking at the various poems and prose texts addressed to specific persons, a network of *udabāʾ* reading and reacting to each other's works emerges. Our authors and Fatḥ al-Dīn b. ʿAbd al-Ẓāhir naturally emerge as central nodes because of the nature of the source material whence I lifted this information, but a few other figures also come into view. We see the earlier mentioned Shihāb al-Dīn Maḥmūd al-Ḥalabī, the famous *adīb* Sirāj al-Dīn al-Warrāq, whom Ibn ʿAbd al-Ẓāhir also quotes once in his biography of Baybars,[468] the chancery author ʿAlāʾ al-Dīn b. al-Ghānim, and al-Ṣafadī himself, who figured so prominently in the literary exchange discussed at the outset of this book. Two of these, as well as Ibn ʿAbd al-Ẓāhir himself are explicitly named by al-Ṣafadī as participating in literary exchanges in al-Ṣafadī's *tarjama* of Ibn al-Ghānim, where he notes that "between the shaykh ʿAlāʾ al-Dīn [b. al-Ghānim], the *qāḍī* Muḥyī al-Dīn b. ʿAbd al-Ẓāhir and al-Shihāb Maḥmūd and other people of the age there were beautiful debates and the usual exchange of correspondence one can expect between *udabāʾ*."[469]

Shihāb al-Dīn Maḥmūd himself referred to exchanges he had with Ibn ʿAbd al-Ẓāhir as well: he mentions that he "received many letters from [Ibn ʿAbd al-Ẓāhir], and I heard a lot of his [expressions] from him personally (*min lafẓihi*), and we exchanged correspondence with poetry, consisting of odes, riddles, and the like."[470] Their close literary relationship is also evident from the relatively high amount of poetry quoted by other authors from these exchanges. One example is found in the chronicle *Durrat al-Aslāk fī Dawlat al-Atrāk* written by Badr al-Dīn b. Ḥabīb al-Ḥalabī (d. 779/1377). Ibn Ḥabīb was himself a renowned *kātib/adīb* and a student of Shihāb al-Dīn Maḥmūd, whom he frequently and admiringly quotes.[471] In his lemma for Ibn ʿAbd al-Ẓāhir he includes three poems: one epigram written by Ibn ʿAbd al-Ẓāhir himself, another epigram by the earlier noted Sirāj al-Dīn al-Warrāq, and then a fifteen-line poem by Shihāb al-Dīn Maḥmūd.[472]

Shihāb al-Dīn Maḥmūd was also one of Shāfiʿ's most important correspondents. One poem sent by him to Shāfiʿ is again recorded by Ibn Ḥabīb,[473] and another one is recorded by al-Ṣafadī. This last poem highlights the importance of reading literary evidence in the light of familial connections: it is a long elegy written for ʿAlāʾ al-Dīn b. ʿAbd al-Ẓāhir's death in 717/1317, addressed to Shāfiʿ. Shihāb al-Dīn

---

468 He cites a poem composed by Sirāj al-Dīn al-Warrāq for the opening of Baybars' madrasa. *Rawḍ*, 184–185.

469 Al-Ṣafadī, *Aʿyān*, 3:498. See also al-Ṣafadī's own literary exchanges with Ibn al-Ghānim cited in *Alḥān*, 1:42–47.

470 Shihāb al-Dīn provides this information in a now-lost historical text, which is quoted by Ibn Taghrī-Birdī in his *tarjama* of Ibn ʿAbd al-Ẓāhir. Ibn Taghrī-Birdī, *Manhal*, 7:98.

471 On Ibn Ḥabīb's own literary writing, see: Jaakko Hämeen Anttila, "The essay and debate," 144.

472 Ibn Ḥabīb, *Durrat al-Aslāk fī Dawlat al-Atrāk*, Universitätsbibliothek Leipzig, MS Vollers 0661, 113b–114a.

473 Ibn Ḥabīb, *Tadkhirat al-nabīh*, 2:209. Also in *Durrat al-aslāk fī Dawlat al-Atrāk*, BnF, MS Arabe 1719, 191b.

Maḥmūd had earlier also written a poem praising ʿAlāʾ al-Dīn's garden.[474] We also have evidence of poetry being exchanged between Shāfiʿ and his cousin Fatḥ al-Dīn: a short poem welcoming Shāfiʿ as a guest built around intertextual references to poems by literary giants Abū l-ʿAlāʾ al-Maʿarrī and al-Fatḥ b. Khāqān (d. 247/861).[475]

The practice of exchanging literary texts was in some cases bound by genre constraints. An interesting case of literary exchange between high-profile scribes was recorded by Shihāb al-Dīn b. Faḍl Allāh al-ʿUmarī (d. 749/1349), a leading *kātib* himself, in his monumental *Masālik al-Abṣār.* In this work, al-ʿUmarī provides an entry for Shāfiʿ in his overview of prominent Egyptian poets while seemingly snubbing Ibn ʿAbd al-Ẓāhir by not mentioning him either in this section or in his overview of prominent scribes.[476] Al-ʿUmarī quotes a good number of Shāfiʿ's poems, as well a few samples of prose text. One such prose piece is a short extract of a variation which Shāfiʿ wrote (*qawluhu muʿāriḍan*) on a piece written by Tāj al-Dīn b. al-Athīr.[477] This Ibn al-Athīr was an important *kātib* in the *dīwān al-inshāʾ* during the reigns of both Baybars and Qalāwūn. Shāfiʿ mentions him once in reverent tones in *al-Faḍl al-Maʾthūr*.[478] The excerpt given by al-ʿUmarī is a variation on or imitation of themes and metaphors used by Ibn al-Athīr in an edict about the freeing of a certain unnamed person, possibly a *ḥājib*.[479] As we shall see below, the concept of *muʿāraḍa* will turn out to be important to understand a particular literary feature of Shāfiʿ's *sīra* output.

An interesting case of literary communication involving Shāfiʿ in the context of chancery tribulations is preserved in an as yet unedited anonymous compilation named *al-Ajwiba al-Muʿtabara ʿan al-Futyā al-Mubtakara* (Esteemable Answers to First Opinions), an anthology of different forms of literary communication amongst schol-

474 Al-Ṣafadī, *Wāfī*, 22:57–61. The lemma effectively spends more space on Shihāb al-Dīn Maḥmūd's writing than on ʿAlāʾ al-Dīn's, of whom only one *risāla* is quoted. In fact, al-Ṣafadī claims that ʿAlāʾ al-Dīn did not write any poetry.

475 Al-Ṣafadī, *Aʿyān*, 2:510.

476 Al-ʿUmarī, *Masālik*, 19:221–226. Unlike Ibn ʿAbd al-Ẓāhir, the earlier mentioned Shihāb al-Dīn Maḥmūd al-Ḥalabī does receive an extensive lemma as one of the most important *kuttāb*. Al-ʿUmarī, *Masālik*, 12:293–330. Al-ʿUmarī did quote a fair amount of Ibn ʿAbd al-Ẓāhir's poetry elsewhere. See for a brief discussion and references Frenkel, "Mamluk Historiography Revisited," 42.

477 Al-ʿUmarī, *Masālik*, 19:224.

478 *Faḍl*, 149. He is also named at (comparatively) considerable length in ʿIzz al-Dīn b. Shaddād's list of *kuttāb* (see chapter four).

479 Al-ʿUmarī, *Masālik*, 19:225. Both the short pieces quoted from Shāfiʿ and Ibn al-Athīr play on the meanings of the word *ḥājib* (pl. *ḥujjāb*), and Ibn al-Athīr even seems to say that the person "was called *ḥājib*."

ars throughout the late medieval period.[480] The last two sections of this manuscript containing collections of *taqārīẓ* (s. *taqrīẓ*, literary appreciations of a book by peers, requested by the book's author) have received some attention from Franz Rosenthal, Amalia Levanoni, and most recently Andreas Herdt,[481] but the manuscript's first few folios deal with a different subject matter: a letter written by the famous poet Ibn Nubāta al-Miṣrī who according to the text's introduction requested Shihāb al-Dīn b. Faḍl Allāh al-ʿUmarī to honour him with a position in the chancery as *kātib al-darj*. When he did not receive a reply, he requested a response (*istaftā*) to this situation from the "people of that age" (*ahl dhālika l-ʿaṣr*). The anonymous compiler notes that he was only able to find one of these responses, written by Shāfiʿ b. ʿAlī.[482] The episode is not dated, and neither is it referred to by Thomas Bauer in his otherwise thorough overview of Ibn Nubāta al-Miṣrī's life.[483] From that overview we do learn that Ibn Nubāta only fully entered the chancery rather late in life in 743/1342 (although he had close links to persons in the *dīwān* of both Damascus and Cairo in the decades before that), indeed in close association with Shihāb al-Dīn b. Faḍl Allāh. This is more than a decade after the death of Shāfiʿ in 730/1330 so the letters must date from a period before that. I would surmise that the events took place at some point in the (late) 720s/1320s when Shihāb al-Dīn b. Faḍl Allāh took over a leading role in the Damascus chancery. For our purposes the case is mostly interesting for the fact that this letter was written at a time when Shāfiʿ likely did not hold an actual position in the chancery and when he had lost his familial connections to it. Nevertheless, his earlier experience in that context and his family relation to recent icons of the chancery allowed him to formulate his opinion here with some authority and above all in the appropriate literary style. This exchange is not included in my visualisation above as the extent to which both authors knew each other and sent their texts directly to each other is unclear.

This example highlights a general feature: the literary exchanges Shāfiʿ engaged in were directly tied to his reputation as (erstwhile) scribe and, perhaps even more so, as member of a scribal dynasty, and this more explicitly than in the case of Ibn ʿAbd al-Ẓāhir. Not all correspondents of our authors were scribes, however. Ibn ʿAbd

---

480 Anonymous, *al-Ajwiba al-Muʿtabira ʿan al-Futyā al-Mubtakira*, Staatsbibliothek zu Berlin MS Wetzstein II, 1473. The manuscript likely dates from the late fifteenth or early sixteenth century, judging by its layout and the fact that it discusses events from the early 9th/15th century. I am grateful to Tarek Sabraa and Mohamad Maslouh for bringing this text to my attention.

481 Franz Rosenthal, "'Blurbs' (*taqrīẓ*) from 14th-Century Egypt," *Oriens* 27–28 (1981), 177–196; A. Levanoni, "Sīrat al-Muʾayyad Shaykh by Ibn Nāhiḍ," in *Texts, Document and Artefacts: Islamic Studies in Honour of D.S. Richards*, ed. C.F. Robinson (Leiden: Brill, 2003), 211–232. Andreas Herdt, "Taqrīẓ, Schein-Taqrīẓ oder Anti-Taqrīẓ? Ein mamlukenzeitliches Beispiel dafür, wie schmal der Grat zwischen Lob und Schmähung sein kann," in *The Racecourse of Literature*, 96–129.

482 *al-Ajwiba*, 1b–3b (Ibn Nubāta's request); 3b–4b (Shāfiʿ's response).

483 Bauer, "Ibn Nubātah al-Miṣrī," 9–35.

al-Ẓāhir for example engaged in a fruitful literary exchange with the poet Muḥyī al-Dīn b. Qirnāṣ al-Ḥamawī (d. 675/1276 or 685/1286), a member of the prominent Āl Qirnāṣ of Hama.[484] He also engaged in an extensive exchange of poems with Athīr al-Dīn Abū Ḥayyān al-Gharnāṭī, another literary heavyweight of the period who is today mostly remembered as a commentator of the Qurʾān and as a grammarian.[485] When al-Gharnāṭī wrote a *qaṣīda* in which a rare expression (*maʿnā gharīb*) was used about a person having a birthmark (*khāl*) on his nose, Ibn ʿAbd al-Ẓāhir promptly wrote no less than eight replies in which he continuously flexed the meaning of the expression.[486] Al-Gharnāṭī's literary relation with Ibn ʿAbd al-Ẓāhir did not end there: al-Jazarī mentions two poems Ibn ʿAbd al-Ẓāhir had heard from other persons and which he transmitted to al-Gharnāṭī.[487]

While all of the above examples are positive exchanges, in which authors praised and commended each other at least ostensibly, there are also uglier sides to literary communication. Ibn ʿAbd al-Ẓāhir's famous rebuttal of a critic cited above is a clear such case, but we also have evidence of such a case for Shāfiʿ. Al-Ṣafadī relates that sometime after he had become blind, Shāfiʿ had consulted a literary writing of the scribe Sharaf al-Dīn b. al-Waḥīd (d. 711/1311) and praised it in an epigram. In response Ibn al-Waḥīd replied with a four-line poem ending on al-Mutanabbī's famous line "I am the one whose *adab* the blind sees." Shāfiʿ took this as an insult and replied with a nine-line poem, of which the first two lines are:

نعم نظرتُ ولكن لم أجد أدبا   يا مَن غدا واحداً في قلة الأدب
جازيت مدحي وتقريظي بمعيرة   والعيب في الرأس دون العيب في الذنب

Yes, I looked but I did not find [true] literature (*adab*)
you who are unique in lacking good manners (*adab*)
you repaid my praise and acclaim with an insult,
but a default in the head is less bad than the disgrace of offending someone![488]

---

484 Al-Ṣafadī, *Wāfī*, 17:262–269. MS Sofia Or. 2026 makes clear that the *maqāma* cited by al-Ṣafadī was not an isolated instance: this manuscript in fact commences with a letter sent by Ibn Qirnāṣ al-Ḥamawī to Ibn ʿAbd al-Ẓāhir to which the *maqāma* is a reply. A further reply by Ibn Qirnāṣ is included as well. MS Sofia Or. 2026, 2a–12b. On Ibn Qirnāṣ al-Ḥamawī, see Ḥusayn ʿAbd al-ʿĀl al-Luhaybī, "Shiʿr Muḥyī al-Dīn b. Qirnāṣ al-Ḥamawī: Dirāsa wa-Tawthīq," *Majallat Markaz Dirāsāt al-Kūfa*, 31 (2013), 74–115.

485 Sidney Glazer, "Abu Ḥayyān A̲th̲īr al-Dīn Muḥammad b. Yūsuf al-G̲h̲arnāṭī," *EI2*.

486 Al-Jazarī, *Ḥawādith*, 1:179–181.

487 Al-Jazarī, *Ḥawādith*, 1:181. One by the famous *muḥaddith* Ibn al-Najjār [al-Baghdādī] (d. 643/1245) and the other by the renowned poet Abū al-ʿAlāʾ al-Maʿarrī (d. 449/1058).

488 al-Ṣafadī, *Wāfī*, vol 3:152. The exchange is summarised by al-ʿAynī, *ʿIqd*, 5:317 who only quotes these first two lines, and replaces the first half of the second line with this variant:

تذكرته أصبحت بعمى عيرتني - "You reproached me by mentioning that I became blind"

Shāfiʿ is employing meaningful terminology here. The term *ʿayb*, or blemish has a rich conceptual history.[489] Already in the 3rd/9th century, it was a major element of Arabic literary criticism. James Montgomery has argued that it should be understood as "a blemish, fault, failing, or defect which besmirches a man's honour and occasions disapproval and condemnation among his peer group and/or society, and which the committer, or possessor (if it is an object), should respond to as a significant diminishment of his social standing."[490] He continues that it was "a socialising response, one which defines and bonds an in-group who subscribe to it and know how to recognise it and, by dividing them off from the rest of society, relegates all others to the out-group."[491] Shāfiʿ was thus not just writing a rebuttal to an insult, he also linked himself to a long-standing tradition of literary challenges and retorts. Once again, he could underline and valorise his mastery of the literary tradition.

The marshalling of such terminology and the extensive citation of material from the rich literary history of the Arabic language are core aspects of literary performance. To briefly return to the anecdotal description of Shāfiʿ presented by al-Ṣafadī with which I started this book, it is this logic of practice that explains why al-Ṣafadī spent so much space on it. Shāfiʿs vigorous book collecting as reflected in the anecdote illustrates the logic of his literary culture's habitus. Shāfiʿ's identification of each book in his collection simply by handling the physical book serves as a metaphor for the ideal *kātib* or *adīb* of the period. It served to portray our author as representative of a self-conscious and self-referential literary culture, in which innovativeness, extensive knowledge of the canon and the ability to quote and associate phrasings from that canon to any given situation were all equally valued.[492] Such a person could associate discrete events to immortal phrasings and idiomatic expressions from the Arabic literary canon at any given time, endlessly reworking them into new contexts.[493] Shāfiʿ did not even need to see the actual works for all the details to appear in his mind, for he had internalised its contents

489 Note that it also appears in the opening lines of Ibn ʿAbd al-Ẓāhir's rebuttal of the Shīʿī cited at the outset of this chapter.

490 Mongomery, *Al-Jāḥiẓ*, 239.

491 Mongomery, *Al-Jāḥiẓ*, 254.

492 Wolfhart Heinrichs has highlighted the central importance of *muḥāḍara*, "or having an apposite quotation at one's fingertips" in literary idioms of pre-modern Arabic. Wolfhart Heinrichs, "Review of Cambridge History of Arabic Literature: ʿAbbasid Belles-Lettres," *al-ʿArabiyya* 26 (1993), 130. See also Bilal Orfali, *The Anthologist's Art:* Abū Manṣūr al-Thaʿālibī *and His* Yatīmat al-dahr (Leiden: Brill, 2016), 2.

493 Notably, al-Ṣafadī records a similar anecdote for the Baghdādī scholar Zayn al-Dīn al-Ḥanbalī (d. after 712/1312) who became blind in old age. The anecdote may thus be part of a topos related to blindness and its concomitant claim to excellent remembering. Paraphrased in Michal Biran, "Libraries, Books, and Transmission of Knowledge in Ilkhanid Baghdad" *JESHO* 62 (2019), 480–481.

and could apply them wherever appropriate, stringing together historiographical topoi, poetry, and rhetorical documents into complex but cohesive textual structures. Literary culture in this period fuelled the sense of a continuous tradition.

5.2 *Sīra* in the literary field

Ibn ʿAbd al-Ẓāhir and Shāfiʿ b. ʿAlī wrote their *sīras* in direct communication with the literary field, embedding poetic and artful prose materials in their texts and showcasing the kind of socio-literary strategies discussed in the preceding section. Participation in the literary field is largely implicit in these choices, but there are also points where they explicitly perform their mastery of cultural capital. In the following two subsections, I look at two examples of how this manifests itself in the *sīras*, respectively in the form of poetry and prose texts. These examples build on the previous chapter's observations on compilation as an integral tool of composition by looking at a number of discrete examples.

5.2.1 Poetry

With the notable exception of ʿAlāʾ al-Dīn b. ʿAbd al-Ẓāhir, all prominent members of the Banū ʿAbd al-Ẓāhir wrote extensively in the domain of poetry. The poetry of both Ibn ʿAbd al-Ẓāhir and Shāfiʿ was compiled into *dīwāns*, although for the latter it has not been preserved as far as I am aware. They also composed works about poetry and poets as noted in the introduction, although I am again not aware of any of these works having been preserved. Shāfiʿ's scribal manual does contain a lot of poetic material to illustrate poetic forms.[494] Poetry also takes up a prominent place in the *sīras*. The quoting of poetry in historical narrative was common practice but has not really been studied at a larger scale. Geert Jan van Gelder devoted two articles to the functions of poetry in "post-classical" historical contexts. He observed that "poetry reflects on history, occasionally it is part of history, and it is an almost indispensable part of historiography" and that "it is valuable in that it shows how the events were interpreted by contemporaries and later generations."[495] In an earlier article he referred to Wolfhart Heinrichs' distinction between two ideal types of poetry that appear in historical narrative: "action poems" and "commen-

494 *Al-Raʾy al-Ṣāʾib*, MS Ahmet III 2583, 88b–121b.
495 Geert-Jan Van Gelder, "Poetry in Historiography: The Case of *al-Fakhrī* by Ibn al-Ṭiqṭaqā," in *Poetry and History: The Value of Poetry in Reconstructing Arab History*, eds. Ramzi Baalbaki, S. Said Agha, & Tarif Khalidi (Beirut: AUB Press, 2011), 73.

tary poems," the first of which serve to drive the action forward, while the second comment upon the events related in the prose parts of the text. However, van Gelder notes that the distinction between the two is not always clear and that they tend to bleed into each other.[496]

Table 2: length of poetical excerpts and poetry percentages per *sīra*.[497]

Number of lines	*Rawḍ*	*Tashrīf*	*Alṭāf*	*Faḍl*	*Ḥusn*	*Sīrat al-Nāṣir*
1	34	1	1	2	3	2
2	22	1		3	2	2
3	5	1	2	1	1	
4	9	1			2	
5	3	1	1		2	
6	2		1			
8	2	1			2	
9–20	5	2	6	1	6	
21–30	2	3	3		1	
36–37				3	1	1
48–60		1		2	1	
77	[1]					
Authorship self-attributed	2	4	None	5	3	2
Percentage of total token count	3,27%	4,79%	17,21%	7,17%	7,36%	2,08%

Table 2 summarises the quantitative prominence of poetry for each text in the *sīra* corpus. As the final line shows, the word count[498] for poetry is not particularly dominant for most of the texts, ranging between only two and seven percent for five of the six texts. This is similar to other historiographical texts of a rhetorical nature from the same period.[499] The big exception is *al-Alṭāf al-khafiyya*, which consists

496 Geert-Jan Van Gelder "Poetry in Historiography: Some Observations" in *Problems in Arabic Literature*, ed. Miklós Maróth (Piliscsaba: The Avicenna institute of Middle Eastern studies, 2004), 5–6; Wolfhart Heinrichs, "Prosimetrical Genres in Classical Arabic Literature," in *Prosimetrum: Cross-Cultural Perspectives on Narrative in Prose and Verse*, ed. Joseph Harris & Karl Reichl (Cambridge: D.S. Brewer, 1997), 249–275.

497 Texts grouped by author: the three on the left by Ibn ʿAbd al-Ẓāhir, the three on the right by Shāfiʿ.

498 In fact, once more a token count. See chapter four, section 4.4.2.

499 Counts were undertaken on digital versions of texts included in the OpenITI corpus. I counted the number of tokens included on lines that included the mARkdown poetry tag and calculated their percentage in relation to the total token count of these texts. Note that these counts are only indicative, as not all the digital texts were proofread closely. For comparison, token counts on semi-contemporary historiographical texts: Ibn al-Dawādārī, *Kanz*: 8,33% (total for all nine volumes); Baybars al-Manṣūrī, *Zubdat*: 5,94% (only for the single volume edited by Donald P. Little); al-Nuwayrī, *Nihāyat*: 6,63% (total for all volumes); ʿIzz al-Dīn b. Shaddād, *Taʾrīkh*, 11,41%. The rel-

for about 17% of poetry. This data already indicates that this last text used poetry differently than the other texts, despite notably not claiming authorship of any of the poems.

While this quantitative data provides a useful overview of poetic prominence per text, it does not tell us much about what this poetry is doing in each text. The pronounced differences in the length and absolute number of the poems quoted already indicate that there is not a single poetic phenomenon governing the use of poetry in these texts or even within a single text. For example, while the surviving volume *al-Alṭāf al-Khafiyya* contains the highest percentage of poetry in our corpus, nearly all of it is found in the volume's first two thirds (if calculated only on that part of the text, the poetry percentage even rises to 26%), while the four *waqf* documents which take up the volume's final third contain no poetry at all, except for one long poem that concludes the introduction to the *waqf*s. In numbers of discrete poems, Ibn ʿAbd al-Ẓāhir's *sīra* of Baybars leads the pack, but in token count it is on the lower end of the scale because of the author's predominant use of one-liners. In this he follows *inshāʾ* practices of citing apt lines from the canon of Arabic literature, largely fitting Wolfhart Heinrichs' category of "commentary poems."

Ibn ʿAbd al-Ẓāhir's *sīra* of Baybars is somewhat exceptional in its reliance on so many epigrams. As the table shows, the other texts contain comparatively few short poems, but they have similar amounts of long poems. Shāfiʿ's penchant for poems of 36 to 37 lines, of which he wrote four (one, a felicitation for the conquest of Acre, is reproduced in two of his texts), is remarkable, especially since neither his uncle nor other contemporary poets appear to have been especially devoted to that specific length. To the *sīra* of Baybars, I have added one extra poem which does not survive in the two defective manuscripts, but which was probably a part of the original text. It appears in abridged form in Shāfiʿ b. ʿAlī's *Ḥusn al-Manāqib* (22 lines) and in its fullest known extent in ʿIzz al-Dīn b. Shaddād's *Taʾrīkh al-Malik al-Ẓāhir* (77 lines) as well as in other texts (see the long first footnote in my introduction to chapter two above).

Only few of the poems cited in the *sīra*s are explicitly attributed to authors. Some of these lines were written by famous poets and perhaps for that reason not explicitly linked to their author—that is, audiences would have been expected to identify these poems instantly. Following established practice in *inshāʾ* writing, our authors regularly cite lines by famous poets such as Imrūʾ al-Qays (d. 544 AD), Ṣaḥib al-Zanj (ʿAlī b. Muḥammad, d. 270/883), al-Buḥturī (d. 284/897), al-Qāḍī al-Fāḍil

atively high count for the latter may be explained by the inclusion of a long chapter compiling elegies for the death of Baybars (pp. 244–264) as well as several obituaries for poets. Compare in that sense the poetry percentage in al-Ṣafadī's biographical dictionary *Aʿyān*: 19,18%.

(d. 596/1200), and several others in their accounts.[500] By far the most quoted poet is al-Mutanabbī (d. 354/965): Ibn ʿAbd al-Ẓāhir quotes him at least fifteen times in the *sīra* of Baybars, and once in *al-Alṭāf al-Khafiyya.*[501] Shāfiʿ also quotes him once in his *sīra* of al-Nāṣir Muḥammad.[502] These quoted lines serve a variety of textual functions, but usually they are commentary poems. They provide a perspective on something just related by direct textual association or by contextual knowledge of the original poem's origins, meanings or interpretations which would be deciphered by the attentive reader.

Many verses included in the texts were probably not attributed because they must have been written by the authors. In the case of *al-Alṭāf al-Khafiyya,* which includes a relatively high number of long poems compared to a limited number of epigrams, it seems likely that the majority if not all its poetic material was written by the author himself. Several of these poems are found at the end of a chapter. They too can be understood as commentary poems, wrapping up the events described in prose in the preceding lines and providing a different perspective from a different literary register.

Ibn ʿAbd al-Ẓāhir's extensive use of self-composed poetry here is one of the ways in which poetry in the *sīra* corpus is distinctive from the works of other historians of the period. The latter routinely quoted poetry composed for specific occasions, but their compilatory approach usually exhibits a more panoramic approach, citing poems written by a range of poets.[503] While our authors do cite poetry written by contemporaries, they gave preferential treatment to poetry they had composed themselves.

While both our authors are keen to include their own poetry, Ibn ʿAbd al-Ẓāhir at one point makes the quoting of other persons' poetry an area of significant authorial agency. One pertinent example of this is found in Ibn ʿAbd al-Ẓāhir's *Tashrīf al-Ayyām,* in a section presenting Qalāwūn's conquest of Marqab as one of the crowning achievements of his sultanate. The prose description of the historical

---

500 It is perhaps notable that while Ibn ʿAbd al-Ẓāhir has a penchant to quote these "superstars" of Arabic poetry, Shāfiʿ more often quotes somewhat more obscure poets.

501 Notably, Shāfiʿ excises the majority of Ibn ʿAbd al-Ẓāhir's quotes in *Ḥusn.*

502 BnF MS Arabe 1705, 27a. Shāfiʿ also claims to have authored what appears to have been a commentary on al-Mutanabbī's poetry entitled *al-Ishʿār bi-mā li-l-Mutanabbī min al-Ashʿār* ("The notification about al-Mutanabbī's poems"). Al-Ṣafadī, *Aʿyān,* 2:507.

503 Indeed, they often quote poetry written by one or both of our authors. For examples of Shāfiʿ being quoted by one semi-contemporary and one later historian: Ibn al-Dawādārī, *Kanz,* 9:190; al-ʿAynī, *ʿIqd,* 5:164, 316, 317. The long elegy for Baybars cited by ʿIzz al-Dīn b. Shaddād is a good case in point for the citation of multiple authors: Ibn ʿAbd al-Ẓāhir's elegy is here the first of eight poems composed by seven different poets. *Taʾrīkh al-Malik al-Ẓāhir,* 244–264.

events is followed by three poems and a prose piece written on the occasion and a short section with historical accounts (*akhbār*) about this castle. Ibn ʿAbd al-Ẓāhir starts his poetical section with a praise poem in which the sultanic excellence of the preceding prose section is amplified by such lines as "[it is] a castle of great fortune, not dealt with in any *sīra* of who preceded you."[504] Following this poem, he includes five lines from a poem written as a reply to the sultan's good tidings (*fī jawābu l-bishārati*) in name of Qalāwūn's son al-Ashraf Khalīl—the name of the poet is not given. Ibn ʿAbd al-Ẓāhir adds the following comment to this poem:

ورأيت قد وقع في مقصورة ابن دريد قوله:
ومرقب مخلولق أرجاؤه   مستصعب الآفاق وعر المرتقى
فاهتدمت جملة من مقصورة ابن دريد ونقلتها إلى مدح مولانا السلطان وكان بها أحق وهي

> I saw that [the following] phrase had been taken from Ibn Durayd's *Maqṣūra*:
> *And beautiful Marqab, its walls*
> *as the horizon beyond reach, and ascending it miserable*
> So I extrapolated a sentence of Ibn Durayd's *Maqṣūra* and relocated it to a panegyric of our lord the sultan, for there it was more proper.[505]

Ibn ʿAbd al-Ẓāhir picked up on an intertextual reference—it should be noted that *ihtidām* actually has a connotation of plagiarism[506]—to the famous poem *Qaṣīdat al-Maqṣūra*, written by the tenth-century poet Ibn Durayd (d. 223/933) in the poem sent by the unnamed poet.[507] The line is indeed similar to a line from the latter part of the *maqsūra*: in fact it only differs from the published version of the poem in its use of *al-āfāq* instead of *al-aqdhāf*—both have similar meanings of distant lands—in the second hemistich.[508] In any case, it is clear that the association triggered Ibn ʿAbd al-Ẓāhir's creativity, for he next produces an entirely new 23-line poem, parts

---

504 *Tashrīf*, 82.

جِصن عظيم القدر في سيرة   لمن مضى قبلك لم يُكتب

505 *Tashrīf*, 83.

506 See however for the problematics of defining where plagiarism starts and intertextuality ends in Arabic rhetorics, Thomas Bauer, "Arabische Kultur," in *Historische Wörterbuch der Rhetorik*, eds. Gert Ueding e.a. (Tübingen: Max Niemeyer, 2007), 119. See also the editor's comment in *Tashrīf*, 83 n. 1.

507 According to Michael G. Carter the *maqṣūra*, so named because of its end-rhyme on the *alif maqṣūra*, is "a pedagogical poem about words," "Ibn Durayd," in *Encyclopedia of Arabic Literature, vol. 1*, eds. Julie S. Meisami & Paul Starkey (London: Routledge, 1998), 322. The poem is actually a eulogy. Its dense rhetorical and stylistic register explains its popularity among later *udabāʾ* and its pedagogical uses.

508 It is thus also possible to read Ibn ʿAbd al-Ẓāhir's first comment as: "I saw that he had been inspired by the [following] phrase from Ibn Durayd's *Maqṣūra*." It remains unclear whether this line was part of the poem sent in the name of al-Ashraf Khalīl, or only that Ibn ʿAbd al-Ẓāhir noted

of which are reminiscent of the *Maqṣūra* in phrasing and wording. We know from manuscript survival and a relative abundance of commentaries that Ibn Durayd's poem was a mainstay of literary culture at the time of Ibn ʿAbd al-Ẓāhir's writing, and we even know that Shāfiʿ also quoted a line from the poem in *Ḥusn al-Manāqib* after mentioning the conquest of Qarqīsiyā, a castle earlier known (and also referenced in the *Maqṣūra*) as al-Zabbāʾ.[509] It is thus not surprising to see two poets engaging with this classic text, but it is perhaps remarkable to see this in the context of a *sīra*. While all the quoted poems are relevant to the topic of praise for the sultan's military achievement at Marqab, Ibn ʿAbd al-Ẓāhir creates a literary dynamic by which the focus is shifted to the poetry and the intertextual communication itself. The topic of that poetry becomes almost secondary to the ways in which its authors participate in practices of literary communication. It furthermore shifts the literary focus to Ibn ʿAbd al-Ẓāhir who performs his superior knowledge of the Arabic poetical tradition.

The just noted example is part of a specific subsection devoted to poetry, but we also find a great deal of short and medium-length verse quoted throughout the historical narratives. One of the sections in which poetry takes a notably prominent place is the section dealing with Baybars' Anatolian campaign for which we have both the probable earlier and later versions found respectively in al-Qalqashandī's *Ṣubḥ al-Aʿshā* and in Ibn ʿAbd al-Ẓāhir's *sīra* of Baybars (see chapter four, section 4.4.2.). Its earlier existence as an *inshāʾ* letter perhaps explains why it contains the most sustained use of poetry as an integral, almost choral textual element in our corpus (as noted above, the original letter contained even more poetry). There are twenty-four poems found throughout the narrative of this section. Of these poems, Ibn ʿAbd al-Ẓāhir only explicitly ascribes four to specific authors: three to al-Mutanabbī and one to Imrūʾ al-Qays. Most are only preceded by something along the lines of "as the poet said" (*ka-mā qāla l-shāʿir*).[510] I could identify eight more of these poetical units as written by al-Mutanabbī, but the remainder of quoted poetry remains unidentified.

This choice for al-Mutanabbī was not random or only inspired by the poet's undeniable stature as one of the greatest panegyric poets of Arabic literature.[511] The association envisaged by Ibn ʿAbd al-Ẓāhir in fact follows a contextual logic.

---

an inspiration, which I do not clearly detect in the lines quoted above the comment, aside from a tendency to end on *alif maqṣūra*.

509 *Ḥusn*, 207. The 42nd line of the *Maqṣūra*.

510 *Rawḍ*, 58, 70, 110, 191, 212, 264 (followed by a poem written by the author himself), 270.

511 Al-Qāḍī al-Fāḍil for example also quoted from al-Mutanabbī's praise poetry to Sayf al-Dawla while addressing Ṣalāḥ al-Dīn. Ernest Sivan, *L'Islam et la croisade: Idéologie et Propaganda dans les Réactions Musulmanes aux Croisades* (Paris: Librairie d'Amérique et d'Orient, 1968), 109.

Al-Mutanabbī served for nine years as court poet to Sayf al-Dawla (d. 356/967), the Ḥamdānid ruler of Aleppo who fought a resurgent Byzantine empire in eastern Asia Minor. For al-Mutanabbī these were fruitful years during which he wrote his most celebrated panegyric poetry.[512] Much of this poetry deals with Sayf al-Dawla's campaigns: it is brimming with evocations of the region where our author and his sultan campaigned. For Ibn ʿAbd al-Ẓāhir it was the ideal place to look for appropriate imagery and phrases to inform his own narrative.[513]

The association of al-Mutanabbī's verses on Sayf al-Dawla's Anatolian campaigns to Baybars' military achievements in the same geographical area aligns with Ibn ʿAbd al-Ẓāhir's oft-noted project of equating Baybars with near-mythical rulers of the distant past. Baybars started out from Aleppo to fight the Armenians and the Mongols, just as Sayf al-Dawla famously started out from the same city to fight the Byzantines in the same region. But the association also goes beyond Sayf al-Dawla. Upon conquering Kayseri, Baybars is seated upon the Saljuq throne in the "House of the Sultanate" (*dār al-salṭana*). Ibn ʿAbd al-Ẓāhir concludes in *sajʿ* that the sultan "sat on the highest point of the Sultanate at the happiest of moments, and by alighting on it he conferred to the throne the greatest felicity."[514] Immediately following this statement, Ibn ʿAbd al-Ẓāhir includes an epigram, the first line of which contains the phrase "*al-malīk al-ẓāhir*," that is, presumably, al-Malik al-Ẓāhir Baybars, so this must be a poem written by the author himself. While it notes that the throne had been unsuitable for anyone but Baybars, who thus excels all other rulers who sat on it before him, the epigram may also communicate another idea by way of the choice for the more rarely attested form "*malīk*," which more literally

512 Julie Scott Meisami, "al-Mutanabbī," in *Encyclopedia of Arabic Literature, vol. 2*, eds. Julie S. Meisami & Paul Starkey (London: Routledge, 1998), 2:559. For a detailed literary discussion of all the poems written during this period, see Andras Hamori, *The Composition of al-Mutanabbi's Panegyrics to Sayf al-Dawla* (Leiden: Brill, 1992).

513 Sayf al-Dawla himself sometimes shows up as an example in political advice literature, such as in the mirror for princes written by Ibn Nubāta l-Miṣrī, as referenced in Syrinx Von Hees, "The Guidance for Kingdoms: Function of a 'Mirror for Princes' at Court and its Representation of a Court," in *Court Cultures in the Muslim World: Seventh to Nineteenth Centuries*, eds. Albrecht Fuess & Jan-Peter Hartung (London: Routledge, 2011), 374.

514 *Rawḍ*, 466. *Martaba* may also literally mean "seat" here, but the connotation of a high summit with a vantage point is strong. This episode is one of the few from the campaign which survive in Shāfiʿ's brief account. It is also one of the few instances in which ʿIzz al-Dīn b. Shaddād resorts to *sajʿ* in the main annalistic section of *Taʾrīkh al-Malik al-Ẓāhir*, 176. The much later historian al-Suyūṭī (d. 911/1505) mentions it as one of the prime achievements of Baybars: *Ḥusn al-Muḥāḍara fī Akhbār Miṣr wa-l-Qāhira*, 2 vols., ed. Muḥammad Abū l-Faḍl Ibrāhīm (Aleppo: Dār Iḥyā al-Kutub al-ʿArabiyya, 1968), 2:96.

means "possessor."[515] In this reading "*ẓāhir*" ("manifest," "apparent," but also more literally "outward appearance") may obliquely claim that the sultan was not a "king manifest" but a "possessor" of the throne only in the literal sense of the word, that is, in appearance only. This is all the more pertinent with the knowledge that after Baybars' return from Anatolia, his conquest of Kayseri and nominal taking up of the Seljuq throne was quickly made undone, not in the least by the sultan's own death.[516] The fact that the sultan is immediately after also described as "*al-nadb*," which has a number of meanings related to "appointment," "mandate," "ingenious,"[517] but also "lamentation" and "weeping," also draws the verse firmly into the domain of ambiguity.

The possible use of *tawriyya* (double entendre) in this poem highlights the strong rhetorical qualities of this entire section,[518] and the ambiguous ways in which Ibn ʿAbd al-Ẓāhir composed it at a moment when Baybars was already on the retreat from his Anatolian campaign. It subtly takes the equation of Baybars' actions to Sayf al-Dawla's beyond the merely glorious actions, for Sayf al-Dawla's later years were also marred by military defeat and the temporary loss of Aleppo. He was eventually even forced to become a tributary to the Byzantines.[519]

Perhaps even more fundamental than Baybars' equation to Sayf al-Dawla is how Ibn ʿAbd al-Ẓāhir performs his position as ideal *kātib* in the narrative. For one, there is a noticeable shift in writing style in this section: Ibn ʿAbd al-Ẓāhir is much more present in his text here, often writing in the first-person plural and talking about his experiences and hardships on the journey as part of the sultan's army. As noted, al-Mutanabbī too, accompanied Sayf al-Dawla on military campaigns and composed

---

515 The poem appears in identical form in the original letter cited in al-Qalqashandī, *Ṣubḥ*, 14:155.

وما كان هذا التخت من حين نصب   لغير المليك الظاهر يصلى الندب

Translated in Khowayṭer, "A Critical Edition," 864 as "Since it was erected this throne had not been suitable for any but the active king al-Ẓāhir."

516 The fact that Shāfiʿ refers to this episode as a "*ghazwa*" (raid) and not a "*fatḥ*" (conquest) is telling in that sense. *Ḥusn*, 333. If al-Qalqashandī's contextual information on the letter in which the poem appears is right, it was likely written still before the death of Baybars, but after the sultan's return to Syria.

517 For the latter, see Lane, *An Arabic-English Lexicon*, 2779, who also describes it as "a man who, when he is sent to accomplish a great, or important, affair, finds it light to him."

518 Ibn ʿAbd al-Ẓāhir was well versed in the art of *tawriyya*, as four centuries after his death ʿAbd al-Ghanī al-Nābulusī (d. 1143/1731) used an example of his to illustrate the working of this poetic technique. Cachia, *The Arch Rhetorician*, 72. However, Cachia or perhaps al-Nābulusī himself mistakenly transcribes the name as Ibn ʿAbd al-Qāhir.

519 Hugh Kennedy, *The Prophet and the Age of the Caliphates: The Islamic Near East from the 6th to the 11th Century* (London: Longman, 1986), 239–240.

poetry for the occasion.[520] By Ibn ʿAbd al-Ẓāhir's time, however, both poetry and prose were essential to literary performance. In the above noted section on Qalāwūn's conquest of Marqab this took the form of Ibn ʿAbd al-Ẓāhir composing separate pieces of poetry and prose to garland the occasion, but in the long section detailing the Anatolian campaign he took a different approach related to its original composition as a *risāla* in the *inshā'* tradition, where poetry and prose were expected to be interwoven.

Ibn ʿAbd al-Ẓāhir's opening claims are suggestive of his undertaking:

ولما كان المملوك قد انتظم في سلك الخدم والعبيد * وأصبح كم له قصيد في مدح هذا البيت الشريف كل بيت منها بيت القصيد * وأنّ في مآثره الرسائل التي قد شاعت * وضاعت نفحاتها في الوجود وكم رسالة غيرها في غيره ضاعت * رأى أن يتحف الخواطر الشريفة من هذه الغزوة بلُمَح يختار منها من يؤلف * ويسند اليها من يؤرخ أو يصنف * وإنما قصد أن يتحف بها أبواب مولانا مع بسط القول وإتساع كلماته * لأن الله قد شرف المملوك بعبودية مولانا "والله أعلم حيث يجعل رسالته" * فإن كان المملوك قد طوّل في المطراحة * فمولانا يتطوّل في المسامحة * وإن قال أحد هذا هذى * فما زال شرح الوقائع مطوّلاً كذا * وتالله ما ورّج مثلها في التواريخ الأول * ولعمري إن خيرًا من سيرة ذلك البطال سيرة هذا البطل * والأمر أعلى في قراءتها واستماعها *

When the *mamlūk* [Ibn ʿAbd al-Ẓāhir] was incorporated in the corps of servants and slaves, and had written a great amount of *qaṣīdas* in praise of this noble house—each verse being as it were the principal verse of the *qaṣīda* (*bayt al-qaṣīd*)—and his writings included letters which had gained fame and whose scents had emanated across the world—(God knows) how many other letters (by him) on other subjects have been lost!—[Ibn ʿAbd al-Ẓāhir] deemed it appropriate to present the [sultan's] notions of this raid by way of a wondrous thing to behold (*lumaḥ*) from which the copyist can choose [what he finds appropriate to copy], and on which the chronicler or compiler may lean. And verily, he has aimed to present it to the gates of our lord [Bahā' al-Dīn b. Ḥinnā] with prolixity and verbosity, because God honoured the *mamlūk* [Ibn ʿAbd al-Ẓāhir] by [bringing him in] the service of our lord—"and God knows to whom he should entrust His message!" [*Qur'ān,* 6:124] And if the *mamlūk* has been long-winded in his proposition, our lord will be generous in his forgiveness; and if one should say: 'this is but empty talk, why did he keep on expounding with such verbosity?,' [I would answer] by God! in the first histories no such [happenings] have been recorded, and by my life! better than a *sīra* of such a vainglorious person (*baṭṭāl*) is the *sīra* of this hero (*baṭal*)![521]

We cannot assess whether these lines were effectively incorporated into the *sīra*, as the folios on which they would have been included are missing in the Istanbul manuscript and it may well be that Ibn ʿAbd al-Ẓāhir excised this bit of text from the original to make it flow more naturally with the rest of the textual construction. But these claims remain telling in relation to the later parts of the text which were reused (be it literally or in different form or wording) in the *sīra*. Ibn ʿAbd al-Ẓāhir

520 "His primary function on these occasions was to record the details of the battles and describe them in celebratory panegyrics. Whether Sayf al-Dawlah was victorious or not mattered little, and the demand for eulogistic renditions sometimes led to ridiculous exaggerations of meager, even non-existent, triumphs." Larkin, *Al-Mutanabbī,* 52–53.

521 *Rawḍ,* 454–455; *Ṣubḥ,* 14:140.

even notes explicitly that his accounts may be helpful to those compiling or writing historical accounts, as it were foreshadowing his own reworking of the text to fit into his *sīra*. The *sīra* also appears here in the last line, and less as a general category than one would think at first sight, as Ibn ʿAbd al-Ẓāhir's project of writing a *sīra* must have been already well advanced when he composed this *risāla*. These comments stress the importance of Ibn ʿAbd al-Ẓāhir's personal association to both the sultan and his vizier. Through this discourse our author effectively establishes that in the following parts of the text he will serve as an intermediary between these two prominent leaders of the sultanate. Ibn ʿAbd al-Ẓāhir is cut out for the task for he is the most adequate eulogist and historian around because of his ample experience in writing praise poems (*qaṣīd*) and letters (*rasāʾil*). This resonates directly with the *sīra*'s introductory claim that no *dawla* can exist without a chronicler. It is even taken one step further here by our author's use of the Qurʾān, by which it is implied that God himself has enabled Ibn ʿAbd al-Ẓāhir to write this text by placing the "message" in the most adequate hands.

This may not necessarily bear any direct relation to the poetic material cited from al-Mutanabbī, but it does highlight how Ibn ʿAbd al-Ẓāhir represented himself *vis-à-vis* Baybars. Ibn ʿAbd al-Ẓāhir's construction of this relation to Baybars, in which he bestows a fundamental role to himself, has a fascinating parallel in al-Mutanabbī's own writings. Just as al-Mutanabbī in his panegyrics to Sayf al-Dawla constantly underlined how only he was worthy of being the ruler's panegyrist,[522] Ibn ʿAbd al-Ẓāhir stressed his importance by way of his stylistic choice in writing the text in such an elaborate register that immediately draws attention to our author's literary dexterity.

Ibn ʿAbd al-Ẓāhir's textual construction here serves both as a laudation (and perhaps veiled criticism) of Baybars and as an equation of Ibn ʿAbd al-Ẓāhir himself to one of the greatest poets of the Arabic literary canon. That he also quotes Imrūʾ al-Qays in passing does not disturb that image but only adds to the timeless qualities of Ibn ʿAbd al-Ẓāhir's literary performance of revisiting and re-signifying the poetic *lieux de mémoire* of eastern Anatolia.[523] If we consider the fact that good letter writing was supposed to interweave famous poetry and artful prose, it may well be a large part of the reason why al-Qalqashandī thought it was a great example of a letter informing about war activities.

---

522 Larkin, *Al-Mutanabbī*, 40. She also notes that "virtually every eulogy of Sayf al-Dawlah is to some extent also a eulogy of the poet." Larkin, *Al-Mutanabbī*, 51–52.

523 A similar practice of prose-poetry interaction and active connection to earlier examples is found in the same text in a section about an earlier raid of Baybars against Sīs, in which a poem by al-Buḥturī (d. 284/897) is followed by several unidentified poems. *Rawḍ*, 434–438.

5.2.2 Prose: *muʿāraḍa*

Having focussed predominantly on Ibn ʿAbd al-Ẓāhir until now, let us now turn to a literary practice found most prominently in the work of Shāfiʿ. As we have seen, Shāfiʿ includes several different texts written for the same occasion by different authors in *al-Faḍl al-Maʾthūr*. He does so for poetry, where multivalence is to be expected, but also for official documents, in which only one such document would have been effectively used or sent. These can be understood as examples of the literary practice of *muʿāraḍa*, generally understood to be an imitation of themes, metrics, metaphors chosen by an earlier writer, but in its imitated form intended to surpass the preceding piece. Maurice Pomerantz notes that it was understood as an "interactive process in which exemplar and copy were compared," and that it involved "a wide range of attitudes toward the initial text, including reverent imitation, conscious emulation, and competitive rivalry."[524] The earliest such document cited by Shāfiʿ is his own version of the marriage contract written for al-Saʿīd Baraka Qān and Qalāwūn's daughter, which he was instigated to write by Ibn ʿAbd al-Ẓāhir, the author of the actual marriage contract. This shows how imitation was an essential part of a scribe's training: he was encouraged to pick up on the purport (*maʿnā*) of an earlier text and come up with a variation of it in a text that both refers to that earlier text and can work as a stand-alone text. In the later thematic sections, he provides us with several more examples—note that his own versions are always the last in the row:

- Two praise poems on the victory at Homs: one by Fatḥ al-Dīn b. ʿAbd al-Ẓāhir, the second by Shāfiʿ.[525]
- Three *tadhkiras* (memoranda) communicating how the sultan's son should rule Egypt in the absence of Qalāwūn: one by Ibn ʿAbd al-Ẓāhir, an abridged one by Fatḥ al-Dīn b. ʿAbd al-Ẓāhir, and one by Shāfiʿ.[526]
- Two *inshāʾ* descriptions of Marqab: one ascribed to Fatḥ al-Dīn b. ʿAbd al-Ẓāhir, another to Shāfiʿ.[527]

524 Maurice Pomerantz, "The Rivalrous Imitator: *The Ruby Red Account of the Fire of Damascus* by Ibn Ḥiǧǧah al-Ḥamawī (d. 838/1434)" in *The Racecourse of Literature*, 129. See also the elegant discussion in Abdelfattah Kilito, *Arabs and the Art of Storytelling: A Strange Familiarity*, (Syracuse, NY: Syracuse University Press, 2014), 6–7. For an earlier example of such a practice in the context of *inshāʾ* writing: Ḍiyā al-Dīn b. al-Athīr (d. 637/1239) cites a prestigious letter informing the Caliph in Baghdad about Ṣalāḥ al-Dīn's victories at Ḥaṭṭīn and Jerusalem, even though it was never sent. Claude Cahen paraphrases Ibn al-Athīr's intention here as "to rival with the *qāḍī* al-Fāḍil." Claude Cahen, "La Correspondance de Ḍiyā ad-Dîn ibn al-Athīr: Liste de lettres et textes de diplômes," *BSOAS* 14, no. 1 (1952), 35.

525 *Faḍl*, 82–85.

526 *Faḍl*, 118–135.

527 *Faḍl*, 142–144. The text here ascribed to Fatḥ al-Dīn is claimed to have been written by Ibn ʿAbd al-Ẓāhir himself in *Tashrīf*, 85.

- Two letters informing the ruler of Yemen about the conquest of Tripoli: one by Tāj al-Dīn b. al-Athīr, a second by Shāfiʿ.[528]
- Two poetry *tahni'as* on the conquest of Acre: one by Ibn ʿAbd al-Ẓāhir, another by Shāfiʿ, which concludes the book.[529]

Two instances from this list will be my focus for the following discussion: the *tadhkiras* and the letters to Yemen.

The *tadhkiras* are introduced by a paragraph in which Shāfiʿ describes the occasion for writing at least the first of these texts: the sultan's departure for Syria (like most of the events in this *sīra*, not specified in time) and the transfer of governorship over Egypt to this son al-Ṣālīh.[530] Shortly before his departure, Qalāwūn is said to have commanded the writing of a *tadhkira* which would detail these tasks.[531] Two scholars have translated and studied the contents of these *tadhkiras*, and Paulina Lewicka argued that these pieces were primarily included "to display the rhetorical skill of [Shāfiʿ] and his kinsmen."[532] A first observation problematises the latter assessment: while Ibn ʿAbd al-Ẓāhir's and Shāfiʿ's *tadhkiras* are given in full, Fatḥ al-Dīn's is presented in abridged form. His *tadhkira* was actually written, in Shāfiʿ's own words, "on the occasion of another journey [of the sultan]" (*fī safra ukhrā*) which may explain the reason for only presenting it in abridged form. However, he also concludes it with the statement that "this is the summary (*mulakhkhaṣ*) of the sections of this *tadhkira*, which are many and long (*kathīra ṭawīla*),[533] and there is sufficiency

528 *Faḍl*, 150–160.
529 *Faḍl*, 178–183.
530 Interestingly, it is said that his brother al-Ashraf Khalīl was "forbidden to vie with his brother" and had to accompany him (*yalzam maʿahu*) in his governing tasks.
531 *Faḍl*, 118. See also Axel Moberg, "Regierungspromemoria eines Ägyptischen Sultans" in *Festschrift Edward Sachau zum siebzigsten Geburtstage gewidmet von Freunden und Schülern*, ed. G. Weil (Berlin: Georg Kremer, 1915), 408. Moberg claims that Ibn ʿAbd al-Ẓāhir stayed in Cairo during this trip, while Shāfiʿ and Fatḥ al-Dīn accompanied Qalāwūn to Syria.
532 Moberg, "Regierungspromemoria" (edition and translation of Ibn ʿAbd al-Ẓāhir's *tadhkira*); Paulina Lewicka, "What a King Should Care About: Two Memoranda of the Mamluk Sultan on Running the State's Affairs," *Studia Arabistyczne i Isamistyczne* 6 (1998), 5–45 (edition and translation of the two other *tadhkiras*). For a later *tadhkira* written by Ibn al-Mukarram, see: Leonor Fernandes, "On Conducting the Affairs of the State: A Guideline of the 14th Century," *Annales Islamologiques* 24 (1988), 81–91.
533 The manuscript would suggest rather *kurra, karra,* or maybe even *kibra, kubra,* or *kabra,* but none of these options seem to make sense here. Tadmurī reads "*kathīra ṭawīla*," *Faḍl*, 127; Lewicka reads "*kabīra ṭawīla*." *Šāfiʿ Ibn ʿAlī's Biography*, 355. Both readings suppose that the copyist did not dot his letters here, while he does do so for most of the text. The line just above undoubtedly contains the word "*kabīr*" written differently and including all the dots. The immediately following

in what we have mentioned (*fī-mā dhakarnāhu maqnaʿ*)."[534] The statement is not only remarkable considering the considerable length of both Ibn ʿAbd al-Ẓāhir's and Shāfiʿ's own *tadhkiras*, it also suggests that Shāfiʿ considered Fatḥ al-Dīn's *tadhkira* to be relatively unimportant. Why Shāfiʿ did not leave the text out entirely then remains unclear, but it does resonate with the two praise texts on the Battle of Homs written by Shāfiʿ and Fatḥ al-Dīn and some general comments about their relationship found in the rest of the text which have made P.M. Holt conclude that Shāfiʿ had "little affection" for his family members "even if he showed them formal respect."[535]

The recording of these three *tadhkiras* was meant in the first place to underline Shāfiʿ's own close association with the two leading *kuttāb* of the type. His text showcased that he was equally worthy, or, considering the crude abridgment of his cousin's text, *more* worthy of being a leading *kātib*, possibly at a point when he did not enjoy such a relation to the chancery anymore. We have seen above that the caliphal *taqlīd* written for al-Nāṣir Muḥammad's third ascension of the throne implicitly communicated competitive practices between Shāfiʿ and ʿAlāʾ al-Dīn b. ʿAbd al-Ẓāhir, which may be seen in a similar light, although there the *taqlīd* was written in direct opposition to rather than as a variation of an earlier document. All these documents attest of a constant need to perform one's fitness to scribal pre-eminence.

The second example takes this beyond Shāfiʿ's family and sees him positioning himself *vis-à-vis* non-family agents. Of the two different letters written to be sent to Yemen to communicate the good news of the conquest of Tripoli the first is written by the well-known *kātib* Tāj al-Dīn b. al-Athīr. We have already come across this author above as the one who wrote a text to which Shāfiʿ wrote a *muʿāraḍa* (see 5.1.).[536] He is also attested as the recipient of a poem in which Shāfiʿ thanks him for having sent him a watermelon from his garden.[537] In *al-Faḍl al-Maʾthūr*, our author introduces Tāj al-Dīn b. al-Athīr and his text as follows:[538]

---

word *ṭawīla* also comprises all necessary dots (except those of the *tāʾ marbūṭa*, which is routinely undotted in the manuscript).

534 Bodleian MS Marsh 424, 92a–92b. *Faḍl*, 127; Lewicka, *Šāfiʿ Ibn ʿAlī's Biography*, 355.

535 Holt, "A Chancery Clerk," 678.

536 As we have seen in chapter four, he is mentioned by ʿIzz al-Dīn b. Shaddād as having joined the central *dīwān al-inshāʾ* during the reign of Baybars, where it is noted that before that he had been active in Damascus in the *dīwān* of al-Nāṣir Yūsuf. ʿIzz al-Dīn b. Shaddād, *Taʾrīkh al-Malik al-Ẓāhir*, 239.

537 The friendly exchange is cited in Ibn al-Ṣuqāʿī, *Tālī*, 23–24.

538 As Tadmurī notes, Ibn al-Athīr's letter is attested in other historical writings with some word variation. The editor notes text variation, but the letter as quoted in al-ʿUmarī, *Masālik*, 12:268–269 actually showcases significant variation compared to the text in *Faḍl*: the latter has several unique phrases, and the ones that do overlap can be quite different, especially in the opening sections which are entirely different. This would suggest that either Shāfiʿ or al-ʿUmarī reworked the letter when including it in their texts or they had access to different versions of it.

وفي فتحها ما كتب الصدر الفاضل البليغ البارع تاج الدين أحمد بن سعيد المعروف بإبن الأثير الكاتب الحلبي وهو الكاتب الذي لا يُباري قلمه * ولا يضاهي كَلِمه * ولا يكمل كاتب لإلاقة دواته * ولا لمعارضة أدواته * كتب مُهَنِّيًا بفتحها للملك المظفر شمس الدين صاحب اليمن كتابًا

> And one of the things written about the conquest [of Tripoli] was by the hand of the honourable, outstanding, eloquent, brilliant Tāj al-Dīn Aḥmad b. Saʿīd, known as Ibn al-Athīr, the *kātib* from Aleppo—the scribe whose pen cannot be vied with, and whose words cannot be imitated; no scribe can reach the lightning[539] of his inkwell, nor could he vie with his utensils. He wrote the following letter in felicitation of its conquest to al-Malik al-Muẓaffar Shams al-Dīn, lord of Yemen.[540]

From the introduction to this letter, it is clear that Shāfiʿ's relationship to this scribe was different than to his relatives. For one, there is no stress on a specific personal relationship: rather, Ibn al-Athīr is merely named as an excellent *kātib*. It is notable that Shāfiʿ specifically mentions that his penmanship is so excellent that it cannot be vied with. The Arabic word used here is *muʿāraḍa*. When introducing his own variation of the text's themes, he does not use the word *muʿāraḍa* but rather writes after noting the conclusion of Ibn al-Athīr's letter (*intahā kalāmahu*, "[here] ends his speech"), on a separate line: "and by the slave, the compiler of this *sīra*" (*wa-liʾl-mamlūki jāmiʿu hādhihi l-sīrati)* and then, separated from the prior statement, *"fī l-maʿnā."*[541] The specific textual position of this statement in the manuscript suggests that it is used here to denote a formal characteristic of the text, meaning something along the lines of, "as an example of *maʿnā*," or "of the same purport." Shāfiʿ was referring here not only to a rhetorical practice intimately concerned with meaning, but he also quite literally meant a *type* of writing. As Adrian Gully notes:

> The Arabic word for 'theme' normally used in the sources is *maʿnā*, probably one of the most loaded, versatile, and significant terms in pre-modern Arabic discourse. Aside from its more general sense of 'meaning'—a term that in itself requires careful reflection—it carries the sense of 'idea', 'motif' or 'concept', all of which are related to the sense of theme. The relationship between idea and theme becomes clear when we examine more closely the unity of the text in a given epistle or even in an example of poetry. The composite structure of a letter is based on the fundamental premise that the main theme should be set by the author in the introductory element (the salutation), and then developed appropriately. Thus the structure of an epistle is made up of several integral components, but all based around one central theme, or idea.[542]

---

539 The word *ilāq* also has a connotation of "lying" and "deceit," however, so the statement may be intentionally ambiguous.

540 *Faḍl*, 149–150. The edition contains an omission (it omits *lā* before *yubārī*, which would make the statement rather strange) which I have corrected based on MS Marsh 424, 109b.

541 MS Marsh 424, 113a. The edition misleadingly renders these two parts as one sentence.

542 Gully, *The Culture of Letter-writing*, 8.

Shāfiʿ's use of the term communicates that his text was intended to participate in the previous letter's "theme," a central aspect of *muʿāraḍa*. Tāj al-Dīn b. al-Athīr's letter communicated the initial "meaning" of the conquest of Tripoli to a foreign ruler, and Shāfiʿ took the opportunity to write a similar text, perhaps to vie with the letter that was sent officially.

Like the *tadhkiras*, this letter was meant to showcase Shāfiʿ's credentials as an excellent *kātib* while also providing relevant context by which the reader could compare and evaluate this claim. This is especially relevant when assessing Shāfiʿ's position in comparison to his family, but this second example takes it even further to the broader social group of prominent scribes. Even if Shāfiʿ in introducing the original letter and its author implied that Ibn al-Athīr's texts were so good that engaging in *muʿāraḍa* with them was futile, he still did so. Rather than a futile exercise, this framing was meant to communicate how Shāfiʿ could vie with any major scribe and write equally appropriate letters on the same themes. Similar ideas may be seen behind the inclusion of different poems: Shāfiʿ in these instances as it were invited his readers to compare the texts and to decide for themselves which was most successful in conveying the relevant meaning.

At least one other relevant example of *muʿāraḍa* by Ibn ʿAbd al-Ẓāhir may be found outside of the *sīra* corpus: a *taqlīd* written for the appointment of a new head of the Jewish community (*tawallā [. . .] riyāsat al-yahūd*) in the year 684/1285. This text was written as a variation of one written by the *kātib al-darj* Ibn al-Mukarram, a contemporary of our authors who, as already noted, may have been the same person as the famous lexicographer Ibn Manẓūr. Ibn al-Furāt provides both versions of the *taqlīd*, in which, interestingly, Ibn ʿAbd al-Ẓāhir's is twice as long as Ibn al-Mukarram's. Ibn ʿAbd al-Ẓāhir's is introduced as follows: "the *qāḍī* Muḥyī al-Dīn b. ʿAbd al-Ẓāhir composed another taqlīd on the same theme (*fī l-maʿnā*) on the [same] date."[543] Neither of these two texts is recorded by Ibn ʿAbd al-Ẓāhir himself (even though it could have fit in *Tashrīf al-ayyām*'s chronological scope), but by an unnamed other historian whose text Ibn al-Furāt must have used as a source. This is possibly Ibn al-Mukarram himself, as the latter wrote a chancery manual that was used as an important source not only by Ibn al-Furāt but also by al-Qalqashandī.[544] Yet the context of a chancery manual is quite different from that of a historiographical text: in the former the focus is entirely on examples of good style and the use of apposite formulae. In such a context, the use of parallel texts is not so much performative, as illustrative of broad literary engagements between *kuttāb*. It may well be the case that both authors com-

543 Ibn al-Furāt, *Taʾrīkh Ibn al-Furāt*, 8:19 (page range for both *taqālīd*: 18–21).
544 Björkman, *Beiträge*, 77. Northrup, *From Slave to Sultan*, 36–37.

posed a version of the *taqlīd*, and that one of these versions would then be chosen as the official version by a higher authority—the vizier or the *dawādār*, presumably.

In historiographical contexts such a sampling of closely related texts seems relevant only from the perspective of a reader or an intended audience of a *kātib* or one specifically interested in the practices of *inshāʾ* writing and/or in the literary practice of *muʿāraḍa*. Ibn al-Furāt thought otherwise, but his chronicle has been noted as somewhat unusual for its patchwork of sometimes contradictory reports about the same events given by different historians.[545] In *al-Faḍl al-Maʾthūr*, the textual relationships between original documents or literary texts and Shāfiʿ's variations on them are made explicit, if sometimes only by the simple fact that Shāfiʿ provides an original text followed by his own take on it. It is possible that other letters included by Shāfiʿ in his other writings functioned along similar lines, as indeed, I have suggested to have been the case for the caliphal *taqlīd* included in his *sīra* of al-Nāṣir Muḥammad. On a more abstract scale, it is even possible to conceive of the whole of *Ḥusn al-Manāqib* as a large scale "variation" in the form of an abridgement of his uncle's initial text.

5.3 Conclusion

Our authors participated in the literary field by exchanging poems and prose pieces with their literary peers, but they also wrote their *sīra* texts following practices common in that field. Demarcating chancery practices from literary practices here is not always possible, given that much of the logic of practice within the chancery has direct cognates in or is directly informed by literary practices. Notably, the *muʿāraḍa* practice dealt with in the final section of this chapter was widespread both within the chancery and in the broader literary field. The permeability of the chancery and all things literary is also why I have dealt with aspects of Ibn ʿAbd al-Ẓāhir's account of Baybars' Anatolian campaign both in the previous chapter and in the present chapter. Nevertheless, the *sīras* were meant to resonate with literary practices cultivated both within and outside of the chancery. The competitive and performative aspects of the period's literary field also strongly influenced how our authors instrumentalised the past and especially how they portrayed their own role in the events alongside the sultans' actions. This goes well beyond the re-enactment discerned by earlier scholars for the portrayal of conquests and battles but is also visible in how authors embedded their own literarising accounts into a continuous tradition of Arabic literary expression.

---

545 Bora, *Writing History*, 46.

Chapter 6
Sīra as courtly phenomenon

ولما أراد مولانا السلطان—خلد الله ملكه—استحضارهم جلس على منبر ملكه في أحسن الهيئات * وأحسن الصور الحسنات * [. . .] ودخلوا على مولانا السلطان وقد تأنق مجلسه العالي الرواق، وظهر في أحسن الخلق وأشرف الأخلاق، ولسان حال كل منهم ينشد

واعذراني فذا مقام يهول   سامحاني إن اعتراني ذهول
ما على الأرض مجلس مثل هذا   يرجع الطرف عنه وهو كليل

And when our lord the sultan—may God perpetuate his kingship—wanted to have [the Mongol messengers] brought before him, he sat on the dais of his kingship in the best of appearances, showcasing the best forms of good practice. [. . .] [The messengers] entered unto the presence of our lord the sultan. The portico had been meticulously prepared for his lofty court, and [the sultan] appeared as the best of creation and of the noblest of character, so that all spectators' tongues would say:

Bear with me, you two, if numbness seizes me
and forgive me, for I am frightened by one of great stature
No majlis *on earth is the equal of this one*
the eye turns away from him [unable to bear the sight]![546]

These lines are part of the elaborate narrative in which Shāfiʿ b. ʿAlī reports about the audience of the envoys bringing Tegüder's first letter communicating his conversion and his proposals to Qalāwūn's court. I already discussed parts of the intricate narrative framing of the documents related to this diplomatic exchange in chapter four, but the episode is interesting to return to for the final chapter of this book. In this chapter I zoom in on the courtly context of *sīra* writing. This involves grappling with the question of how we can delineate what the sultan's "court" was, what norms governed it, and especially how scribes fit into it. Building on these investigations, I will consider how this was relevant to the production of *sīra* texts in the late 7th/13th and early 8th/14th centuries. While I have not foregrounded the courtly aspect of the *sīra*s as much as previous scholars have done because it tends to overwhelm other important communicative layers of these texts, the direct relationship between sultan and scribe in the courtly setting remains an important building block to understand the complex layers of these texts. Bringing the court back into focus also involves circling back to the issue of legitimisation, as this is

546 *Faḍl*, 101. Slight moderations based on Bodleian MS Marsh 424, 72a. Shāfiʿ recycled the poem cited at the end here—though with some variant phrasings—in his later *sīra* of al-Nāṣir Muḥammad in a section dealing with the return of envoys who had been sent out to the Ilkhan Ghāzān in the year 704/1305. BnF MS Arabe 1705, 33b.

https://doi.org/10.1515/9783110753028-007

the context where the performance of legitimising panegyric is generally believed to have been situated.

Many events along the lines of the one cited above are detailed throughout the biographies, but this example is relatively extensive and highlights some features that will be important to my discussion of the courtly environment in 7th/13th century Egypt. On the level of terminology, the first phrase uses two verbal forms that are central to the courtly phenomenon: *istiḥḍār*, which I rendered as "brought before him" and *jalasa*, referring to the sultan's "sitting" on the "dais of his kingship" (*minbar mulkihi*). The first of these terms is derived from the base radicals *ḥ-ḍ-r* which convey a sense of presence. The idea of the sultan's physical presence is central to many descriptions of courtly ceremonial. It was the node around which courtly phenomena revolved. The sitting conveyed by *jalasa* speaks to the physical rituals which were central to the initiation of interaction with the sultan—standing up, sitting, and kissing the ground. These terms thus speak to how we should conceptualise the court itself, but also the habitus that governed its workings. The idea of sitting also brings into focus the phenomenon of the *majlis*, highlighted recently by Christian Mauder as an important aspect of courtly life in Egypt in a later period but appearing somewhat more ambiguously in the scope of the *sīra* corpus. Importantly, however, it appears literally in the poem cited here.

Below I translate another extract which directly follows the previously translated extract. Here the interactions between the sultan, the envoys, and the leading scribe in his *dīwān*, at this point Shāfiʿ's cousin Fatḥ al-Dīn b. ʿAbd al-Ẓāhir, are foregrounded. It is this dynamic which will be of central interest to the following chapter.

ولما حصلوا في الحضرة * ومثلوا واقفين بين يديه مشاهدين ما هو للعين قرة * وللقلوب مسرة * طلب مولانا السلطان الصاحب فتح الدين بن عبد الظاهر صاحب ديوان المكاتبات، فحين حضر انتصب له قائما وإن كان رب وظيفة لا يتكلف له القيام، وأمر بجلوسه، فجلس ميمنة على عادة الكتاب من سالف الأيام. ثم أخذ يسأل بالتركي ما المقصود بسفير معرب بينه وبينهم * وما المراد الذي أوجب عن وطنهم بينهم *

فقال قطب الدين الشيرازي: ثم مشافهة وكتاب.

فأمر مولانا السلطان أن يسلم الكتاب لصاحب ديوانه هذا، وأن تعاد عليه المشافهة إذ هو أفهم للخطاب، فتوقف وقال: إنما أمرت أن أشافه مولانا السلطان لا من سواه. فكان الجواب: إنني ما أعرف ما تقول، وهذا الذي يعرف فحواه، فلم يسعه إلا أن سلم له الكتاب المشروح نصه * المثبت فصه * وأعاج عليه المشافهة * ولم تفده تلك المجابهة *

When [the envoys] arrived in the [sultan's] presence and stood before him—observing how he was a delight for the eye and a pleasure for the heart—our lord the sultan called in the leader of the composition bureau (*ṣāḥib dīwān al-mukātabāt*) Fatḥ al-Dīn b. ʿAbd al-Ẓāhir. When he arrived in [the sultan's presence] he stood before [the sultan], but since he held an official position (*rabb waẓīfa*) that did not require standing up, [the sultan] ordered him to sit. [Fatḥ al-Dīn] then sat down to the right [of the sultan] according to the habit of the *kuttāb* since the olden days. Then [the sultan] commenced to ask [the envoys] in Turkish with the assistance of an Arabic intermediary (*bi-safīr muʿarrab*) about their intentions and the objective that brought them here from their homeland.

> So Quṭb al-Dīn al-Shīrāzī said: "There is an oral message and a letter."
>
> Our lord the sultan ordered to hand over the letter to this leader of his chancery (*ṣāḥib dīwānihi hādha*), and for the oral message to be delivered to him [as well] so that he might understand the message. [Quṭb al-Dīn al-Shīrāzī] thought this over and then said: "I have been ordered only to speak to our lord the sultan, none other than him." To which [the sultan's] answer was: "I do not understand what you say. [The leader of the chancery] is the one who can make sense of it," so [the envoy] could not but hand over the letter [to the leader of the chancery so that] its text could be examined precisely (*bi-naṣṣihi wa-faṣṣihi*), and to render the oral message to him. [The envoy] could not avoid this confrontation.[547]

The anecdote next goes on to detail how Fatḥ al-Dīn and the other scribes of the *dīwān*, including Shāfiʿ himself, retired to their apartments to form an understanding of the letter and to write a proper response. This process is portrayed as a collaborative process in which scribes wrote individual responses and finally worked together to improve Fatḥ al-Dīn's version—apparently the superior version of all those drafted—of which the text is then given. The anecdote is thus interesting for the insight it gives into how chancery agents composed high-profile texts—already hinted at in the previous chapter with the practice of *muʿāraḍa*—but it is perhaps even more insightful for how it presents the sultan interacting with his scribes. This includes the positions scribes were supposed to take in courtly ceremonial—to the right hand side of the sultan. This position is also evident from famous depictions of sultans from the period, such as in a prominent medallion on the inner rim of the 14th century basin known today as the Baptistère de Saint-Louis where the ruler is flanked to his right by a scribe holding a writing case (*dawāh*) and to his left by a military figure holding a sword.[548] But it also includes the dynamic of interpreting both on a literal linguistic level, even if Qalāwūn's lack of Arabic may be exaggerated here, and on the diplomatic level of decoding a rival ruler's messages and translating the sultan's reply into appropriate prose.

The anecdote thus highlights several features of the dynamics and representations of the "court." In this chapter I approach the court as a set of practices in which various agents came together around the "presence" of the ruler. I am specifically

547 *Faḍl*, 101–102. Slight emendations to the Arabic edition based on Bodleian MS Marsh 424, 72b–73a.

548 Muḥammad b. al-Zayn, *Bassin dit 'Baptistère de Saint Louis'*, Metal, second quarter of the 8th/14th century, Musée du Louvre, Paris, https://collections.louvre.fr/en/ark:/53355/cl010318774 A similar item seemingly manufactured by the same artisan is also held by the Louvre and carries a similar image of a sultan flanked by a scribe and a military advisor. Muḥammad b. al-Zayn, *Bol*, Metal, second quarter of the 8th/14th century, Musée du Louvre, Paris, https://collections.louvre.fr/en/ark:/53355/cl010320012 See also Frédéric Bauden, "'The Caligrapher'" and Behrens-Abouseif, "A Mamluk Pen Box" for a discussion of preserved pen boxes from the period, notably one that is inscribed with poems written by Ibn ʿAbd al-Ẓāhir and Fatḥ al-Dīn b. ʿAbd al-Ẓāhir.

interested in how normative practices are reflected in the textual universe of the *sīras*. This textual reflection of the idea of the court is both an act of reproduction—that is, of memorialising—and of production—that is, of creating a normative image. Our authors, as members of several sultans' entourages—sitting as it were on their righthand side—rendered images of the courts of individual sultans throughout their texts. These images attest to how these sultans recreated earlier norms of ideal courtly behaviour, and at the same time establish a norm for future sultans to emulate.[549] The spectacle of sultanship comes into play here again then. It is in the strongly regulated norms of courtly interaction we can locate Kirstie Fleckenstein's "decorous spectacle," and in the literary rendering of it in the *sīras* that a reader can ponder its meanings.

If it is primarily through the lens of our authors' experiences and representations that I approach the court, that is because I want to consider how they used it as an arena to perform their social status. I aim to delineate the field of social practice, as well as the habitus active within that field by comparing what our authors write with references from contemporary or semi-contemporary texts. These texts often present idealised portrayals of social contexts and their descriptions do not necessarily correspond to historical reality. Despite this I will refer to these social contexts as institutions, but one must bear in mind that I am only referring to the textual logic in which they are presented as institutions.[550] Because the source material used in my analysis derives predominantly from the *sīra* corpus, it is fundamental to form an understanding of these textual representations of court, chancery, and the social practices described if we also want to understand other information contained within our texts that refers to these representations of institutions. This means also coming to grips with the presence of literature in the courtly environment, as well as situating courtly dynamics within the literary field, if not as its primary locus, at least as an important one that existed in continuous dialogue with the wider field.

From this situation of literature in the courtly environment, I will revert to the issue of legitimisation problematised in the introduction to this book and most fruitfully engaged with from the courtly angle. Legitimisation is most clearly aligned with

549 Compare for an insightful discussion of a much earlier text which memorialised norms and customs of the Abbasid court: Antonella Ghersetti, "Enseigner en racontant: les anecdotes dans L'Étiquette de la cour califale (Rusūm dār al-ḫilāfa) d'al-Ṣābi'" *Synergies Monde arabe* 6 (2009), 27–40.

550 Though see the insightful discussion on the unwillingness to recognise institutional dynamics in some research on the period by Kristof D'hulster, "The Road to the Citadel as a Chain of Opportunity: Mamluks' Careers Between Contingency and Institutionalization," in *Trajectories of State Formation across Fifteenth-Century Islamic West-Asia: Eurasian Parallels, Connections and Divergences*, ed. Jo Van Steenbergen (Leiden: Brill, 2019), 159–200. See also the discussion about the state and its institutions for an earlier period in Marina Rustow, *The Lost Archive.*

conceptualisations of the court and scribes' position within it, as it has been generally understood within that context: scribes offering their panegyric services to the sultan, reading their laudations out loud in front of the sultan. This representation is quite different to the dynamic of interaction between scribes and sultans represented in the anecdote cited above, and there is little evidence for such performances of *sīra* as panegyric. It will be shown that we must understand the *sīra* corpus from a broader courtly angle, situated in the social network of the sultan's household, but not necessarily in a direct patronage relationship to the sultan himself.

6.1 Defining court: terms, spaces, practices

Insofar as the courtly environment forms part of the state, I conceive of it in line with the theorisation of the late medieval state in Syro-Egypt as a Military Patronage State. Political practice in the Cairo Sultanate should be understood in a continuum with that of several other post-Saljuq polities, most prominently of course the Ayyubid sultanate. Building on the pioneering research of Marshall S. Hodgson and Michael Chamberlain, Jo Van Steenbergen's convincingly applied the concept of the Military Patronage State to the 7th/13th and 8th/14th century Cairo Sultanate, focussing especially on the Qalāwūnid dynasty. Citing Chamberlain, he defines the "Military Patronage State" as a conceptualisation that:

> eschews the idea of the polity as a unitary state and as an institutional body that existed autonomously from its ruling elite. Instead, it sees politics and government as an integrative process of acquiring and devolving power and revenue resources along lines of extended family memberships and patronage; it sees the state or polity as no more than a fragile 'collection of powerful households kept in check by the most powerful among them'; it sees 'the ruling household's adoption of monarchical and legal arguments for legitimate authority [as] one way of fending off the claims of the other [elite] households'; and it considers frontier warfare against crusaders, Mongols or any other external threat as time and again benefiting charismatic military leaders and their households to advance successfully their claims and arguments against those of others. 'The military patronage state,' concludes Chamberlain, 'thus permitted the [Islamic] ideal of the universal cosmopolitan empire to survive within a political-economic context that tended towards fragmentation,' ensuring that, 'although individual dynasties were short lived, the practices that sustained them were enduring.'[551]

551 Jo Van Steenbergen, "The Mamluk sultanate as a Military Patronage State: household politics and the case of the Qalāwūnid *bayt* (1279–1382)," *JESHO* 56 (2013), 194; Michael Chamberlain, "Military Patronage States and the Political Economy of the Frontier, 1000–1250." in *A Companion to the History of the Middle East*, ed. Youssef M. Choueiri (Blackwell 2005), 141–152.

If the central integrative node of social practice in the Military Patronage State was the household (referred to as *bayt* in the sources), led by an amir or by the sultan himself, it follows that "court" in this period should be understood within the social logic of the *bayt* as well. Like the state itself, it was not a fixed institution, but a set of practices and norms (Pierre Bourdieu's *habitus*) continuously produced and reproduced in relationship to whoever holds the effective reins of power. Matthieu Eychenne confirmed this insight in his extensive study of household patronage relations. He defined a *kātib*'s role in the household of an amir as "an informal relation, because of the lack of contract, between persons of unequal status." He further noted that it is a relation based on the "exchange of services relative to the respective power of patrons and clients."[552] The relational dynamic in a household, and perhaps even more so in the semi-public courtly setting, is not just one of hierarchy, but one of "ambiguous bonds" between socially disparate individuals.[553]

In a recent study of the courtly phenomenon during the reign of the last major sultan of Cairo, Qāniṣawḥ al-Ghawrī (r. 906/1501–922/1516) and especially of the *majālis* that took place during his reign, Christian Mauder offers an elaborate definition of the court. He defines the court as "on the one hand [. . .] performatively constituted through sequences of spatially manifested communicative events performed by, in the presence of, or on behalf of rulers, and on the other hand, as social groups made up by those who usually participate in these events and thus enjoy regular access to their rulers."[554] This is in fact close to the understanding of the *bayt* developed by Hodgson, Chamberlain and Van Steenbergen. Distinctive is that Mauder centers the *majlis* as one of the most important courtly occasions, although he acknowledges that the textual representations of Qāniṣawh's *majālis* are unique sources with no direct equivalent in earlier periods. As we shall see, the *majlis* appears with a somewhat different set of connotations in our sources.

Despite his foregrounding of the *majlis* as an important occasion for the performance of courtly rituals, Mauder underlines that there is in fact no clear-cut equivalent for "court" in classical Arabic, and that accommodating the various rituals, performances, and the general habitus that one would intuitively understand as courtly requires careful consideration. One reason for there not being a direct translation for court is because it was in the first place a social phenomenon rather than a fixed institution tied to a particular place.[555] It was a field of action generated when ruler, retinue, and guests came together to perform certain rituals that had

552 Eychenne, *Liens personnels*, 63.

553 Eychenne, *Liens personnels*, 72.

554 Mauder, *In the Sultan's Salon*, 14.

555 Compare Jeroen Duindam's discussion of the court as a "fixed institution," the rites of which were performed in "many different locations." Duindam, "Prince, Pen, and Sword: Eurasian Perspectives,"

throughout earlier periods converged to form a normative lexicon of appropriate actions and expressions, a *habitus* of courtly practice.[556] Central to Mauder's definition of the court, and in the view of the state in the Military Patronage State, is the ruler himself: it is he who embodies power as the head of the *bayt* and he is thus also the only one who can initiate the courtliness.

In our sources, the ruler's centrality is most commonly visible in repeated use of verbal forms derived from the root letters *ḥ-ḍ-r*, essentially denoting "presence." Unlike other common verbs used in contexts of courtly rituals in relation to the sultan, such as *akrama* (to treat reverentially), *anʿama* (to bestow favours) and *aḥsana* (to act well towards someone, or to be conversant) which are intimately related to the specific etiquette of receiving and honouring guests, *ḥ-ḍ-r* is also used beyond ritual: it denotes the sultan's personal presence as the embodiment of the court. This presence is as it were transitive, for the subject of the verb *ḥ-ḍ-r* is usually not the ruler, but the guest(s) who arrive(s) in his presence, thus initiating the courtliness. Similarly, sometimes authors note that guests arrived in front of the sultan by the term "*bayna yaday*" ("between the two hands of"), which is a common expression to denote "in front of," but it emphasises the personal and physical nature of the encounter.[557] Ibn ʿAbd al-Ẓāhir for example notes that he read out loud the caliph al-Ḥākim's genealogy during Baybars' allegiance ceremony: "the sultan ordered that a genealogical tree should be drawn up, so I drew it up (*ʿamaltuhā*) and read it out loud for the elites (*al-nās*) in his presence (*bayna yadayhi*)."[558]

Because of the inherently social and specifically relational character of "court"—that is, it is to be situated in direct or indirect social interaction with the sultan—it becomes highly transferrable in terms of spatiality: *ḥ-ḍ-r* is used in audiences irrespective of its context in the citadels of Cairo and Damascus, or elsewhere. On 5 Rajab 685 / 3 Septemer 1286 Qalāwūn for example received the Ayyubid prince of Hama and his retinue in his recently erected *qubba* (mausoleum) in central Cairo.[559] Courtly rituals were also performed in a military encampment.[560] The verb is also used irrespective of the ruler: when Ibn ʿAbd al-Ẓāhir describes the experiences of three envoys sent by Qalāwūn to the Castilian court in Seville where they were not allowed to leave, an envoy of the Marinid sultan of Marrakesh Abū Yūsuf Yaʿqūb b. ʿAbd al-Ḥaqq (d. 685/1286) describes Qalāwūn's envoys' presence at

---

in *Prince, Pen, and Sword: Eurasian Perspectives*, eds. M. van Berkel and J. Duindam (Leiden: Brill, 2018), 548–549.

556 Compare E. Naaman, *Literature and the Islamic Court*, 21–24.

557 BnF MS Arabe 1705, 22; *Tashrīf*, 103.

558 *Rawḍ*, 142.

559 *Tashrīf*, 139–140.

560 *Tashrīf*, 91.

king Alfonso X's (d. 1284) court with the verbal form *ḥaḍarū*, and Alfonso replies by using another form of the same verb (*yaḥḍur*).[561] There are also instances in which the term is used to denote enemies, such as defeated rebels from Karak who were brought before sultan Qalāwūn to become beneficiaries of "his natural disposition for forgiveness and beneficence for every human being."[562] Only a few pages further he uses the verb to denote the arrival of Qalāwūn himself in the city during the ceremonial opening of his grand complex in the city centre.[563]

Of course, certain places were more suitable than others. The primary location for courtly ceremonial was without a doubt the Citadel, the seat of power in Cairo first built during the reign of Ṣalāḥ al-Dīn on an outcrop of the Muqaṭṭam hills, towering over the city as an effective symbol of the sultan's authority.[564] Most of the sultans to whom biographies were devoted by our authors engaged in major building activity on this site. The mosque built by al-Nāṣir Muḥammad in the Citadel is still standing today. The most imposing building in the Citadel complex was however the sultan's *qubba* or *īwān*, commonly rendered in English as audience hall or throne hall. This structure on the southern part of the Citadel was rebuilt or updated several times by Baybars, Qalāwūn, and al-Nāṣir Muḥammad. Al-Ashraf Khalīl possibly left his imprint on it as well.[565] It was still standing in the early 19th century but was replaced by Muḥammad ʿAlī's mosque which today still dominates Cairo's skyline. That visual dominance was likely also a feature of the *īwān*, even if it was a significantly smaller structure than the modern mosque. As these places "conveyed an image of royal grandeur appropriate for the ceremonies they

---

561 *Tashrīf*, 112. Ibn ʿAbd al-Ẓāhir is in this part presumably paraphrasing a letter sent by these envoys when they returned to Tunis. The account also includes some information about the enthronement of Sancho IV in which the author uses terminology typically found in descriptions of courtly performances of the Egyptian sultans themselves, claiming among other things that Sancho was "crowned sultan (*tasalṭana*), and he rode out with the *ṭabalkhānāt*." *Tashrīf*, 113. See also Van Den Bossche, "Muḥyī al-Dīn b. ʿAbd al-Ẓāhir" (forthcoming).

562 *Tashrīf*, 123–124. In the same context, Ibn ʿAbd al-Ẓāhir even uses the verb to refer to the arrival of "good tidings" (*bishāra*) about the capture of the citadel of Karak. Similarly, Ibn Shaddād reproduces Mongol direct speech in which a person being sent to Abaghā Khān is referred to by way of a similar form: "***aḥḍarū*** *maʿa-nā ilā l-urdū bayna yaday Abaghā li-yafṣil bayna-nā wa bayna-kum.*" *Taʾrīkh al-Malik al-Ẓāhir*, 153.

563 *Tashrīf*, 126. Compare al-Qalqashandī's discussion of various ways to write to non-Islamic rulers, in which *ḥaḍra* is an important element. *Ṣubḥ* 6:165–170.

564 On the architectural features of the Citadel and the rituals performed there, see: Doris Behrens-Abouseif, "The Citadel of Cairo: Stage for Mamluk Ceremonial," *Annales Islamologiques* 24 (1988), 25–79; Nasser Rabbat, *The Citadel of Cairo: A New Interpretation of Royal Mamluk Architecture* (Leiden: Brill, 1995). See now also Mauder, *In the Sultan's Salon*, 310–314 for a specific discussion of the Citadel in its early 10th/16th century guise.

565 Nasser Rabbat, "Mamluk Throne Halls: *Qubba* or *Iwān*?," *Ars Orientalis* 23 (1993), 201.

were built for," the association with ceremonial and the sultan's outward image is not surprising.[566] The citadel itself is sometimes used as a narrative signifier of authority in the *sīras*. Ibn ʿAbd al-Ẓāhir for example refers to "[the sultan's] citadel" (*qalʿatuhu*),[567] to "the abode of his kingship" (*mustaqarr mulkihi*),[568] or to the more abstractly formulated "his resting place in the secure fortified place" (*qāmatuhu fī ḥirzi l-salāmati*).[569] Several decades later, his grandson ʿAlāʾ al-Dīn b. ʿAbd al-Ẓāhir (d. 717/1317) even described the Cairo citadel (*qalʿatu Miṣr*) as "God's shelter on His earth" (*kinānat Allāh fī arḍihi*).[570]

A more commonly used term by which our authors refer to something that can be identified as "court" is the compound construction of *al-abwāb*, "the gates," followed by a variety of adjectives such as *al-sharīfa* ("revered"), *al-ʿālīya* ("exalted"), *al-sulṭānīya* ("sultanic"), or more directly, *mawlānā al-sulṭān* ("of our lord the sultan"), or sometimes simply *abwābuhu* ("his gates"). Shāfiʿ at one point uses the term *al-abwābu l-Saʿīdiyya* to specifically refer to the sultanate of al-Saʿīd Baraka during that sultan's struggles with Qalāwūn.[571] It was also often used for the vizierate of Bahāʾ al-Dīn b. Ḥinnā.[572] The 14th-century Christian *kātib* Ibn al-Ṣuqāʿī (d. 726/1325–1326), a contemporary of Shāfiʿ, refers to a certain *kātib* known as Shihāb al-Ḥanafī[573] who served the Syrian viceroy as a "*kātib* at the gate [of the viceroy Badr al-Dīn Baylīk al-Jāshnikīr al-Ḥalabī al-Ẓāhirī] in the *dawla* of al-Ẓāhir [Baybars]."[574] This reminds one of the lexically similar Ottoman *bāb-i ʿālī*, commonly rendered as "Sublime Porte," which could refer to the Grand Vizier himself, the state position he represented, and to his "personal dwelling."[575]

When used in sultanic contexts the *abwāb* compound is used relatively interchangeably with the forms of *ḥ-ḍ-r* mentioned above. Both terms commonly occur in the same context.[576] But the compound has the advantage that it can also be used outside of the context of an audience. Where "presence" is usually invoked in contexts where persons came to the sultan, *abwāb* is sometimes also used in the

566 Nasser Rabbat, "Mamluk Throne Halls," 208.
567 *Alṭāf*, 27. See also BnF MS Arabe 1705, 72r.
568 *Tashrīf*, 115, 139.
569 *Tashrīf*, 129.
570 ʿAlāʾ al-Dīn b. ʿAbd al-Ẓāhir, *Rawḍ*, 42.
571 *Faḍl*, 42.
572 ʿIzz al-Dīn b. Shaddād, *Taʾrīkh al-Malik al-Ẓāhir*, 81; *Rawḍ*, 454.
573 This is not the famous *kātib* Shihāb al-Dīn Maḥmūd whom I have discussed already.
574 Ibn al-Ṣuqāʿī, *Tālī*, 31. When this amir died of lepra, the *kātib* started working for another amir, which is again rendered via a similar expression: "*lazima Shihāb al-Dīn bāb Badr al-Dīn al-Masʿūdī.*"
575 J. Deny, "Bāb-i ʿĀlī," *EI2*.
576 *Tashrīf*, 68, 89, 92; *Alṭāf*, 45, 51; BnF MS Arabe 1705, 35a, 40b, 45a, 105b.

reverse direction, i.e. when people are sent out by the sultan,[577] or when letters or news arrives at court.[578]

Syrinx Von Hees has argued that the use of the term "*bāb*" foremost denotes the spatial separation of the ruler from his flock, essential to medieval Islamic rulership, "the border offering controlled access to the ruler."[579] It is true that behind these (metaphorical) gates elaborate rituals had to be performed. These are sometimes described in some detail, so we can form an impression about how the attendants would interact in the sultan's presence. Much of this has been described in earlier research, so in the following section I will limit myself to discuss relevant insights from that earlier research and add data taken specifically from the *sīra* corpus to formulate some ideas about how exactly our authors would have fit into these rituals.[580]

6.2 Performing court: Ritual, ceremony, and the courtly habitus

If courtliness was initiated by the sultan's presence it follows that its rituals could be performed anywhere, be it "behind the gates" of the Citadel or in a *majlis* initiated elsewhere. These rituals were strongly intertwined with social and literary conceptions of proper etiquette and behaviour (*adab*). From the later Abbasid period important literary sources have survived which speak about the proper comportment of caliphal courtiers, although they are not specifically defined but rather exemplified through anecdotes.[581] While not nearly as systematic, some aspects of adequate courtly composure can be inferred from the more fragmentary descriptions in the *sīra* corpus. The description translated at the outset of this chapter is a good example: it presupposes that the reader accepts the details about what was considered appropriate for whom. The fact that informal rules governed the habitus can also be seen in Ibn ʿAbd al-Ẓāhir's detailed account of the ritualised inauguration of Qalāwūn's Manṣūriyya complex: many robes of honour were dealt out to anyone from *qāḍīs* to craftsmen (*ṣunnāʿ*), and during the sultan's procession from the northern Bāb al-Naṣr

577 *Tashrīf*, 30; Arabe 1705, 59b.

578 Arabe 1705, 67a.

579 Von Hees, "Guidance," 375.

580 Karl Stowasser, "Manners and Customs at the Mamluk Court," *Muqarnas* 2 (1984), 13–20. See also the studies mentioned above on the Citadel.

581 One important such source is Hilāl al-Ṣābīʾs (d. 448/1056) *Rusūm dār al-khilāfa* ("Rules at the Court of the Caliphate"), of which the narrative and normative strategies are discussed by Antonella Ghersetti in "Enseigner en racontant."

to his complex further south in the middle of the city, the "people" (*al-nās*) are said to have been "arranged according to their ranks" (*ḥaḍara mawlā-nā al-sulṭān min jihat Bāb al-Naṣr wa'l-nās qad tarattabū fī amākinihim*).[582] Once the sultan and others had entered the madrasa they sat at large banquets (*asmiṭa*, literally "eating cloths") where all ate in the sultan's presence (*bayna yadayhi*).[583]

The sharing of food and drink at banquets was an important part of participating in the sultan's presence. Correctly presiding over such a ceremony was a marker of fitness to rule, as can be gleaned from an account by Shāfiʿ in his *sīra* of al-Nāṣir Muḥammad. After this sultan left Cairo to perform the *ḥajj* in 709/1309—in fact a ruse for his defection to Karak whence he would abdicate—he had provided for his harem to follow him—also a ruse to evacuate his harem from the capital. Shāfiʿ writes:

> وحين خرج الركب من الديار المصرية خرج ولده المشار اليه وصحبته الأدر المصونة وخيموا ببركة الجب—وهي بركة الحجاج—وخرجت أدر الأمرا في خدمتهم للوداع وبكر نائب السلطنة وأستاددارها الأميران المذكوران وصحبتهم الأمرا لوداع السلطان الملك [المنصور علاء الدين علي؟] ولده فمد لهم سماطًا متنوّعًا * وجلس على رأس السماط كعادة أبيه—اعزّ الله سلطانهما—وهو في دست أبيه متودّعا مودعا * فلما قضوا الخدمة من الأكل قبلوا الأرض بين يديه * وعادوا بعد أن أبدوا ما يجب من التعظيم لديه *

> When the caravan left the Egyptian lands the aforementioned son [presumably al-Manṣūr ʿAlī] also left accompanied by the Harem women camping next to Birkat al-Jubb, that is, The Pond of the Pilgrims, and the women of the amirs in their service left to make their farewells.[584] The sultanate's viceroy and *ustāddār*, the two aforementioned amirs [Salār and Baybars al-Jāshnikīr] and their accompanying amirs woke up early to say farewell to sultan al-Malik [al-Manṣūr] his son, and he laid down for them a varied meal. He sat at the head of the food cloth *according to his father's habit*—may God strengthen the power of both [father and son]—thus occupying the seat that his father occupied when taking leave. And when they finished the session as far as the food was concerned [the amirs] *kissed the ground in front of him*, and they returned after they had expressed the necessary salutations towards him.[585]

The ritualised nature of interaction with the ruler, even by the two most highly placed amirs in the sultanate—Baybars and Sallār effectively directed the affairs of the sultanate during al-Nāṣir's second reign—is again clear here. What is more,

---

582 *Tashrīf*, 126. On the typical itinerary of such processions, see Flinterman, "Cult," 117; Nasser Rabbat, "Staging the City: Or How Mamluk Architecture Coopted the Streets of Cairo," *Ulrich Haarmann Memorial Lecture* 9 (2014).

583 *Tashrīf*, 127.

584 Reading *ādur* instead of *adur*. The first is a plural form of *dār* which was often used to denote noble wives. Another option would be to read *adurr* as an unattested plural form of *durra*. *Al-durra al-maṣūna* is still a common way to describe chaste, virtuous women. For both forms (though with *durra* only in the singular) see: Aḥmad ʿAbd ar-Rāziq, "La femme au temps des mamlouks en Egypte" (Unpublished PhD thesis, Université De Paris-I (Sorbonne), 1972), 99–101.

585 Arabe 1705, 75a–75b. My italics.

these interactions were regulated according to an ingrained habitus: the infant son of al-Nāṣir Muḥammad is said to have behaved "according to the habit of his father" (*ka-ʿādat abīhi*) and the concluding actions are described as "what is necessary" (*mā yajibu*). The anecdote thus shows al-Nāṣir's son as a worthy heir of the sultanate, who not only performed what was necessary but was also able to command the respect for a sultan from those who serve him. Similar representations of courtly behaviour also regularly appear in the context of hunting trips, where the sultan would hold banquets and hand out robes of honour. These were presented as instances in which the rituals of power distribution were symbolically performed.[586]

Another context in which the sultan's public image was performed were the regular sessions of dealing out justice in the *dār al-ʿadl*, or "court of justice," where *maẓālim* or "grievances" cases were heard. Our sultans inherited this tradition from earlier rulers—Nūr al-Dīn Zengi (d. 569/1174) is said to have initiated the practice of doing so in a *dār al-ʿadl*—but extensively used it to perform their status as protectors of justice. They also used it as a context in which to receive foreign ambassadors and collect the *jizya* tax on non-Muslim subjects. In Jonathan Berkey's words, it was "an important architectural manifestation of the sultan's authority."[587] Many researchers have seen the *dār al-ʿadl* foremost as a place for sultanic legitimisation and highlighted the tension between the sultan's justice, or *siyāsa*, and traditional Islamic law, or *sharīʿa*. Yossef Rapoport has however drawn attention to the period's important legal innovations in which the *maẓālim* courts—held in the *dār al-ʿadl*—played an active role as mediators between the relatively rigid tenets of *sharīʿa* and the realities of social practice.[588]

The *dār al-ʿadl* theoretically functioned as a means of public access to the sultan, but the descriptions of these sessions still suggest a high degree of ritualised interaction. This is confirmed by repeated references to such sessions following "regular" (*ʿalā l-ʿāda*) practice.[589] Not only were the rituals of power performed in the *dār*

---

586 *Rawḍ*, 221, 264–265; *Ḥusn*, 153–154; *Tashrīf*, 3, 53: *Alṭāf*, 23–29; Arabe 1705, 23b–24b, 62b–63b.

587 J.P. Berkey, *The Formation of Islam: Religion and Society in the Near East, 600–1800* (Cambridge: Cambridge University Press, 2003), 222.

588 Yossef Rapoport, "Royal Justice and Religious Law: *Siyāsah* and Shariʿah Under the Mamluks," *MSR* 16 (2012), 71–76.

589 *Ḥusn*, 143. In one of the three *tadhkiras* written by members of the Banū ʿAbd al-Ẓāhir cited by Shāfiʿ b. ʿAlī in his *sīra* of Qalāwūn—this one written by Shāfiʿ's cousin Fatḥ al-Dīn—explicit provision is made about ceremonies in the *dār al-ʿadl*: "[As for] the *dār al-ʿadl* [the prince, that is Qalāwūn's first son and heir at the time, al-Ṣāliḥ ʿAlī] calls on the representatives associated to [this institution] (*nuwwābahā bi-mulāzamatihā*) in the first ten days of the month Dhū l-Ḥijja, and [makes sure] that he who is usually present in its sessions is present during the time of the sultan's absence because of his partaking in battle, and that the representatives may make decisions

al-ʿadl, they were also to some degree negotiated there. Shāfiʿ includes a telling anecdote in his *sīra* of Baybars—it is one of several anecdotes not found in Ibn ʿAbd al-Ẓāhir's original *sīra*—about the sultan's behaviour in this context:

وحضر للطعام فأكل السلطان والأمراء والتفت للأمراء وقال: نحن بدار عدل وهذا الطعام الحاضر لكل فيه حق وقد إنفردنا به فما تقول في ذلك يا قاضي القضاة تاج الدين؟ فقال: بك تستخلص الحقوق واستحسن من السلطان هذا الكيس وهذه المداعبة.

> [The sultan] arrived to eat,[590] so the sultan and the amirs ate. Then [the sultan] turned to the amirs and said: 'we are in a *dār al-ʿadl*, and everybody is entitled to a share in the food present, while we have taken it for ourselves individually. What do you say to that, chief judge Tāj al-Dīn [b. Bint al-Aʿazz]?' [The latter] replied: 'Rights derive from you and such cleverness and pleasantry from the sultan is commendable.'[591]

As we have seen, sharing food with courtiers was a crucial part of sultanic behaviour, but Baybars here criticises the fact that the courtiers have done so "individually." In the context of the *dār al-ʿadl*, where all could come to the sultan to present their grievances, this courtly behaviour effectively sealed off the *dār al-ʿadl* again from the general population. Considering Yossef Rapoport's evaluation of the *dār al-ʿadl* as a socially necessary institution in which the populace could receive more legally flexible judgements, this is a telling intervention. This is strengthened by the fact that the sultan asks the opinion of the Shāfiʿī chief *qāḍī* Tāj al-Dīn b. Bint al-Aʿazz. It has been argued that Baybars' instatement of four chief judgeships, one for each of the four law schools, was a way of breaking the legal power of Ibn Bint al-Aʿazz who had been unwilling to accept rulings from judges who belonged to another *madhhab* than his own.[592] With the knowledge of this power struggle in mind, this initially obscure anecdote in the *dār al-ʿadl* can be read as Baybars asserting his supreme legal authority when it came to *maẓālim*. The judge is portrayed as going along with Baybars' decision, minor as it may be, but in doing so symbolically acknowledging the sultan's authority. The specific words used by the *qāḍī* are suggestive as well, for they seem to belong partly in the context of an informal gathering, where a pleasant atmosphere was cultivated, yet it also adheres to the respectful tone required of a courtier. The sultan is called "clever" (*kays*) and

concerning the grievances of the world and settle the stipulation of the complaints, and cut off injustices." *Faḍl*, 126.

590 Al-Khuwayṭir, the editor of the text, suggests that this might be a misspelling for "*ḥaḍara al-ṭaʿām*" (the food arrived).

591 Shāfiʿ, *Ḥusn*, 143–144. Al-Khuwayṭir split up the last sentence (written continuously in the manuscript, BnF MS Arabe 1707, 45r), implying that Tāj al-Dīn only replied "rights derive from you" and that the rest of the sentence was said by the sultan. I think this makes little sense in the context of the anecdote.

592 Sherman A. Jackson, "The Primacy of Domestic Politics: Ibn Bint al-Aʿazz and the Establishment of Four Chief Judgeships in Mamlûk Egypt," *JAOS*, 115, no. 1 (1995), 52–65.

"pleasant" *(mudāʿaba)*, but these comments are ultimately submissive, for they acknowledge the sultan's prerogative to decide what was lawful and what was not.

6.3 Court and literary culture

The above description of ceremonial in the *dār al-ʿadl* is reminiscent of the dynamics of the *majālis* discussed at length by Mauder.[593] In our sources at least one gathering in the *dār al-ʿadl* is denoted with the term *majlis*.[594] The term appears much more commonly in other contexts, however. It is most commonly invoked in courtly ceremonial involving gatherings of leading amirs, the caliph, and the sultan's retinue in general, often for important state occasions,[595] with audiences with foreign representatives or subservient rulers being of particular note.[596] Because of this high profile nature of *majālis*, the title of *amīr majlis* was accorded to a leading amir from the sultan's immediate circle (*khawāṣṣ*), whose responsibility was to manage these *majālis*.[597] The term *majlis* is however also invoked at somewhat less high profile occasions, such as when the sultan gathers with courtly agents who are not in the highest circles of political authority, for example with scribes[598] and jurists.[599]

Conspicuously absent, however, are *majālis* as literary gatherings presided over by the sultan. In earlier periods, such *majālis* convened around a powerful ruler or dignitary had been a major arena of courtly behaviour. There is also some evidence for such practices in other periods of the Cairo Sultanate.[600] By contrast,

593 Most of the topics discussed in al-Ghawrī's *majālis* were of a legal nature. Mauder, *In the Sultan's Salon*, 414–417.

594 *Rawḍ*, 85.

595 *Rawḍ*, 94 (*majlis ʿāmma*), 141–142; *Faḍl*, 80; *Ḥusn*, 80; Arabe 1705, 95a–95b; *Tashrīf*, 127, 140.

596 *Rawḍ*, 116 (paired with *ḥ-ḍ-r*), 151, 452; *Tashrīf*, 25; *Faḍl*, 101, 145; *Ḥusn*, 263. In at least one case a *majlis* held by a foreign dignitary (the Mongol general Kitbughā) is described: *Rawḍ*, 66.

597 *Rawḍ* 363, 443. The function is briefly discussed by al-Qalqashandī who rather unhelpfully notes that "the function [of the office] is obvious" (*maʿnāhu ẓāhir*) in *Ṣubḥ*, 5:428.

598 *Faḍl*, 148. This anecdote includes direct speech by Shāfiʿ, "we are in a *majlis* to judge (*taḥākum*), to demand justice, and to prescribe, not a *majlis* to oppress." The same anecdote is related in different wording in *Ḥusn*, 274. Note the resonance of this comment by our author with the anecdote involving Baybars and Ibn Bint al-Aʿazz cited above.

599 Note, however, that in most cases these legal *majālis* did not involve the sultan. *Ḥusn*, 233; Arabe 1705, 2bis b, 67a–67b.

600 For earlier periods, see Samer Ali, *Arabic Literary Salons in the Islamic Middle Ages: Poetry, Public Performance, and the Presentation of the Past* (Notre Dame, IN: University of Notre Dame Press, 2010); for the 9th/15th century, see: Syrinx von Hees, "Ein Lobgedicht," 215.

we know little about such practices in the period studied here.[601] This is not to say that rulers were not interested in literature. The Ayyubid rulers of Hama al-Malik al-Muʾayyad Abū l-Fidāʾ (d. 732/1331), a notable historian and geographer himself, and his son al-Malik al-Afḍal (d. 742/1342) were great patrons of literature and facilitated an atmosphere of creative expression at their regional court.[602] The closest we get to this in the *sīra* corpus, is in the mentioning of rewards for poets who composed appropriate odes for certain occasions.[603] The texts also abound with verses lauding the sultan's achievements. In most cases these were (probably) written by our authors themselves. At the same time, entertainment and poetry are sometimes derided and used as a topos concomitant to the portrayal of incompetence.[604] Apparently, while the writing, performance and rewarding of appropriate praise poetry was accepted as integral to courtly behaviour, the more frivolous singing and poetry associated with such courtly *majālis* was seen negatively. This suggests that praise poetry still held a position of some importance at court, or at least that various authors considered it fitting to present such practices as happening within broadly defined courtly settings.

The idea that courts did not constitute an important avenue of literary performance anymore in the later Middle Period has remained a stubborn truism in research despite evidence to the contrary. In part the observation is of course relevant: courts were indeed not the primary avenue of literary activity anymore, but rather one arena among several: horizontal communication between literary agents had become much more the norm. On the other side, however, part of the unwillingness to recognise the continued importance of courts as important stimuli of literary production is related to the still powerful cliché of an uncultured warrior class ruling over a mass with which it did not communicate directly.[605] The presentation of

601 ʿIzz al-Dīn b. Shaddād does refer to *majālis* held by the slightly earlier Anatolian Seljuq ruler ʿAlāʾ al-Dīn Kayqubādh (d. 634/1237) in which a certain Muhadhdhab al-Dīn ʿAlī distinguished himself in Arabic linguistics (*ʿilm al-ʿArabiyya*). ʿIzz al-Dīn b. Shaddād, *Taʾrīkh al-Malik al-Ẓāhir*, 185. In an obituary for the poet Ṣafī al-Dīn al-Bazāʿī he also refers to a poem being improvised in a *majlis*, but he does not specify whether this was a sultanic *majlis* or one among peers. ʿIzz al-Dīn b. Shaddād, *Taʾrīkh al-Malik al-Ẓāhir*, 89.

602 Bauer, "The Dawādār's Hunting Party," 295.

603 *Rawḍ*, 185.

604 *Rawḍ*, 62, 77, 425, 466; *Faḍl*, 39.

605 Christian Mauder has devoted several studies to this theme: *Gelehrte Krieger: Die Mamluken als Träger arabischsprachiger Bildung nach al-Ṣafadī, al-Maqrīzī und weiteren Quellen* (Hildesheim: Georg Olms Verlag, 2012); Mauder, "The Development of Arabo-Islamic Education among Members of the Mamluk Military," in *Knowledge and Education in Classical Islam*, 963–983; Mauder, "Education and Learning among Members of the Mamluk Army: Results of a Quantitative Analysis of Mamluk Biographies" in *History and Society during the Mamluk Period (1250–1517): Studies of*

Qalāwūn in the anecdote cited at the outset of this chapter is of course also part of the reason why such an idea remains present: Shāfiʿ presents him as a glorious sultanic presence, an image of authority, but at the same time he unmistakably notes that the sultan's grasp of Arabic is not good enough to understand the messengers' oral message. At other points Shāfiʿ also presents Qalāwūn as speaking colloquial Arabic, a distinctive feature of late medieval historiography which has been suggested to convey a sense of derision about non-Arab *mamlūks*.[606] In Shāfiʿ's case, however, this presentation of the sultan is not meant to deride his authority but rather to create a necessary layer of mediation in which the importance of the chancery can be highlighted. Even if Qalāwūn's limited grasp of proper Arabic may have been real, this anecdote is in the first place meant to underline how scribes functioned as the sultan's mouthpiece and interpreted important messages conveyed to him.

While Qalāwūn may not have been a refined speaker of Arabic, we should be careful not to accept his portrayal in the historical sources as the end of the story as far as the circulation of literary material at his court goes. There is good evidence of highly placed amirs engaging in literary culture via patronage or even authoring literary texts themselves. One such example relevant to the circles in which our authors moved is Badr al-Dīn Baylīk al-Khazindār, already noted above as Baybars' Syrian viceroy (*nāʾib al-salṭana*). The earliest evidence for Shāfiʿ's professional writing activities is in his service, as our author notes that he wrote an official letter in name of the viceroy informing al-Saʿīd Baraka Qān of the death of his father Baybars.[607] Shāfiʿ does not expound on his service on that occasion, but we know from other sources that this viceroy had an interest in Arabic poetry and history writing.[608] Similarly, the vizier Tāj al-Dīn b. Ḥinnā (d. 707/1307)—son of Bahāʾ al-Dīn b. Ḥinnā who was vizier under Baybars and ʿIzz al-Dīn b. Shaddād's direct patron—is said to have surrounded himself with poets and wrote poetry himself which was compiled in a *dīwān*.[609]

For other leading amirs or sultans the biographical dictionaries do not tend to highlight literary interests, but material evidence paints a different picture. Single manuscripts bearing ex-libris marks from amirs' libraries exist for example,

---

the Annemarie Schimmel Institute for Advanced Study III, eds. Bethany J. Walker & Abdelkader Al Ghouz (Bonn: V&R University Press/Bonn University Press, 2021), 61–88.

606 Nasser O. Rabbat, "Representing the Mamluks in Mamluk Historical Writing," in *The Historiography ofn Islamic Egypt (c. 950–1800)*, ed. Hugh Kennedy (Leiden: Brill, 2001), 59–75. See for an assessment of colloquial usage by historians more broadly: Koby Yosef, "Language and Style in Mamluk Historiography," in *New Readings in Arabic Historiography*, 112–164.

607 *Ḥusn*, 342.

608 al-Ṣafadī, *Wāfī*, 10:366–367.

609 Al-Ṣafadī, *Aʿyān*, 5:113 ("He was a greatly praised man, choosing the greatest of poets to praise him in verse") and 118 (mention of the *dīwān* followed by a poem attributed to him).

although no systematic study of such texts exists to the best of my knowledge.[610] Due to the lucky survival of a catalogue of the books included in a *madrasa* library incorporating the court library of the Ayyubid ruler of Damascus al-Ashraf Mūsā (d. 635/1237), Konrad Hirschler could show that a large part of this court library consisted of poetry and other literary volumes. From this we may assume that he promoted or at least welcomed the production of poetry, despite his portrayal in narrative sources of the period giving little indication for such an interest.[611] Closer in space and time, a major example is Balabān al-Rūmī, Baybars' *dawādār*, whom we have come across in chapter three as the one responsible for promoting Shāfiʿ to the service of al-Saʿīd Baraka Qān. A two-part note on one of the earliest surviving manuscripts of Bahāʾ al-Dīn b. Shaddād's biography of Ṣalāḥ al-Dīn, Berlin Wetzstein II 1893, which is dated to 625/1228 can be attributed to Balabān. It is written in a stylised hand reminiscent of chancery edicts—though unfortunately on a page with a cut-off bottom-left corner. The page is reproduced in Figure 7 (in appendix) and can be transcribed and translated as follows:

اللهم أرحم ملوك الإسلام وأرحم مولانا السلطان الملك الظاهر الغازي المجاهد ركن الدنيا والدين بيبرس الصالحي قسيم أمير المؤمنين فاتح القلاع الكفار الحصينة مقاتل الفرسان الفرنجية ناصر دين الإسلامية مقصد الحـ[. . .] التتار في بلدانهم[612] مشتت سملهم متصـ[-.. على] بهادريتهم[613] مسبي حريم . . .[614]

> God have mercy on the kings of Islam, and may He have mercy on our lord the sultan al-Malik al-Ẓāhir the warrior (*ghāzī*), the wager of *jihād*, the support of this world and of the religion (*Rukn al-Dunyā wa'l-Dīn*) Baybars al-Ṣāliḥī, companion of the commander of the believers [the Caliph], conqueror of the strong castles of the unbelievers, fighter against the Frankish knights, helper of the Islamic religion, the striver for [. . .] the Tatars in their lands, disperser of their remainders[. . .] by their heroism, capturer of the sanctuary[. . .]

610 For a codicological description of a single such manuscript, see Élise Franssen "What was there in a Mamluk Amīr's Library? Evidence from a Fifteenth-Century Manuscript" in *Developing Perspectives in Mamluk History. Essays in Honor of Amalia Levanoni*, ed. Yuval Ben-Bassat (Leiden: Brill, 2017), 311–332.

611 Konrad Hirschler, *Medieval Damascus: Plurality and Diversity in an Arabic Library* (Edinburgh: Edinburg University Press, 2016), 27, 106. According to Hirschler's table of "external thematic categories," 32% of the library's contents was devoted to poetry and 16,5% to general *adab* works.

612 Reading *buldānihim* instead of *baladh ʾanhum* (بلذأنهم) as written in manuscript, assuming this is a misspelling.

613 The word here would appear to be a derived form of the Persian noun *bahādur*, "hero" or "champion". This term was a common name for *mamlūks*. I am grateful to Kristof D'hulster and Boris Liebrenz for their suggestions on this term.

614 I am grateful to Boris Liebrenz for his corrections on an earlier transcription of this note and for sharing his transcriptions of other notes from this manuscript.

In a similar but slightly freer hand we then find an identification of its writer:

كتبه العبد الفقير بلبان الدوادار عفا الله عنه سادس عسر ربيع الاخر سنة تسع سبعين

This was written by the humble servant Balabān, the *dawādār*, may God forgive him, on the 16th of Rabīʿ II, in the year [6]79 [June 12, 1280].[615]

The dating of the note praising Baybars' deeds to a year after Qalāwūn's ascent of the throne, in a manuscript of a well-known biography about a revered earlier sultan raises some questions concerning Balabān's attitude towards this regime change. His laudation of Baybars could be read as nostalgic or even subversive knowing that Qalāwūn effectively wrested power from the hands of Baybars' sons. Its subsequent circulation in the outer courtly circles of Qalāwūn himself is indicated by an ownership note on the reverse of the same folio which is attributed to a servant of Qalāwūn's viceroy Ḥusām al-Dīn Ṭurunṭāy (d. 689/1290–1291).[616] There is also a consultation note by a man who appears to have been an otherwise unattested son of Balabān,[617] and a vending note which may allude to Balabān's role in facilitating the sale of the manuscript.[618] While the evidence is disparate, the manuscript does suggest that it was circulating in the households of amirs with important courtly roles, who furthermore had close professional ties to our two authors of sultanic biographies. In the absence of direct evidence for the circulation of the *sīra*s themselves in the same environments due to the patchy survival of the material corpus—missing first volumes or title pages where patronage dedications would most likely have appeared in five of the relevant manuscripts, and bearing only an ambiguous designation on the one manuscript that does bear a patronage note—it does give an indication that their texts at least spoke to historiographical and literary interests prevalent in the courtly environment of late 7th/13th century Cairo.

This latter observation is confirmed by the holograph of ʿAlāʾ al-Dīn b. ʿAbd al-Ẓāhir's panegyric on al-Nāṣir Muḥammad's victory at Shaqḥab. This manuscript copy, currently held in St. Petersburg, carries a patronage dedication note on its luxuriously executed title page in which the text is dedicated to al-Muẓaffar Mūsā (d. 718/1318–1319),[619] the son of Qalāwūn's eldest son al-Ṣāliḥ ʿAlī. The manuscript

615 Berlin MS Wetzstein II 1893, 234a.

616 Berlin MS Wetzstein II 1893, 234b. The servant's name is Abū al-Faḍl b. Abī al-Majd b. al-Sunbāṭī.

617 Berlin MS Wetzstein II 1893, 235b.

618 Berlin MS Wetzstein II 1893, 235b. I am grateful to Boris Liebrenz for deciphering this note and for pointing my attention to it.

619 Reproduced in L.A. Mayer, *Saracenic Heraldry: A Survey* (Oxford: Clarendon Press, 1933), plate XIV. The dedication reads: *bi-rasm al-khizāna al-ʿāliyya al-mawlawiyya al-sayyidiyya al-makhdūmiyya al-Muẓaffar[iyya?] / Mūsā b. al-sulṭān al-shahīd al-Malik al-Ṣāliḥ . . . Allāh*

also contains a laudatory appendix describing this patron's virtues (*manāqib*).[620] The historian al-Nuwayrī notes that ʿAlāʾ al-Dīn read it to sultan al-Nāṣir Muḥammad and was rewarded for it.[621] Whether the surviving holograph is a second copy of the text offered to another member of the Qalāwūnid dynasty, or whether it is the only copy that was produced is unknown, but it does at least bring a text close in spirit to the *sīra* corpus into the circles of the sultan's family. As discussed above, one part of Shāfiʿ's *al-Faḍl al-Maʾthūr*, his description of the Battle of Homs, was a similar kind of battle treatise that he claimed to have offered to the royal library (*al-khizāna al-ʿāliyya al-mawlawiyya al-sulṭāniyya*) before embedding it in his *sīra* of Qalāwūn.[622] This evidence suggests that *sīra* texts should most definitely be situated in those contexts as well.

6.4 Court and *sīra*

Unlike for later periods, only relatively few manuscripts survive that can unequivocally be situated in the libraries of the sultans of the 7th/13th and the early 8th/14th century.[623] Scholars have generally imagined the *sīra* corpus to be some of the best examples of such texts. These assessments appear to have been made based on a supposition that direct sultanic or courtly patronage is how much historiography and panegyric material worked in earlier periods. Several works for example explicitly state in their introductions how a certain ruler or dignitary requested the author to write or compile a work on a specific topic, after which the author would usually claim to only have acquiesced to the request upon strong insistence.[624] As

620 This prince's birth date is not known but it must have been at some point between 681/1282 or 1283 when al-Ṣāliḥ ʿAlī married Mankabak bint Nughāy and 687/1288 when al-Ṣāliḥ ʿAlī died. He was thus of a roughly similar age as al-Nāṣir Muḥammad who was born 684/1285. Bauden, "The Qalāwūnids: A Pedigree."

621 al-Nuwayrī, *Nihāyat*, 32:33.

622 *Faḍl*, 85.

623 The particularly rich material evidence for the library of Qāniṣawḥ al-Ghawrī has been compiled and discussed extensively by Kristof D'hulster in *Browsing the Sultan's Bookshelves* and in various addenda he has been self-publishing on his academia.edu profile. Similarly good evidence exists for the library of al-Ghawrī's predecessor Qāyitbāy.

624 Freimark, "Das Vorwort," 36–40. Houari Touati defines the practice in "l'institution dédicatiare" as follows: "Un écrivain, en offrant son oeuvre à un grand personnage, atteste de sa grandeur et de son bon goût; en retour, le puissant, en gratifiant l'écrivain, donne une reconnaissance publique à son talent. Dans cette transaction, pouvoir et savoir trouvent leur compte; pendant que l'un voit son prestige rehaussé, l'autre est publiquement consacré." Touati, "La dédicace des livres en Islam médiévale," *Annales: Histoire, Sciences Sociales*, 55, no. 2 (2000), 330.

we have seen, none of the preserved introductions in our corpus make such specific claims of having been requested; they instead argue that their circumstances—that is, the authors' privileged positions as eyewitnesses and close collaborators of the sultans—necessitated their writing a biography.

There is thus no evidence to claim that rulers specifically requested the writing of these texts. A more likely claim would be that these texts were directly received and commended by the sultan, that they came to be in a process of oral performance upon which the authors would receive feedback. The works themselves would then only be completed after the sultan's death because their function as running laudatory annals of the sultan's deeds did not allow them to be finished during the sultan's life. The sultan's death itself is a fitting closer to such texts, upon which they may be revised and offered as completed *sīras* to a successor. The surviving manuscripts would be only the final products of an extended writing process. The fact that a good deal of their content was the result of compilatory processes seems to support this interpretation.

Ibn ʿAbd al-Ẓāhir at one point provides some information about the composition of a high-profile reply to a letter sent in the name of the Mongol ruler of the Golden Horde, Bereke Khan—neither letter is quoted—which may also be suggestive about the writing of *sīra.* He notes that he "composed an answer on seventy pages of half-size Baghdādī paper" and details some of its contents before concluding that he "read the letter to the sultan in the presence of the gathered amirs, and he made additions to it, as did the *atabeg* who had dictated it. When this letter had been completed the revered presents [for the Mongol ruler] were prepared."[625] While the letter is presented as a product of the scribe's composition in the first place, it is also a collaborative project in which the sultan and the *atabeg*, one of his most prominent advisors, played an important part. It is even claimed that the *atabeg* "dictated" the text (he is described as *mumlīhi*), although it is unlikely that this would have amounted to more than its general idea (that is, the *maʿnā*), considering how Ibn ʿAbd al-Ẓāhir stresses his own role in composing the actual contents which he enumerates in some detail.

In how far can we see the composition of a *sīra* as a similar process? Scholars have routinely highlighted two reports of (parts of) Ibn ʿAbd al-Ẓāhir's *sīra* of Baybars being read out to the sultan. These mentions are not made by Ibn ʿAbd al-Ẓāhir but by Shāfiʿ b. ʿAlī in *Ḥusn al-Manāqib.* Although these two excerpts are taken from different parts of the text, they are insightful not only about the literal performance of the text, but also more generally concerning the process of writing and subsequently abridging a *sīra.* P.M. Holt has translated these excerpts and

625 *Rawḍ,* 171–172. On the size and type of Baghdādī paper, see al-Qalqashandī, *Ṣubḥ,* 6:182.

argued that they prove that Ibn ʿAbd al-Ẓāhir's *sīra* of Baybars should be seen as the sultan's "memoir,"[626] or even as a "ghosted autobiography."[627] The first excerpt is taken from the introduction and has been dealt with before:

> The situation demanded [of him] that he register of these accounts [both] the lean and the fat, and if [in doing so] he reiterated what he had uttered orally, [it is because] his sultan gave ear to eulogisers and though he was truthful in this, he was not under oath.[628]

As I have argued, the importance of this claim should be seen in the context of Shāfiʿ's argumentative build-up: it is the gap he identifies by which his own endeavour of abridging the *sīra* of Baybars becomes a necessity. This statement claims that Ibn ʿAbd al-Ẓāhir embellished the life and times of Baybars by his penchant for encomiastic discourse which Baybars is said to have appreciated, and in which "truth" was of secondary importance. However, this does not yet mean that Ibn ʿAbd al-Ẓāhir was urged to construct the sultan's legitimacy in writing. For that argument, Holt lifts another quote from *Ḥusn al-Manāqib*'s concluding section:

> إذ كان رحمه الله شاملاً له بإحسانه * مبالغاً في رفعة شأنه * رافعاً من مكانه * مجزلاً مراد إمكانه * أطلعه على سره * منوهاً بترادف الخلع والأنعام من ذكره * مشيراً إليه بسنح من مهماته * معتمداً عليه في محوه وإثباته * مجزياً له عن حسنه هذه السيرة بأمثاله * مصيغاً ببشاشة إستحسانه إلى أقواله * كان السلطان—رحمه الله—إذا أكمل الجزء منها جلس وأجلسه لسماعه * وأحسن جراه بالخلع النفيسة * وما يتبعه مكافأة لإمتاعه وإبداعه

> When [the late sultan]—may God have mercy on him—engulfed him with his beneficence, exerting himself to raise his rank, elevating his station, and generously bestowing as much as he wanted; he disclosed to him his inmost secret, hereby commending him with a succession of robes and gifts on account of what he said, pointing out to him whatever important matter, depending on him when it came to effacement and reaffirmation,[629] remunerating him for embellishing this beautiful *sīra* with exemplary tales of him, listening with a smile of approval to his accounts. When [Ibn ʿAbd al-Ẓāhir] had completed a portion of it, [the sultan]—may God have mercy on him—would take his seat and bid [Ibn ʿAbd al-Ẓāhir] to be seated so that he might hear it. He would recompense him with precious robes and so forth as a reward for the enjoyment of this remarkable creation.[630]

This quote does not claim that the sultan told Ibn ʿAbd al-Ẓāhir what to write, but that he *rewarded* him for the creative act of rendering the sultan's life in writing based on the information he received orally. It is stated that the sultan depended on his secretary *(muʿtamidan ʿalayhi)* to create this literary image, which resonates

---

626 Holt, "The Sultan as Ideal Ruler," 134.

627 The first to use this phrase was Peter Thorau in *The Lion of Egypt*, transl. P.M. Holt (Harlow: Longman, 1992), 270. It was afterwards echoed by Holt, first in "Qalawun's Treaty," 325 and then in *Early Mamluk Diplomacy*, 2.

628 *Huṣn*, 26. See chapter two, section 2.3.3. for its context and the Arabic original.

629 This is a reference to the *Qurʾān* 13:39. I am grateful to Kristof D'hulster for pointing this out to me.

630 *Huṣn*, 339. Compare the translation in Holt, "The Sultan as Ideal Ruler," 134.

with the pervasive argument of a *kātib*'s essential contribution to a sultan's state. There is a reciprocal relation implied here. While acknowledging that historical truth was not Ibn ʿAbd al-Ẓāhir's primary aim, Shāfiʿ explains that this should be understood within the context of the specific relation to the sultan required by his uncle's position of patronage. He does not claim that Ibn ʿAbd al-Ẓāhir altered the facts of history to *legitimise* a wrongfully taken political position, but that he embellished history because that is what was expected of a panegyrist and, presumably, also of a biographer.

As I have highlighted above, it is important to interpret Shāfiʿ's claims here in the context of him validating his own project to abridge and update his uncle's masterwork. The first excerpt should be understood in the context of the introduction's argument, and the second immediately follows Shāfiʿ's quotation of Ibn ʿAbd al-Ẓāhir's elegy for the death of Baybars, after which the remainder of the *sīra* consists of texts written by Shāfiʿ himself: a section in *sajʿ* describing the events that took place after Baybars' death; a letter written by Shāfiʿ to Baybars' son al-Saʿīd Baraka Qān in name of the viceroy Badr al-Dīn Baylīk al-Khazindār (already noted above as the earliest official text Shāfiʿ claims to have written); and finally a letter sent to al-Muẓaffar Shams al-Dīn, the ruler of Yemen, which was likely written by Shāfiʿ as well. This excerpt discussing Ibn ʿAbd al-Ẓāhir's relationship to Baybars serves as part of a transitional section then: it wraps up the material taken from the original *sīra* on both a laudatory and critical tone and introduces the concluding part in which the abridger takes centre stage. These quotes talk about the relation between Baybars and his chief *kātib*, with the *sīra* being the epitome of that relationship, the culmination of years of close service and advice in a masterful literary work. That work is precisely because of that relationship flawed in the changing context of political patronage under Baybars' successors. These excerpts do not convincingly support the idea that Baybars asked Ibn ʿAbd al-Ẓāhir to write a *sīra* about him then. Rather, Shāfiʿ's description indicates that the process of composing a *sīra* followed the logic of patronage, with Ibn ʿAbd al-Ẓāhir offering a literary feat praising the sultan and Baybars encouraging him to write more. The relationship is one of reciprocal negotiation of status in Baybars' household.

For the other *sīras* we have no information whatsoever about them being requested or originating within a context of oral performance in courtly *majālis*. If we wish to say something about their textual intentions more creative readings are thus necessary. As far as deriving such insights from the texts' contents, the previous chapters have shown how they speak to an array of concerns, only some of which are directly linked to sultanic legitimacy, and one of the most pervasive aspects being a consistent underlining of the importance of the chancery to the sultan's *dawla*.

Some of the social intentions of the *sīra* corpus can be inferred from their material survival. As noted already, all but one of the texts exists in single manuscripts, and all of these are likely holographs—the one text for which we cannot be at least reasonably certain that it is a holograph is also the one that exists in more than one copy: Ibn ʿAbd al-Ẓāhir's *sīra* of Baybars. In the following paragraphs I turn to the material evidence and discuss what this can tell us about the texts' links to court. In Table 3 some of the basic material data is summarised.[631]

Three of the preserved frontispieces of the *sīra* manuscripts—four if we count the single manuscript of ʿIzz al-Dīn b. Shaddād's biography of Baybars and five if we count the battle treatise written by ʿAlāʾ al-Dīn b. ʿAbd al-Ẓāhir[632]—were produced at considerable expense with extensive use of coloured and gold ink, text in cloud bands and decorative roundels. The manuscript of *al-Faḍl al-Maʾthūr* will be discussed at more length below. The manuscripts of *al-Alṭāf al-Khafiyya* and *Tashrīf al-Ayyām* are rather large volumes, and their body text is written with wide spacing.[633] This is also the case for the manuscript of the *sīra* of al-Nāṣir Muḥammad, of which the title page has not been preserved. This evidence indicates that these were no personal draft copies (*musawwada*), or copies aimed at a broad audience—these manuscripts were produced to be gifted to high profile audiences.

Of the three remaining manuscripts, both copies of Ibn ʿAbd al-Ẓāhir's *sīra* of Baybars are missing their title pages as well as the final folios which may have included colophons. Both manuscripts are executed with a denser page layout than the luxurious manuscripts noted above, at 17 lines per page. That said, however, the manuscript of Ibn Shaddād's biography of Baybars bears 15 lines per page as well as an illuminated title page—although I would venture that it is less luxuriously produced than the other three illuminated title pages in the corpus. The size of the British Library manuscript of Ibn ʿAbd al-Ẓāhir's *sīra* of Baybars is also smaller than

---

631 The measurements in the table are based on catalogue information and digital scans, except British Library MS Or. Add 23331 which I measured myself and Bodleian MS Marsh 424 for which Alasdair Roberts of the Bodleian kindly provided me with the measurements of the manuscript. For BSB MS Cod. arab 405 and BnF MS Arabe 1707 I calculated the writing surface based on scale relationship to paper size, as only paper size was noted in the relevant catalogues.

632 I have not been able to consult a full scan of this manuscript, nor have I been able to get more precise data on it, so I have not included it in the table.

633 Compared to other works produced for courtly settings, especially in the Persianate tradition, these manuscripts are still of relatively modest size. Compare the statistics in Elaine Wright, *The Look of the Book: Manuscript Production in Shiraz, 1303–1452* (Washington, DC: Freer Gallery of Art Occasional Papers, 2012), 136–137 and the observations in Karjoo-Ravary, "Adorning the King of Islam." Closer in time and space, compare the size and opulence of the Qurʾān copy prepared for al-Muẓaffar Baybars around 704–705/1304–1306, measuring 475 x 320 mm. Ursula Sims-Williams, "Over 2,000 pages in gold: Sultan Baybars' Qur'an now online," British Library, Asian and African Studies Blog, 8 May 2018. https://blogs.bl.uk/asian-and-african/2018/05/over-2000-pages-in-gold-sultan-baybars-quran-now-online.html

Table 3: Material data for manuscripts of the *sīra* corpus.

	BL MS Or. Add 2331 (*sīra* of Baybars)	**Süleymaniye MS Fatih 4366 (*sīra* of Baybars)**	**BnF MS Arabe 1704 (*Tashrīf*)**	**BSB MS Cod. Arab 405 (*Alṭāf*)**	**Bodleian MS Marsh 424 (*Faḍl*)**	**BnF MS Arabe 1707 (*Ḥusn*)**	**BnF MS Arabe 1705 (*Sīra* of al-Nāṣir Muḥammad)**	**Selimiye MS 2306 (Ibn Shaddād's biography of Baybars)**
Title page preserved	No	No	Yes (vol. 2)	Yes (vol. 3)	Yes	Yes	No	Yes (vol. 2)
Title page style	N/A	N/A	Illuminated in gold, blue and red; floral motifs and cloud bands; author not noted	Illuminated in gold and blue, floral motifs and cloud bands, separate panel with author noted	Illuminated in gold and blue; floral motifs and cloud bands; three vertically asymmetrically stacked panels of unequal size; author named in cloud bands left of middle panel	Plain undecorated title page noting title and author (*ta'līf*)	N/A	Illuminated in gold and blue; cloud bands and floral motifs; horizontal panel on top and shamsa in the middle; author not named
Paper size	245 x 170 mm	Unknown	260 x 190 mm	250 x 190 mm	259 x 176 mm	205 x 140 mm	255 x 175 mm	Unknown
Writing surface	185 x 115 mm	Unknown	155 x 120 mm	160 x 115 mm	185 x 117 cm	150 x 100 mm	175 x 115 mm	Unknown
Lines per page	17	17	7	7	13	13	9	15
Page layout features	Red rubrication and vocalisation throughout	Vocalisation, gold roundels as text separators and section highlighters	Vocalisation, gold roundels as text separators and section highlighters	Vocalisation, gold roundels as text separators and section highlighters	Vocalisation, no roundels for text separation, left justification for poetry	No vocalisation, no text separators, larger script section headers	Some vocalisation, red highlighting and text separators only at start of the MS, larger script section headers	Vocalisation, large script section headers

his later *sīras* preserved in holographs. The smallest manuscript on which I could gather size data is that of *Ḥusn al-Manāqib*. Its title page is preserved but significantly less elaborately executed. Its general page layout is however close to that of the same author's *sīra* of al-Nāṣir Muḥammad, though with more lines per page. These two manuscripts' section headers are even executed in a similar manner as can be seen in Figure 8.

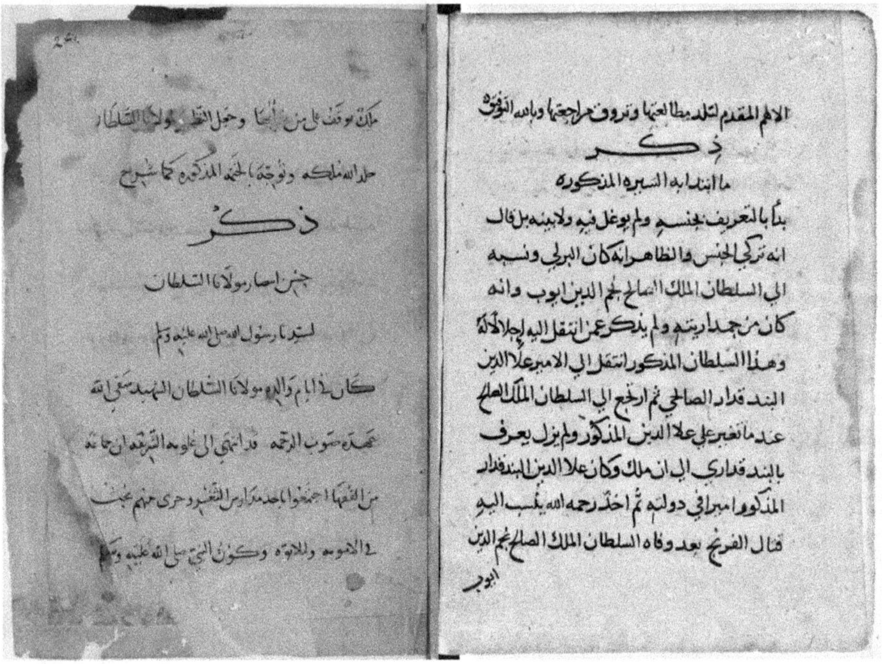

Figure 8: Page layout in BnF MS Arabe 1705 folio 2bis a and BnF MS Arabe 1707 folio 4b.

Only one of the manuscripts from the corpus, Bodleian Marsh 424—the manuscript of Shāfiʿ's *al-Faḍl al-Maʾthūr*—names a dedicatee on its decorated title page (see Figure 9 in appendix), in the middle panel of its three vertically stacked panels, flanked to the left by the author identification:

برسم الخزانة العالية المولوية المخدومية المالكية الشهابية

Intended for the sublime library of the possessing lord the employer Shihāb [al-Dīn].[634]

634 Bodleian Marsh 424, 1r.

The only thing we can be certain of is that this person had the *laqab* Shihāb al-Dīn. If we start from the assumption that he must have been a sultan or someone at the highest—that is, military or sultanic—echelons of power, a first possibility is al-Nāṣir Shihāb al-Dīn Aḥmad b. Muḥammad b. Qalāwūn (d. 744/1344), a son of al-Nāṣir Muḥammad who reigned as his third successor for about three months in 742/1342, well after Shāfiʿ's death in 730/1330. Shihāb al-Dīn Aḥmad was born in 716/1316 and was thus only about 14 years old when Shāfiʿ himself died. He is unlikely to have played a role of any importance before our author's death. Frédéric Bauden also notes that we hear little of this son before the early 730s/1330s.[635] Furthermore, as the text contains no mentions of events or updates beyond the conquest of Acre, it seems unlikely that Shāfiʿ would have waited this long to offer it to a patron.

More likely candidates are found in the higher echelons of the *dīwān al-inshāʾ*. One is immediately inclined to accord the honour to Shihāb al-Dīn b. Faḍl Allāh al-ʿUmarī (d. 749/1349). A handful of manuscripts offered to the library of Muḥyī al-Dīn Yaḥyā or to libraries of other family members are known.[636] This makes a dedication of the Bodleian manuscript to his library possible, but the time frame again does not quite add up: Shihāb al-Dīn b. Faḍl Allāh al-ʿUmarī was born only in 700/1301. He became a chancery agent of some prominence by the 720s/1320s, but only came to Egypt in 728/1328 as an assistant to his father Muḥyī al-Dīn Yaḥyā b. Faḍl Allāh (d. 738/1337) who was appointed *kātib al-sirr* in Egypt after having served for several years in this function in Syria. Shihāb al-Dīn only took office as *kātib al-sirr* himself in 739/1339. Thus, it seems a little early in his career to be offered such a text. Furthermore, considering the text's time frame—ending with a congratulation poem for the conquest of Acre—it would again have meant Shāfiʿ waited rather long to donate this text.

---

635 Frédéric Bauden, "The Sons of al-Nāṣir Muḥammad and the Politics of Puppets: Where Did It All Start?," *MSR* 13, no. 1 (2009), 67–72.

636 Al-Ṣafadī owned a work that was at an earlier point donated to Muḥyī al-Dīn Yaḥyā's library: Rağıp Paşa Kütüphanesi MS 1078. For a discussion and reproductions of some folios of the manuscript, see: Franssen, "al-Ṣafadī: the Scholar as Reader," 96–97, 133. The same article mentions that al-Ṣafadī himself offered a work on lexicography to an unnamed "head of the chancery" in 757/1356. Franssen, "al-Ṣafadī: the Scholar as Reader," 95 (footnote 45). A copy of al-Ṣafadī's *al-Iqtiṣār ʿalā Jawāhir al-Silk fī ʾl-Intiṣār*, an abridgement of a text by the poet Ibn Sanāʾ al-Mulk (d. 608/1211) was copied apparently by al-Ṣafadī himself for the library of an unspecified member of the Ibn Faḍl Allāh family. It was part of the library of the Dār Ṣadām liʾl-Makhṭūṭāt in Baghdad (now the Library of the Museum of Baghdad), with the call number 9112. It being a literary offering to Ibn Faḍl Allāh is stated in a short journalistic listicle dating to shortly after the American invasion of Iraq, and presumably to shortly after the looting of the Baghdad Museum: "al-Makhṭūṭāt al-adabiyya al-latī kānat taḍummuhā Dār Ṣadām liʾl-makhṭūṭāt," *al-Sharq al-awsaṭ* 21 Ṣafar 1424/24 April 2003, https://archive.aawsat.com/details.asp?issueno=8800&article=167034#.Yt5khJDMIc8

Given those ending contents the most likely candidate is the Syrian *kātib al-sirr* Shihāb al-Dīn Maḥmūd b. Fahd al-Ḥalabī, whom we have come across already as one of the great stylistic masters of the age and as one of the most prominent agents in the literary field of the period.[637] He was born in 644/1246–1247 and was thus a contemporary of Shāfiʿ. He furthermore held office in the Cairo chancery during the last decade of the 7th/13th century and during most of the first two decades of the 8th/14th centuries. He returned to Damascus in 717/1317 and served the chancery there until his death in 725/1325.[638] Modern scholarship has not paid much attention to him beyond noting him as an important littérateur of the period.[639] His service in Cairo is especially badly documented, but when going through historical and other works dealing with this period he appears several times as a courtly agent. Shihāb al-Dīn b. Faḍl Allāh al-ʿUmarī tells us that he was active in the service of *(bayna yaday)* Ibn al-Salʿūs, al-Ashraf Khalīl's powerful vizier, after being invited to take up the vacant position in the chancery left by the death of Fatḥ al-Dīn b. ʿAbd al-Ẓāhir.[640] He appears to have remained in service during the tumultuous period following the near-simultaneous murder of both al-Ashraf Khalīl and Ibn al-Salʿūs, the first sultanate of al-Nāṣir Muḥammad, and the following years. Al-Qalqashandī for example quotes him as the author of the diplomas of investiture for the sultans al-ʿĀdil Kitbughā (r. 694/1294–695/1296) and al-Manṣūr Lājin (r. 696/1296–698/1299), both of whom reigned between the first and second reign of al-Nāṣir Muḥammad.[641] Al-Nuwayrī also notes Shihāb al-Dīn Maḥmūd as the one who composed a

637 Frédéric Bauden has noted that a later hand added the name "Maḥmūd" near the bottom of the title page, possibly as a further identification of the patron. Frédéric Bauden, "Maqriziana XVI: al-Maqrīzī as a Reader," in *Authors as Readers*, 260, note 81.

638 Extensive biographical lemmata are given for him in, among others, al-ʿŪmarī, *Masālik*, 12:293–330 (note that al-ʿŪmarī refers to him as "my shaykh", p. 330); al-Ṣafadī, *Wāfī*, 301-361. A short obituary is provided by al–Nuwayrī, *Nihāyat*, 33:193.

639 His relatively obscure position in modern research has for example resulted in Li Guo referring to him as "an obscure figure" and "a low-ranking clerk" who could not be identified in much detail (a quick look in the biographical dictionaries of the period would have sufficed to dispel this notion), although he does note the importance of his writings as source material for Quṭb al-Dīn al-Yūnīnī. Li Guo, *Early Mamluk Syrian Historiography*, 63–64. Exceptions to the dearth of studies on this important author are two papers by the Iraqi scholar ʿAbd al-Hādī ʿAbd al-Raḥmān al-Shāwī, "Rasāʾil Shihāb al-Dīn Maḥmūd al-Ḥalabī (h. 725): Ittijāhātuhā al-Mawḍūʿiyya wa-Samātuhā al-fanniyya" (2011) unpublished paper, in *https://www.academia.edu/11638350/رسائل_شهاب_الدين_الحلبي_ت725هـ_اتجاهاتها_الموضوعية_وسماتها_الفنية*; al-Shāwī and Ḥusayn ʿAbd al-ʿĀlī Buʿaywī, "Shihāb al-Dīn al-Ḥalabī wa-Juhūduhu al-Adabiyya," *al-ʿAdad*, 40 (2016), 211–237.

640 Al-Ṣafadī, *Aʿyān*, 5:254–256; al-ʿŪmarī, *Masālik*, 12:295.

641 Al-Qalqashandī, *Ṣubḥ*, 11:47–58. Al-Ṣafadī relates an anecdote about an exchange between Shihāb al-Dīn Maḥmūd as scribe and al-Manṣūr Lājin as sultan, in which the former composed a short witty epigram followed by a long panegyric to the sultan. *Wāfī*, 24:387–389.

tawqīʿ which al-Nuwayrī had to bring to Tripoli in 710/1310, shortly after al-Nāṣir Muḥammad's third ascension of the throne.[642] In addition to his professional activities, some of his poetic works are well attested in manuscript form, including a number of lavishly produced copies of his compilation of love and erotic poetry *Manāzil al-Aḥbāb wa-Manāzih al-Albāb* ("The Lovers' Resting Places and the Breastbones' Pleasure Gardens").[643] His most active years in the chancery thus coincide with the period in which Shāfiʿ most likely finished and offered this text to its dedicatee—i.e. the final year of the reign of al-Ashraf Khalīl—considering its conclusion on the conquest of Acre but without any reference to the death of that sultan.

Reading the information contained in *al-Faḍl al-Maʾthur* as being communicated to an agent in the *dīwān* and not to the sultan or a prominent amir is helpful to understand the author's penchant for detailing his own participation in chancery affairs and his extensive showcasing of his writerly abilities, sometimes to the detriment of (or at least in competition with) his (erstwhile) colleagues. Shihāb al-Dīn Maḥmūd's ascent in the Cairene chancery followed the deaths of Ibn ʿAbd al-Ẓāhir and Fatḥ al-Dīn b. ʿAbd al-Ẓāhir who were likely our author's most important connections to court at the time. As noted above, a poem of al-Sirāj al-Warrāq cited by al-Ṣafadī as sent to Shāfiʿ was apparently meant to mediate between the poet and Fatḥ al-Dīn b. ʿAbd al-Ẓāhir in some unspecified business. The fact that it was sent to Shāfiʿ highlights that the close family connection also had professional ramifications. I have also noted that when Fatḥ al-Dīn's son ʿAlāʾ al-Dīn b. ʿAbd al-Ẓāhir died in 717/1317, Shihāb al-Dīn Maḥmūd is reported to have written an elegy for him which he addressed to Shāfiʿ. Considering the literary entanglements of these agents, and the fact that much of this interaction consisted of sending each other poems and prose texts, it is reasonable to assume that *sīra* texts could be used in such exchanges as well.

The manuscript of *al-Faḍl al-Maʾthur* having been offered to an official in the *dīwān al-inshāʾ* rather than to the sultan is not so unusual given that several anecdotes attest to the appointment of *kuttāb* by other more highly placed *kuttāb*. We have for example seen that Fatḥ al-Dīn was appointed by Ibn Luqmān, and that Ibn

---

642 Al-Nuwayrī, *Nihāya*, 32:122. Elias Muhanna suggests that his dispatch to Tripoli was the end for al-Nuwayrī's possible (never explicitly stated) ambitions to attain the high position of *wakīl al-khāṣṣ*. *The World in a Book*, 98.

643 A copy with a lavish title page dated to 720/1320 and apparently copied by the author himself was sold by Christies in 2011 (Art of the Islamic and Indian Worlds Lot 146). Two further important copies of the text may be noted here (information based on catalogue data): Leiden Universiteitsbibliotheek MS Or. 798 (an old copy from well before 780/1378-1379); Bodleian MS Arab f. 71 (dated to 1351, belonged to al-Ṣafadī). The text was edited by ʿAbd al-Raḥīm Muḥammad ʿAbd al-Raḥīm (Cairo: Maṭbaʿa al-Taysīr, 1989).

ʿAbd al-Ẓāhir is said to have addressed a *risāla* to a number of high-ranking *kuttāb* during the reign of Baybars' predecessor al-Muẓaffar Quṭuz. This last example demonstrates that texts could be used in the context of career advancement. There is furthermore evidence that the practice of dedicating works to the libraries of prominent *kuttāb* was not uncommon.[644] Considering the most likely time frame for finalising and offering this text to the patron "Shihāb al-Dīn"—that is, following the deaths of Shāfiʿ's uncle and cousin in the early 690s/1290s and his eyesight likely worsening more than a decade after his injury—the new agent taking over the leading position in the chancery would be a relevant person to offer such a text to. A text attesting both in content and form to the scribal qualities of its author would make an effective gift to advance or secure its author's position in the circles of the chancery. The important claim advanced in this and the other *sīra*s that the *kātib* was necessary for the sultan's *dawla* to ably communicate its political ambitions would have resonated with such an audience, who could see in such a text both their own crucial role confirmed and a peer's mastery performed.

This is not to say that a sultanic audience or one of agents in the military elite is unlikely for the other *sīra*s, but only that there is little actual evidence for this supposition and that internal evidence rather suggests a broader audience. Much of the correspondence and other official documents found in the texts of course emanated from sultanic policy, but the common evaluation of diplomacy as an arena for claims of legitimacy does overstate the influence of rulers and ruling elites on the forms that diplomacy took. It does not fully take into account the central importance of chancery scribes on the specific forms and contents of these documents. Letters were as much a display of a scribe's claim to status as that of the sultan. It is no coincidence that much diplomatic correspondence was included in our authors' texts, as it showcased their own crucial role in the execution of the sultan's project of state formation. While the sultan and his immediate entourage must have been part of the wider intended audience of the texts, there is only little evidence that his (or their) influence on the larger textual constructions was fundamental. The conceptualisations of ideal rule found in these texts should not only be read as functioning as forms of legitimisation, but also as displays of rhetorical and literary prowess, as cultural capital applied in a negotiation of social position in the courtly

644 In addition to the examples related to the Ibn Faḍl Allāh al-ʿUmarī family cited above, consider the following later example: Najm al-Dīn al-Qalqashandī, son of the well-known al-Qalqashandī who wrote *Ṣubḥ*, offered two copies of his father's work to the libraries of the two important chancery officials Nāṣir al-Dīn Muḥammad b. Muḥammad al-Bārizī and Badr al-Dīn Muḥammad b. Muḥammad b. Muzhir in the early decades of the 9th/15th century. Bauden, "Maqriziana XIII: An Exchange of Correspondence," 203. On Nāṣir al-Dīn Muḥammad b. Muḥammad al-Bārizī's patronage, see also Von Hees, "Ein Lobgedicht."

environment, in the household of the sultan or one of his agents, and especially in the literary field dominated by the *dīwān al-inshā'*.

6.5 Conclusion

In the introduction to this chapter, I referred to one of the engravings on the so-called Baptistère de Saint-Louis in which a seated sultan is represented flanked by a military advisor on his lefthand side and a scribe on his righthand side. The scribe carries a pen case, itself explicitly engraved with the word *dāwāh* (pencase), as the symbol by which his service to the sultan is best encapsulated, while the military advisor carries a sword: the debate between pen and sword personified in a visual conception of ideal rule. Much of this chapter has been concerned with the question of whether we can replace that pencase with a book of regnal biography, and whether the writing of *sīra* was indeed a phenomenon that should be understood as part of the scribe's service to the sultan. I have argued throughout this book, and in this chapter in particular, that the writing of sultanic biography should be understood more broadly: rather than a scribe's pen being put to work to legitimise a ruler's position on the throne, *sīra* functioned as an important part of the negotiation of social status in the courtly sphere and beyond. Having first established how we can understand the scribe's actual relationship to the sultan based on the evidence offered in the *sīra* corpus, I then argued that legitimisation was only part of what they aimed to communicate. More fundamentally than a larger-than-life image of the sultan, the *sīra*s as it were project the engraved image of the sultan flanked by his assistants: they provide accounts of his military endeavours in which amirs often take centre stage and balance these with extensive accounts of diplomatic dealings in which scribes and their verbal command become the central focus. It is because of the pervasiveness of that last feature, as well as the patronage evidence on one of the manuscripts, that I have posited leading agents of the *dīwān al-inshā'* to have been part of, perhaps even the primary audience of these texts. Because of the importance of the *dīwān al-inshā'* to a sultan's political project and their crucial role in the management and recording of courtly gatherings, the *sīra*s too function as courtly literature.

Chapter 7
Final conclusions

تعجبت من أمر القرافة إذ غدت   على وحشة الموتى بها قلبنا يصبو
فألفيتُها مأوى الأحبة كلّهم   ومستوطن الأصحاب يصبو لهُ القلبُ

I marvelled at the graveyard's command,
as my heart started yearning for the desolation of its dead.
I found it to be the refuge of all my beloved ones
those companions for whom my heart yearns[645]

Let us return to that moment in time with which I started this book: Shāfiʿ b. ʿAlī's poetical musings on old age, uttered in an exchange with the young al-Ṣafadī. These seem to be the words of acceptance of an old man who has led a life rich in experiences and achievements, who has seen many members of his generation including three of his close family members and several sultans pass away. Of course, the subject matter and imagery dominating this exchange was in large part given in by the fact that the old Shāfiʿ and his young visitor al-Ṣafadī stumbled on the time-worn topic of old age as an inspiring topic for their meeting.[646] It does not literally represent our author's yearning for the grave. Yet, it is tempting to imagine him with this mix of melancholy and pride: old and blind, sitting in a room surrounded by his bookcases, recalling the various poems and books he wrote in earlier days and promptly adding a few extra verses in the literary exchange with his guest. One wonders how he would look back on the three *sīras* he wrote which we have been able to read at least in part. Did he reminisce about the memories of his professional life, the sediments of a literary culture now changed by the inevitable passing away of many of its agents, and of course the remnants of the political state of sultans, most long dead and another—al-Nāṣir Muḥammad—now at the height of his powers? Did he perhaps observe how tastes were ever so slowly changing among those who wrote and received historical works in the courtly context, from the biographical monograph to the multi-volume universal history? There may be a layer of bittersweet nostalgia behind these poems, but there is in fact little evidence for Shāfiʿ assessing his past as such. By most accounts—and of course with the major exception of the traumatic incident that resulted in his blinding—he had led a rather successful life. So much so that by the end of his life younger scholars

645 Al-Ṣafadī, *Aʿyān*, 2:504.
646 For a study of this topic, see Hasan Shuraydi, *The Raven and the Falcon: Youth versus Old Age in Medieval Arabic Literature* (Leiden: Brill, 2014).

https://doi.org/10.1515/9783110753028-008

like al-Ṣafadī and al-Jazarī sought him out to devote substantial entries to him in their biographical dictionaries. Unlike some of his peers, there is also no indication that he was in financial trouble at any time—as he noted to al-Jazarī, his service in the chancery was rewarded with continued remuneration through his pension and ration. That he included all his *sīras* in his auto-bibliography also suggests that he was prepared to take full responsibility for his authorship so many years later. For one of these *sīras* (*al-Faḍl al-Ma'thūr*) he even added the note that "[its] merits are on the tongues of many citizens," implying that he considered the work to be well appreciated.[647]

In the end, we know relatively little about this man's life, even compared to many of his contemporaries. Perhaps this is why I have gravitated towards these poems to open and close this book, as these lines accord some humanity to Shāfiʿ's personality. We arguably know even less about his uncle, despite more of his writing having survived. The most personal notes surviving from him are poems addressed to his son Fatḥ al-Dīn, including a touching elegy where he writes how his son's "dwelling is in my heart, whence it does not vanish."[648] It has often been noted that biographical writing in the Arabic tradition rarely provides such personal insights, even in the face of tremendous sadness and suffering. The *sīra* corpus does not provide such insights either, and the sultans these texts portray remain larger than life figures in these texts, unknowable rulers and unfathomable warriors. For example, when Qalāwūn's eldest son al-Ṣāliḥ ʿAlī died, Shāfiʿ presents the sultan as a paragon of virtuous patience (*ṣabr*), noting how the sultan "was reassured by patience and endurance, sacrificing in anticipation of God's reward what he lost from this son."[649] The sultan keeps his grief to himself and as such exemplifies ideal rule, but for a modern reader this creates a distance where the sultan's thoughts and emotions become unknowable.[650] The section further exemplifies

647 Al-Ṣafadī, *Aʿyān*, 2:507. المتضمنها جزء واحد التي حسنتها على ألسنة الرعايا متعددة

The only evidence for this text indeed being appreciated by later historians is in the material notes left on the holograph manuscript. Only one of these speaks specifically about the merits of the book, and is coincidentally by al-Maqrīzī, who notes that he "benefited from it." For a discussion of al-Maqrīzī's reading notes, see Bauden, "Maqriziana XVI: al-Maqrīzī as a Reader" (reproduction of the note on Marsh 424 at p. 260).

648 Al-Ṣafadī, *Wāfī*, 3:367.

أيها الفتح أنت عَوني وسكنا　　　كَ بقلبي فليس عنه تغيبُ

Compare a poem he addressed to his son while he was still alive where he addresses him as "qalbī" (my heart): Al-Ṣafadī, *Wāfī*, 17:285.

649 *Faḍl*, 164.

650 For the representation of royal emotions in two other regnal biographies, see Van Den Bossche, "Narrative Construction."

once more the ideal literary observer, as our author ends the section with a poetic elegy he composed for the death of Qalāwūn's son.[651] Rather than informing us unambiguously about what happened or about the decisions made by the ruler, this kind of information is mostly informative about what made sense for an author to write about such events. It suggests a lot about conceptions of ideal rule prevalent at the time, but mostly it is informative about what Shāfiʿ himself deemed relevant to include and how he made sense of the past by way of established literary forms and narrative horizons of expectation.

The prevalence of this kind of material is why in this book I have aimed to shift the attention away from what these texts tell us about sultanic policies of legitimisation and towards the agency of authors in writing texts that spoke to concerns of sultanic legitimacy as much as they spoke to authors' concerns about the memory of their own role in a sultan's state. These texts tell us a lot about what it meant to turn memory into history, given how close to the events these authors wrote, both in time and social proximity, but for any such study we must consider that they did so through certain literary and historiographical prisms that defined how they could write about his past. Reading them for historical facts is bound to be disappointing but reading them solely from an angle of legitimising discourse is too narrow as well. I have argued for the desirability of a holistic evaluation of the different layers of meaning employed by these authors to create literary spectacles of sultanship.

Much as I have argued how these texts can provide rewarding reading experiences for critical modern readers who endeavour to appreciate the different strands of literary agency employed in these texts, it remains the case that historical readers do not seem to have been particularly impressed by most of these texts. What to make of the rather disappointing pre-modern reception of these texts? As noted, only Ibn ʿAbd al-Ẓāhir's *sīra* of Baybars showcased a modicum of circulation through citation, but this still resulted in only two known manuscript witnesses. Most of the other manuscripts from the corpus show relatively little evidence of consultation or even circulation. What can a small corpus of six not very widely circulated texts tell us about literary culture of late medieval Egypt and Syria then? Unlike Baybars' sultanate, which is still widely remembered in the Arab world and even beyond, the names of our authors do not ring bells anymore beyond a small circle of scholars.

And what about these poems about old age and death which I have started and ended with? Even though the poems seem to have little to do with the actual corpus of texts studied, they are equally representative of the literary world within

651 *Faḍl*, 165.

which our authors wrote their biographies. I have argued that these texts were ultimately meant to be communicative, in the sense that they invited their readers to engage with their contents, to marvel at the narrative and linguistic spectacles of a sultan's reign, and especially to ponder the presentation of the relationship between this sultan and his *kuttāb*. For that is the central relationship being presented in these texts, always implicitly through the textual negotiation of time by way of which our authors embedded their authorial personality in their texts, but often also explicitly, by way of compiled documents and poems, discussions of the importance of *kuttāb* in the sultan's *dawla*, or via anecdotes in which the *kātib*'s actions were shown to be essential for a happy end to political events. To reiterate Ibn ʿAbd al-Ẓāhir's explicit words: "no *dawla* whatsoever could exist without a chronicler to write down its accounts and entrust its traces to paper" (see chapter two, section 2.3.1.). The *sīra*s were the ultimate proof of this major claim, for they textually translated the sultan's life. The reasons why they did so was to showcase these claims to their peers and to negotiate their position within the literary field. The ambitions of the poems about death are of course much humbler, but they also show authors eager to display their rhetorical inventiveness in a specific area and in a profoundly relational context: they were explicitly improvised to provoke response and to engage an opponent in improvising a variation of the theme (*maʿnā*) expressed in the other's poem.

It should be clear from the preceding pages that I see the *sīra*s as idiosyncratic engagements with historiographical and literary idioms of the period. Yet, even if they were somewhat singular and specific in their approach to writing about the life and rule of a sultan, I have also demonstrated that these were no revolutionary texts either: the interpretation of *sīra* by our authors was not a new development, but one that made perfect sense compared to how contemporary authors engaged with the inheritance of seven centuries of Arabic textual practice. Perhaps the importance of this book lies in the fact that it is one of relatively few detailed engagements with the life and works of individual authors, showcasing how this close reading technique reveals a lot of information that is easily glossed over when merely consulting these works for a particular bit of information. I hope to have demonstrated the importance of this close approach to studying historiography and in doing so to have contributed to a small contemporary surge of such studies, as evidenced by the works of Konrad Hirschler, Elias Muhanna, and a growing list of studies on the life and texts of al-Maqrīzī, and several 9th/15th century historians.[652]

652 Hirschler, *Medieval Arabic Historiography*; Muhanna, *The World in a Book*; Van Steenbergen, *Caliphate and Kingship*; Nasser Rabbat, *Writing Egypt: Al-Maqrizi and his Historical Project* (Edinburgh: Edinburgh University Press, 2022); and the Bibliotheca Maqriziana series edited by Frédéric Bauden. See also the studies compiled in the thematic issue "Fifteenth-Century Arabic Historiog-

The last chapter of this book has furthermore highlighted how we should be careful in interpreting statements about the social performance of texts as expressed in the texts themselves. While I have not disproven the hypothesis that these texts were offered to the sultan, I have highlighted how this is little more than a hypothesis as neither the manuscripts as social objects nor the textual contents provide any clear-cut information about such practices and instead even suggest other channels of performance and reception. Furthermore, I have challenged the still all too common legitimisation narrative and offered some perspectives on how we might more fruitfully conceive of patronage and courtly textual production as a multidirectional, especially reciprocal effort by which agents negotiated their social positions within the field. It is within the performance of literary sensibility and the panegyric negotiation of status between patron and author that we should interpret the production and consumption of *sīra*.

Our authors were not the final ones to compose *sīra*s for contemporary rulers. I have referred to some later examples in passing. Most of these texts from the late 8th/14th and the 9th/15th century seem to have interpreted the valence of *sīra* differently. A cursory look would suggest that in these later works the chronographical focus loses in importance while the panegyrical and virtue-focused approach gains a more central position in works that make the *istiṭrād* ("digression") principle a central element of their endeavour.[653] These and other historiographical texts invite future research by way of the close reading approach used in this study. Further studies may even disclose more commonalities of these later traditions and the interpretation of *sīra* by our two authors than I have allowed in my interpretation here.

For our authors, who knew each other intimately as members of the same family, *sīra* meant something particular and in a way also something quite personal. It was their way of making sense of a sultan's life and reign, of the chaos of history, but also of their own experiences in serving the sultan whose life they depicted. Perhaps most importantly, it was their way of trying to secure benefit from important patrons by showcasing their mastery of specific literary discourses: they used this form to negotiate their social position at or in relation to courtly circles, the chancery, and their peers in the literary field. In the case of Shāfiʿ, who

raphy: A New Research Agenda" in *MSR* 23 (2020). We may start to speak of an important shift of focus in the field from the historical-critical interest in historians, to more specific engagements with the practices of historiography.

653 For a discussion of some relevant examples, see P.M. Holt, "Literary Offerings: A Genre of Courtly Literature," in *The Mamluks in Egyptian Politics and Society*, eds. Thomas Philipp & Ulrich Haarmann (Cambridge: Cambridge University Press, 1998), 3–16. For two closer studies of 9th/15th century examples see: Weintritt, *Formen*; Banister, "Professional Mobility."

likely did not hold a position in the chancery after having become severely visually impaired at a relatively young age, we may even imagine the major personal stakes of such a performance. Remember the poem in which he rebutted a contemporary poet's appropriation of al-Mutanabbī's line "I am the one whose *adab* the blind sees" by decrying the poet's lack of manners and literary quality (*adab*). One could imagine Shāfiʿ writing his many books as proof that blindness did not hinder his eloquence and productivity. If we return to imagining the blind Shāfiʿ in old age, remembering his literary career, we might think of him not only as longing for the peace of a final resting place, but also as it were exclaiming proudly: "I am the blind whose *adab* the seeing read!"

Bibliography

Manuscript sources

Anonymous, *al-Ajwiba al-Muʿtabira ʿan al-Futyā l-Mubtakira*, Berlin: Staatsbibliothek, Wetzstein II 1473.
al-Bandanījī, *Kitāb al-Tafqīh fī al-Lugha*, Istanbul: Süleymaniye Kütüphanesi, Aya Sofya 4670.
Al-Fayyūmī, *Nathr al-Jumān fī Tarājim al-Aʿyān*, Dublin: Chester Beatty Library, Ar. 4113.
Ibn ʿAbd al-Ẓāhir, Muḥyī al-Dīn, *Dīwān*, Cairo: Dār al-Kutub waʾl-Wathāʾiq, Shiʿr Taymūr 101
Ibn ʿAbd al-Ẓāhir, Muḥyī al-Dīn, *Dīwān*, Cairo: Maktabat al-Azhar, Adab 657
Ibn ʿAbd al-Ẓāhir, Muḥyī al-Dīn, *Dīwān*, Leiden: Universiteitsbibliotheek, Or. 2688
Ibn ʿAbd al-Ẓāhir, Muḥyī al-Dīn, *al-Rawḍa al-Bahiyya al-Zāhira fī Khiṭaṭ al-Muʿizziyya al-Qāhira*, London: British Library Or. 13317 folios 142–180.
Ibn ʿAbd al-Ẓāhir, Muḥyī al-Dīn, [*Sīra* of Baybars],[654] Istanbul: Süleymaniye Kütüphanesi, Fatih 4366.
Ibn ʿAbd al-Ẓāhir, Muḥyī al-Dīn, [*Sīra* of Baybars], London: British Library, O/C Add. 23331.
Ibn ʿAbd al-Ẓāhir, Muḥyī al-Dīn, *Tashrīf al-Ayyām waʾl-ʿUṣūr bi-Sīrat al-Malik al-Manṣūr*, Paris: BnF, Arabe 1704.
Ibn ʿAbd al-Ẓāhir, Muḥyī al-Dīn, *al-Alṭāf al-Khafiyya min al-Sīra al-Sharīfa al-Sulṭāniyya al-Malikiyya al-Ashrafiyya*, Munich: Bayerische Staatsbibliothek, orientalische and asiatische Handschriften, Cod. arab 405.
Ibn ʿAbd al-Ẓāhir, Muḥyī al-Dīn, [Correspondence and literary exchanges], Sofia: St. Cyril and Methodius National Library, MS Or. 2026.
Ibn ʿAqīl, *al-Durr al-Naḍīḍ fī Manāqib al-Malik al-Ẓāhir Abī Saʿīd*, Berlin: Staatsbibliothek, Wetzstein I 133.
Ibn ʿArabshāh, *al-Taʾlīf al-Ṭāhir fī Shīm al-Malik al-Ẓāhir*, London: British Library Or. 3026.
Ibn Ḥabīb, *Durrat al-Aslāk fī Dawlat al-Atrāk*, Leipzig: Universitätsbibliothek, Vollers 0661
Ibn Ḥabīb, *Durrat al-Aslāk fī Dawlat al-Atrāk*, Paris: BnF, MS Arabe 1719.
Ibn Shaddād, Bahāʾ al-Dīn, *al-Nawādir al-sulṭāniyya waʾl-maḥāsin al-Yūsufiyya*, Berlin: Staatsbibliothek, Wetzstein II 1893.
Ibn Shaddād, ʿIzz al-Dīn, *Tārīkh al-Malik al-Ẓāhir*, Edirne: Selimiye Kütüphanesi, 2306.
Shāfiʿ b. ʿAlī, Nāṣir al-Dīn, *Ḥusn al-Manāqib al-Sirriyya al-Muntazaʿa min al-Sīra al-Ẓāhiriyya*, Paris: BnF, Arabe 1707.
Shāfiʿ b. ʿAlī, Nāṣir al-Dīn, *al-Faḍl al-Maʾthūr min Sīrat al-Sulṭān Malik al-Manṣūr*, Oxford: Bodleian, Marsh 424.
Shāfiʿ b. ʿAlī, Nāṣir al-Dīn, [*Sīrat al-Malik al-Nāṣir Muḥammad*], Paris: BnF, Arabe 1705.
Shāfiʿ b. ʿAlī, Nāṣir al-Dīn, *al-Raʾy al-Ṣāʾib fī Thibāt mā lā Budda minhu liʾl-Kātib*, Istanbul: Topkapı Sarayı Müzesi Kütüphanesi: Ahmet III 2583.
al-Suyūṭī, Jalāl al-Dīn, *al-Qawl al-Ashbahu fī man ʿArafa Nafsahu faqad ʿArafa Rabbahu*, Paris: BnF, Arabe 773.

Published primary sources

al-ʿAynī, Badr al-Dīn, *ʿIqd al-Jumān fī Taʾrīkh Ahl al-Zamān*, ed. Maḥmūd Rizq Maḥmūd (Cairo: Maṭbaʿat Dār al-kutub, 2003–2009), 5 vols.
Baybars al-Manṣūrī, *Zubdat al-Fikra fī Taʾrīkh al-Hijra*, ed. D.S. Richards (Beirut: Dār al-nashr, 1998).

654 Square brackets denote presumed titles which do not appear on the manuscripts themselves.

https://doi.org/10.1515/9783110753028-009

al-Birzālī, *al-Muqtafī ʿalā Kitāb al-Rawḍatayn al-Maʿrūf bi-Tārīkh al-Birzālī*, 4 vols., ed. ʿUmar Tadmurī (Ṣaydā/Beirut: al-Maktaba al-ʿAṣriyya, 2006).

Ḥajjī Khalīfa, Kātip Çelebi, *Kashf al-Ẓunūn ʿan Asāmī l-Kutub waʾl-Funūn*, ed. Mehmed Şerafeddin Yaltkaya (Beirut: Dār iḥyāʾ al-turāth al-ʿarabī, n.d.), 2 vols.

al-Ḥarīrī, *Maqāmāt*, ed. Yūsuf al-Biqāʿī (Beirut: Dār al-Kutub al-Lubnānī, 1981).

al-Ḥusaynī, Aḥmad b. Muḥammad, *Ṣilat al-Takmila li-Wafayāt al-Naqala*, 2 vols., ed. Bashshār ʿAwād Maʿrūf (Dār al-gharb al-islāmī, 2007).

al-Ḥuṣrī, Abū Isḥāq, *Zahr al-Ādāb wa-Thamar al-Albāb*, 4 vols., ed. Muḥammad Muḥyī al-Dīn ʿAbd al-Ḥamīd (Beirut: Dār al-Jīl, 2011).

Ibn ʿAbd al-Ẓāhir, Muḥyī l-Dīn, *Baybars I of Egypt*, ed. Syedah Fatima Sadequi (London: Oxford University Press, 1958).

Ibn ʿAbd al-Ẓāhir, Muḥyī l-Dīn, *al-Rawḍ al-Zāhir fī Sīrat al-Malik al-Ẓāhir*, ed. ʿAbd al-ʿAzīz al-Khuwayṭir (Riyadh: n.p., 1976).

Ibn ʿAbd al-Ẓāhir, Muḥyī l-Dīn, *Tashrīf al-Ayyām waʾl-ʿUṣūr bi-Sīrat al-Malik al-Manṣūr*, ed. Murad Kāmil (Cairo: n.p., 1961).

Ibn ʿAbd al-Ẓāhir, Muḥyī l-Dīn, *Chronicles of Qalawun and His Son al-Ashraf Khalil*, transl. David Cook (London-New York: Routledge, 2020).

Ibn ʿAbd al-Ẓāhir, Muḥyī l-Dīn, *Ur ʿAbd Allah B. ʿAbd eẓ-Ẓâhir's biografi over sultanen el-malik al-Aśraf Halîl*, ed. Axel Moberg (Lund: Gleerupska Univ.-Bokhandelen, 1902).

Ibn ʿAbd al-Ẓāhir, Muḥyī l-Dīn, *al-Darr al-Naẓīm min Tarassul ʿAbd al-Raḥīm*, ed. Aḥmad Aḥmad Badawī (Cairo: Maktaba Nahḍat Miṣr, 1959).

Ibn ʿAbd al-Ẓāhir, Muḥyī l-Dīn, *al-Rawḍa l-Bahiyya al-Zāhira fī Khiṭaṭ al-Muʿizziyya l-Qāhira*, ed. Ayman Fuʾād Sayyid (Cairo: al-Dār al-ʿarabiyya li-l-kutub, 1996).

Ibn ʿAbd al-Ẓāhir, Muḥyī l-Dīn, *Dīwān: Dirāsa wa-taḥqīq*, ed. Gharīb Muḥammad ʿAlī Aḥmad (Cairo: Maṭbaʿat Dār al-Bayān, 1990).

Ibn ʿAbd al-Ẓāhir, ʿAlāʾ al-Dīn, *al-Rawḍ al-Zāhir fī ghazwat al-Malik al-Nāṣir, wa-bi-dhaylihi: al-Manāqib al-Muẓaffarīyah*, ed. ʿUmar Tadmurī (Ṣaydā: al-Maktabah al-ʿAṣrīyah, 2005).

Ibn al-Dawādārī, *Kanz al-Durar wa-Jāmiʿ al-Ghurar*, eds. U. Haarmann, H.R. Roemer e.a. (Beirut, Cairo, Stuttgart: Sāmī al-Khanjī, Schwarz, e.a., 1960-1994), 9 vols.

Ibn Durayd, *Qaṣīdat al-Maqṣūra*, in https://ar.wikisource.org/wiki/%D9%85%D9%82%D8%B5%D9%88%D8%B1%D8%A9_%D8%A7%D8%A8%D9%86_%D8%AF%D8%B1%D9%8A%D8%AF

Ibn al-Furāt, *Taʾrīkh Ibn al-Furāt [= Taʾrīkh duwal al-mulūk], volume 7*, ed. Q. Zurayq (Beirut: al-Maṭbaʿa al-Amīrikāniyya, 1942).

Ibn al-Furāt, *Taʾrīkh Ibn al-Furāt [= Taʾrīkh duwal al-mulūk], volume 8*, Q. Zurayq & N. ʿIzz al-Dīn (Beirut: al-Maṭbaʿa al-Amīrikāniyya, 1939).

Ibn al-Fuwaṭī, *Talkhīṣ Majmaʿ al-Ādāb fī Muʿjam al-Alqāb*, 6 vols, ed. Muḥammad al-Kāẓim (Tehran: Muʾassasat al-Ṭibāʿa waʾl-Nashr, Wizārat al-Thaqāfa waʾl-Irshād al-Islāmī, 1416/1995–1996).

Ibn Ḥabīb, *Tadkhirat al-nabīh fī ayyām al-Manṣūr wa-bānīhi*, ed. Muḥammad Muḥammad Amīn (Cairo: al-Hayʾa al-Miṣriyya l-ʿāmma li-l-kitāb, 1976–86), 2 vols.

Ibn Ḥajar al-ʿAsqalānī, *al-Durar al-Kāmina fī Aʿyān al-Miʾa al-Thāmina*, ed. Muḥammad Sayyid Jād al-Ḥaqq (Cairo: Dār al-Kutub al-Ḥadītha, 1966), 5 vols.

Ibn Ḥijja al-Ḥamawī, *Khizānat al-adab wa-ghāyat al-arab*, ed. ʿIṣām Shuʿaytū (Beirut: Dār Maktabat al-Hilāl, 2004).

Ibn Iyās, Muḥammad b. Aḥmad, *Badāʾiʿ al-Zuhūr fī Waqāʾiʿ al-Duhūr*, ed. M. Mustafa (Wiesbaden: Franz Steiner, 1975), 2 vols.

Ibn Manẓūr, Muḥammad b. Mukarram, *Lisān al-ʿArab*, in http://ejtaal.net/aa

Ibn Shaddād, Bahā' al-Dīn, *al-Nawādir al-Sulṭāniyya wa'l-Maḥāsin al-Yūsufiyya, aw Sīrat Ṣalāḥ al-Dīn,* ed. Jamāl al-Dīn al-Shayyāl (Cairo: Maktabat al-Khānjī, second edition, 1994).
Ibn Shaddād, ʿIzz al-Dīn, *Ta'rīkh al-Malik al-Ẓāhir,* ed. Aḥmad Ḥuṭayṭ (Wiesbaden: Franz Steiner, 1983).
Ibn al-Shiḥna, *al-Badr al-Zāhir fī Nuṣrat al-Malik al-Nāṣir Qāyitbāy,* ed. ʿUmar Tadmurī (Beirut: Dār al-Kitāb al-ʿArabī, 1983).
Ibn al-Ṣuqāʿī, *Tālī Kitāb Wafayāt al-Aʿyān*, ed. Jacqueline Sublet (Damascus: Presses de l'IFPO, 1973).
Ibn Taghrī-Birdī, *al-Manhal al-ṣāfī wa'l-Mustawfī baʿda l-Wāfī,* ed. Muḥammad Muḥammad Amīn (Cairo: al-Hay'a l-Miṣriyya al-ʿāmma li-l-kutub, 1984-2009), 13 vols.
Ibn Taghrī-Birdī, *al-Nujūm al-Zāhira fī Mulūk Miṣr wa'l-Qāhira,* ed. Muḥammad Ḥusayn Shams al-Dīn (Beirut: Dār al-Kutub al-ʿIlmiyya, 1992), 16 vols.
Ibn Wāṣil, *Mufarrij al-Kurūb fī Akhbār Banī Ayyūb,* eds. Jamāl al-Dīn Shayyāl, Ḥasanayn Muḥammad Rabīʿ and Saʿīd ʿAbd al-Fattāḥ ʿĀshūr (Cairo: Dār al-Lutub wa'l-Wathā'iq al-Qawmiyya, 1957), 5 vols.
al-Iṣfahānī, ʿImād al-Dīn, *al-Fatḥ al-Qussī fī al-Fatḥ al-Qudsī,* ed. Carlo de Landberg (Leiden: Brill, 1888).
al-Iṣfahānī, *Conquête de la Syrie et de la Palestine par Saladin (al-Fatḥ al-qussî fî al-fatḥ al-qudsî),* transl. Henri Massé, ed. Charles Pellat (Paris: Paul Geuthner, 1972).
al-Jazarī, *Ḥawādith al-Zamān fī Anbā'ihi wa-Wafayāt al-Akābir wa'l-Aʿyān min Abnā'ihi,* ed. ʿUmar Tadmurī (Ṣaydā/Beirut: al-Maktaba al-ʿAṣriyya, s.d.), 2 vols.
al-Kutubī, Ibn Shākir, *Fawāt al-Wafāyāt,* ed. Iḥsān ʿAbbās (Beirut: Dār Ṣādir, 1973–1974), 5 vols.
al-Maqrīzī, Tāqī al-Dīn, *al-Sulūk li-Maʿrifat Duwal al-Mulūk,* 4 vols. Ed. Muḥammad M. Ziyāda and Saʿīd 'Abd al-Fattāḥ 'Ašūr (Cairo: Lajna al-ta'līf wa'l-nashr, 1939–1972),
al-Maqrīzī, Tāqī al-Dīn, *al-Muqaffā l-Kabīr,* ed. Muḥammad al-Yaʿlāwī (Beirut: Dār al-gharb al-islāmī, 1991), 8 vols.
al-Maqrīzī, Tāqī al-Dīn, *Histoire des sultan mamlouks,* tr. Marc Etienne Quatremère (Paris: Oriental Translation Fund of Great Britain and Ireland, 1837–1845), 4 vols.
al-Nābulsī, ʿAbd al-Ghanī, *The Arch Rhetorician, or, The Schemer's Skimmer: A Handbook of Late Arabic badīʿ*, ed. and transl. Pierre Cachia (Wiesbaden: Harrassowitz, 1998).
al-Nuwayrī, Shihāb al-Dīn, *Nihāyat al-Arab fī Funūn al-Adab,* ed. Ibrāhīm Shams al-Dīn (Beirut: Dār al-kutub al-ʿilmiyya, 2004), 33 vols.
al-Nuwayrī, Shihāb al-Dīn, *The Ultimate Ambition in the Arts of Erudition,* transl. Elias Muhanna (New York City: Penguin Books, 2016).
al-Qalqashandī, Shihāb al-Dīn, *Ṣubḥ al-Aʿshā fī Ṣināʿat al-Inshā'*, no editor (Cairo: Maṭbaʿat Dār al-kutub, 1922), 14 vols.
al-Ṣafadī, Khalīl b. Aybak, *Alḥān al-Sawājiʿ bayna 'l-Bādī' wa'l-Murājiʿ,* ed. Ibrāhīm Ṣāliḥ (Damascus: Dār al-Basha'ir, 2004), 2 vols.
al-Ṣafadī, Khalīl b. Aybak, *Aʿyān al-Aṣr wa-Aʿwān al-Naṣr,* ed. Abū Zayd e.a. (Beirut-Damascus: Dār al-fikr al-muʿāṣir & Dār al-fikr, 1998), 6 vols.
al-Ṣafadī, Khalīl b. Aybak, *Kitāb al-Wāfī bi'l -Wafāyāt,* eds. Hellmut Ritter e.a. (Wiesbaden: Franz Steiner, 1982), 25 vols.
al-Ṣafadī, Khalīl b. Aybak, *Tamām al-Mutūn fī Sharḥ Risālat Ibn Zaydūn,* ed. Muḥammad Abū l-Faḍl Ibrāhīm (Ṣaydā /Beirut: Manshūrāt al-Maktaba l-ʿAṣriyya, 1969).
al-Ṣafadī, Khalīl b. Aybak, *Nakt al-Himyān fī Nukat al-ʿUmyān,* ed. Aḥmad Zakī Bak (Cairo: al-Maṭbaʿah al-Jamālīyah, 1911).
Shāfiʿ b. ʿAlī, Nāṣir al-Dīn, *al-Faḍl al-Ma'thūr min Sīrat al-Malik al-Manṣūr,* ed. ʿUmar Tadmurī (Ṣaydā / Beirut: al-Maktaba l-Aṣriyya, 1998).
Shāfiʿ b. ʿAlī, Nāṣir al-Dīn, *Šāfiʿ Ibn ʿAlī's Biography of the Mamluk Sultan Qalāwūn,* ed. P. Lewicka (Warsaw: Dialog, 2000), Orientalia Polona 2.

Shāfiʿ b. ʿAlī, Nāṣir al-Dīn, *Ḥusn al-Manāqib al-Sirriyya al-Muntazaʿa min al-Sīra al-Ẓāhiriyya*, ed. ʿAbd al-ʿAzīz al-Khuwayṭir, second edition (Riyadh: n.p., 1989).
Shihāb al-Dīn Maḥmūd , Abū al-Thanāʾ Ibn Fahd, *Ḥusn al-Tawassul ilā Ṣināʿat al-Tarassul* (Cairo: Maṭbaʿat Amīn Afandī Hindīyah, 1315 [1897]).
Shihāb al-Dīn Maḥmūd , Abū al-Thanāʾ Ibn Fahd, *Manāzil al-Aḥbāb wa-Manāzih al-Albāb*, ed. ʿAbd al-Raḥīm Muḥammad ʿAbd al-Raḥīm (Cairo: Maṭbaʿa al-Taysīr, 1989).
al-Suyūṭī, Jalāl al-Dīn, *Ḥusn al-Muḥāḍara fī Akhbār Miṣr waʾl-Qāhira*, ed. Muḥammad Abū l-Faḍl Ibrāhīm (Aleppo: Dār Iḥyā al-Kutub al-ʿArabiyya, 1968), 2 vols.
al-Ṭabarī, Abū Jaʿfar *Tārīkh al-Rusul waʾl-Mulūk*, ed. Muḥammad Abū l-Faḍl Ibrāhīm, (Cairo: Dār al-Maʿārif bi-Miṣr, 1960), 11 vols.
al-ʿUmarī, Shihāb al-Dīn b. Faḍl Allāh, *Masālik al-Abṣār fī Mamālik al-Amṣār*, ed. Kāmil Salmān al-Jubūrī & Mahdī al-Najm (Beirut: Dār al-kutub al-ʿilmiyya, 2010), 27 volumes.
al-ʿUmarī, Shihāb al-Dīn b. Faḍl Allāh, *al-Taʿrīf biʾl-Muṣṭalaḥ al-Sharīf*, ed. Muḥammad Ḥusayn Shams al-Dīn (Beirut: Dār al-kutub al-ʿilmiyya, 1988).
al-ʿUmarī, ʿIṣām al-Dīn, *al-Rawḍ al-naḍir fī tarjama udabāʾ al-ʿaṣr*, ed. Salīm al-Nuʿaymī, (Baghdad: al-Mujammaʿ al-ʿilmī al-ʿIrāqī, 1975), 3 vols.
al-Zabīdī, Muḥammad Murtaḍā, *Tāj al-ʿArūs min Jawhar al-Qāmūs*, ed. Ḍāḥī ʿAbd al-Bāqī e.a. (Kuwait: Muʾassasat al-Kuwayt li-l-taqaddum al-ʿilmiyya, 2001), 40 vols.

Secondary sources

ʿAbd ar-Rāziq, Aḥmad, "La femme au temps des mamlouks en Egypte" (Unpublished PhD thesis, Université De Paris-I (Sorbonne), 1972).
Afsaruddin, Asma, *Excellence and Precedence: Medieval Discourse on Legitimate Leadership* (Leiden: Brill, 2002).
Aigle, Denise, *The Mongol Empire between Myth and Reality: Studies in Anthropological History* (Leiden: Brill, 2015).
Ali, Samer, *Arabic Literary Salons in the Islamic Middle Ages: Poetry, Public Performance, and the Presentation of the Past* (Notre Dame, IN: University of Notre Dame Press, 2010).
Allouche, Adel, "Tegüder's Ultimatum to Qalawun," *IJMES*, 22, no. 4 (1990), 437–446.
Ambros, Arne A., "Beobachtungen zu Aufbau und Funktion des gereimten klassisch-arabischen Buchtitels," *Wiener Zeitschrift für die Kunde des Morgenlandes* 80 (1990), 13–57.
Anonymous, "al-Makhṭūṭāt al-Adabiyya al-latī kānat Taḍummuhā Dār Ṣadām liʾl-Makhṭūṭāt," *al-Sharq al-awsaṭ* 21 Ṣafar 1424/24 April 2003, https://archive.aawsat.com/details.asp?issueno=8800&article=167034#.Yt5khJDMIc8
Anthony, Sean W., *Muhammad and the Empires of Faith: The Making of the Prophet of Islam* (Oakland: University of California Press, 2020),
Antrim, Zayde, "Ibn Shaddād, ʿIzz al-Dīn," *EI3*.
Ashtor, Eliyahu (as E. Strauß), "Muḥyîʾddîn b. ʿAbdaẓẓâhir," *Wiener Zeitschrift für die Kunde des Morgenlandes* 45 (1938), 191–202.
Ashtor, Eliyahu (as E. Strauß), "Some Unpublished Sources for the Baḥrī Period," in *Studies in Islamic History and Civilization*, ed. U. Heyd (Jerusalem: The Magnes Press, 1961), 24–27.
ʿĀṣī, Ḥusayn, *Muḥyī al-Dīn b. ʿAbd al-Ẓāhir, Aṣruhu wa-Turāthuhu al-Taʾrīkhī* (Beirut: Dār al-kutub al-ʿilmiyya, 1413/1993).
Assmann, Aleida, *Cultural Memory and Western Civilization* (Cambridge: Cambridge University Press, 2011).

Banister, Mustafa, "The *ʿĀlim*-caliph: Reimagining the Caliph as a Man of Learning in Eighth/Fourteenth and Ninth/Fifteenth-Century Egypt," in *Knowledge and Education in Classical Islam: Religious Learning Between Continuity and Change*, 2 vols., ed. Sebastian Günther (Leiden: Brill, 2020), 741–769.

Banister, Mustafa, *The Abbasid Caliphate of Cairo: Out of the Shadows* (Edinburgh: Edinburgh University Press, 2021).

Banister, Mustafa, "Professional Mobility in Ibn ʿArabshāh's Fifteenth-Century Panegyric Dedicated to Sultan al-Ẓāhir Jaqmaq," *MSR* 23 (2021), 133–164.

Bauden, Frédéric, "Les relations diplomatiques entre les sultans mamlouks circassiens et les autres pouvoirs du Dār al-islām: l'apport du ms. ar. 4440 (BNF, Paris)," *Annales Islamologiques* 41 (2007), 1–29.

Bauden, Frédéric, "The Sons of al-Nāṣir Muḥammad and the Politics of Puppets: Where Did It All Start?," *MSR* 13, no. 1 (2009), 53–81.

Bauden, Frédéric, "Maqriziana XIII: An Exchange of Correspondence between al-Maqrīzī and al-Qalqashandī," in *Developing Perspectives in Mamluk History: Essays in Honor of Amalia Levanoni*, ed. Yuval Ben-Bassat (Leiden: Brill, 2017), 201–229.

Bauden, Frédéric, "Mamluk Diplomatics: The Present State of Research," in *Mamluk Cairo, a Crossroads for Embassies: Studies on Diplomacy and Diplomatics*, eds. Frédéric Bauden and Malika Dekkiche (Leiden: Brill, 2019), 1–104.

Bauden, Frédéric, "Maqriziana XVI: al-Maqrīzī as a Reader," in *Authors as Readers in the Mamlūk Period and Beyond*, ed. Élise Franssen (Venice: Edizione Ca'foscari, 2022), 195–266.

Bauden, Frédéric, "'The Calligrapher Is an Ape!' Arabic Epigrams on Pen Boxes (Sixth/Twelfth-Ninth/Fifteenth Centuries" in *Inscriptions from the Islamic World*, ed. Bernard O'Kane, Andrew Peacock, and Mark Muehlheusler (Edinburgh: Edinburgh University Press, forthcoming), 436–534.

Bauden, Frédéric, "Ibn ʿAbd al-Ẓāhir," *EI3*.

Bauden, Frédéric, "The Qalawūnids: A Pedigree" s.d., in: http://mamluk.uchicago.edu/qalawunids/qalawunid-pedigree.pdf.

Bauer, Thomas, "Mamluk Literature: Misunderstandings and New Approaches," *MSR* 9, no. 2 (2005), 105–130.

Bauer, Thomas, "Arabische Kultur," in *Historische Wörterbuch der Rhetorik* ed. Gert Ueding e.a. (Tübingen: Max Niemeyer, 2007), 111–137.

Bauer, Thomas, "The Dawādār's Hunting Party: a Mamluk *Muzdawija Ṭardiyya*, probably by Shihāb al-Dīn ibn Faḍl Allāh," in *O Ye Gentlemen: Arabic Studies on Science and Literary Culture in Honour of Remke Kruk*, eds. A. Vrolijk & J.P. Hogendijk (Leiden: Brill, 2007), 291–312.

Bauer, Thomas, "Ibn Nubātah al-Miṣrī (686–768/1287–1366): Life and Works. Part I: The Life of Ibn Nubātah," *MSR* 12, no. 1 (2008), 1–35.

Bauer, Thomas, "Mamluk Literature as a Means of Communication," in *Ubi sumus? Quo vademus? Mamluk Studies – State of the Art*, ed. Stephan Conermann (Bonn: V&R unipress/Bonn University Press, 2013), 23–56.

Behrens-Abouseif, Doris, "The Citadel of Cairo: Stage for Mamluk Ceremonial," *Annales Islamologiques* 24 (1988), 25–79.

Behrens-Abouseif, Doris, *Practicing Diplomacy in the Mamluk Sultanate: Gifts and Material Culture in the Medieval Islamic World* (London-New York: I.B. Tauris, 2016).

Behrens-Abouseif, Doris, "A Mamluk Pen Box Connected to the *Thousand and One Nights* and the Historian Ibn ʿAbd al-Ẓāhir," *Muqarnas* 39 (2022), 23–36.

Berkey, Jonathan P., "Culture and Society during the Late Middle Ages," in *The Cambridge History of Egypt, vol. 1, Islamic Egypt, 640–1517*, ed. Carl F. Petry (Cambridge: Cambridge University Press, 1998), 386–411.

Berkey, Jonathan P., *The Formation of Islam: Religion and Society in the Near East, 600–1800* (Cambridge: Cambridge University Press, 2003).
Biran, Michal, "Libraries, Books, and Transmission of Knowledge in Ilkhanid Baghdad" *JESHO* 62 (2019), 464–502.
Björkman, Walter, *Beiträge zur Geschichte der Staatskanzlei im islamischen Ägypten* (Hamburg: Friedrichsen, De Gruyter & co., 1928).
Bora, Fozia, "A Mamluk Historian's Holograph: Messages from a *Musawwada* of *Taʾrīkh*," *Journal of Islamic Manuscripts* 3 (2012), 119–153.
Bora, Fozia, *Writing History in the Medieval Islamic World: The Value of Chronicles as Archives* (London: I.B. Tauris, 2019).
Bosworth, C.E., "A 'maqāma' on Secretaryship: al-Qalqashandī's 'al-Kawākib al-durriyya fī'l-manāqib al-Badriyya'," *BSOAS*, 27, no. 2 (1964), 291–298.
Bosworth, C.E., "The Heritage of Rulership in Early Islamic Iran and the Search for Dynastic Connections with the Past" *Iranian Studies* 9 (1978), 7–34.
Bourdieu, Pierre, "Le champ littéraire," *Actes de la recherche en sciences sociales* 89 (1991), 3–46.
Broadbridge, Anne F., "Mamluk Legitimacy and the Mongols: The Reigns of Baybars and Qalāwūn," *MSR* 4 (2000), 91–118.
Broadbridge, Anne F., *Kingship and Ideology in the Islamic and Mongol Worlds* (Cambridge: Cambridge University Press, 2007).
Broadbridge, Anne F., "Careers in Diplomacy among Mamluks and Mongols, 658–741/1260–1341," in *Mamluk Cairo, a Crossroads for Embassies: Studies on Diplomacy and Diplomatics*, eds. Frédéric Bauden and Malika Dekkiche (Leiden: Brill, 2019), 276–277.
Burke, Seán, *The Death and Return of the Author: Criticism and Subjectivity in Barthes, Foucault and Derrida* (Edinburgh: Edinburgh University Press, 1992).
Buylaert, Frederik & Haemers, Jelle, "Record-Keeping as Status Performance in the Early Modern Low Countries," *Past and Present* 230 (2016), 131–150.
Cahen, Claude, "La Correspondance de Ḍiyā ad-Dîn ibn al-Athīr: Liste de lettres et textes de diplômes," *BSOAS* 14, no. 1 (1952), 34–43.
Campbell, Joseph, *The Hero with a Thousand Faces* (Princeton: Princeton University Press, 1968).
Carmona, Alfonso, "Sobre la estructura convencional del título en los libros árabes," *al-Qantara* 21, no. 1 (2000), 85–96.
Carter, Michael G., "Ibn Durayd," in *Encyclopedia of Arabic Literature*, 2 vols., eds. Julie S. Meisami & Paul Starkey (London: Routledge, 1998), vol. 1:322.
Casanova, P., "L'historien Ibn ʿAbd aḍh-Ḍhāhir," in *Mémoires publiés par les members de la Mission Archéologique française au Caire, vol. 6*, ed. M.Urbain Bouriant (Paris: Ernest Leroux, 1893), 493–505.
Chamberlain, Michael, *Knowledge and Social Practice in Medieval Damascus, 1190–1350* (Cambridge: Cambridge University Press, 1994).
Chamberlain, Michael, "Military Patronage States and the Political Economy of the Frontier, 1000–1250," in *A Companion to the History of the Middle East*, ed. Youssef M. Choueiri (New Jersey: Wiley-Blackwell, 2008), 125–153.
Chartier, Roger, *Forms and Meanings: Texts, Performances, and Audiences from Codex to Computer* (Philadelphia: University of Pennsylvania Press, 1995).
Chraïbi, Aboubakr, "L'émergence du genre 'muqaddima' dans la littérature arabe" in *Entrer en matière: les prologues*, eds. Jean-Daniel Dubois & Bernard Roussel (Paris: Cerf, 1998), 89–101.
Clifford, William W., *State Formation and the Structure of Politics in Mamluk Syro-Egypt, 648–741 A.H./1250–1340 C.E.*, ed. S. Conermann (Bonn: V&R unipress/Bonn University Press, 2013).

Cureton, W. & Rieu, Charles, *Catalogus codicum manuscriptorum orientalium qui in Museo Britannico asservantur: partem secundam codices Arabicos amplectentem* (London: 1846–1871).
Dekkiche, Malika, "The Letter and Its Response: The Exchanges between the Qara Qoyunlu and the Mamluk Sultan: MS Arabe 4440 (BnF, Paris)," *Arabica,* 63, no. 6 (2016), 579–626.
Dekkiche, Malika, "Diplomatics, or Another Way to See the World," in *Mamluk Cairo, a Crossroads for Embassies: Studies on Diplomacy and Diplomatics*, eds. Frédéric Bauden and Malika Dekkiche (Leiden: Brill, 2019), 185–213.
Deny, J. "Bāb-i ʿĀlī," *EI2.*
de Slane, M. le Baron, *Catalogue des manuscrits arabes* (Paris: Imprimerie nationale, 1883–1895).
D'hulster, Kristof, "The Road to the Citadel as a Chain of Opportunity: Mamluks' Careers between Contingency and Institutionalization," in *Trajectories of State Formation across Fifteenth-Century Islamic West-Asia: Eurasian Parallels, Connections and Divergences,* ed. Jo Van Steenbergen (Leiden: Brill, 2019), 159–200.
D'hulster, Kristof, *Browsing the Sultan's Bookshelves: Towards a Reconstruction of the Library of the Mamluk Sultan Qāniṣawh al-Ghawrī (r. 906–922/1501–1516)* (Bonn: V&R unipress/Bonn University Press, 2021).
Diem, Werner, *Ehrendes Kleid und ehrendes Wort: Studien zu Tašrīf in mamlūkischer und vormamlūkischer Zeit* (Würzburg, 2002).
Duff, David (ed.), *Modern Genre Theory* (London: Routledge, 1999).
Duindam, Jeroen, "Prince, Pen, and Sword: Eurasian Perspectives," in *Prince, Pen, and Sword: Eurasian Perspectives,* eds. M. van Berkel and J. Duindam (Leiden: Brill, 2018), 542–565.
Eddé, Anne-Marie, *Saladin,* transl. Jane Marie Todd (Cambridge, MA: The Belknap Press of Harvard University Press, 2011).
Eddé, Anne-Marie, "Baybars et son double: De l'ambiguïté du souverain ideal" in *Le Bilad Al-Šam face aux mondes extérieurs. La perception de l'autre et la représentation du souverain,* ed. Denise Aigle (Damascus/Beirut: Presses de L'Ifpo, 2012), 73–86.
Elbendary, Amina A., "The Sultan, the Tyrant, and the Hero: Changing Medieval Perceptions of al-Zāhir Baybars," *MSR* 5 (2001), 141–157.
Elisséeff, Nikita, "Ibn ʿAsākir," *EI2.*
El-Merheb, Mohamad, *Political Thought in the Mamluk Period: The Unnecessary Caliphate* (Edinburgh: Edinburgh University Press, 2022).
Escovitz, J.H., "Vocational Patterns of the Scribes of the Mamlūk Chancery," *Arabica* 23, no. 1 (1976), 42–62.
Eychenne, Matthieu, *Liens personnels, cliéntelisme et réseaux de pouvoir dans le sultanat mamelouk (milieu XIIIe-fin XIVe siècle)* (Damascus/Beirut: Presses de l'ifpo, 2013).
Fernandes, Leonor, "On Conducting the Affairs of the State: A Guideline of the 14th Century," *Annales Islamologiques* 24 (1988), 81–91.
Fleckenstein, Kristie S., "Decorous Spectacle: Mirrors, Manners, and Ars Dictaminis in Late Medieval Civic Engagement," *Rhetoric Review* 28, no. 2 (2009), 111–127.
Flinterman, Willem, "The Cult of Qalāwūn: *Waqf*, Commemoration, and Dynasty in early Mamluk Cairo, ca. 1280–1340" (Unpublished PhD thesis, Universiteit Amsterdam, 2017).
Flinterman, Willem & Van Steenbergen, Jo, "Al-Nasir Muhammad and the Formation of the Qalawunid State," in *Pearls on a String: Art in the Age of Great Islamic Empires*, ed. Amy Landau (Baltimore/Seattle: The Walters Art Museum/University of Washington Press, 2015), 87–113.
Franssen, Élise, "What was there in a Mamluk Amīr's Library? Evidence from a Fifteenth-Century Manuscript" in *Developing Perspectives in Mamluk History. Essays in Honor of Amalia Levanoni,* ed. Yuval Ben-Bassat (Leiden: Brill, 2017), 311–332.

Franssen, Élise, "al-Ṣafadī: the Scholar as a Reader" in *Authors as Readers in the Mamlūk Period and Beyond*, ed. Élise Franssen (Venice: Edizione Ca'foscari, 2022), 83–152.
Freimark, Peter, "Das Vorwort als literarische Form in der arabischen Literatur" (Unpublished PhD thesis, Westfalischen Wilhelms-Universität zu Münster, 1967).
Frenkel, Yehoshua, "Baybars and the Sacred Geography of Bilād al-Shām: A Chapter in the Islamization of Syria's Landscape," *Jerusalem Studies in Arabic and Islam* 25 (2001), 153–170.
Frenkel, Yehoshua, "Mamluk Historiography Revisited: Narratological Perspectives in Damascene Chronicles" in *Mamluk Historiography Revisited: Narratological Perspectives*, ed. S. Conermann (Bonn: V&R Unipress/Bonn University Press, 2018), 27–50.
Frye, Northrop, *Anatomy of Criticism: Four Essays* (Princeton, NJ: Princeton University Press, 1957).
Fück, Johann W. "Ibn Manẓūr," *EI2*.
Fuess, Albrecht, "Sultans with horns: The Political Significance of Headgear in the Mamluk Empire" *MSR* 12, no. 2 (2008), 71–94.
Gabrieli, Francesco, *Arab Historians of the Crusades*, transl. E.J. Costello (London: Routledge, 2010).
Geertz, Clifford, *The Interpretation of Cultures: Selected Essays* (New York: Basic Books, 1973).
Ghersetti, Antonella, "Enseigner en racontant: les anecdotes dans L'Étiquette de la cour califale (Rusūm dār al-ḫilāfa) d'al-Ṣābi" *Synergies Monde arabe* 6 (2009), 27–40.
Glazer, Sidney, "Abu Ḥayyān Athīr al-Dīn Muḥammad b. Yūsuf al-Gharnāṭī," *EI2*.
Gould, Rebecca, "Inimitability versus Translatability," *The Translator*, 19, no. 1 (2013), 81–104.
Gruendler, Beatrice, *Medieval Arabic Praise Poetry: Ibn al-Rūmī and the Patron's Redemption* (London: Routledge, 2003).
Gully, Adrian, *The Culture of Letter Writing in Pre-Modern Islamic Society* (Edinburgh: Edinburgh University Press, 2008).
Guo, Li, "Mamluk Historiographic Studies: The state of the Art" *MSR* 1 (1997), 15–43.
Guo, Li, *Early Mamluk Syrian Historiography: Al-Yūnīnī's* Dhayl Mirʾat al-zamān, *Volume One* (Leiden: Brill, 1998).
Haarmann, Ulrich, *Quellenstudien zur frühen Mamlukenzeit* (Freiburg: Robischon, 1969).
Haarmann, Ulrich, "Auflösung und Bewahrung der klassischen Formen arabischer Geschichtsschreibung in der Zeit der Mamluken," *ZDMG*, 121, no. 1 (1971), 46–60.
al-Ḥāfiẓ, Muḥammad Muṭīʿ, *Al-Ḥāfiẓ Ibn ʿAsākir: Muḥaddith al-Shām wa-Muʾarrikhhā al-kabīr* (Damascus: Dār al-qalam, s.d.).
Al-Hajji, Hayat Nasser, *The Internal Affairs in Egypt during the Reign of Sultan al-Nāṣir Muḥammad b. Qalāwūn (709–741/1309–1341)* (Kuwait: Kuwait University, 1978).
Hämeen Anttila, Jaakko, "The essay and debate (al-risāla and al-munāẓara)," in *Arabic Literature in the Post-Classical Period*, eds. R. Allen and D.S. Richards (Cambridge: Cambridge University Press, 2008), 134–144.
Hamori, Andras, *The Composition of al-Mutanabbī's Panegyrics to Sayf al-Dawla* (Leiden: Brill, 1992).
Harb, Lara, *Arabic Poetics: Aesthetic Experience in Classical Arabic Literature* (Cambridge: Cambridge University Press, 2021).
Heinrichs, Wolfhart, "Review of Cambridge History of Arabic Literature: ʿAbbasid Belles-Lettres," *al-ʿArabiyya* 26 (1993), 129–162.
Heinrichs, Wolfhart, "Prosimetrical Genres in Classical Arabic Literature," in *Prosimetrum: Cross-Cultural Perspectives on Narrative in Prose and Verse*, eds. Joseph Harris & Karl Reichl (Cambridge: D.S. Brewer, 1997), 249–275.
Herdt, Andreas, "Taqrīẓ, Schein-Taqrīẓ oder Anti-Taqrīẓ? Ein mamlukenzeitliches Beispiel dafür, wie schmal der Grat zwischen Lob und Schmähung sein kann," in *The Racecourse of Literature: An-Nawāǧī and His Contemporaries*, eds. Alev Masarwa & Hakan Özkan (Baden-Baden: Ergon Verlag, 2020), 96–129.

Herzog, Thomas, "Romans populaires arabes: de l'historiographie au roman, du roman à l'historiographie," in *Écrire l'histoire de son temps (Europe et monde arabe)*, ed. R. Jacquemond (Paris: L'harmattan, 2005), 95–108.

Herzog, Thomas, *Geschichte und Imaginaire: Entstehung, Überlieferung und Bedeutung der Sirat Baibars in ihrem sozio-politischen Kontext* (Wiesbaden: Harrassowitz, 2007).

El-Hibri, Tayeb, *Reinterpreting Islamic Historiography: Hārūn al-Rashīd and the Narrative of the 'Abbāsid Caliphate* (Cambridge: Cambridge University Press, 1999).

Hirschler, Konrad, *Medieval Arabic Historiography: Authors as Actors* (London: Routledge, 2006).

Hirschler, Konrad, "Islam: The Arabic and Persian Traditions, Eleventh-Fifteenth Centuries," in *The Oxford History of Historical Writing, volume 2: 400–1400*, eds. S. Foot & C.F. Robinson (Oxford: Oxford University Press, 2012), 267–286.

Hirschler, Konrad, "From Archive to Archival Practices: Rethinking the Preservation of Mamluk Administrative Documents," *JAOS* 136, no. 1 (2016), 1–28.

Hirschler, Konrad, *Medieval Damascus: Plurality and Diversity in an Arabic Library* (Edinburgh: Edinburg University Press, 2016).

Holt, P.M., "Qalāwūn's treaty with Acre in 1283," *The English Historical Review* 81, vol. 361 (1976), 802–812.

Holt, P.M., "The Virtuous Ruler in Thirteenth-Century Mamluk Royal Biographies," *Nottingham Medieval Studies* 24 (1980), 27–35

Holt, P.M., "Three Biographies of al-Ẓāhir Baybars," in *Medieval Historical Writing in the Christian and Islamic Worlds*, ed. David O. Morgan (London: School of Oriental and African Studies, University of London, 1982), 19–29.

Holt, P.M., "Saladin and His Admirers: A Biographical Reassessment," *BSOAS* 46, no. 2 (1983), 235–239

Holt, P.M., "Some Observations on Shāfiʿ b. ʿAlī's Biography of Baybars," *Journal of Semitic Studies* 29 (1984), 123–130.

Holt, P.M., "The Īlkhān Aḥmad's Embassies to Qalāwūn: Two Contemporary Accounts," *BSOAS* 49, no. 1 (1986), 128–132.

Holt, P.M., "A Chancery Clerk in Medieval Egypt," *The English Historical Review* 101/400 (1986), 671–679.

Holt, P.M., "The Presentation of Qalāwūn by Shāfiʿ b. ʿAlī" in *Essays in Honor of Bernard Lewis: The Islamic World. From Classical to Modern Times*, eds. C.E. Bosworth, C. Issawi, R. Savory, & A.L. Udovitch (eds.) (Princeton: The Darwin Press, 1989), 141–150.

Holt, P.M., "The Sultan as Ideal Ruler: Ayyubid and Mamluk Prototypes," in *Süleyman the Magnificent and His Age: The Ottoman Empire in the Early Modern World*, eds. Metin Kunt & Christine Woodhead (New York: Longman, 1995), 122–137.

Holt, P.M., "Literary Offerings: A Genre of Courtly Literature," in *The Mamluks in Egyptian Politics and Society*, eds. Thomas Philipp & Ulrich Haarmann (Cambridge: Cambridge University Press, 1998), 3–16.

Holt, P.M., *Early Mamluk Diplomacy (1260–1290): Treaties of Baybars and Qalāwūn with Christian Rulers* (Leiden: Brill, 1995).

Holtzman, Livnat, "The Dhimmi's Question on Predetermination and the Ulama's Six Responses: The Dynamics of Composing Polemical Didactic Poems in Mamluk Cairo and Damascus," *MSR* 16 (2012), 35.

Irwin, Robert, "Mamluk History and Historians," *The Cambridge History of Arabic Literature: Arabic Literature in the Post-Classical Period*, ed. R. Allen & D.S. Richards (Cambridge: Cambridge University Press, 2006), 159–170.

Jackson, Sherman A., "The Primacy of Domestic Politics: Ibn Bint al-Aʿazz and the Establishment of Four Chief Judgeships in Mamlûk Egypt," *JAOS* 115, no. 1 (1995), 52–65.

Karjoo-Ravary, Ali, "Adorning the King of Islam: Weaving and Unraveling History in Astarabadi's *Feasting and Fighting*," *MAVCOR Journal* 6, no. 2 (2022).

Kazimirski, Albert de Biberstein, *Dictionnaire arabe-français: contenant toutes les racines de la langue arabe, leurs dérivés, tant dans l'idiome vulgaire que dans l'idiome littéral, ainsi que les dialectes d'Alger et de Maroc*, 2 vols. (Paris: Maisonneuve et Cie, 1860).

Keegan, Matthew L., "Commentators, Collators, and Copyists: Interpreting Manuscript Variation in the Exordium of Al-Ḥarīrī's Maqāmāt," *Arabic Humanities, Islamic Thought: Essays in Honor of Everett K. Rowson*, ed. Joseph Lowry & Shawkat Toorawa (Leiden: Brill, 2017), 295–316.

Keegan, Matthew L., "Throwing the Reins to the Reader: Hierarchy, Jurjānian Poetics, and al-Muṭarrizī's Commentary on the *Maqāmāt*," *Journal of Abbasid Studies* 5, vol. 1–2 (2018), 105–145.

Keegan, Matthew L., "Review of Adam Talib, *How do you Say Epigram in Arabic?*," *Middle Eastern Literatures* 21, nos. 2–3 (2018), 251–252.

Keegan, Matthew L., "*Adab* without the Crusades: The Inebriated Solidarity of a Young Officer's Hunting Epistle," *Al-ʿUṣūr al-Wusṭā* 28 (2020): 272–296.

Keegan, Matthew L., "Rethinking Poetry as (Anti-Crusader) Propaganda: Licentiousness and Cross-Confessional Patronage in the *Ḫarīdat al-qaṣr*," *Intellectual History of the Islamicate World* (2022 forthcoming).

Kennedy, Hugh, *The Prophet and the Age of the Caliphates: The Islamic Near East from the 6th to the 11th Century* (London: Longman, 1986).

Khalidi, Tarif, *Arabic Historical Thought in the Classical Period* (Cambridge: Cambridge University Press, 1994).

Khowaiter, Abdul-Aziz, *Baibars the First: His Endeavours and Achievements* (London: Green Mountain Press, 1978).

al-Khowayter, Abdul Aziz, "A Critical Edition of an Unknown Source for the Life of al-Malik al-Ẓāhir Baibars, with introduction, translation, and notes" (Unpublished PhD thesis, School of Oriental and African Studies, University of London, 1960) 3 vols.

Kilito, Abdelfattah, *Arabs and the Art of Storytelling: A Strange Familiarity*, transl. Mbarek Sryfi and Eric Sellin (Syracuse, NY: Syracuse University Press, 2014).

Koch, Yoel, "ʿIzz al-Dīn ibn Shaddād and his Biography of Baybars," *Annali (Istituto Universitario Orientale)* 43, no. 2 (1983), 249–287.

Kruk, Remke, "History and Apocalypse: Ibn Al-Nafīs' Justification of Mamluk Rule" *Der Islam* 72, no. 2 (1995), 324–337.

Kühn, Hans-Ulrich, *Sultan Baibars und seine Söhne: Frühmamkūkische Herrschaftssicherung in ayyūbidischer Tradition* (Bonn: V&R unipress/Bonn University Press, 2019).

Lane, Edward William & Lane-Poole, Stanley (ed.), *An Arabic-English Lexicon* (Beirut: Librairie du Liban, 1863–1893), in *Mawrid Reader*, http://ejtaal.net/aa

Langner, Barbara, *Untersuchungen zur historischen Volkskunde Ägyptens nach mamlukischen Quellen* (Freiburg: Klaus Schwartz 1983).

Larkin, Margaret, *Al-Mutanabbi: Voice of the ʿAbbasid Poetic Ideal* (London: OneWorld, 2007).

Lee, Joo-Yup, *Qazaqlïq*, or *Ambitious Brigandage, and the Formation of the Qazaqs: State and Identity in Post-Mongol Central Eurasia* (Leiden and Boston: Brill, 2016).

Levanoni, Amalia, A *Turning Point in Mamluk History: The Third Reign of al-Nāṣir Muḥammad Ibn Qalāwūn (1310–1341)* (Leiden: Brill, 1995).

Lewicka, Paulina, "What a King Should Care About: Two Memoranda of the Mamluk Sultan on Running the State's Affairs," *Studia Arabistyczne i Isamistyczne* 6 (1998), 5–45.

Little, Donald P., *An Introduction to Mamluk Historiography: An Analysis of Arabic Annalistic and Biographical Sources for the Reign of Al-Malik An-Nāṣir Muḥammad Ibn Qalāʾūn* (Wiesbaden: Franz Steiner Verlag, 1970).

Little, Donald P., "The Recovery of a Lost Source for Bāḥrī Mamlūk History: Al-Yūsufī's Nuzhat Al-Nāẓir Fī Sīrat Al-Malik Al-Nāṣir," *JAOS* 94, vol. 1 (1974), 42–54.

Little, Donald P., "Historiography of the Ayyubid and Mamluk epochs," in *The Cambridge History of Egypt, Volume One: Islamic Egypt, 640–1517,* ed. C.F. Petry (Cambridge: Cambridge University Press, 1998), 412–444.

al-Luhaybī, Ḥusayn ʿAbd al-ʿĀl, "Shiʿr Muḥyī al-Dīn b. Qurnāṣ al-Ḥamawī: Dirāsa wa Tawthīq," *Majallat Markaz Dirāsāt al-Kūfa,* 31 (2013), 74–115.

Malti-Douglas, Fedwa, "Dreams, the Blind, and the Semiotics of the Biographical Notice," *Studia Islamica* 51 (1980), 137–162.

Mansouri, Tahar, "Le Portrait Du Sultan Al-Manṣūr Qalāwūn D'après *Al-Faḍl Al-Ma'ṯūr Min Sīrat Al-Malik Al-Manṣūr* De Šāfiʿ B. ʿalī" in *Le Bilad Al-Šam face aux mondes extérieurs. La perception de l'autre et la représentation du souverain,* ed. D. Aigle (Damascus/Beirut: Presses de L'Ifpo, 2012), 87–97.

Marlow, Louise, "Advice Literature," *EI3.*

Marlow, Louise, "Ḥasab o Nasab," *EIr.*

Martel-Thoumian, Bernadette, *Les civils et l'administration dans l'état militaire mamelouke (IXe/XVe siècle)* (Damascus: Institut français, 1992).

Mauder, Christian, *Gelehrte Krieger: Die Mamluken als Träger arabischsprachiger Bildung nach al-Ṣafadī, al-Maqrīzī und weiteren Quellen* (Hildesheim: Georg Ulms Verlag, 2012).

Mauder, Christian, "The Development of Arabo-Islamic Education among Members of the Mamluk Military," in *Knowledge and Education in Classical Islam: Religious Learning Between Continuity and Change*, 2 vols., ed. Sebastian Günther (Leiden: Brill, 2020), 963–983.

Mauder, Christian, "Being Persian in Late Mamluk Egypt: The Construction and Significance of Persian Ethnic Identity in the Salons of Sultan Qānīṣawh al-Ghawrī (r. 906–922/1501–1516)" *Al-ʿUṣūr al-Wusṭā* 28 (2020), 376–408.

Mauder, Christian, "Education and Learning among Members of the Mamluk Army: Results of a Quantitative Analysis of Mamluk Biographies" in *History and Society during the Mamluk Period (1250–1517): Studies of the Annemarie Schimmel Institute for Advanced Study III*, eds. Bethany J. Walker & Abdelkader Al Ghouz (Bonn: V&R University Press/Bonn University Press, 2021), 61–88.

Mauder, Christian, *In the Sultan's Salon: Learning, Religion, and Rulership at the Mamluk Court of Qānīṣawh Al-Ghawrī (r. 1501–1516)* (Leiden: Brill, 2021).

Mayer, L.A., *Saracenic Heraldry: A Survey* (Oxford: Clarendon Press, 1933).

Mazor, Amir, *The Rise and Fall of a Muslim Regiment: The Manṣūriyya in the First Mamluk Sultanate, 678/1279–741/1341* (Bonn: V&R Unipress/Bonn University Press, 2015).

Meisami, Julie Scott, "Review of *Arabic Historical Thought in the Classical Period,*" *JAOS* 116, no. 2 (1996), 309–313.

Meisami, Julie Scott, "Rulers and the Writing of History" in *Writers and Rulers: Perspectives on Their Relationship from Abbasid to Safavid Times,* eds. Beatrice Gruendler & Louise Marlow (Wiesbaden: Reichert Verlag, 2004), 73–96.

Meisami, Julie Scott, "History as Literature," in *A History of Persian Literatuere X: Persian Historiography,* ed. Charles Melville & Ehsan Yarshater, (New York: I.B. Tauris, 2012), 1–53.

Meisami, Julie Scott, "al-Mutanabbī," in *Encyclopedia of Arabic Literature,* 2 vols., eds. Julie S. Meisami & Paul Starkey (London: Routledge, 1998), 2:559.

Melchoir-Bonnet, Sabine, *Histoire du miroir* (Paris: Editions imago, 1994).

Moberg, Axel, "Regierungspromemoria eines Ägyptischen Sultans" in *Festschrift Edward Sachau zum siebzigsten Geburtstage gewidmet von Freunden und Schülern,* ed. Gotthold Weil (Berlin: Georg Kremer, 1915), 406–421.

Moberg, Axel, "Zwei ägyptische Waqf-Urkunden aus dem Jahre 691/1292" in *Le monde oriental* 12 (1918), 1–64.
Monroe, James T. & Pettigrew, Mark F., "The Decline of Courtly Patronage and the Appearance of New Genres in Arabic Literature," *JAL* 34 (2003), 138–177.
Montgomery, James E., "Serendipity, Resistance, and Multivalency: Ibn Khurradadhbih and his Kitāb al-Masālik wal-Mamālik," in *On fiction and adab in medieval Arabic literature,* ed. Philip F. Kennedy (Wiesbaden: Harrassowitz, 2005), 177–232.
Montgomery, James E., *Al-Jāḥiẓ; In Praise of Books* (Edinburgh: Edinburgh University Press, 2013).
Mourad, Suleiman, *Ibn ʿAsakir of Damascus* (London: OneWorld, 2021)
Muhanna, Elias, "Why was the 14th century a century of Arabic encyclopaedism?" in *Encyclopaedism from Antiquity to the Renaissance*, eds. Jason König & Greg Woolf (Cambridge: Cambridge University Press, 2013), 343–356.
Muhanna, Elias, *The World in a Book: al-Nuwayrī and the Islamic Encyclopedic Tradition* (Princeton, NJ: Princeton University Press, 2017).
al-Musawi, Muhsin J., "Vindicating a Profession or a Personal Career? Al-Qalqashandī's *Maqāmah* in Context," *MSR* 7, no. 1 (2003), 111–135.
al-Musawi, Muhsin J., "Pre-Modern Belletristic Prose" in *Arabic Literature in the Post-Classical Period*, eds. Roger Allen and Donald S. Richards (Cambridge: Cambridge University Press, 2008), 101–133.
al-Musawi, Muhsin J., *The Medieval Islamic Republic of Arabic Letters: Arabic Knowledge Construction* (Notre Dame, IN: University of Notre Dame Press, 2015).
Naaman, Erez, *Literature and the Islamic Court: Cultural Life Under al-Ṣāḥib b. ʿAbbād* (London: Routledge, 2016).
al-Nāṣir, Ṣafwān Ṭaha Ḥasan, "'Sīrat al-Malik al-Ẓāhir Baybars' li-Muḥyī al-Dīn b. ʿAbd al-Ẓāhir (t. 692 / 1293): Dirāsa naqdiyya fī taḥqīq al-kitāb," *Majallat al-tirbiyya wa'l-ʿilm* 17, no. 3 (2010), 80–99.
Nielsen, Jorgen S., *Secular Justice in an Islamic State: Maẓālim Under the Baḥrī Mamlūks (662/1264–789/1387)* (Istanbul: Nederlands Historisch-Archeologisch Instituut, 1985).
Northrup, Linda S., *From Slave to Sultan: The Career of al-Manṣūr Qalāwūn and the Consolidation of Mamluk Rule in Egypt and Syria (678–679 A.H./1279–1290 A.D.)* (Stuttgart: Franz Steiner, 1998).
Noth, Albrecht, *Quellenkritische Studien zu Themen, Formen und Tendenzen frühislamischer Geschichtsüberlieferung* (Bonn: Orientalisches Seminar der Universität, 1973).
Noth, Albrecht & Conrad, Lawrence I., *The Early Arabic Historical Tradition: A Source-Critical Study* (London: Darwin Press, 1994).
Onimus, Clément, *Les maîtres du jeu: Pouvoir et violence politique à l'aube du sultanat mamlouk circassien (784–815/1382–1412)* (Paris: Editions de la Sorbonne, 2019).
Orfali, Bilal, *The Anthologist's Art:* Abū Manṣūr al-Thaʿālibī *and His* Yatīmat al-dahr (Leiden: Brill, 2016).
Pellat, Charles, "Manāḳib," *EI2.*
Pfeiffer, Judith, "Aḥmad Tegüder's Second Letter to Qalā'ūn (682/1283)," in *History and Historiography of Post-Mongol Central Asia and the Middle East,* ed. Judith Pfeiffer & Sholeh A. Quinn (Wiesbaden: Harrassowitz, 2006), 167–202.
Pomerantz, Maurice, "The Rivalrous Imitator: *The Ruby Red Account of the Fire of Damascus* by Ibn Ḥiǧǧah al-Ḥamawī (d. 838/1434)" in *The Racecourse of Literature: An-Nawāǧī and His Contemporaries,* eds. Alev Masarwa & Hakan Özkan (Baden-Baden: Ergon Verlag, 2020), 130–147.
Propp, Vladimir, *Morphology of the Folktale,* transl. Laurence Scott (Austin: University of Texas Press, 1968).
Qutbuddin, Aziz K. "A Literary Analysis of *Taḥmīd*: A Relational Approach for Studying the Arabic-Islamic Laudatory Preamble," in *Reflections on Knowledge and Language in Middle Eastern*

Societies, eds. Hussain Qutbuddin, Yonatan Mendel & Bruno De Nicola (Newcastle: Cambridge Scholars Publishing, 2010), 63–89.

Rabbat, Nasser, "Mamluk Throne Halls: *Qubba* or *Iwān*?," *Ars Orientalis* 23 (1993), 201–214.

Rabbat, Nasser, *The Citadel of Cairo: A New Interpretation of Royal Mamluk Architecture* (Leiden: Brill, 1995).

Rabbat, Nasser, "Representing the Mamluks in Mamluk Historical Writing," in *The Historiography of Islamic Egypt (c. 950–1800)*, ed. Hugh Kennedy (Leiden: Brill, 2000), 59–76.

Rabbat, Nasser, "Staging the City: Or How Mamluk Architecture Coopted the Streets of Cairo," *Ulrich Haarmann Memorial Lecture* 9 (2014).

Rabbat, Nasser, *Writing Egypt: Al-Maqrizi and his Historical Project* (Edinburgh: Edinburgh University Press, 2022).

Radtke, Bernd, "Einleitung" in *Kanz al-durar wa-jāmiʿ al-ghurar, Erster Teil: Kosmographie*, (Cairo-Wiesbaden: Franz Steiner, 1982).

Radtke, Bernd, "Zur 'Literarisierten Volkschronik' Der Mamlukenzeit," *Saeculum* 41, no. 1 (1990), 44–52.

Radtke, Bernd, *Weltgeschichte und Weltbeschreibung im mittelalterlichen Islam* (Beirut-Stuttgart: Orient Institut-Franz Steiner, 1992).

Radtke, Bernd, "Die Literarisierung der mamlukischen Historiografie: Versuch einer Selbstkritik," in *O ye Gentlemen: Arabic Studies on Science and Literary Culture. In Honour of Remke Kruk*, eds. Arnoud Vrolijk & Jan P. Hogendijk (Leiden: Brill, 2007), 263–274.

Rapoport, Yossef, "Legal Diversity in the Age of *Taqlīd*: The Four Chief *Qāḍī*s Under the Mamluks," *Islamic Law and Society*, 10, no. 2 (2003), 210–228.

Rapoport, Yossef, "Royal Justice and Religious Law: *Siyāsah* and Shariʿah Under the Mamluks," *MSR* 16 (2012), 71–102.

Raven, Wim, "Sīra," *EI2*.

Raven, Wim, "Biography of the Prophet," *EI3*.

Reynolds, Dwight F., *Interpreting the Self: Autobiography in the Arabic Literary Tradition* (Berkeley-Los Angeles-London: University of California Press, 2001).

Ricoeur, Paul, *Temps et récit 1: L'intrigue et le récit historique* (Paris: Editions du Seuil, 1983).

Richter-Bernburg, Lutz, *Der Syrische Blitz: Saladins Sekretär zwischen Selbstdarstellung und Geschichtsschreibung* (Stuttgart: Steiner, 1998).

Robinson, Chase F., *Islamic Historiography* (Cambridge: Cambridge University Press, 2003).

Rosenthal, Franz, *A History of Muslim Historiography, Second edition* (Leiden: Brill, 1968).

Rosenthal, Franz, "Ibn Sayyid al-Nās," *EI2*.

Rosenthal, Franz, "'Blurbs' (*taqrīẓ*) from 14th-Century Egypt," *Oriens* 27–28 (1981), 177–196.

Rowson, Everett K. "An Alexandrian Age in 14th-Century Damascus: Twin Commentaries on Two Celebrated Arabic Epistles," *MSR* 7, no. 1 (2003), 97–110.

Rubin, Uri, *The Eye of the Beholder: The Life of Muhammad as Viewed by the Early Muslims (A Textual Analysis)* (Princeton: The Darwin Press, 1995).

Rustow, Marina, *The Lost Archive: Traces of a Caliphate in a Cairo Synagogue* (Princeton: Princeton University Press, 2020).

Salibi, Kamal, "Ibn Faḍl Allāh," *EI2*.

Sauer, Rebecca, "Al-Qalqašandī's maqāma *al-Kawākib ad-durrīya:* A Re-Consideration Within the Framework of Ego-Document," *Islamische Selbstbilder: Festschrift für Susanne Enderwitz*, ed. Sarah Kiyanrad, Rebecca Sauer & Jan Scholz (Heidelberg: Heidelberg University Publishing, 2020), 253–269.

Seidensticker, Tilman, "How Arabic Manuscripts Moved to German Libraries", in *Manuscript Cultures* 10 (2017), 73–82.

Sellheim, Rudolf, “Faḍīla,” *EI2*.

al-Shāwī, ʿAbd al-Hādī ʿAbd al-Raḥmān, “Rasāʾil Shihāb al-Dīn Maḥmūd al-Ḥalabī (h. 725): Ittijāhātuhā al-Mawḍūʿiyya wa-Samātuhā al-Fanniyya” (2011) unpublished paper, in https://www.academia.edu/11638350/سائل_شهاب_الدين_الحلبي_ت725هـ_اتجاهاتها_الموضوعية_وسماتها_الفنية

al-Shāwī, ʿAbd al-Hādī ʿAbd al-Raḥmān & Ḥusayn ʿAbd al-ʿĀlī Buʿaywī, “Shihāb al-Dīn al-Ḥalabī wa-Juhūduhu al-Adabiyya,” *al-ʿAdad*, 40 (2016), 211–237.

Shuraydi, Hasan, *The Raven and the Falcon: Youth versus Old Age in Medieval Arabic Literature* (Leiden: Brill, 2014).

Sims-Williams, Ursula, “Over 2,000 pages in gold: Sultan Baybars’ Qur’an now online,” *British Library, Asian and African Studies Blog*, 8 May 2018. https://blogs.bl.uk/asian-and-african/2018/05/over-2000-pages-in-gold-sultan-baybars-quran-now-online.html

Sivan, Ernest, *L’Islam et la croisade: Idéologie et Propaganda dans les Réactions Musulmanes aux C roisades* (Paris: Librairie d’Amérique et d’Orient, 1968).

Somogyi, Jozsef, “Ibn al-Jauzī’s School of Historiography,” *Acta Orientalia Academiae Scientiarum Hungaricae* 6, no. 1/3 (1956), 207–214.

Sperl, Stefan, “Islamic Kingship and Arabic Panegyric Poetry in the Early 9th Century,” in *JAL* 8 (1977), 20–35.

Spiegel, Gabrielle M., *Romancing the Past: The Rise of Vernacular Prose Historiography in Thirteenth-Century France* (Berkeley: University of California Press, 1993).

Stephen Humphreys, R., *From Saladin to the Mongols: The Ayyubids of Damascus, 1193–1260* (Albany: State University of New York Press, 1977)

Stewart, Angus, “Between Baybars and Qalāwūn: Under-age Rulers and Succession in the Early Mamlūk Sultanate,” *Al-Masaq: Journal of the Medieval Mediterranean* 19, no. 1 (2007), 47–54.

Stowasser, Karl, “Manners and Customs at the Mamluk Court,” *Muqarnas* 2 (1984), 13–20.

Talib, Adam, *How Do You Say ‘Epigram’ in Arabic? Literary History at the Limits of Comparison* (Leiden: Brill, 2017).

Talib, Adam, “Al-Ṣafadī, His Critics, and the Drag of Philological Time,” *Philological Encounters* 4 (2019), 109–134.

Taragan, Hanna, “Sign of the Times: Reusing the Past in Baybars’s Architecture in Palestine,” in *Mamluks and Ottomans: Studies in Honour of Michael Winter*, ed. David J. Wasserstein and Ami Ayalon (London-New York: Routledge, 2006), 54–66.

Thorau, Peter, *The Lion of Egypt*, transl. P.M. Holt (Harlow: Longman, 1992).

Touati, Houari, “La dédicace des livres en Islam médiévale,” *Annales: Histoire, Sciences Sociales* 55, no. 2 (2000), 325–353.

Troadec, Anne, “Les Mamelouks dans l’espace syrien: stratégies de domination et résistances (658/1260–741/1341)” (Unpublished PhD thesis, Ecole Pratique des hautes-études, 2014).

Troadec, Anne, “Baybars and the Cultural Memory of Bilād al-Shām: The Construction of Legitimacy,” *MSR* 18 (2014), 113–147

van Berkel, Maaike, “The People of the Pen: Self-Perceptions of Status and Role in the Administration of Empires and Polities,” in *Prince, Pen, and Sword: Eurasian Perspectives*, eds. Maaike van Berkel and Jeroen Duindam (Leiden: Brill, 2018), 384–451.

van Berkel, Maaike, “Archives and Chanceries: pre-1500, in Arabic,” *EI3*.

Van Den Bossche, Gowaart, “Narrative Construction, Ideal Rule, and Emotional Discourse in the Biographies of Ṣalāḥ al-Dīn and Louis IX by Bahāʾ al-Dīn b. Shaddād and Jean Sire de Joinville,” *al-Masaq* 30, no. 2 (2018), 133–147.

Van Den Bossche, Gowaart, “Literarisierung Reconsidered in the Context of Sultanic Biography: The Case of Shāfiʿ b. ʿAlī’s *Sīrat al-Nāṣir Muḥammad* (BnF MS Arabe 1705),” in *New Readings in*

Arabic Historiography from Late Medieval Egypt and Syria: Proceedings of the themed day of the Fifth Conference of the School of Mamluk Studies, eds. J. Van Steenbergen & M. Termonia (Leiden: Brill, 2021), 466–489.

Van Den Bossche, Gowaart, "Muḥyī al-Dīn b. ʿAbd al-Ẓāhir," in *Arabic Textual Sources for the Crusades* ed. Alex Mallett (Leiden: Brill, forthcoming).

Van Gelder, Geert-Jan H., "The Conceit of Pen and Sword: On an Arabic Literary Debate," *Journal of Semitic Studies*, 22, no. 2 (1987), 329–360.

Van Gelder, Geert-Jan H., "Poetry in Historiography: Some Observations" in *Problems in Arabic Literature*, ed. Miklós Maróth (Piliscsaba: The Avicenna institute of Middle Eastern studies, 2004), 1–13.

Van Gelder, Geert-Jan H., "Poetry in Historiography: The Case of al-Fakhrī by Ibn al-Ṭiqṭaqā," in *Poetry and History: The Value of Poetry in Reconstructing Arab History*, eds. Ramzi Baalbaki, S. Said Agha, & Tarif Khalidi (Beirut: AUB Press, 2011), 61–94.

Van Steenbergen, Jo, "Qalāwūnid Discourse, Elite Communication and the Mamluk Cultural Matrix: Interpreting a 14th-Century Panegyric," *JAL* 43 (2012), 1–28.

Van Steenbergen, Jo, "The Mamluk Sultanate as a Military Patronage State: Household Politics and the Case of the Qalāwūnid *bayt* (1279–1382)," *JESHO* 56 (2013), 189–217.

Van Steenbergen, Jo, *Caliphate and Kingship in a Fifteenth-Century Literary History of Muslim Leadership and Pilgrimage* (Leiden: Brill, 2016).

Van Steenbergen, Jo, "Revisiting the Mamluk Empire: Political Action, Relationships of Power, Entangled Networks, and the Sultanate of Cairo in Late Medieval Syro-Egypt," in *The Mamluk Sultanate from the Perspective of Regional and World History: Economic, Social and Cultural Development in an Era of Increasing International Interaction and Competition*, eds. Reuven Amitai and Stephan Conermann (Bonn: V&R unipress/Bonn University Press, 2019), 75–106.

Van Steenbergen, Jo, "Introduction – History Writing, *Adab*, and Intertextuality in Late Medieval Egypt and Syria: Old and New Readings" in *New Readings in Arabic Historiography from Late Medieval Egypt and Syria: Proceedings of the themed day of the Fifth Conference of the School of Mamluk Studies*, eds. J. Van Steenbergen & M. Termonia (Leiden: Brill, 2021), 1–29.

Veeser, H. Aram (ed.). *The New Historicism* (London: Routledge, 1989).

Vermeulen, Urbain, "Une note sur les insignes royaux des mamelouks," in *Egypt and Syria in the Fatimid, Ayyubid and Mamluk Eras*, eds. Urbain Vermeulen & Daniel De Smet (Leuven: Peeters, 1995), 355–362.

von Grunebaum, Gustav, *Medieval Islam: A Study in Cultural Orientation* (Chicago-London: The University of Chicago Press, 1953).

Von Hees, Syrinx, "The Guidance for Kingdoms: Function of a 'Mirror for Princes' at Court and its Representation of a Court," in *Court Cultures in the Muslim World: Seventh to Nineteenth Centuries*, eds. Albrecht Fuess and Jan-Peter Hartung (London: Routledge, 2011), 370–382.

Von Hees, Syrinx, "Ein Lobgedicht auf den obersten Staatssekretär zum Anlass eines 'House-sitting': Überschneidungen von Herrschaftshof und Bildungsbürgertum und ihre Reflexian bei an-Nawāǧī" in *The Racecourse of Literature: An-Nawāǧī and His Contemporaries*, eds. Alev Masarwa & Hakan Özkan (Baden-Baden: Ergon Verlag, 2020), 213–262

Wehr, Hans, *Arabic-English Dictionary: The Hans Wehr Dictionary of Modern Written Arabic*, ed. J.M. Cowan (Ithaca, NY: Spoken Language Services, 1994).

Weintritt, Otto, *Formen spätmittelalterlicher Islamischer Geschichtsdarstellung: Untersuchungen zu an-Nuwairī al-Iskandarānīs* Kitāb al-ilmām *und verwandten zeitgenössischen Texten* (Beirut-Stuttgart: Orient Institut-Franz Steiner, 1992). Beiruter Texte und Studien 45.

Wickens, George M., "Notional Significance in Conventional Arabic "Book" Titles: Some Unregarded Potentialities" in *The Islamic World From Classical to Modern Times: Essays in Honor of Bernard Lewis*, eds. Clifford E. Bosworth e.a. (Princeton: The Darwin Press, 1989), 369–388.
Witkam, Jan-Just, *Inventory of the Oriental Manuscripts of the Library of the University of Leiden, volume 3: Manuscripts Or. 2001 – Or. 3000, registered in Leiden University Library in the Period between 1871 and 1883* (Leiden: Ter Lugt Press, 2008).
Woolf, Virginia, "'I Am Christina Rossetti'," in *The Common Reader, Second Series* (London: The Hogarth Press, 1965).
Wright, Elaine, *The Look of the Book: Manuscript Production in Shiraz, 1303–1452* (Washington, DC: Freer Gallery of Art Occasional Papers, 2012).
Yosef, Koby, "Dawlat al-Atrāk or Dawlat al-Mamālīk? Ethnic Origin or Slave Origin as the Defining Characteristic of the Ruling Elite in the Mamluk Sultanate," *Jerusalem Studies in Arabic and Islam* 39 (2012), 387–411.
Yosef, Koby, "Language and Style in Mamluk Historiography," in *New Readings in Arabic Historiography from Late Medieval Egypt and Syria: Proceedings of the themed day of the Fifth Conference of the School of Mamluk Studies,* eds. J. Van Steenbergen & M. Termonia (Leiden: Brill, 2021), 112–164.

Digital resources

Muther, Ryan & Seydi, Masoumeh, *KITAB passim run stats 2022.1.6* [data set] (2022).
Nigst, Lorenz; Romanov, Maxim; Savant, Sarah Bowen; Seydi, Masoumeh and Verkinderen, Peter, *OpenITI: A Machine-Readable Corpus of Islamicate Texts (Version 2022.1.6)* [data set] (2022), Zenodo, http://doi.org/10.5281/zenodo.4513723.
Verkinderen, Peter, "KITAB diffViewer", in https://kitab-project.org/diffViewer/ ; code at https://github.com/kitab-project-org/diffViewer.

Material artwork

Muḥammad b. al-Zayn, *Bassin dit 'Baptistère de Saint Louis'*, Metal, second quarter of the $8^{th}/14^{th}$ century, Musée du Louvre, Paris, https://collections.louvre.fr/en/ark:/53355/cl010318774
Muḥammad b. al-Zayn, *Bol,* Metal, second quarter of the $8^{th}/14^{th}$ century, Musée du Louvre, Paris, https://collections.louvre.fr/en/ark:/53355/cl010320012

Appendix

Figure 7: Staatsbibliothek zu Berlin, MS Wetzstein II 1893: folio 234a. Public domain, available at http://resolver.staatsbibliothek-berlin.de/SBB000239DD00000471

https://doi.org/10.1515/9783110753028-010

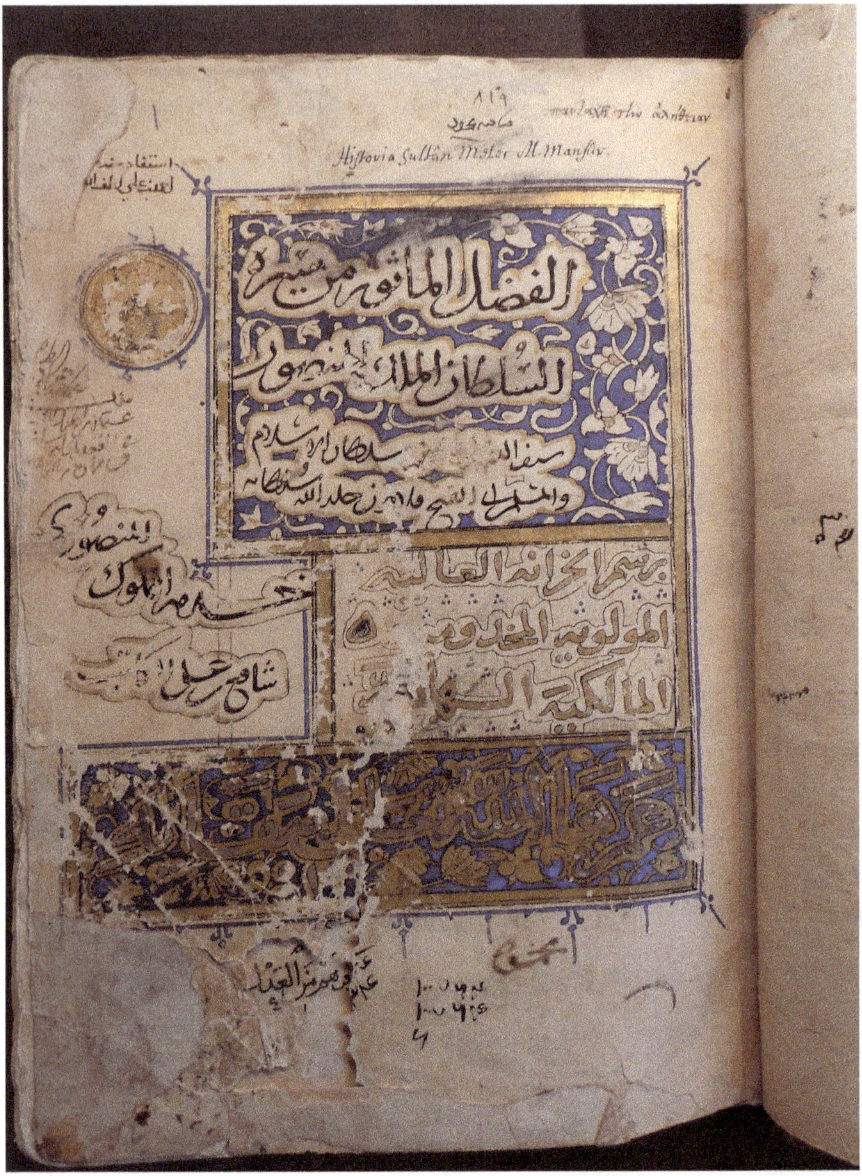

Figure 9: Bodleian Library, Marsh 424, folio 1a (title page). Reproduced with permission

Figure 10: Bayerische Staatsbibliothek Munich, Cod. Arab. 405, 1a (title page). Reproduced with permission

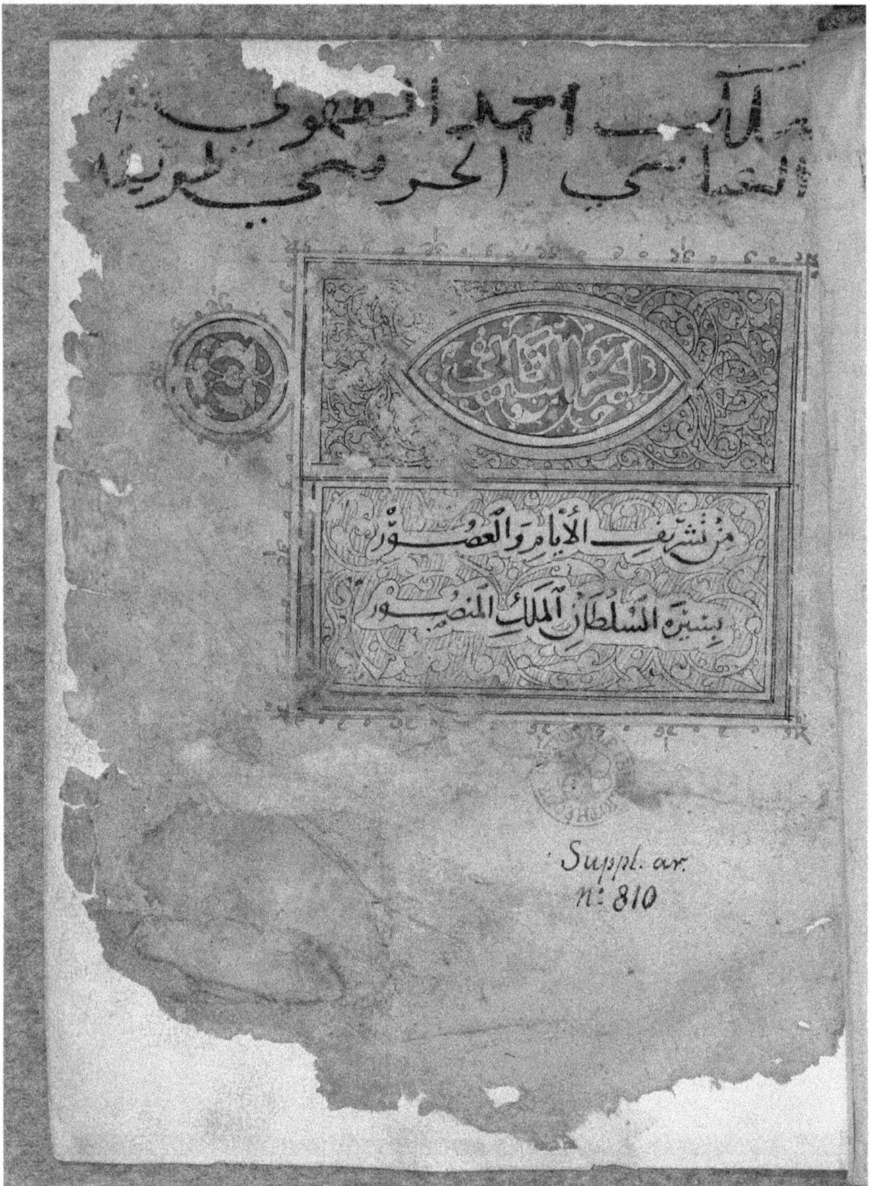

Figure 11: BnF, Arabe 1704, 1a (title page). Reproduced with permission

Index

Abaghā 131, 134, 177 n. 562
ʿAbbās, ʿImād al-Dīn Abū l-Faḍl 37
Abbasid 19, 85, 90, 173 n. 549, 179
Abbasid caliphate of Cairo 19, 85, 113, 118
ʿAbd al-Raḥmān (shaykh of Aḥmad Tegüder) 135, 140
Abu al-ʿAlāʾ al-Maʿarrī 145 n. 462, 150, 152 n. 487
Abū Bakr 52 n. 149
Abū al-Fidāʾ, al-Muʾayyad 184
Abulustayn (Elbistan) 20
Acre 21, 40, 87, 91, 98, 99 n. 314, 108 n. 337, 114, 116, 156, 165, 195, 197
Adab 49, 71, 84, 92, 152, 179, 186 n. 611, 205
Adab al-kātib 38, 112
Aḥmad b. Muḥammad b. Qalāwūn, al-Nāṣir Shihāb al-Dīn 195
Aḥmad Tegüder 91, 96, 131–32, 133, 135, 136, 139–40, 170
Aleppo 18, 53, 135, 137, 160, 161, 167
Alexander 78
Alexandria 78 n. 231
Alfonso X of Castile 177
ʿAlī, al-Manṣūr ʿAlāʾ al-Dīn (son of al-Nāṣir Muḥammad) 103 n. 324,
ʿAlī, al-Ṣāliḥ b. al-Manṣūr Qalāwūn 21, 44, 91, 98, 181 n. 589, 187, 188 n. 620, 203
al-Amīn (Abbasid caliph) 90
Anatolia 6, 20, 84, 120, 140, 159–161, 163, 169, 184, n. 601
Anecdotes 2, 38, 54, 88, 90, 93, 98, 112 n. 346, 122 n. 388, 121–22, 153, 171–73, 179, 180–81, 182, 183 n. 598, 185, 196 n. 641, 203
Annals/annalistic historiography 11, 31, 48, 54–55, 79, 80, 82–83, 89, 95, 102, 148, 189
ʿAntara b. Shaddād 67, 94 n. 299
Antioch 20, 84, 85
Anūshirwān 52 n. 149
ʿAqd (marriage contract) 120–21, 130, 164
Aqṭāy, Fāris al-Dīn 18, 80, 82
Aragon 99, 101
Ardashīr 52 n. 149
Arsūf 84 n. 249
Athīr al-Dīn Abū Ḥayyān al-Gharnāṭī 152
Aybak, al-Muʿizz 18–19, 80, 117, 118, 127
ʿAyn Jālūt, Battle of 19, 79, 80
Ayyūb, al-Ṣāliḥ 17–18, 19, 37, 80, 86, 89, 92, 118 n. 364 and 367
Ayyubid sultans/dynasty/period 16–18, 27, 53, 111, 117, 174, 176, 184, 186
al-Azhar 83 n. 248

Badīʿ al-Zamān al-Hamadhānī 124
Badr al-Dīn al-Mawṣilī 114, 115
Baghdād 85, 164 n. 524, 195,
Baghrās 84
Balabān al-Rūmī 121–23, 186–87
Balāṭunus 84
Banū al-Jarrāḥ 52 n. 149
Baraka Qān, al-Saʿīd 17 n. 40, 20, 21, 29 n. 59, 37, 46, 89–91, 92, 93, 121–22, 164, 178, 185, 186, 191
al-Basāsīrī 85
Baybars al-Jāshnikīr, al-Muẓaffar 21, 22, 101, 103–5, 120, 180
Baybars al-Manṣūrī 120, 155 n. 499
Baybars, al-Ẓāhir Rukn al-Dīn 3, 5, 7, 9, 16, 17–20, 26 n. 56, 27, 31, 37, 40, 46, 54, 55, 61–62, 70–71, 74, 78–85, 86, 87, 89, 90, 92, 93, 99, 102, 108, 112 n. 346, 113, 114–16, 117–19, 121–23, 134, 127 n. 438, 140–41, 150, 159–61, 163, 166 n. 536, 169, 176, 177, 182, 185–87, 190, 191, 198, 202
Baylīk al-Khazindār, Badr al-Dīn 121, 185, 191
Bereke Khan (Mongol ruler) 189
Berthereau, Dom 33 n. 80, 108
Birkat al-Jubb (Pond of the Well) 102–103, 180
Blind/blindness 1–3, 37–38, 93 n. 295, 123, 152, 200, 205
Buḥayra 113
al-Buḥturī 34 n. 80, 56
al-Bunduqdārī, ʿAlāʾ al-Dīn Aydikīn 86
al-Būṣīrī, Sharaf al-Dīn 98
Byzantines 101, 141 n. 450, 160–161

Caesarea 20, 84
Cairo 1, 2, 5, 19, 21, 22, 25, 27, 28, 43, 102, 104, 111, 113, 118, 131, 132, 134, 135, 136, 140, 147, 165 n. 531, 176, 177, 180, 187, 196

https://doi.org/10.1515/9783110753028-011

Cairo Citadel 37, 103, 139, 176, 178, 179
du Camboust, Herni-Charles 33 n. 80
Chancery 2, 3, 4, 10, 13, 14, 15, 22, 23, 27–28, 37–38, 43–45, 47 n. 130, 51, 77, 94, 107–44, 150, 151, 166, 169, 172, 173, 185, 186, 191, 195–98, 201, 204, 205
Chancery manual 64–65, 107, 109, 110–11, 112, 154, 168
Cilicia (Sīs) 84, 101, 141 n. 450
Colloquial Arabic 93, 122 n. 384, 185
Court/courtly 3, 6, 7, 9–10, 14, 24, 47 n. 130, 48, 51, 62, 77, 82, 94, 99, 102, 109, 123, 126, 138, 147, 170–99, 200, 204

Damascus 18, 19, 20, 21, 43, 53, 90, 91, 101, 115, 116, 117, 118, 122 n. 388, 134, 137 n. 436, 138, 151, 166, 176, 186, 196
Dār al-ʿadl 37, 112 n. 350, 113, 121 n. 380, 181–83
Darj, kuttāb al- 37 n. 100, 113–16, 151, 168
Dast, kuttāb al- 112–15, 121 n. 380
Dawādār 13, 111, 112 n. 346, 113, 115 n. 358, 117, 121–23, 169, 186–87
Dawla 4, 23, 48, 55, 60–62, 85, 89, 92, 99, 119, 122 n. 388, 127, 129, 144, 163, 178, 193, 198, 203
Digression (*istiṭrād*) 10, 55, 84, 87–88, 142, 204
Dīwān (poetry) 28, 154
Dīwān al-inshāʾ 2, 13, 38, 55, 93, 94, 96, 97, 98, 108, 109, 111, 112, 115, 116, 117, 119, 120

Fakhr al-Dīn b. Luqmān 93, 114, 115, 116, 118–19, 120, 197
al-Fatḥ b. Khāqān 150
Fatimids/Fatimid dynasty/period 21, 38, 85, 111, 113 n. 351
Futuwwa 130

Genhis Khān 5
Ghazal 47 n. 129
Ghāzān 44, 170 n. 546
Golden Horde 101, 119, 189

Ḥajjī Khalīfa 31–32, 64 n. 185
al-Ḥākim bi-Amr Allāh (Cairo caliph) 85, 113
Hama 54, 118 n. 364, 152, 176, 184
al-Ḥarīrī 124
Hijra, 18, 81, 82
al-Ḥillī, Ṣafī al-Dīn 28 n. 60
Ḥisn ʿAkkār 84
Ḥisn al-Akrād 84
Ḥisn al-Kaff 84
Historiography 6, 8, 10, 11, 16, 47–51, 53, 63, 125, 154, 185, 203
Holograph 6, 13, 40, 111 n. 345, 187–88, 192, 194, 201 n. 647
Homs, Battle of 2, 3, 20, 37, 91, 92, 93 n. 295, 95, 123, 131, 140, 164, 166, 188
Hülegü 19

Ibn ʿAbd al-Ẓāhir, ʿAlāʾ al-Dīn 26, 43–44, 45, 100, 103, 105, 120, 128 n. 412, 149–50, 154, 166, 178, 187, 188, 192, 197
Ibn ʿAbd al-Ẓāhir, Fatḥ al-Dīn 25, 26, 28, 43, 45, 91, 93, 95, 112, 116 n. 361, 120, 119, 122 n. 384, 123, 135 n. 430, 148, 150, 164, 165–166, 171–172, 196, 197, 201
Ibn ʿAbd al-Ẓāhir, Rashīd al-Dīn 27, 36
Ibn al-ʿAjamī, Kamāl al-Dīn 114, 115, 116 n. 360
Ibn ʿAsākir, Abū al-Qāsim ʿAlī 36
Ibn al-Athīr, Ḍiyāʾ al-Dīn 164 n. 524
Ibn al-Athīr, Tāj al-Dīn Aḥmad b. Saʿīd 96 n. 303, 115, 116 n. 360, 148, 150, 165, 166–68
Ibn Bint al-Aʿazz, Tāj al-Dīn 182
Ibn al-Dawādārī 56
Ibn Durayd 158–59
Ibn Faḍl Allāh, Muḥyī al-Dīn Yaḥyā 195
Ibn Faḍl Allāh al-ʿUmarī, Shihāb al-Dīn 110, 111 n. 345, 112, 116 n. 360, 150, 151, 195, 196, 198 n. 644
Ibn al-Fuwaṭī 43 n. 118
Ibn al-Ghānim, ʿAlāʾ al-Dīn 148–49
Ibn Ḥabīb, Badr al-Dīn al-Ḥalabī 149
Ibn Ḥajar al-ʿAsqalānī 37, 103 n. 324
Ibn Ḥijja al-Ḥamawī 28 n. 60
Ibn Hilāl al-Dawla, Badr al-Dīn 45
Ibn Ḥinnā, Bahāʾ al-Dīn 5, 53, 115, 118 n. 367, 120, 123 n. 388, 141–42, 162, 178, 185
Ibn Ḥinnā, Tāj al-Dīn 185
Ibn Khallikān 5
Ibn Manẓūr, Muḥammad Ibn al-Mukarram 45 n.125, 51, 64, 127 n. 406, 165 n. 532, 168
Ibn al-Mukarram, see Ibn Manẓūr.

Ibn al-Muqaffaʿ 52 n. 149
Ibn al-Nadīm 52 n. 149
Ibn Nubāta al-Miṣrī 151, 160 n. 513
Ibn al-Qaysarānī, Fatḥ al-Dīn 114, 115, 116 n. 360,
Ibn al-Qaysarānī, Ibrāhīm 56
Ibn Qirnāṣ al-Ḥamawī, Muḥyī al-Dīn 148, 152
Ibn Rāfiʿ al-Salāmī 37
Ibn al-Salʿūs 43, 127, 196
Ibn Sayyid al-Nās 52 n. 148
Ibn Shaddād, Bahāʾ al-Dīn 4, 51 n. 141, 79, 186,
Ibn Shaddād, ʿIzz al-Dīn 5, 32, 44, 47 n. 128, 53–56, 82, 95 n. 302, 115–17, 118, 119, 120, 123, 141, 156, 157 n. 503, 160 n. 514, 166 n. 536, 177 n. 562, 184 n. 601, 185, 192
Ibn al-Ṣuqāʿī 178
Ibn al-Waḥīd, Sharaf al-Dīn 148, 152–53
Ibn Wāṣil 54
Ijāza 1, 100, 124
Ilkhanate/Ilkhanids 9, 19, 20, 96, 101, 131, 134
ʿIlm 49, 184 n. 601
Imrūʾ al-Qays 156, 159, 163
Inshāʾ 48, 68, 74, 92, 97, 106, 109, 112, 124–29, 130, 139, 145, 156, 159, 162, 164, 169
al-Iṣfahānī, ʿImād al-Dīn 4, 55–56, 125,
Ismāʿīl, al-Ṣāliḥ b. al-ʿĀdil 117, 118 n. 364
Ismāʿīl, al-Ṣāliḥ b. al-Nāṣir Muḥammad 56
Istiṭrād. See digression.

Jaffa 84
al-Jazarī 2 n. 3, 36, 37, 152, 201
Jerusalem 4 n. 9, 164 n. 524
Jinās (paronomasia) 65 n. 191, 135

Kakhkhuta 97
Karak 20, 22, 97, 102, 103 n. 324, 177, 180
Kātib al-sirr (confidential secretary) 68, 71, 111–13, 120, 195, 196
Kaynūk 84, 142
Kayseri (Qaysariyyat al-Rūm) 84, 160–61
Khalīl, al-Ashraf 3, 17 n. 40, 21, 28, 35, 42 n. 111, 43, 56 n. 162, 64, 77, 88, 91–92, 96 n. 303, 98, 99, 119, 120, 126–27, 158, 165 n. 530, 177, 196, 197
Khiḍr b. Baybars 91
Khuṭba 85, 89, 92, 119, 130
Kināna 37
Kitbughā, al-ʿĀdil, 21 196
Kitbughā (Mongol commander) 19

Lājīn, al-Manṣūr 21, 122 n. 388
Literarisierung 48–51
Louis IX 16, 17, 172, 199

Madhhab 19, 182
Mamlūk 7, 16–18, 34, 35 n. 88, 39 n. 105, 41 n. 111, 43, 62 n. 179, 102, 105, 122, 162, 185
Mankabak bint Nughāy 188 n. 620
al-Manṣūra, Battle of 85
Maqāma 124, 152
al-Maqrīzī 29, 44, 99, 108, 201, 203
Marcel, Jean-Joseph 35 n. 87
Marj al-Suffar/Saffar. See Shaqḥab, Battle of.
Marqab, conquest of 20, 91, 94 n. 299, 96, 97, 157–59, 162, 164
Materiality 6, 24, 39, 40, 192–93
Metaphor 11, 52, 56, 62 n. 182, 71, 73, 104, 150, 153, 164, 179
Mirror for princes 82 n. 245, 160 n. 413
Military patronage state 174
Mongols 2, 9, 19, 20, 21, 22, 44, 80, 81, 89 n. 268, 90–91, 100, 101, 119, 131–40, 160, 170, 174, 177 n. 562, 183 n. 596, 189,
Muʿāraḍa 23–24, 147, 150, 164–69, 172
Muʾarrikh 53 n. 152, 61
Muʿāwiyya 52 n. 149, 135 n. 428
Muḥammad b. Abī Zakariyā 54
Muḥammad, Prophet 18, 25, 52, 68, 78, 81, 82
Murtaḍā al-Zabīdī, Muḥammad 51
Mūsā, al-Ashraf (underage Ayyubid ruler of Cairo) 18
Mūsā, al-Ashraf (Ayyubid ruler of Damascus) 186
Mūsā, al-Muẓaffar b. al-Ṣāliḥ ʿAlī 44, 187
al-Mustanṣir (Abbasid caliph of Cairo) 85, 118
al-Mutanabbī 145, 147, 157, 159–60, 161, 163, 205
al-Muẓaffar Shams al-Dīn 167, 191

al-Nāṣir Muḥammad b. Qalāwūn 3, 21–22, 40, 41 n. 111, 42–45, 56, 71, 77, 94, 100–106, 112, 118 n. 365, 120, 157, 166, 169, 177, 180–81, 187–88, 195, 196–97, 200
Naẓm 13
al-Nuwayrī 2 n. 3, 3 n. 6, 36, 44, 107, 110, 119, 188, 196–97

Obituary chronicle 54

Panegyric 6 9, 10, 23, 44, 46, 48, 50, 55, 56, 58, 67, 78, 81, 106, 158–60, 163, 171, 174, 187, 188, 196 n. 641, 204
Paronomasia. See *Jinās*.
Patronage, patron 9, 11–14, 39, 46, 48, 94, 106, 111, 117–23, 139, 141, 174, 175, 184–88, 191, 195, 198–99, 204
Persian 6, 96, 125, 134, 137–38, 186 n. 613, 192 n. 633
Poetry 3, 13, 14, 21, 23, 28, 38, 46, 47 n. 129, 48, 51, 53, 54, 63, 76, 90, 97, 106, 124, 129, 141, 142, 143, 144, 147–50, 155–63, 165, 167, 184, 185, 186, 197
Prose 13, 14, 28, 46, 53, 56, 77 n. 227, 94, 106, 124, 126, 128, 134, 139, 144, 147, 148, 150, 154, 155, 157, 158, 162, 163, 164, 169, 172, 197

al-Qāḍī al-Fāḍil, ʿAbd al-Raḥīm 29, 32, 111, 125 n. 398, 156, 159 n. 511, 164 n. 524
Qalʿat al-Rūm 43
Qalāwūn, al-Manṣūr 3, 7, 9, 16–17, 20–21, 28, 33–35, 37, 38, 39, 40, 41 n. 111, 43, 56 n. 162, 64, 67, 71, 87–98, 102, 108, 111, 112 n. 346, 113, 119, 122, 123, 127 n. 406, 131–40, 150, 157, 158, 164, 165, 170–72, 176, 177, 178, 179, 181 n. 589, 185, 187, 201–2
Qalāwūnid dynasty 17, 20, 174, 188
al-Qalqashandī, Shihāb al-Dīn 26 n. 56, 29, 99, 110, 113 n. 351, 114, 117, 118 n. 365, 125, 141–43, 159, 161 n. 515, 163, 168, 177 n. 563, 183 n. 597, 196
al-Qalqashandī, Najm al-Dīn 198 n. 644
Qānişawḥ al-Ghawrī 175, 188 n. 623
Qaṣīda 47 n. 129, 81, 152, 158, 162
Quatremère, Étienne Marc 35 n. 87, 108
Quṭuz, al-Muẓaffar 19, 61, 80, 86, 89, 116, 118, 198

Rhymed prose and rhyming cadenced prose. See *sajʿ*.
Risāla 117, 141, 145, 147, 162, 163, 198

Safad 84 n. 249
al-Ṣafadī 1–2, 3, 25 n. 51, 29, 30, 36, 37 n. 100, 42, 100, 105, 111 n. 345, 117, 119, 121 n. 381, 124, 128, 145, 147–49, 152–3, 195 n. 636, 196 n. 641, 197, 200–1
Ṣāḥib dīwān al-inshāʾ 27–28, 112 n. 347, 113, 171–72
Sajʿ (rhyming cadenced prose) 2, 56, 66, 101, 104, 124, 126, 140, 145, 160, 191, 137
Ṣalāḥ al-Dīn 4, 51 n. 141, 55, 78, 79, 84, 111, 123, 164 n. 524, 177, 186,
Sallār 44, 101, 103, 105, 120, 180
Sayf al-Dawla 160–61, 163
Séguier, Pierre 33 n. 80
Seljuq/Saljuq 20, 84–85, 160–61, 174, 184 n. 601
Shaqḥab, Battle of (Battle of Marj al-Suffar) 22, 44, 100, 187
Shaqīf Arnūn 84
Shihāb al-Dīn Maḥmūd 94, 110, 112, 148–50, 196–97
Ṣiffīn, Battle of 135 n. 428
Spectacle 7, 11–14, 48, 61, 66, 77, 143, 173, 202–203
Sufi/sufism 98, 132, 137–39
Sulāmish, al-ʿĀdil 91
Sunqur al-Ashqar, Shams al-Dīn 91, 92–93, 20

Tadbīr 128
Tadhkira (memorandum) 91, 130, 164–66, 168, 181 n. 589
Taḥmīd (laudatory preamble) 59, 65–66, 70
Tahniʾa 130, 165
Taqlīd (diploma of investiture) 102, 105–106, 111, 118, 130–31, 166, 168–69
Taʾrīkh 47, 53
Tawqīʿ 113, 133, 197
Tawriyya 161
Tripoli 20, 84, 87, 91, 94 n. 299, 95, 96 n. 303, 98, 122 n. 388, 123, 165, 166–68, 197
Truce 87–88, 99, 130–31
Tūrān Shāh 16, 17–18, 20, 61, 80, 89, 90
Ṭurunṭāy, Ḥusām al-Dīn 148, 187

ʿUmar b. al-Khaṭṭāb 52 n. 149, 78

Venetians 101
Vizier (*wazīr*) 5 n. 11, 13, 43, 53, 111, 112, 113, 114, 115, 117, 118, 119, 120, 123 n. 388, 127, 141, 163, 169, 178, 185, 196

Wādī al-Khaznadār, Battle of 100
Waqf/waqf documents 35, 83 n. 248, 99–100, 130–31, 156
al-Warrāq, Sirāj al-Dīn 25, 45, 121 n. 381, 148–49, 197
Wazīr. See vizier.

Yaʿqūb b. ʿAbd al-Ḥaqq, Abū Yūsuf (Marinid ruler of Marrakesh) 176
Yemen 96 n. 303, 101, 118 n. 365, 165, 166–67, 191
Yūsuf b. Quraysh, Shams al-Dīn 37, 114 n. 356, 115, 123
Yūsuf, al-Muẓaffar (Rasūlid sultan) 118 n. 365
Yūsuf, al-Nāṣir (Ayyubid ruler of Damascus and Aleppo) 18, 53, 166 n. 536